The Other Zulus

POLITICS, HISTORY, AND CULTURE

A series from the International Institute at the University of Michigan

Series Editors

George Steinmetz and Julia Adams

Series Editorial Advisory Board

Fernando Coronil	Nancy Rose Hunt	Julie Skurski
Mamadou Diouf	Andreas Kalyvas	Margaret Somers
Michael Dutton	Webb Keane	Ann Laura Stoler
Geoff Eley	David Laitin	Katherine Verdery
Fatma Müge Göcek	Lydia Liu	Elizabeth Wingrove

Sponsored by the International Institute at the University of Michigan and published by Duke University Press, this series is centered around cultural and historical studies of power, politics, and the state—a field that cuts across the disciplines of history, sociology, anthropology, political science, and cultural studies. The focus on the relationship between state and culture refers both to a methodological approach—the study of politics and the state using culturalist methods—and a substantive one that treats signifying practices as an essential dimension of politics. The dialectic of politics, culture, and history figures prominently in all the books selected for the series.

THE OTHER ZULUS

THE SPREAD OF ZULU ETHNICITY
IN COLONIAL SOUTH AFRICA

Michael R. Mahoney

DUKE UNIVERSITY PRESS
Durham & London 2012

Printed in Designed by Jennifer Hill. Typeset in
Minion Pro by Keystone Typesetting, Inc.

Library of Congress Cataloging-in-Publication
Data appear on the last printed page of this book.

To Molly

CONTENTS

ACKNOWLEDGMENTS

The research for this book was funded by the United States Department of Education's Foreign Language Area Studies Fellowship, by various fellowships and teaching assistantships from the University of California, Los Angeles (UCLA), and by various grants, including the Morse, Griswold, and Macmillan, from Yale University. My thanks are therefore due to the people of the United States of America and of the State of California and to Yale University.

In South Africa, the University of KwaZulu-Natal (UKZN), the Pietermaritzburg Archives Repository (PAR), the University of the Witwatersrand, the South African National Archives Repository in Pretoria, the Durban Archives Repository, and the Campbell Collections in Durban facilitated my research in many different ways at little or no cost to myself, so thanks are also due to the people of that country. Numerous individuals associated with these institutions proved enormously generous and helpful, including Pieter Nel, Unnay Narrine, Thami Ndlovu, and Zakhele Ntombela at the PAR, and Bobbie Eldridge at the Campbell Collections.

This book has also benefited from insights offered by and conversations with scholars in South Africa and "overseas." The University of KwaZulu-Natal history departments in both Pietermaritzburg and Durban proved to be particularly fruitful locations for me intellectually. In Pietermaritzburg, Jabulani Sithole, John Wright, John Laband, Tim Nuttall, and Bill Guest were most helpful. Jeff Guy, Keith Breckenridge, and Catherine Burns and numerous other participants at the Durban campus's African Studies Seminar provided me with valuable feedback and, perhaps more important, resistance. This seminar was very important in the development of this book. It would be a loss if the seminar were not to survive the changes at UKZN. Participants, including visiting foreign scholars, who provided me with feedback and fellowship included Prinisha Badassy, Julian Brown, Mwelela Cele, Suryakanthie Chetty, Mxolisi Mchunu, Bernard Dubbeld, Marijke Du Toit, Bill Freund, Muzi Hadebe, Robert Houle, Heather Hughes, Mark Hunter, Eva Jackson, Vashna Juganath, Vukile Khumalo, Gerhard Maré, Jeremy Martens, Sarah Mathis, Mandisa Mbali, Percy Ngonyama, Vanessa Noble, Fiona Scorgie, Yonah Seleti, Nafisa Essop Sheik, Stephen Sparks, Glen Thompson, Thembisa Waetjen, and Cherryl Walker.

My education in South Africa goes beyond what turns up in the endnotes of this book. For this I must heartily thank the Groeners of Port Elizabeth and their extended family, the Moodleys of Pietermaritzburg and their extended family, and David Kinyua, who was such a valuable friend.

I have also had the pleasure of being a member of a community of scholars and friends at the University of California, Los Angeles. Several students and faculty members helped make me both a better scholar and a better human being: Nuando Achebe, Tony Adedze, Christine Ahmed, Edward Alpers, Houri Berberian, Mary Dillard, Karen Flint, Catherine Cymone Fourshey, Lloys Frates, Elham Gheytanchi, Sondra Hale, David Hoyt, Tony Iaccarino, Kairn Klieman, Ron Kunene, Dennis Laumann, Shirley Lim, Laura Mitchell, Patrick Molloy, Surer Noor, Merrick Posnansky, Kendahl Radcliffe, Jasamin Rostam-Kolayi, Bridget Teboh, Brian Thompson, Nhlanhla Thwala, and the late George Vilakazi. My committee members have also been helpful long since I left UCLA, in particular Chris Ehret and my supervisor William Worger. All these people made UCLA more collegial than competitive.

My ten years at Yale University were an extremely enriching experience. Undergraduates too numerous to mention taught me as much as I taught them, pardon the cliché. Bob Harms proved to be extremely helpful in every way. Others who blessed me with their intellectual and social fellowship included Allison Alexy, Jennifer Baszile, Ann Biersteker, Jon Butler, Rurami-sai Charumbira, Kamari Clarke, Sue Cook, Seth Curley, Jacob Dlamini, Laura Engelstein, William Foltz, Joseph Hill, Emily Horning, Jennifer Klein, Mary Lui, Kay Mansfield, Thomas McDow, Richard Payne, Brian Peterson, Steve Pitti, Mridu Rai, Mieka Rietsemma, Lamin Sanneh, Sandra Sanneh, Alicia Schmidt-Camacho, James Scott, Henry Trotter, Dorothy Woodson, and Eric Worby.

Colleagues at universities other than UKZN, UCLA, and Yale have also been very helpful. Among these I want to mention Doug Anthony, Misty Bastian, Norman Etherington, Carolyn Hamilton, Amanda Kemp, Paul La Hausse, John Lambert, Elizabeth MacGonagle, Greg Mann, Shula Marks, Maria Mitchell, Derek Peterson, and Marcia Wright. Special mention must also be made of Sakkie Niehaus, who was a great support both in Pretoria and during his year's residence at Yale.

Most important of all, for this book at least, were my experiences in Mapumulo, where this book is set. Those experiences, brief though they were, made the narrative of this book more responsive to the on-the-ground realities of the people living there. In the Qwabe chiefdom, Chief Makhosini Qwabe, Tom Ntuli, and Mboneni Gumede were incredibly hospitable and informative. The most thanks, however, must go to the late Thuthukani Cele and his family, to whom I owe an enormous debt. I am sorry that he did not live to see this book completed.

Thanks of the deepest order must also go to Julie Parle, my dearest friend in South Africa, who also aided in the completion of this project through her intellectual engagement and above all her friendship.

I must also thank my mother, father, brothers, and sister, for all the support they provided in allowing me to reach my present age as complete as I am.

Finally, I dedicate this book to Molly Margaretten. Her love and her shared immersion in all things South African have made writing (and revising and revising) this book a much less solitary process.

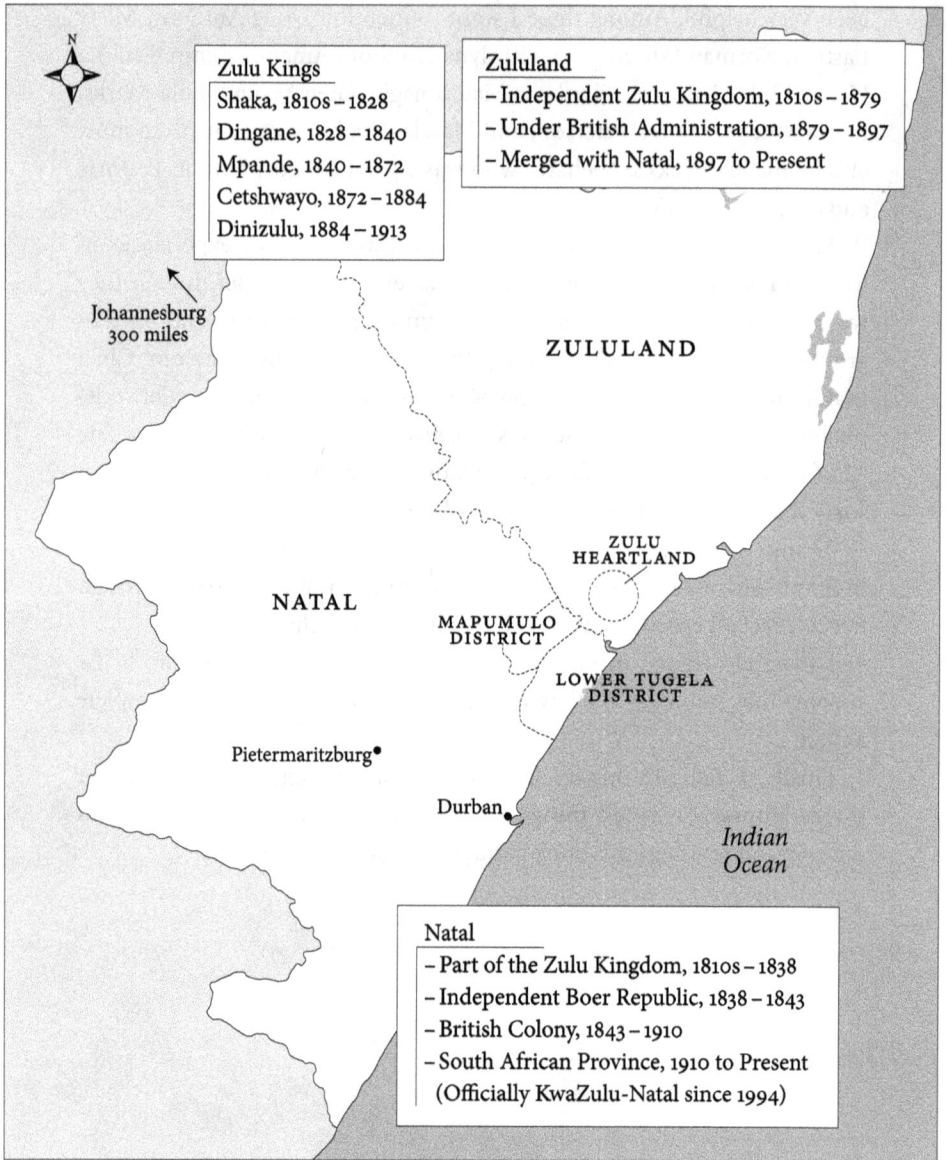

Zulu Kings

Shaka, 1810s – 1828
Dingane, 1828 – 1840
Mpande, 1840 – 1872
Cetshwayo, 1872 – 1884
Dinizulu, 1884 – 1913

Zululand

– Independent Zulu Kingdom, 1810s – 1879
– Under British Administration, 1879 – 1897
– Merged with Natal, 1897 to Present

Johannesburg
300 miles

ZULULAND

ZULU
HEARTLAND

NATAL

MAPUMULO
DISTRICT

LOWER TUGELA
DISTRICT

Pietermaritzburg

Durban

Indian
Ocean

Natal

– Part of the Zulu Kingdom, 1810s – 1838
– Independent Boer Republic, 1838 – 1843
– British Colony, 1843 – 1910
– South African Province, 1910 to Present
  (Officially KwaZulu-Natal since 1994)

ZULULAND AND NATAL

MAGISTERIAL DIVISIONS IN NATAL COLONY

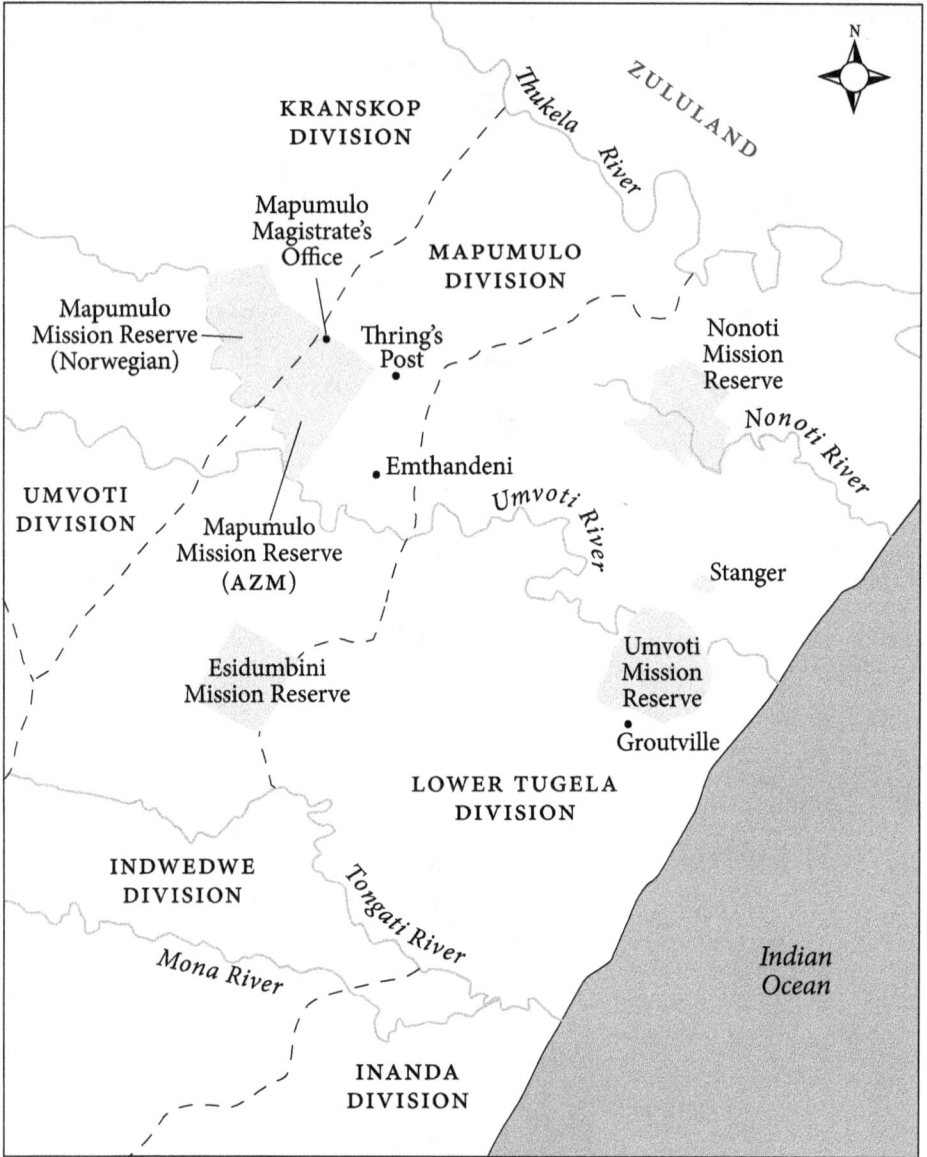

MAPUMULO AND LOWER TUGELA DISTRICTS

INTRODUCTION

In 1879, the British colony of Natal went to war against the neighboring Zulu kingdom. Large numbers of Natal Africans fought on the British side in this war, enabling the British victory over and ultimately the annexation of the Zulu kingdom. One of my objectives is to explain why Natal Africans would do this. My other primary objective is to explain why, twenty-seven years later, many of those same Natal Africans, or their children or grandchildren, rebelled against the British in the name of the Zulu king. The reason, I maintain, is that in the intervening period Natal Africans became Zulus, whereas they had not been before. Ethnic groups, so important in the past and present of Africa and indeed the entire world, are not unchanging givens. Rather, they are phenomena with histories that help us to understand them and their effects, such as ethnic conflict and traditionalist politics, extremely important issues in a continent still living under the shadow of the Rwandan genocide and similar, albeit far more restrained, episodes in other countries. And, it must be added, these issues are by no means limited to Africa, but are truly global.

But this is only the first of three main arguments that I wish to make. The second argument is that it was not elites, whether whites or Africans, who played the leading role in the process of what might be called "Zulu-ization," but rather ordinary Africans, the bulk of Natal's population. The insight that "traditions" could be "invented" and that "tribes" could be "created" is not a new one, least of all in Africa.[1] Ethnicity is an abstraction that gets its reality and its significance when people assert ethnic self-identification or are assigned ethnic identity by others. People have to do the work of naming an ethnic group, defining its characteristics (history, culture, language, ancestry), and identifying who is a member and who is not. Somebody also has to persuade others that ethnicity is important and has to try to mobilize ethnic constituencies in the promotion of certain political ends. In Africa and elsewhere, much scholarly attention has focused on the influence that the most powerful people have had in these processes. Government officials have promoted ethnic identification through censuses, identification cards, education, and the like, sometimes to promote ethnic homogeneity (as in nineteenth-century France) and sometimes quite explicitly to divide and rule subject populations (as in white-ruled Africa).[2] In Africa, white missionaries have also been important in this process, especially by defining different ethnic groups that must be served by different languages in school and in the liturgy. But social construction has not just been the business of white elites. The emerging African Christian middle class has used ethnicity to legitimize its position and mobilize support from traditionalists. At the same time, the African traditional elite of chiefs and headmen used ethnicity to shore up their power as it was being undermined by colonialism, capitalism, and other forces of modernity.

Within South Africa, no African ethnic group has been as large or as assertive of its own ethnic self-identification as the Zulus.[3] This fact acquired particular significance when, in 2009, Jacob Zuma became the first Zulu president of South Africa. Zuma has used his Zulu ethnicity and his traditionalism to develop a particularly enthusiastic following among other Zulus, but his support extends far beyond that ethnic group. Much more divisive has been the conflict between Zuma's African National Congress (ANC) and the Inkatha movement that emerged in the 1970s under the leadership of Chief Mangosuthu Gatsha Buthelezi, since 1968 chief minister to the Zulu king Goodwill Zwelethini. Inkatha attracted a much more conservative and traditionalist constituency than did the ANC, and Buthelezi was willing to work within the apartheid system to bring about change, as opposed to the ANC, which preferred peaceful mass protest and armed struggle. Throughout the 1980s and 1990s, supporters of the ANC and Inkatha fought a low-level civil war, mostly in Natal province, but also to some extent in the Johannesburg area. In Natal in particular, this was not a conflict between ethnic groups (there were large numbers of Zulus in the ANC), but rather within the Zulu ethnic group. Many different groups of people used their ANC or Inkatha ties to attract and mobilize followers in local struggles that often had very little to do with national politics. The white South African government was also accused of covertly supporting Inkatha, even militarily, in order to divide the opposition. Thousands died in the low-level war between the ANC and Inkatha.[4] When South Africa's first free, multiracial election took place in 1994, Natal was renamed KwaZulu-Natal partly in order to placate Inkatha, which gained control of the provincial government, one of only two provincial governments that were not under the control of the ANC. Thereafter, Inkatha's support declined, and they lost the provincial government to the ANC in the 2004 elections.

During Inkatha's heyday, historians such as Shula Marks and Nicholas Cope demonstrated that Inkatha's key supporters were the urban, Christian middle class and the rural, traditional elite, as well as some influential whites in both government and business. More important, these historians also showed that this alliance could be traced back to the 1920s, and that it had historically served the interests of the wealthier classes of Natal, both black and white. Members of the black and white elite had founded various organizations, some of which were also called "inkatha," a reference to the large grass coil kept by the Zulu king as a symbol of the unity of the nation. These organizations tended to preach obedience to authority: subjects to chiefs, women to men, youths to elders, workers to bosses, tenants to landlords, and even blacks to whites. They discouraged their members from joining unions or political parties that promoted equality and mass protest. Zulu ethnicity and the Zulu king were the linchpins of the ideology of the movements led by the conservative elite. Whether in the 1980s–90s or the 1920s–30s, Zulu nationalist organizations like Inkatha and its predecessors used not only pride in Zulu ethnicity, but also the privileges of gender and generation to attract not only the elite, but also men and women of modest means who derived what little power they had from their positions as heads of households.[5]

Already in the 1990s, however, some scholars began to express dissatisfaction with the limitations of explanatory frameworks that emphasized both the elite dominance and the supposedly uncontested politics of Zulu nationalism and, by extension, ethnic and nationalist movements in other cases as well. For example, the sociologist Ari Sitas called on scholars "to depart from naïve beliefs about the 'captive' nature of the audience" toward which Inkatha has directed its message, and to break the "unproblematic link between 'Zulu-ness' and Inkatha," a break made not only by scholars, but also by Zulus who felt betrayed by Inkatha.[6] The historian Paul La

Hausse argued, "Particular ethnicities in South Africa, whilst they have been structured by the state, have also been actively shaped by the experience and vocabulary of ordinary people. . . . [N]either the historical strength of Zulu ethnic nationalist sentiment nor, paradoxically, the innovative, contested and contradictory nature of politicised Zulu ethnicity have been adequately recognised or explored by historians."[7] La Hausse has demonstrated how, in the early twentieth century, the groundwork for the more elite and conservative Zulu nationalism of the 1920s and beyond was laid by Christian intellectuals of lower-middle-class origins. They often had very different views than did either the traditional or modern Zulu elites on various issues of the day, such as the proper relationship between rich and poor, chief and subject, Christian and traditionalist, and black and white. The lectures, sermons, and writings of these lower-middle-class Zulu nationalists also spawned further debate about these issues among Zulus in the press, the churches, and all manner of public and private spaces. And where historians like Marks and Cope demonstrated how white and Zulu elites used Zulu nationalism to contain the threat posed by the Industrial and Commercial Workers Union (ICU) in the 1920s and 1930s, La Hausse and Helen Bradford showed how the ICU's members themselves used Zulu nationalism to challenge those same elites.[8]

This broader, more internally contentious picture of Zulu ethnic politics could emerge as scholars produced more fine-grained and localized histories, and extended the history of Zulu ethnicity back further in time. Histories situated at the level of an entire province or nation have tended to exaggerate the power of the elites who dominate such large-scale units and the documents they produce. Local histories, on the other hand, can highlight the difference between rhetoric and practice, as well as the complex micropolitics that unfold at the community level. Meanwhile, histories with greater time-depth can show how contingent and changeable any given social order can be.

The history that I am presenting tries to negotiate a path between geographical localization and chronological specificity on the one hand and a geographically and chronologically broad synthesis on the other. Thus I extend the narrative of Zulu history back before the twentieth century to the nineteenth, and I look at the history not of the Zulu people as a whole, but rather of particular segments. Others have written extensively on the Zulu royal family and the Zulu kingdom during the nineteenth century, and in the process demonstrated precisely how much contention there was within it. Members of the royal family vied with one another for the Zulu crown and often challenged the authority of the person who won it. Conquered chiefs and royal officials were likewise prone to acting independently. Low-level civil wars broke out on numerous occasions, and the kingdom fragmented into little bits quite quickly after both the Boer invasion of 1837 and the British invasion of 1879, fragmentation that these invading Europeans did their best to promote.[9] Clearly it would be very difficult to speak of a strong sense of Zulu ethnicity in the Zulu kingdom of the nineteenth century.

But my focus is not on the Zulu royal family or the Zulu kingdom proper, but rather on Natal, which was politically distinct from the Zulu kingdom across the Thukela River from the late 1830s—when the Boers conquered Natal, which was at that time part of the Zulu kingdom—until 1897—when the British, who had taken Natal from the Boers in the 1840s, completed the process of annexation of Zululand that had begun with the Anglo-Zulu War of 1879. During this period, Natal was a British-ruled colony, while Zululand continued to be an independent African kingdom. Even before the Boer invasion, Zulu rule had been weaker in Natal, and the British found in Natal large numbers of Africans willing to fight against the Zulu kingdom in 1879. Zulu ethnicity was far weaker in Natal than it was in Zululand, which contained the heartland of the Zulu people and the graves of its kings. Thus, the spread of Zulu ethnicity in colonial Natal was more dramatic. My effort to tell this history is indebted to the work of other historians of KwaZulu-Natal, who I will cite throughout. I weave together their various arguments, as well as my own extensive primary source research, into a coherent whole that aims to tell the history of Zulu ethnicity during the colonial period, a history that has not been examined this thoroughly before.

One thing that quickly becomes apparent from such a study is that the Zulu ethnic identity of virtually the entire African population of Natal was itself not a given; it had to be established. The historians John Wright and Carolyn Hamilton have done the most to show that the creation of the Zulu kingdom under Shaka (d. 1828) in the early 1800s did not lead to the assimilation of the peoples of the various conquered chiefdoms into one Zulu ethnicity. Indeed, the kingdom's elite made a point of identifying some of these people as *not* Zulu, and even many of those that they tried to assimilate fully resisted, sometimes violently.[10]

The chiefdom that will serve as a case study throughout this book, the

Qwabe, was one of the latter. Indeed, a close examination of this particular chiefdom's history reveals an extremely close but also extremely antagonistic relationship with the Zulu, from its origin stories well into the nineteenth century. This makes it doubly surprising that the Qwabe chiefdom saw more of its members participate in the 1906 rebellion than did any other chiefdom. One might conclude that the Qwabe became Zulu during the colonial period as a result of the colonial "creation of tribalism" that occurred throughout Africa. But as late as the Anglo-Zulu War of 1879, forty years after the white conquest of Natal (at that point part of the Zulu kingdom), the Qwabe were still so antagonistic toward the Zulu as to fight alongside the British against them. And while the colonial government of Natal did engage in the "creation of tribalism," for officials there this meant bolstering local chiefdom identification and doing whatever they could to prevent the emergence of a broader identity such as Zulu ethnicity represented. The colonizers succeeded in this for most of the nineteenth century, but the 1906 rebellion clearly demonstrated that most Natal Africans—including those who did not rebel—considered themselves to be Zulus.[11]

My own work in this book could be seen as an attempt to fill the gap between the story of precolonial Zulu ethnicity told by Carolyn Hamilton and John Wright and the story of twentieth-century Zulu ethnicity told by Shula Marks, Nicholas Cope, Paul La Hausse, Helen Bradford, Gerhard Maré, and others. I would like to find out how Zulu ethnicity went from a category that excluded many Natal Africans and was resisted by many others, to a category that united a very diverse assortment of people: Zululanders and Natalians, traditionalists and Christians, men and women, elders and youths, chiefs and subjects, rich and poor, members of different chiefdoms. How does an examination of Zulu ethnicity affect our understanding of the social transformations that took place during this period, the era of British colonial rule in Natal (1840s–1910)?

ZULU ETHNICITY, CONFLICT, AND COHESION WITHIN ZULU SOCIETY

This takes us back to the arguments that I started to enumerate at the beginning of this introduction: that Natal Africans' ethnic self-identification changed, and that this change resulted from the initiative of the lower classes and not the elites of Natal African society. Following from these two points is my third, and most important, argument, which tries to answer the question "Why did this happen?" I maintain that young men in particular cultivated this new, broader conception of Zulu ethnicity in order to foster social cohesion in a Natal African society that was characterized by intense internal conflict, especially in the late 1800s and early 1900s. This internal conflict was of two sorts: between chiefdoms and within chiefdoms. Between chiefdoms, violent feuding over land and other issues was particularly frequent during this period. Within chiefdoms, on the other hand, conflict between chiefs and subjects, and between elders and youths, was peaking in intensity. Certain long-standing hegemonic ideas, such as patriarchy and chiefship, that had provided a degree of social cohesion were under severe stress, while the relatively new Zulu ethnicity was emerging to provide even broader-based unity. How to account for the coexistence of conflict and consensus that seems to have characterized all societies at every point in each of their histories is one of the most important questions in African studies, and indeed in the study of human society in general.

Shula Marks, John Lambert, Benedict Carton, and Jeff Guy have all examined the conflicts in colonial Natal between classes, generations, and chiefdoms, and the reasons for them.[12] My own work owes a great deal to their efforts, which I hope to build on by considering the relationship between these conflicts and the spread of Zulu ethnicity. I am indebted to these historians for having done so much to draw attention to these conflicts and to show how they shaped African responses to white racial domination as well as interethnic relations among Africans themselves. However, these historians have emphasized conflict so much that it is sometimes difficult to understand how Africans could ever have acted in concert, as they did in the 1906 rebellion. Carton, for example, focuses on generational conflict, which was certainly a major issue in Natal during this period. But generational conflict does not help to explain the two most violent manifestations of conflict within colonial Natal: the 1906 rebellion, and the endemic feuding between African chiefdoms that has plagued Natal from the 1800s to the present day. The rebellion, after all, saw young African men organize themselves under the leadership of their chiefs and elders. And the feuding pitted young African men from different chiefdoms against each other, in the name of their respective chiefs. Intergenerational conflict cannot be considered without also examining the investment in both chiefship and patriarchy that young men shared with their elders. Young men did indeed change the balance of power between themselves and their elders somewhat, but not entirely: chiefs and elders still ruled the roost. The difference was that youths now had more say in how society functioned. This is not surprising considering the fact that, though generations separated young men and elders, they all benefited from male privilege, and young men could look forward to becoming elders themselves.

Greater power and influence for youths was just one change in late-colonial Natal African society. Growing interchiefdom unity and the closely related spread of Zulu ethnicity to the area were others. It is precisely these transformations that Marks fails to take into account in some of her over-arching arguments about the 1906 rebellion. Marks asserts that the various conflicts among Africans helped to determine who would rebel, who would fight on the side of the colonial state, and who would sit on the sidelines: "At the level of final commitment to armed rebellion, it was the minutiae of local-level politics which seemed to tip the balance."[13] No wonder that she attributes so much of the failure of the rebellion to what she calls "the continuing validity of the earlier moral universe of the peasantry."[14] But, ironically, my own close examination of "the minutiae of local-level politics" shows how irrelevant they were in 1906, how bitter enemies could become allies overnight, although perhaps not permanently. I will also show that, despite the appearance of continuity in the institutions of chief-ship and patriarchy, "the earlier moral universe of the peasantry" had in fact changed substantially. The new Zulu ethnicity was a tool that did not eliminate conflict, but rather channeled it so as not to undermine unity.

The coexistence of conflict and cohesion, resistance and collaboration, in virtually all social and political orders is a paradox that has perennially puzzled social scientists. This paradox is particularly apparent in Zulu history. The Zulus' bitter anticolonial resistance in 1838, 1879, and 1906 made them a symbol of black pride and resistance worldwide, but that history stands alongside a history of unusually close collaboration with whites and the Zulus' long-standing role as the black soldiers, policemen, and security guards of white society. The Zulus' strong sense of ethnic identity contrasts with the high levels of interchiefdom feuding among them. The history of Zulu youths and women contains episodes of both gross insubordination against and the most enthusiastic compliance with the demands of elder Zulu men.[15]

It is therefore no coincidence that the first researcher specializing in

Africa to examine in depth the ambiguities and ideological bases of the relationship between rulers and ruled in Africa was also the foremost specialist in Zulu anthropology from the 1930s to the 1970s, Max Gluckman. Gluckman distinguished between social conflict that produced revolutionary social change and that which produced mere rebellion and superficial change. Social conflict was a constant and a given, but only on rare occasions did it lead to true revolution. Gluckman highlighted two instances of such revolutionary change in Zulu history: the rise of King Shaka in the 1810s and 1820s, and the European conquest of the Zulu kingdom during the decades that followed. At other times, social conflict led to rebellions against constituted authority that merely exchanged one king or chief for another without calling into question the very institution of kingship or chiefship.[16] Indeed, kingship or chiefship disputes have been extremely common in KwaZulu-Natal from earliest times down to the present day.

However, I intend to demonstrate that social conflict led to real change more often than Gluckman allowed, that superficial continuities masked—and in fact facilitated—major shifts in the balance of power in Zulu society. Specifically, youths became stronger at the expense of their chiefs and elders. But this was no Manichean struggle between sharply delineated and clearly opposed sides. Rather, youths succeeded precisely because they worked within existing structures of chiefship and patriarchy. This change was connected with the other main change in African society during the colonial era in Natal: the spread of Zulu ethnicity. In one sense Zulu ethnicity was well established; certainly, it had been around for at least decades before it spread throughout Natal in the 1890s and 1900s. But the ideas associated with it during this latter period—greater power for youths, rebellion against colonial authority—were new.

The Zulu ethnicity that is the subject of this book was new in several senses. First, it was new to the Natal Africans who started adopting it in the late 1800s but had not considered themselves Zulus up to that point. Second, it was new in the sense that its promoters were not the Zulu kings and their states, but rather young men. Third, it was new in that these young men used it to challenge, but not overturn, patriarchal authority and to try to end colonial rule. The content of this new Zulu identity was explicit self-identification by Natal Africans as Zulus, and the use of various symbols to indicate this Zulu self-identification: professions of allegiance to the Zulu king, and the use of his war badges, war cries, and war medicine. The content also consisted of the many stories that Natal Africans told to each other and to Natal Europeans from the 1890s onward that expressed all these ideas. The people who used the symbols and spread these stories were mainly young men, and their message was that Dinuzulu, and neither their chiefs nor the British monarch, was their king. The youths gained power by being the conduits for Dinuzulu's orders, which had precedence over the orders of the youths' own parents and chiefs and reflected the youths' desire for things that they wanted more than their elders did, most notably anti-colonial rebellion. But the youths' own versions of Dinuzulu's orders also kept chiefs and elders in leadership positions over youths, and the youths sought out and accepted that leadership, as long as it involved a more confrontational stance toward the colonial state.

The very ambiguity of the new Zulu ethnicity—serving youths' interests while reassuring elders of their continued authority—was what made it so popular in the 1890s and 1900s, and today. In this sense, Zulu ethnicity is not unlike similar ideas that from all over the world and throughout history have bound communities together and legitimated authority while at the same time providing space for dissent, debate, and change. Some scholars call such ideas "moral economies," because they distribute goods on the basis of shared notions of rights and obligations, rather than on the basis of supply, demand, and price. Moral economies usually permit, and even legitimate, some inequality among members of the community, but they also create obligations for the powerful to help the less powerful, and mechanisms for the less powerful to call the more powerful to task for failing to fulfill those obligations. Moral economies create what the Italian sociologist Antonio Gramsci called "hegemony": legitimacy for the ruling classes, common acceptance of ideas that support that legitimacy, but also some space for dissent. Hegemony grants power and constrains power at the same time. Indeed, as Michel Foucault has pointed out, power that accepts constraints is actually increased because those constraints minimize people's resistance to the exercise of that power.[17]

Ethnicity can serve as the basis on which membership in a moral economy is defined, and within which its nature is debated. John Lonsdale, a historian of Kenya, has developed the notion of moral ethnicity by way of analogy with moral economy. Lonsdale shows how ethnicity does not necessarily have inherent political implications. Rather, it can serve as an arena of contention. Ethnicity does not preclude debate; it facilitates it. Different assertions of ethnicity are often associated with different visions of the way things should be within that ethnic group. These different visions are in debate with one another, explicitly or implicitly. Ethnicity determines who may participate in the debate, who is affected by it, and by what rules that debate is to proceed. Different sides in the debate may also use ethnicity to legitimate their arguments.[18] Historians, such as Paul La Hausse, who deal with the contested nature of Zulu ethnicity show how such ideas are relevant to the Zulu case. My own research demonstrates that Zulu ethnicity was an arena for late-colonial debates over generational power, chiefly authority, interchiefdom conflict, and the proper response to colonialism.

Zulu ethnicity emerged as the basis for a moral economy in late colonial Natal that existed alongside two other moral economies. One was based on African ideas of chiefship and patriarchy. The other was a colonial moral economy, based in part on European notions of government, but also in part on the African moral economy. The fortunes of these alternative moral economies determined the attractiveness of Zulu ethnicity to Natal Africans. As long as the colonial moral economy and the African moral economy were robust, most Natal Africans would continue to reject Zulu ethnicity. But when those other moral economies came into crisis between the 1880s and the 1900s, Zulu ethnicity became more popular.

By speaking of a colonial moral economy, I do not mean to suggest that colonialism was legitimate and accepted in Natal Africans' eyes. Rather, I argue that colonizers tried to legitimate their rule and not rely on force alone, and the colonizers' quest for legitimacy enabled the colonized to have some say in the shape of colonial society and government, and to insist that the colonizers fulfill certain obligations to them. This was how the colonizers created a sort of hegemony, in the Gramscian sense. Some historians have argued that while the colonizers may have tried to create hegemony, they failed. Such arguments depend on very narrow definitions of hegemony in two respects: first, they see hegemony only as operating through the sorts of European idioms and institutions that Gramsci discussed; second, they see hegemony as little different from legitimacy. For example, Shula Marks and Dagmar Engels make the absolutely valid point that European ideas and institutions were weakly implemented or ignored in colonial Africa and Asia. However, from this they conclude that the colonizers were thus incapable of achieving hegemony outside of the small minority of colonized subjects who assimilated most to European culture and even converted to

Christianity. Marks and Engels prefer to talk of the colonizers' hegemonic projects, which usually failed, leaving the colonizers to rely much more on coercion and working through political structures inherited from the pre-colonial era.[19] But it was precisely in these indigenous political structures that the colonizers managed to achieve hegemony. Similarly, the Indian historian Ranajit Guha characterizes British colonial rule in India as "dominance without hegemony." But the failed hegemonic projects that Guha discusses have to do with the creation of a "civilized" class of indigenous collaborators who asserted some authority through British-style parliaments, courts, and bureaucracies. He does not examine the "princely states" of colonial India, where indigenous modes of governance were yoked to the British colonial state.[20]

The colonial state pursued two different types of hegemonic projects. One, the civilizing mission, was premised on the assimilation of the colonized through European ideas and institutions, such as Christianity, Western medicine, Western education, capitalism, urban planning, and so on.[21] Marks, Engels, and Guha are correct when they say that such hegemonic projects failed to impact more than a tiny, assimilated minority. But they neglect the other colonial hegemonic project, namely indirect rule, or rule through indigenous modes of governance. To a very large extent, the European colonial moral economy in Natal depended on the African moral economy. Chiefship and patriarchy were yoked to the colonial project through the colonial recognition of chiefs, customary law, and communal land tenure in African reserves. Natal Africans were more cooperative with colonial officials when the latter comported themselves like African chiefs and used African political idioms. Following Karen Fields, a historian of Zambia, I will show that the colonial state was essentially a parasite, living off the legitimacy produced by the precolonial political structures it had conquered but not eliminated.[22]

The civilizing mission has received far more attention than it deserves, and indirect rule far less. European cities, transportation networks, trading systems, medical clinics, schools, and churches only ever covered a small portion of colonial society in Africa and Asia. The number of European colonial officials, missionaries, traders, and settlers was extremely small, especially in rural areas. In both respects, the European presence in colonial Africa and Asia was weak, especially compared with European culture's far greater impact in the colonial Americas, north and south. Some scholars of colonialism have gotten around this by suggesting that the power of symbolic representation, especially in the worlds of written documents and the visual arts, greatly enhanced the impact of the civilizing mission. All too often, scholars have failed to demonstrate how, or even whether, the representations that they discuss (and attribute so much power to) reached the bulk of colonial society. For most of the colonized, the ideological, symbolic, and cultural struggles that mattered most to them took place in their own idioms and indigenous social structures.[23]

The tradition of fine-grained, localized social history in Natal that I have discussed, and of which I consider my own work a part, is thus a necessary counterweight to histories of colonialism that have focused on the power of colonizers to represent, categorize, and legislate for Africans. This is true even of works that have focused more on indirect rule than on the civilizing mission. Take, for example, two books that have garnered a fair amount of attention in the field of colonial studies: Carolyn Hamilton's *Terrific Majesty* and Mahmood Mamdani's *Citizen and Subject*. Hamilton's book examines how the Zulu king Shaka in particular and the Zulu in general were represented by British colonizers in explorers' and traders' accounts, literature, amateur ethnography, and, most crucially, government documents and actions. She makes the compelling argument that this power to represent was constrained by the reality of Zulu life: the power of these representations of Zulu tradition risked losing their effectiveness if their "creation" or "invention" was too obvious. Mamdani, on the other hand, sees the colonial state as having been far more powerful. Through indirect rule, the identification and delineation of "tribes," the recognition of chiefs and other "native authorities," and the incorporation of customary law into colonial law, the colonial government created the ethnic divisiveness and the undemocratic local government structures that plague Africa to this day. Crucially, Mamdani identifies colonial Natal as the birthplace of this system, which was then reproduced throughout South Africa, British-ruled Africa, and in some ways even in the African colonies of other European powers.[24] As much as both books have contributed to our understanding of this history, they are both "big picture" books that have much to say about the grand actions of the colonizers, but much less, indeed far too little, to say about the day-to-day interactions between colonial officials, chiefs, and their subjects. This latter history is important because it was how colonialism was experienced by the colonized, but also because it allows us to test how effective the

colonizers were in translating their elaborate schemes and guiding princi-
ples into effective action. The power of colonial texts, policies, and laws
must not be assumed; it must be proven. Indeed, there was often a large gap
between colonial policy and colonial practice.

A close examination of the government of colonial Natal, and in particular its interactions with chiefdoms like the Qwabe, reveals just how dependent the colonial state was on African chiefship and patriarchy. The colonial
moral economy was liable to fall apart directly because of the colonizers' own
excesses, and indirectly because of how those excesses undermined the authority of chiefs and homestead heads over young men in particular. The
colonial state's claims to be merely an extension of precolonial African
government, and its efforts to bolster the flagging authority of chiefs and
homestead heads, shaped Africans' responses to colonialism. When a "Great
White Chief" of colonialism or a local African chief crossed a line, young
Natal African men found another chief to replace him: the Zulu king. If the
Great White Chief had to be ousted, and the African chiefs were too oppressive, compromised, or divided (owing to feuds) to lead the effort to do so, the
Zulu king was the perfect alternative. It helped that the Zulu king was weak
and his image in Natal Africans' minds had little to do with his real nature:
Natal Africans were free to conjure up the sort of Zulu king they desired. The
spread of Zulu ethnicity in Natal was thus intimately connected with colonialism, generational conflict, and the travails of chiefs.

SOURCES OF THE ZULU PAST AND THE DEBATES ABOUT THEM

Before we examine this history more closely, we first have to consider the
available evidence. Written sources from the precolonial era were composed
entirely by Europeans. At worst these sources suffer from the racist biases of
their authors; at best they suffer from their authors' status as newly arrived
foreigners thoroughly unfamiliar with the intricacies of African culture.
Since the 1960s, African historians working in other parts of the continent
have tried to address the lack of sources written by Africans by collecting
vast numbers of African oral traditions. Armed with two years of formal
Zulu instruction at the university level and aided by native Zulu-speaking
translators and interpreters, I have taken some steps in this direction myself.
However, oral traditions collected in the present about events that occurred
almost two hundred years ago raise more questions than they answer. Most

obviously, the passage of time inevitably leads to distortions and a lack of detail relative to older accounts. Moreover, the sources for many of these oral traditions now include schoolbooks, radio programs, and even made-for-television movies. As a result, I have found, these oral traditions reveal far more about the present than they do about the past. I have therefore decided to focus on them in another book, where I can deal with these issues at greater length.[25] I do, however, refer to them occasionally in the argument that follows.

By any measure, the best available source for the history of precolonial KwaZulu-Natal is the James Stuart Archive, a compendium of oral traditions collected from Africans by the British colonial official James Stuart between the 1890s and the 1920s. It is far larger and more detailed than any other source, and the informants were indigenous Africans who were alive during the precolonial era, or whose parents or grandparents had been. Nevertheless, it has been criticized, most notably by the historian Julian Cobbing, for two reasons in particular: the first being, as Cobbing maintains, that James Stuart was a racist; the second being, as Cobbing argues, that Stuart may have forged much or all of the archive, or at least may have been biased in the questions he chose to ask and the evidence he chose to include, in order to legitimate white racial domination in the region.[26]

Another historian, Carolyn Hamilton, has thoroughly refuted Cobbing's criticisms of the James Stuart Archive. First, while Stuart did believe in white racial domination, he was also favorably impressed by Zulu culture and critical of many aspects of white rule in Natal. He was born and raised on a white-owned farm with numerous African tenants and laborers, and was a fluent Zulu speaker. He vigorously opposed calls from other Natal Europeans for the abolition of African chiefship, customary law, and communal land tenure. Second, Stuart never published, nor intended to publish, his archive, so he would have had no reason to forge it. Indeed, Stuart was meticulous and scrupulous in his oral research. Every interview was written out word for word, sometimes in Zulu and sometimes in English. Stuart also provided the date and location of each interview, as well as the names, ages, and biographical information for each interviewee. Stuart seems to have been particularly interested in collecting numerous versions of different oral traditions, even (perhaps especially) if those versions contradicted one another. Many of the views expressed in the archive also contradict Stuart's own published views on various subjects.[27]

An examination of the actual recorded testimony of Stuart's informants does not support Cobbing's contention that it uniformly depicts the Zulu kings—especially Shaka (ruled c. 1816–28) and Dingane (ruled c. 1828–40)—in a negative light, or that it provides an apologia for colonialism. What we have instead are debates. Take, for example, attitudes toward the Zulu kings. Many of the informants were critical of Shaka. One, Baleka, was a woman from the Qwabe chiefdom who was about sixty-three years of age when Stuart interviewed her in 1919. She called Shaka a "madman." Dinya was about seventy-eight years old when Stuart interviewed him in 1905. Dinya belonged to the Cele chiefdom and now lived on a Christian mission station. His father had fought in Shaka's army and died in battle. Dinya said, "We do not care for the Tshaka regime. We were all killed off there." Lunguza, about eighty-six or eighty-seven years old when Stuart interviewed him in 1909, was a member of the Thembu chiefdom, which was conquered by Shaka, and later served in the Zulu army under Dingane. He said that under Shaka and Dingane, an oft-heard prayer was "Would that some other king might reign!" and that some people had paid with their lives when the kings heard they had said such a thing.[28] But other informants had more positive things to say about Shaka. Mayinga, about sixty-six when Stuart interviewed him in 1905, was a member of the Gaza chiefdom conquered by Shaka. In 1856, when he was about seventeen, he fought in a short-lived succession dispute between rivals for the Zulu kingship. He said of Shaka and Dingane, "The old regime was good, even though they killed off frequently." Ndukwana, who Stuart interviewed more extensively than any other person, was a fifty-seven-year-old member of the Thembu chiefdom, yet another of Shaka's conquests, when Stuart started interviewing him in 1897. Ndukwana said, "Tshaka did not scatter the nations; he unified them. . . . People will forget their old customs and find Tshaka's government good."[29]

Stuart also recorded extensive African and European criticisms of colonialism. A careful examination of the testimony of Stuart's informants demonstrates that it could hardly be read as one extended apologia for colonialism. It is true that some excerpts could be read this way. For example, Qalizwe was one of Stuart's servants, and his father, Dlozi, had worked for Stuart's family. Qalizwe's chiefdom was the Chunu. He said, "Living under British rule is more preferable than living under the Zulu regime when people were killed for the slightest offence."[30] At the same time, however, Stuart's informants also suggested that the turn to the British had more to do with the shortcomings of the Zulu kings than with the supposed blessings of British civilization. Qalizwe's own father, Dlozi, for example, said, "At first Europeans were regarded as saviours from the oppressions of the Zulus, but now they are looked on as more tyrannical and oppressive than Tshaka's wildest schemes." If Natal Africans still seemed to be contented with European rule, this was because, as Dlozi put it, "to Europeans' faces they pretend to be satisfied, whereas amongst themselves they speak discontentedly."[31] Similar testimony came from Sijewana, a devout Christian convert in his late seventies who had fought in the Zulu army under Dingane and his successors. Sijewana was of two minds. On the one hand, he said, "Natives appreciate English rule because of the security of life and property under it. They are not killed off indiscriminately as under Tshaka without any trial being held." But Sijewana also complained that Africans "are not allowed a voice in the making of laws which concern their own welfare," and that "the system of taxation and collection of taxes [under the British] is a real hardship on the people, and there is much severe suffering in consequence."[32] Stuart's informant Lunguza felt the same way. At one point he said, "We are better off now that the whites have come. People are permitted to die natural deaths, a far more preferable system of government." And yet Lunguza felt that this peace came at a cost, for people were inclined to crime as a result: "The misbehaviour of nowadays is due to its being impossible to kill off people as formerly. For people are confident that nothing, or very little, can happen, for there is a great chief [the colonial government] who will stand up for them even though they have done wrong."[33] Even one of Stuart's European informants, the judge and former Natal secretary for native affairs John Shepstone, argued that Natal Europeans had generally misinterpreted African quiescence: "If Natives were wanting protection or anything, they appreciated our protection. They wanted protection whilst the Zulu menace lasted. They never asked for or desired our rule."[34]

Ambivalence toward Shaka is not limited to Stuart's informants, but rather is characteristic of both African oral traditions and contemporary popular opinion. My own interviews among Zulu speakers in the late 1990s confirmed that memories of the depredations of the Zulu kings in the early 1800s were alive and well.[35] In 1925, the South African writer Thomas Mofolo wrote a novel about Shaka based on southern Sotho oral traditions, and the picture he paints is also somewhat negative.[36] Two decades earlier, Magema

Fuze, a middle-class Christian with close ties to missionaries who had been publicly critical of British colonial policies toward Africans, wrote the first Zulu-language book. In it, he both praised and criticized Shaka and Dingane, and also had some bad things to say about Europeans' actions in the region.[37] What is important from my standpoint is not whether Shaka and his successors were indeed bad, but simply that many Africans, including Zulus, voiced severe criticisms of the Zulu kings and acted in ways that demonstrated opposition to the Zulu kings.

When it comes to the colonial period, the focus of this book, the bulk of the sources that I use come from the official colonial archive. These sources suffer from many of the same problems as do the sources for precolonial history: they were overwhelmingly written by European colonialists and thus reflect their biases or even misunderstandings and ignorance of African culture. What little there is in the way of African testimony is also potentially distorted by the severe imbalance in colonial power relations. Africans said what they thought the European colonial officials wanted to hear, and had reason to fear the consequences if they were to say the wrong thing, regardless of whether it was true or not.

In practice, however, it is not difficult to correct for the biases of colonial sources. Numerous historians, studying southern Africa and other regions, have come to the conclusion that elite sources can nevertheless yield accurate histories of the masses who could not write for themselves. In her history of African work culture in colonial Natal, Keletso Atkins reads colonialist sources against the grain, giving more sympathetic interpretations of African behavior in the events colonialists describe. Ranajit Guha does the same thing for colonial India, arguing that the colonial state had a vested interest in the accuracy of the "official eavesdropping" by its intelligence network. Carlo Ginzburg maintains that even a "hostile chronicle" could not entirely transform or suppress the reality of what it was hostile to. Allen Isaacman concludes that "careful readings" of such written sources have produced "much of the best work on the social history of rural South Africa" and elsewhere, if only insofar as such work has kept an eye open to "differing peasant perspectives."[38]

Colonial officials were inclined to see colonialism as a good thing and to see Africans as inferior to Europeans, but these are value judgments and interpretations that historians can easily identify and dismiss because they are so obvious and so general. At the level of particularities and specifics—

what happened when, who said what—there is little room for these biases to distort facts. After all, the highest priority for colonial officials was to prevent African resistance and to squelch it when it did occur. They were torn by a tendency to see "their" Africans as grateful colonial subjects on the one hand and potential rebels who could strike at any moment on the other hand. These tendencies created countervailing biases that had a way of canceling each other out, especially as officials debated among themselves. The resulting debates had extremely important implications for the documents that Natal Europeans produced: opposing sides criticized each other's arguments and the evidence on which those arguments were based, much like lawyers or even historians would. Nobody was calling for an end to European rule, but there were some who called for limiting or even ending European immigration into Natal, for liberalizing racially discriminatory legislation, and, like Stuart, for preserving African chiefship, customary law, and land tenure. There were many who argued that if Africans resisted or even rebelled, Natal Europeans only had themselves to blame. Some Natal Europeans went so far as to call themselves "friends of the Native," and some had grown up among Zulu speakers, spoke Zulu fluently themselves, and had a thorough familiarity with Zulu culture. I do not want to push this argument too far, but certainly it would be wrong to argue that Natal European society was so uniformly and unremittingly hostile toward and ignorant about Natal Africans that colonial documents can tell us nothing about the realities of African life.

There is voluminous testimony from Africans in the colonial archive, mainly in the form of testimony in various official proceedings, but also including reports from government informants and requests for government action, the latter often involving implicit or explicit criticism of colonialism. In many cases Africans were quite able to tell European colonial officials what they did not want to hear. In many other cases, it was not even clear what it was that the Europeans wanted to hear in the first place. Did the Europeans want to hear about African loyalty or African disloyalty? When disputes emerged between Africans—and a large portion of the colonial archive is devoted to documenting such disputes—what did the Europeans want to hear? It is true that the African voices recorded by colonial officials were overwhelmingly elder and male, but they were often complaining about women and youths whose actions and motivations can be discerned by historians, even when reported by others. When I looked at these colonial sources, I was trying to determine the level of conflict or cooperation among Africans, as well as the level of conflict and cooperation between Africans and Europeans. Europeans were not predisposed to see either conflict or cooperation, and the Africans who talked to them were not predisposed in this way either.

Still, the limitations of the colonial archive are to some extent insuperable. The perspectives of the white authors of the various source documents are hard to escape, and indeed must be included considering that the development of Zulu ethnicity was a dialogic process with the development of colonialism. More important, we cannot go to the Natal Africans of the colonial era and interview them about their ethnic self-identification or their attitudes toward their fathers, chiefs, colonial officials, or the Zulu king. Ethnicity is an aspect of one's consciousness, and it is difficult enough to find out what other people today, or even we ourselves, are truly thinking, let alone people from another a culture a century or two in the past, whose history has been transmitted to us by people alien to that culture. There are some explicit declarations, but for the most part the historian must rely on the implicit testimony of collective actions. Similarly, with such indirect and usually anecdotal evidence, it is impossible to generalize. Some Natal Africans may always have considered themselves Zulus. Indeed, some of them were refugees from the Zulu royal family itself and became chiefs in Natal. Conversely, even after the rebellion there may still have been some Natal Africans who did not consider themselves Zulus. Many Zululanders may very well have always been ambivalent about Zulu ethnicity, and one must also acknowledge, alongside the wars and flights of refugees between Zululand and Natal, substantial peaceful interaction between the peoples on both sides of the Thukela River. Like some vastly larger and far more significant epistemic shifts, such as the industrial and scientific revolutions, the spread of Zulu ethnicity to Natal was probably neither instantaneous nor complete, but the exceptions and ambiguities should not blind us to the reality of the changes in any of these cases.

1

THE FAILURE OF ZULU ETHNIC INTEGRATION
IN THE PRECOLONIAL ZULU KINGDOM

Ask Zulus today when their ancestors first became Zulus, and they may greet the question with puzzlement. Those with a little more historical consciousness may trace the creation all the way back to the 1810s and 1820s and the actions of King Shaka, in some senses the founder of the Zulu kingdom and certainly the most prominent figure in Zulu history. But even the accounts of Shaka's life most popular among Africans include some reference to how violent his conquests were and how much resistance they produced among the conquered. Scratch the surface a little more, probe the written historical record, examine living oral traditions, seek out local histories as opposed to national ones, and it quickly becomes apparent that the dozens of chiefdoms that now make up the Zulu kingdom had an independent existence not only before Shaka's rule but often after it as well. Many of the people in those chiefdoms resented and resisted Shaka's rule to the degree that they never came to identify themselves as Zulus. Instead they continued to identify themselves as members of their chiefdoms, of which the Qwabe was among the largest. The Qwabe had a closer relationship to the Zulu than did any other chiefdom in the region, but that relationship was also even more vexed than were those of the other chiefdoms. The Qwabe would ultimately become Zulu, but Shaka's reign did more to hinder that process than to promote it, and the same was true for many other chiefdoms.

To understand the rivalry between chiefdoms and the degree to which people identified with one chiefdom or another, one must also understand another, more basic, unit of precolonial African society in the region: the homestead (*umuzi*). The continuity and stability of homesteads stand in striking contrast to the upheaval surrounding chiefdoms during this era. Chiefdoms without households were chiefdoms without followers. Chiefs tried to attract, co-opt, and control homestead heads. But homestead heads were not just subordinates, or even intermediaries; they were authority figures in their own right who competed with chiefs for the allegiances of their followers. Shaka tried to circumvent the authority of homestead heads and make young men and women directly answerable to him. But the system he introduced was less attractive to these youths than the one that homestead heads had established, and in many chiefdoms, like the Qwabe, it was the homesteads that prevailed. Identification with the Zulu king would only trump identification with the homestead head and the chief when there emerged changes that undermined the legitimacy and popularity of these more local authority figures and the institutions they represented.

MALANDELA, QWABE, AND ZULU: SOCIAL CATEGORIES AND IDENTITIES IN THE PRECOLONIAL ERA

The histories of the categories "Qwabe" and "Zulu" were joined from the very beginning, for the two share a common origin story. According to this story, the Qwabe and the Zulu (whose name means "sky") are descended from two brothers with those names, and their father was named Malandela. James Stuart collected numerous versions of this story from his informants around the turn of the century.[1] These stories were still circulating among Africans in Natal fifty years later.[2] Indeed, some people from the Qwabe chiefdom are able to relate the story even today, one hundred years after Stuart began his work. In 1997, a schoolteacher named Mboneni Gumede, who lived in the Qwabe chiefdom in the Mapumulo district of KwaZulu-Natal, told a version of the story to me and Thuthukani Cele, my translator and interpreter. According to Gumede, Malandela came from the north to Zululand and settled near the Mhlatuze River. His senior wife, Nozidiya, was a daughter of the Zungu clan. Nozidiya's oldest son by Malandela was Qwabe, and her second son was Zulu. Malandela stayed with his family. Before he died, he started to divide his wealth among his children. Malandela said Qwabe would inherit everything that belonged to him, mainly livestock, but also Malandela's position as chief. While Qwabe would inherit Malandela's property, he would not inherit the property of Malandela's wives. After Malandela died, however, Qwabe took everything, including Zulu's property. Nozidiya complained that this was unfair. She insisted that something be given to Zulu. One day, a dog sat down in front of the homestead and its penis became erect. Qwabe saw this, and knew that by this action the ancestors were saying something, namely that Zulu no longer belonged to this homestead. Lufenulwenja (dog's penis) became Zulu's new salutation, and he was to leave the homestead. Some people did not like this name, preferring Ufalwenja, the "crack of the dog." Many were also very unhappy with Qwabe's insult of Zulu and left with Zulu, crossed the White and Black Mfolozi rivers, and settled at Babanango. These were all Malandela's people. Those who followed Zulu were called the Zulu, while those who stayed with Qwabe were called the Qwabe.[3]

Many aspects of Gumede's version of the story, including the ribald bits, can be found in many other versions of the story collected over the last hundred years. It is true that there is virtually no point on which all versions agree. Besides the basic question of whether or not Malandela, Qwabe, and Zulu were related to each other, other issues are also treated differently from account to account: the prior ancestry of Malandela, the relationship of Nozidiya to Malandela and the others, Nozidiya's very gender, the identity of the siblings Qwabe and Zulu, and the resultant interrelationship of the various lineages of the region, the subsequent genealogies of the Qwabe and Zulu lineages, the story of the name Lufenulwenja, the reasons for the conflict between Qwabe and Zulu or indeed whether or not there was such a conflict, the role of chiefship in the story, and the residence and migration patterns of the story's protagonists. Even the question of who was in the wrong, Qwabe or Zulu, has varying answers.[4] Nevertheless, two motifs are particularly common: that the progenitors of the Qwabe and Zulu were brothers, and that they came into a conflict that led to the separation of the two peoples. Memories of these events, regardless of whether or not they actually happened, would lend additional significance to the many later conflicts between the two groups.

This was how the Zulus (singular, iZulu; plural, amaZulu), and for that matter the Qwabes (singular, iQwabe; plural, amaQwabe), first came to be. But the name Zulu can refer to at least four different kinds of categories: the Zulu ethnic group, the Zulu kingdom, the Zulu chiefdom, and the Zulu lineage. Members of each of these groups can be called, and may call themselves, Zulu. The Zulu ethnic group is made up of those who identify themselves, and are identified by others, as Zulus, based on their common language, culture, and ancestry. But the size and indeed the very existence of the Zulu ethnic group resulted from the creation of the Zulu kingdom. Before the 1810s, the peoples who would become Zulu had no overarching name for themselves. Instead, they identified with their chiefdoms or lineages, of which the Zulu was just one among many. To the extent that people recognized themselves as belonging to wider categories, they spoke of *Lala, Mbo, Ntungwa, abaSenhla, abaSenzansi*, and, most notably, *Nguni*, each of which included many different lineages and chiefdoms. None of these categories was coterminous with the present-day Zulu ethnic group, and many included groups that are not Zulu today, such as the Xhosa and Swazi. Three different, although closely related, languages were spoken during the pre-Shakan era in what is now KwaZulu-Natal province: tekela or tekeza (spoken along the Drakensberg escarpment from Swaziland to the Eastern Cape, and in most of the country south of the Thukela), thefula (spoken in the coastal regions from Durban northward into Thongaland), and Zunda (spoken in the heartland north of the Thukela, sandwiched between tekela and thefula speakers). It was only during Shaka's reign and afterward that Zunda came to be known as isiZulu, the Zulu language, and the others went from being independent languages in their own right to being seen as mere dialects of Zulu.[5]

In contrast to the Zulu ethnic group, the Zulu kingdom and Zulu chiefdom may be defined as social groups ruled by the Zulu king, or *inkosi* (plural *amakhosi*). The difference between a kingdom (*izwe* or *isizwe*) and a chiefdom (*uhlanga*) is that in a kingdom the inkosi rules over other amakhosi. Although in Zulu both a king and a chief could be referred to as an inkosi, one could also make a distinction between an *inkosi yezwe* (a "king," the ruler of an izwe) and *inkosi yohlanga* (a "chief," the ruler of an uhlanga).[6] In this sense, the Zulu chiefdom only became a kingdom under Shaka.

Thus, before Shaka's time, the Zulu ethnic group and the Zulu kingdom did not exist, so the only way to be a Zulu was to be a member of the Zulu chiefdom or the Zulu lineage. A chiefdom and a lineage were similar, and indeed both were called *uhlanga* in Zulu, which also means "stem," "stock," "ancestry," "genealogy," and "dynasty." The main difference is that a lineage was the descent group one was born into, while a chiefdom was the polity ruled by a chief to whom one pledged fealty. People could change their chiefdom affiliations, but not their lineages. The name of one's lineage would also be one's surname, which remained constant, except when women married into another lineage. Thus, not all members of the Qwabe lineage belonged to the Qwabe chiefdom, nor did all Zulus belong to the Zulu chiefdom. There have long been, in fact, Qwabes in the Zulu chiefdom and vice versa. Each of the dozens of chiefdoms in KwaZulu-Natal has always included members of many different lineages.[7]

Another difference between lineages and chiefdoms was that not every lineage had a chief. Submitting oneself to the authority of a particular chief was known as *ukukhonza* (the verb means "pay homage, pay respect to; subject oneself to, serve; send compliments, best wishes, regards; worship"). This submission was made with the declaration, "Ngizokhonza, Nkosi; ngifake ikhanda lapha kuwe" ("I have come to serve, O Chief; that I may put my head in your control").[8] Even before Shaka's time, people "khonza'd" whenever they changed their allegiance from one chief to another. People spoke of khonza'ing not only chiefs within present-day KwaZulu-Natal province, but even those beyond, such as Pondos and even Sothos. People could also khonza one chief, then switch their allegiances and khonza another, or even a third.[9] Sometimes they were forced to do so, but often it was a choice, made for many different reasons: to go where there was better and more abundant land for grazing and crops, to live closer to the friends and family of the husband or wife, or to leave one chief for a better one. In fact, the ability to change chiefdom allegiances has long been one of the main checks subjects have been able to exert on the authority of their chiefs; a chief who ruled poorly ran the risk of losing his subjects.[10]

Before Shaka's time, the Zulu had not particularly distinguished themselves in the competition among chiefdoms and lineages. When Shaka became the Zulu inkosi, several chiefdoms in the region were larger and more powerful than the Zulu, among them the Mabhudu, the Mthethwa, the Ndwandwe, the Ngwane, and the Qwabe. And members of the Zulu lineage, those who traced their patrilineal descent directly back to Zulu himself, were a large but hardly preponderant group. Even today, after almost two centuries of Zulu ethnic consolidation, Zulu is still only the tenth most common surname in KwaZulu-Natal, after Mkhize, Dlamini, Ngcobo, Ndlovu, Gumede, Cele, Khumalo, Mthembu, and Mhlongo, and there are numerous other surnames (and therefore lineages) besides.[11]

As institutions, chiefdoms and lineages have been extraordinarily stable for centuries, perhaps since the time of Malandela, who is supposed to have ruled in the late 1500s or early 1600s, seven to nine generations before Shaka.

Evidence from archaeology, oral traditions, and historical linguistics, not to mention documentary evidence from the time of Shaka to the present, all suggest a high degree of continuity in these basic patterns of social and political organization.[12] While individual chiefdoms may have been in constant flux and individual chiefs may have been under constant threat of regicide or secession, the chiefdom as an institution was widely accepted, and seemingly permanent. The anthropologist Max Gluckman, long the most prominent ethnographer and analyst of Zulu society, first noted this decades ago. Gluckman pointed out that while there was no lack of contestation and struggle, even rebellion, in pre-Shakan southeastern Africa, true revolution—reorganization of the social and political structure—was rare. He characterized this stability as an "equilibrium": people might reject the authority of their chiefs by overthrowing them, assassinating them, supporting rival claimants to the throne, or seceding, but every case involved merely a change in the officeholder, not a transformation of the political structure. The establishment of the Zulu kingdom under Shaka and the onset of European rule were more genuinely revolutionary, but even here new large-scale structures have often simply been grafted onto old structures of local governance. Though many European colonial officials, settlers, and missionaries called for the abolition of African chiefship, both the colonial state of the nineteenth century and the white-dominated South Africa of the twentieth century found they had little choice but to continue to recognize chiefs. Even the African National Congress, which over the course of the last century became progressively more inclined to portray chiefs as apartheid collaborators, had to become more accommodating towards chiefship after coming to power, in 1994.[13] In short, chiefdom, lineage, and khonza have long been hegemonic ideas, accepted even by people who have otherwise disagreed about many things.

Chiefdom, lineage, and khonza may have derived their hegemonic power from the fact that they were based on patriarchy, the most basic unit of social and political organization in this area, operating on the level of the individual household or homestead (umuzi). In many ways, chiefship simply replicated on a larger scale the patriarchy of the homestead. Each individual chief was the head of his lineage, which was the family writ large, and, with very few exceptions, chiefs were always men. Moreover, the political hierarchy at the chiefdom merged imperceptibly with the social hierarchy on the homestead level. The chief was at the top of this hierarchy;

below him were the headmen (singular *induna*, plural *izinduna*), who governed individual districts; and below the headmen were the homestead heads (singular *umnumzane*, plural *abanumzane*), who were the patriarchs or paterfamilias of each individual homestead.

The homestead has been the primary unit of social and political organization among the Nguni-speaking peoples (including the Zulu, Xhosa, Swazi, and Ndebele) for a very long time indeed. Archaeology and oral traditions demonstrate a fundamental continuity in Nguni household structure stretching back centuries before the political innovations of the 1700s. Although the rise of mining, urbanization, and migrant labor were to fundamentally transform the institution from the 1880s onward, many of these earlier patterns survive to the present. The typical household has consisted of the homestead head, his wives, their unmarried children, and various dependents, both related and unrelated. All homesteads, from the most humble to those of the Zulu kings, have tried to follow the same basic plan: several round, one-roomed huts arranged in an arc or, if the homestead is large enough, in a circle, around a central cattle byre. At the center of the arc, facing east, is the house of the homestead head, with one house for each individual wife arranged on either side, and additional houses beyond for each unmarried son. One wife, usually but not necessarily the first, is designated chief wife. The homestead is surrounded by fields used for farming. Archaeologists have found homesteads built in this pattern dating as far back as the seventh century, and the same structure is still to be found in the rural, communal land-tenure areas of KwaZulu-Natal province.[14]

The foremost markers of wealth were the number of wives in a household and the number of cattle owned by the household. Cattle were used sparingly for meat, usually only on ceremonial occasions, their main contributions to the southeastern African diet coming in the form of milk. Cattle also provided leather. But their importance lay more in their exchange value than in their use value. Cattle could be accumulated in ways that, say, grain stores could not. Requiring very little labor input compared to crops, and given decent conditions, cattle herds could increase like capital investments earning interest or dividends.[15] Cattle thus came to serve as a particularly prized form of currency. However, even their exchange value did not quite capture the entirety of the significance of cattle in southern African culture. Cattle had a ritual significance, as well, which could be seen in their roles in sacrifice, the centrality of the cattle byre to the homestead, and the fact that homestead members were buried beneath the byre. All this made southeast African society a classic example of the "cattle culture" so common to the savanna areas throughout Africa, from South Africa to the Sudan, from Senegal to Somalia.[16]

Although the household structure I have described was hegemonic, stable, and common to many southern African societies, it was neither unchanging, nor uniform, nor free from internal contestation. Wealth in cattle was unequally distributed, and this had important consequences for household structure. The institution of bridewealth exchange, almost universal in sub-Saharan Africa, called for the husband's family to give the bride's family a certain amount of wealth upon marriage. In southern Africa this was usually, though not always, in the form of cattle, at least ideally. Wealth in cattle therefore allowed some men to marry more women than other men could: even in the best of times, most married men had only one wife, while the very wealthiest men could have dozens. The situation for men was particularly dire, for the poorest stood little chance of getting married at all and were often forced into clientship with richer households. The situation for women was somewhat better, for there was always the possibility that they could marry into a wealthier household. But even in a polygamous society some women remained unmarried, particularly the very old and the very young. If they did not have a family to support them, they too drifted into clientship. Clientship also awaited those married couples too poor to afford their own homesteads.

But in precolonial society in southeastern Africa, class was not nearly so important as gender and generation. In fact, strictly speaking, class hardly existed: differences of wealth tended to be quantitative, not qualitative, and marriage and adoption usually absorbed those who fell through the cracks. And since the homestead was a political unit as much as a social unit, every homestead head essentially held a political office with the same privileges as others in the same office. Within the homestead, however, the situation was very different.

The homestead head controlled not only the fruits of the labor of the other homestead members, but also what might be called their "labor power."[17] In marrying off his daughter, the homestead head lost both the young woman's productive labor and her reproductive labor. By accumulating cattle, however, he was able to acquire wives whose productive and reproductive labor made up for what might be lost. Similarly, as long as a son remained unmarried he was subject to his father's authority, which the father was able to enforce through control of the primary means by which the son could attain his independence: bridewealth cattle. In other words, the father could punish the son's insubordination by effectively prolonging his subordination. The labor power of young women and men was symbolized by cattle, and these people and things were connected through the institution of bridewealth exchange, which was controlled by the homestead head.

Although women and youths did on occasion challenge the power structure of the homestead, this challenge was limited and for a long time failed to fundamentally transform it. Oral traditions are replete with evidence of women, in particular, challenging the authority of their husbands and fathers. We see this "in the struggles described within the homestead, in the many accounts of daughters escaping from dominating fathers and unwanted husbands, and of mothers pursued by their sons and fleeing from their husbands."[18] In the case of sons, patricide is also a common theme in Nguni oral traditions. Yet there were many factors that mitigated potential conflict between patriarchs on the one hand, and women and youths on the other. Most notably, the homestead head had numerous obligations to redistribute the homestead's wealth to its members. For their part, women enjoyed numerous privileges, especially over children, younger siblings, and junior wives. Women's prestige was not purely symbolic, but derived from the value of their manual labor and their reproductive labor (giving birth to and raising children). Both gender and generational conflict were mitigated by the fact that both women and youths stood to gain privileges as they became older themselves. As James Scott has noted, the most stable and legitimate social hierarchies throughout the world and throughout history have tended to be those, like generational hierarchies, in which the lowest-ranking members are virtually guaranteed to become high-ranking members themselves one day.[19] The stability and legitimacy of patriarchy, in turn, ensured the stability and legitimacy of the social and political institutions based on it, the chiefdom, and the lineage.

SHAKA AND PHAKATHWAYO: THE BEGINNINGS OF THE ZULU KINGDOM AND ZULU ETHNICITY

Thus, until the early 1800s only the members of the Zulu chiefdom and lineage called themselves amaZulu, and they were only a small proportion of the total population of what would later become KwaZulu-Natal. The other people in the region called themselves by the names of the numerous chiefdoms or lineages to which they belonged: amaNgwane, amaThembu, amaChunu, amaQwabe, and so on. They were aware of overarching categories of common ancestry that linked people across chiefdom boundaries, but these categories had names like Lala, Mbo, Ntungwa, abaSenhla, abaSenzansi, and Nguni, not Zulu. They were also aware of shared languages that also crossed chiefdom boundaries, but these were tekela/tekeza, thefula, and Zunda, not isiZulu. If it had not been for the Zulu king Shaka's conquests and his ethnolinguistic policies, the category of amaZulu would never have become as broad and as inclusive as it is today.

The political and ethnic consolidation that Shaka brought about was not the first of its kind. There is some evidence from both archaeology and the study of oral traditions that suggests that there had been earlier cycles of political centralization and fragmentation. For example, the prevalence of the related categories Mbo and Langa/Langeni may have been the legacy of a Mbo or Langa kingdom that once existed but had broken up. Similarly, the concept of the kingdom (izwe or isizwe) that incorporated many different chiefdoms and was ruled by an inkosi yezwe (king, paramount chief) with several different inkosi yohlanga (chiefs, heads of chiefdoms/lineages) under him was perhaps too elaborate already in the 1820s to have been developed just during Shaka's reign or even during the reigns of his predecessors. Perhaps there was an already existing template for how a kingdom would operate, a template sustained in oral tradition, which could simply be reactivated when fragmentation gave way once more to centralization. But even if this notion of the cyclical nature of state formation in the region were true, it would also be further proof of the weakness and instability of kingdoms compared to chiefdoms and households as institutions, which showed much greater continuity and staying power.[20]

A more recent wave of political consolidation hit the region after about 1750. When Shaka was born in the 1780s or 1790s, the Zulu chiefdom's most powerful neighbors were the Mthethwa kingdom, ruled by Dingiswayo, and the Ndwandwe, ruled by Zwide. The ultimate catalyst behind their sudden growth seems to have been the intensification of trade during this period at Delagoa Bay, in the extreme south of present-day Mozambique, between the Portuguese and neighboring Africans. Certainly one of the main rivals of the Mthethwa and Ndwandwe, the Mabhudu kingdom, in the immediate hinterland of the bay, became a major conduit for this trade and used the proceeds to simultaneously expand and centralize the state under the authority of the king. The Ndwandwe and Mthethwa were expanding as well at this time, perhaps also because of trade, and military competition between these states and others was becoming more intense. Trade would have given the Mthethwa and the Ndwandwe kings, like their Mabhudu counterpart, more wealth to redistribute to their followers and prospective followers, effectively buying more legitimacy. Failing this, the wealth could also be used to create larger and stronger military forces which could coerce people into pledging allegiance to one or another king. Trade with the Portuguese thus provided both the motive and the means to engage in predatory raiding to secure what the Portuguese wanted: at first ivory, then increasingly cattle, and a trickle of slaves that became a significant flow only in about 1823. Abstaining from either trade or military competition was simply not an option.[21]

Crucially, in the case of the new Mthethwa kingdom at least, political consolidation was not accompanied by the ethnic assimilation of conquered peoples. Chiefdoms of this era tended to incorporate conquered peoples as equals, often by developing myths of common ancestry ("fictive kinship"). The inkosi of the once-independent chiefdom might be eliminated, but the old chiefdom's izinduna and abanumzane would quickly become full members in the new chiefdom's elite. This was standard practice with the Mthethwa until its expansion and consolidation had reached such a level, and its coercive powers had become sufficiently strong, that it no longer needed to make such concessions to its newly conquered subjects. Instead, the latter came to form a subordinate class, while the core inhabitants of the Mthethwa kingdom became a privileged class. Although the evidence is scanty, there is some indication that the Ndwandwe were able to do the same with their conquests.[22]

Among the Zulu, on the other hand, and their neighbors such as the Qwabe, Ngcobo, Hlubi, and Ngwane, ethnic assimilation of conquered peoples continued into Shaka's reign. This was because the leaders of these chiefdoms lacked the power to fully subordinate their new subjects. In these cases, military aggression had to be accompanied by some sort of positive inducement in order to defeat the opposing chief and his subjects and to get them to accept conquest. One of these inducements was security: the power of the heads of these chiefdoms grew, not so much because they had new and greater coercive powers at their disposal, but rather because their subjects, and the subjects of the chiefdoms they conquered, were more willing to unite and submit to a chief's authority in the face of military threats from the Mthethwa and the Ndwandwe farther north. In other words, many people preferred conquest by these smaller chiefdoms, including the Zulu, precisely because they lacked the coercive power of the Mthethwa and Ndwandwe, and might defend them from it. The other inducement was more egalitarian ethnic incorporation: instead of becoming a subordinate and ethnically marked class of helots under the Mthethwa and Ndwandwe, conquered peoples in the Zulu chiefdom and the other smaller chiefdoms like it became full-fledged members of the chiefdom, neither outsiders nor subordinates.[23]

Before Shaka became the Zulu chief, in about 1816, his own personal experience was of differential ethnic incorporation. Though Shaka was a son (probably illegitimate) of the Zulu inkosi Senzangakhona and was born in the Zulu chiefdom, conflicts between Senzangakhona and Shaka's mother, Nandi, forced her into exile, and she took Shaka with her. Shaka then spent most of his youth as an outsider in various other chiefdoms, first in the Langeni, with Nandi's family, and later in the Qwabe, where Nandi married a commoner and had another child. Though the Langeni and the Qwabe, like the Zulu at this time, tended to incorporate conquered subjects as ethnic, social, and political equals, Shaka's situation was different. Throughout the region, one's lineage and chiefdom were determined by that of the father. But Shaka had been rejected by his father, and many Langeni and Qwabe refused to see him as one of their own as well. Many oral traditions relating to Shaka's childhood and youth tell of the ostracism and humiliation to which the Langeni and Qwabe subjected him. Later, Shaka went to live among the Mthethwa, who also treated him badly at first and, unlike the Qwabe or Langeni, generally consigned outsiders to a subordinate caste. Ironically, among the Mthethwa Shaka managed to overcome this status by virtue of his military acumen, becoming one of the favorite soldiers of the Mthethwa inkosi Dingiswayo.[24]

In about 1816, Shaka returned to the Zulu chiefdom, killed both Senzangakhona and his heir, and became Zulu inkosi himself. In the beginning, Shaka's position was weak, for two reasons. First, many people in the Zulu chiefdom saw Shaka as a usurper of the Zulu chiefship, whose claim to that position was not entirely legitimate. Second, the very existence of the Zulu chiefdom was in jeopardy, regardless of who was chief. When the Ndwandwe defeated the Mthethwa shortly after Shaka became chief, Shaka lost a benefactor and protector, and the Ndwandwe now seemed to be without a serious rival to check their conquests in the area.

Shaka sought to strengthen his position by getting the weaker chiefdoms in his immediate neighborhood to submit to his authority, whether by force or by persuasion, and to unite with him against the Ndwandwe. One of his first conquests was the Qwabe chiefdom, now ruled by Phakathwayo. During the reign of Phakathwayo's father and predecessor, Khondlo, the Qwabe chiefdom was stronger and more powerful than any other in the Thukela Valley and adjacent areas.[25] Numerous stories about this period refer to the weakness of the Zulu and other neighboring chiefdoms, and to the contempt the Qwabe had for them. This general contempt intersected with the contempt that many Qwabe, including Phakathwayo himself, had expressed toward Shaka while he had lived among them. Shaka and Phakathwayo had a quarrel as boys, and Phakathwayo called Shaka a "little Ntungwa, a little nothing in hiding, with a little penis that points upwards."[26]

The young Shaka left the Qwabe for the Mthethwa at precisely the time when Mthethwa expansion was threatening the Qwabe. Toward the end of Khondlo's reign, a succession dispute emerged between the supporters of two of his sons, Nomo and Phakathwayo. Khondlo nominated Nomo, but most of the Qwabe izinduna protested that this would make the chief mother a Mthethwa. The izinduna therefore favored Phakathwayo and helped him secure the Qwabe chiefship.[27] At stake in the dispute between Nomo and Phakathwayo was not only the chiefship, but the relative power of the chief and the izinduna. The izinduna had checked the chief's power by refusing to accept the successor he nominated. Once he became chief, however, Phakathwayo was eager to shore up his power. He therefore raided the Makhanya, a subchiefdom recognizing the supremacy and authority of the Qwabe chief while at the same time retaining its own chief, for cattle.[28] Phakathwayo must have done so in order to gain leverage over the izinduna, for otherwise the cattle raid is inexplicable in light of the support he had received from the Makhanya. They had sheltered him after an earlier defeat by Nomo, helped him attack and overcome Nomo, and continued to khonza him.[29]

After Phakathwayo defeated him, Nomo and many other Qwabes left the chiefdom and joined Shaka, who welcomed them into the chiefdom. Notable among these was Zulu ka Nogandaya, also known as Komfiya. Komfiya went to the Zulu chiefdom and became one of Shaka's favorites and a famous warrior. Komfiya found refuge among the Zulu, was able to rise to prominence through achievement rather than through noble birth, and, perhaps most important, willingly fought for Shaka against the Qwabe: "He [Shaka] said, 'Zulu, are you prepared to go among your people, the Qwabe, and kill?' Zulu replied [calling Shaka by his praise name], 'Ndabezita, I am.'"[30] The stories of Komfiya's exploits helped bolster Zulu hegemony over the Qwabe by showing how a man could transfer his allegiance from the Qwabe chief to the Zulu king and profit by doing so.[31]

Perhaps an even more important Qwabe who found refuge under Shaka was Nqetho, younger brother to Nomo and Phakathwayo. Nqetho deserted the Qwabe because members of the chiefdom claimed he was violating law and custom by trying to marry a woman he was prohibited from marrying. Nqetho apparently also said, in leaving, "We do not have enough to eat," suggesting that material want pushed him into Shaka's camp.[32] Nqetho then went to the Zulu chiefdom and khonza'd Shaka.[33] Shaka allowed Nqetho enormous discretion both before and after the Zulu conquest of the Qwabe. Nqetho was able to publicly challenge Shaka, behave in a familiar manner toward him, and claim the same level of protocol.[34] Several sources remark that Nqetho was the only person who could spit in Shaka's presence.[35] Nevertheless, "Shaka kept Nqetho close to him" so as to keep him from mounting any rebellions against Shaka's rule.[36]

Shaka's incorporation of prominent Qwabe refugees like Nomo, Komfiya, and Nqetho was a prelude to his invasion and conquest of the Qwabe chiefdom itself, the first major conquest of his reign. Shaka may have attacked the Qwabe in order to force the Qwabe into a defensive alliance in response to the threat represented by Zwide's Ndwandwe chiefdom.[37] Indeed, the Zulu probably attacked the Qwabe before they attacked any of the trading states to the north or the various Thukela valley chiefdoms to the south and west. Traditional views that the Qwabe were contemptuous of the Zulu chiefdom for being so small and weak, and that the Qwabe were surprised by the Zulu attack, both suggest that the Zulu had not had any major conquests before the Qwabe.[38] Stuart's informant Madikane, in an explicit consideration of the order of Shaka's conquests, says that Shaka "attacked Tayi of the amaLangeni section of the Ngcobo people, then Pakatwayo, then conquered Zwide."[39] Meanwhile, Mayinga, another one of Stuart's informants, claimed that Shaka attacked Phakathwayo for Dingiswayo.[40] This suggests that the Qwabe conquest came at such an early point in Shaka's career that he was still so weak as to be bound to some sort of subservient relationship to Dingiswayo as Mthethwa chief.

The battle between Phakathwayo and Shaka was a pivotal point in the histories of both the Zulu and Qwabe chiefdoms. As the schoolteacher Mboneni Gumede told me, there were many chiefdoms in the area at the time, compared to Malandela's day, and this made things very difficult. Zwide of the Ndwandwe started to fight all the chiefs in the area. He wanted to conquer them. Phakathwayo moved from the Mhlathuze to eSangoya. Shaka came to Phakathwayo to ask for his opinion about Zwide's actions. Phakathwayo said, "I am happy that you [Shaka] can see that Zwide is not doing good. You must think carefully about what to do." Shaka reported back to his people, the Zulu, about his discussions with Phakathwayo. They decided to kill some of the cattle to make shields. Shaka sent spies among Zwide's people to find out how they made their shields so that they could make ones themselves that were just as strong. This system worked for Shaka. When they fought, Zwide's people were fooled and thought that Shaka's people were Ndwandwe. The Zulu defeated the Ndwandwe. Shaka was convinced that his defeat of Zwide meant that he had conquered all the people in the area. At midnight, Shaka sent his warriors to raid Phakathwayo's homestead. Phakathwayo was killed there, along with his heir, Khathide.[41]

Different chiefdoms responded differently to Shaka's aggression. While he had to resort to warfare to get Phakathwayo's Qwabe and others like the Nyuswa to submit, some, like Zihlandlo's Mkhize, submitted peacefully. The two other large chiefdoms in the area, Macingwane's Chunu and Ngoza's Thembu, fled across the Thukela and Mzinyathi rivers, respectively, into Natal proper, beyond Shaka's effective authority.[42] Despite Shaka's failures with the Chunu and Thembu, his successes with the Qwabe, Nyuswa, and Mkhize were sufficient to repel a second Ndwandwe invasion (the first having come after Shaka's accession but before his first conquests). Finally, in 1819, instead of merely trying to withstand a third Ndwandwe invasion, the Zulu counter-attacked, defeated, and conquered the Ndwandwe, although many of the Ndwandwe fled northward rather than accept Shaka's rule.[43] This left the Zulu the most powerful force between Delagoa Bay and the Mzimkhulu River—that is, throughout the whole of modern KwaZulu-Natal province—although Shaka did not even pretend to rule most of this territory.

Many people, especially those south of the Thukela River, who would later become Zulus, were either totally independent of the Zulu or effectively defied Shaka's claims over them.

As a result of these conquests, the Zulu chiefdom became the Zulu kingdom. The many conquered chiefdoms retained their identities as sections of the Zulu kingdom, and their chiefs retained their titles as amakhosi, although many had been installed by Shaka himself after he had eliminated those who refused to accept his overrule. This greatly expanded the number of people who could be considered "Zulus" by adding a third category of "Zulus." Besides the members of the Zulu lineage and of the Zulu chiefdom proper (the Zulu heartland, that part of the Zulu kingdom which had been ruled by Shaka's predecessors), now there were also the subjects of the Zulu king, who belonged to dozens of chiefdoms.

Shaka's reign also saw the beginning of the Zulu ethnic group. This was defined in terms of both language and ancestry. Linguistically, the Zulu elite promoted their Zunda dialect as a sort of standard language, isiZulu, that all the people of the kingdom should adopt, while they mocked and denigrated other ways of speaking. Like the common Zulu language, the notion of common ancestry was both a legacy of the pre-Shakan era and the result of active social engineering by the Zulu elite. The overarching categories of Lala, Mbo, Ntungwa, and Nguni were all based on traditions claiming that the progenitors of different lineages shared common ancestors, as was the case with the Qwabe and the Zulu. While many of these traditions probably predated Shaka, there is also evidence that other traditions were either manipulated or even invented out of whole cloth during Shaka's reign in order to assimilate and foster unity between the Zulu elite and the people they had conquered.[44]

But there were limits to the integration of Shaka's conquered subjects into the Zulu ethnic group. To begin with, Shaka and the Zulu leadership explicitly excluded many of these people from what would become the Zulu ethnic group. The Zulu elite promoted the idea that both they and those lineages that had been ethnically incorporated on equal terms belonged to the category of people that became known as the Ntungwa, a precursor to the Zulu ethnic group. But the counterpart of this inclusion and incorporation was exclusion and differentiation. After Shaka's initial round of conquests and the defeat of the Ndwandwe, his power was much more secure. Therefore he no longer had to purchase the loyalty of newly conquered subjects by giving them the benefits of incorporation into the Zulu ruling class. One of the myths of Shaka's rule is that he replaced genealogy with merit as the main criterion for promotion and appointment to high offices in the state and the army. In fact, these offices became an Ntungwa monopoly. Those belonging to other chiefdoms (mainly on the coast and in the extreme north and south of Zulu-ruled territory) were said to belong to other, inferior ethnic groups such as the Lala, Nhlengwa, Thonga, or iNyakeni. These categories may have predated Shaka, but under his rule and afterward they became imbued with derogatory connotations, and the people to whom they applied became a sort of helot class, mere sources of labor and tribute without the privileges of the Ntungwa.[45] Thus, Shaka and the Zulu leadership did not even attempt to make all their subjects Zulu.[46]

Perhaps more important, many people resisted incorporation, whether it was political or ethnic. The reason was that the more local forms of social organization, namely the chiefdom and the household, were far more legitimate than either the Zulu kingdom or the Zulu ethnic group in many people's eyes, and chiefs and homestead heads were more legitimate than the Zulu king. The latter thus posed challenges to Shaka's authority. Shaka and other kings recognized this and tried to usurp the authority not only of chiefs, but of homestead heads as well. The introduction of the regiments, or *amabutho*, was perhaps the clearest case of this usurpation. Before the political consolidation of the late 1700s, young men and women were initiated into adulthood in their local communities. As long as they were unmarried, their homestead heads, usually their fathers, controlled their labor and the fruits of it. They could only become independent of their homestead heads by becoming married themselves, but they could only do so with the permission of their homestead heads. In the late 1700s, centralizing chiefs and kings developed the amabutho, which initiated young men and women in central places under the jurisdiction of the chief or king, rather than the homestead head. The young men's amabutho made up the bulk of the manpower serving in armies in the region, both under Shaka and elsewhere. While serving in the amabutho, the youths' labor and its fruits were controlled by the chief or king, and marriage now depended on the permission of the king, not that of the homestead head. Many homestead heads were also either persuaded or forced to send some of their daughters to the *isigodlo*, a special regiment of women for whom the king arranged marriage and collected bridewealth. While popular in some quarters, these developments were also resented and even resisted in others, by both youths and their parents.[47]

The clearest evidence for the Qwabes' rejection of incorporation into the Zulu kingdom and ethnic group is their often violent resistance to the Zulu even *after* the Qwabe had been conquered. The rejection in this case is all the more striking because the Qwabe were ethnically incorporated on more equal terms than were many other chiefdoms. On the one hand, some prominent Qwabe like the chief Nqetho and the soldier Komfiya were among Shaka's greatest favorites. According to one of Stuart's informants, many Qwabe accepted their own conquest by Shaka, saying, "We are now Tshaka's people."[48] But the available traditions are also replete with references to rather intense violence between the two groups during and after conquest. Arguably, Shaka's most severe depredations were carried out against the Qwabe, especially after some members of the chiefdom were implicated in an assassination attempt against him in 1824. Stuart's informant Jantshi provided the following account of the incident.

> I know Tshaka was stabbed in the left arm, the assegai slightly entering his left side. He drew the assegai out himself and ran into a hut. Looking at the assegai he found it had a shaft blunted at the top, and so concluded it belonged to the Qwabe people, whereas it was one of his own people's. After this there was an order that the Qwabe people were to be killed. Having already konza'd, they, like the Zulus themselves, lived at Tshaka's kraal at Bulawayo. Those members of the Qwabe tribe found at the king's kraal were killed, a search was made for fugitives at their homes, and the saying arose that members of that tribe would be known by a habit men had of always placing wood on the hearth with the right arm. When caught, they were to be stabbed in the left side. Many members of the tribe were accordingly killed. The people scattered in all directions to hide themselves.[49]

Many of Stuart's informants say Shaka targeted all Qwabe indiscriminately in reprisal. Thus, according to Baleka, "Tshaka said that the Qwabe people should be picked out and all put to death."[50] Another, Mbovu, was more graphic,

> It was said in respect to the great massacre of the Qwabe people that Tshaka is said to have caused dongas [ditches] to be filled with corpses. So vast was the massacre that the whole people left Zululand to settle in Natal,

Pondoland, and elsewhere. There is nowadays no section of the Qwabe tribe in Zululand. On seeing a member of the Qwabe tribe in Zululand, some old woman of the amaCunu tribe is said to have expressed the greatest surprise, believing, as the slaughter was so thorough, that every one must have been killed.[51]

Similar stories tell of atrocities committed by Shaka against numerous other chiefdoms. As with the Qwabe, personal revenge may help to explain the severity of Shaka's actions against the Mthethwa and the Langeni. Revenge was clearly his main motive for doing so.

One day Tshaka called all the Langeni people together to a certain euphorbia tree at some hill. Finding that they were not all assembled, he sent and directed that even the very old men should come. They came, believing that he had it in mind to make them presents of cattle, as his mother was a member of their tribe. When as many as possible had congregated, he proceeded to call to mind the way they had brought him up when a boy; how they had given him a small black beast with horns . . . saying he was to eat that; how they used to send him out herding cattle and, during his absence, dig a hole, and on his getting back say, "There's a bird in that hole over there, my child; go and take it out," (and how) he then put his hand in to find nothing but faeces buried there; how they would ask, "Do you know what a porcupine's egg looks like?," and on his saying, "No," they would say, "There it is; take it out," and when he attempted to do so he would find nothing but excrement there; how they would pour curds in such quantities into his hands for him to eat that it would run down both arms to the elbows and become quite hot as he ate. In fact they had treated him just like a dog. He then said that on account of all this, of their ill-treatment of him, he would have them put to death, and forthwith, on (his) giving the order, all were massacred on the spot. He was afterwards very sorry for what he had done, and directed all the orphans to be carried off to the Mtetwa district (for that was where he himself had grown up), where, he said, the country was a pleasant one to live in and where they would get nice curds for their children. They were accordingly accommodated with land.[52]

Shaka acted in a similar way against the Mthethwa themselves because some of them had treated him badly, as well. Baleni said, "Tshaka did however kill those of the Mtetwa tribe who had bullied him whilst he was a young men." Nhlekele told of how the Mthethwa king Mondiso was "caught and killed at the dancing place. . . . Many of Mondiso's followers, of the *indhlunkulu*, were killed at the same time.[53] But revenge was not a factor for the many other groups that Shaka targeted without having any personal history with them. In these cases, Shaka's violence was a simple response to resistance against him. The sheer number of chiefdoms affected attests to the extent of the resistance: Bhaca, Nganga, Ndwandwe, Thembu, Ntshali, Tshangala, Qadi, Gasa, Chunu, Mabaso, Cele, and others.[54] Even if Africans' accounts of Shaka's depredations were exaggerated, what matters is that they believed that those stories were true. As such, oral traditions critical of Shaka are evidence of widespread animosity toward the Zulu king, which precluded people who saw themselves as the Zulu king's victims from identifying themselves as Zulus.

DINGANE AND NQETHO: CONTINUED RESISTANCE TO ZULU POLITICAL AND ETHNIC INTEGRATION

The same points that have been made about Shaka's reign could be made about that of Dingane, Shaka's half-brother who had also led the conspiracy to assassinate him. Dingane failed, or did not even try, to extend his rule south of the Thukela beyond the narrow coastal strip north of Durban. Shaka had established a new capital, KwaDukuza, south of the Thukela after the Qwabe assassination attempt of 1824, in order to strengthen his influence in Natal proper, where many of the Qwabe lived. Dingane, on the other hand, moved his capital, Mngungundlovu, back to the north of the river. Dingane also continued Shaka's policy of differential ethnic incorporation —with privileges for the Ntungwa elite and exclusion for the despised Lala and others. But resistance continued, mainly in the form of flight, and Dingane both provoked and responded to this resistance with violence reminiscent of Shaka's.

It is indicative of the widespread resentment aroused by Shaka's violence that Dingane was fairly popular at first, even though he had been involved in the plot to assassinate Shaka. Indeed, early on the most effective means by which Dingane acquired legitimacy in the eyes of his subjects was by saying that he had saved the Zulu kingdom from Shaka's depredations. However, Dingane himself soon felt obliged to renege on his earlier promises to end the violence, even though this was widely seen as hypocritical and his popularity plunged as a result.[55] Dingane soon became as arbitrary in his violence as Shaka, for example by waging war against the Amabaso because they had complained to Dingane about the chief he had appointed to rule over them.[56] People of the Tshangala and Gasa kingdoms were killed off because their doctors, while having succeeded in bringing rain to the kingdom, also brought lightning. These particular episodes seem puzzling until one realizes that the Gasa doctors, at least, had also been favorites of Shaka's.[57] Similarly, Dingane attacked the Mbo because their chief publicly lamented Shaka's death in 1828.[58]

After the stories of Malandela, Qwabe, and Zulu, and later of Shaka and Phakathwayo, the third and final episode of precolonial Qwabe–Zulu antagonism that was to be remembered by Natal Africans throughout the colonial era was Dingane's destruction and scattering of the Qwabe chiefdom, now ruled by Shaka's favorite, Nqetho. Coinciding with the era of European penetration and conquest, this episode was a fitting end for precolonial Qwabe history and the generations-long feud between Qwabe and Zulu. The dispute had started with a fight between Malandela's sons, Qwabe and Zulu, which led to the separation of the two peoples and the founding of two different lineages and chiefdoms. In the second phase, after Shaka defeated Phakathwayo, Qwabe independence was lost and Zulu dominance decisively established. With the annihilation of Qwabe chiefship in the third phase, the story seemed to be over.

Ironically, it took a successful attempt on Shaka's life to bring in a Zulu regime that would repress the Qwabe chiefdom far more thoroughly than Shaka ever had. Soon after Dingane's accession to the Zulu kingship, he promptly initiated a purge of Shaka's favorites from the kingdom's administration. As vulnerable as this made Nqetho, as one of Shaka's greatest favorites, Nqetho exacerbated the situation by defying Dingane.[59] Nqetho then preempted any attempt on his own life by fleeing the kingdom with a retinue of his followers, as well as herds of cattle and oxen that had belonged to Shaka.[60] Finally, to add insult to injury, members of Nqetho's party cut off the tails of whatever cattle and oxen they left behind, depriving the owners of these important ritual symbols.[61]

The provocations by Nqetho and his followers only gave Dingane more reason to come down hard on them, but the fleeing Qwabe proved more than a match for their Zulu pursuers. Dingane sent numerous *izimpi* in pursuit of Nqetho and his followers, who frequently managed to avoid being caught by lighting fires at nightfall and then moving off again under cover of darkness. The izimpi would see the fires and carefully approach them, intending to ambush the people now that they had encamped, only to find that the camps had been abandoned and the fires left burning. Such tactics could not work forever, though, and Nqetho's followers fought with Dingane's izimpi in several minor engagements. The climax came at Ezimbokodweni, on the Umlazi River in the Natal midlands. Nqetho's forces routed the Zulu, though not without several of their own party, including women, dying.[62]

While Qwabe in Zululand suffered from Dingane's wrath, the Qwabe refugees under Nqetho were more victimized by people from other chiefdoms than by the Zulu. The reason seems to be that Nqetho and his followers did little to garner support from other people. Although they managed to recruit members from some of the territories through which they passed on their journey southward, suggesting they enjoyed favor in at least some quarters, they also earned widespread animosity by stealing cattle from others.[63] Even Stuart's Qwabe informants compared Nqetho unfavorably to Shaka. Both Nqetho and Shaka terrorized the people of the region through their raiding. However, Stuart's informants argued that Nqetho was worse because he did not settle, preferring to live purely off what he and his followers could steal. Nqetho refused to settle even when his followers began to pressure him to do so. Instead, he pressed on toward the land of the Amapondo and their chief, Faku.[64]

Nqetho's encounter with Faku led to war and the eventual destruction of this last straggling branch of the Qwabe chiefdom. Nqetho and Faku got along well at first. Nqetho sent some oxen and one of his izinduna to offer his allegiance to Faku, and Faku received Nqetho "as one of his children."[65] Soon, however, minor depredations by Nqetho or his followers began to trouble the Amapondo. A force of Amapondo was organized, led by Klaas Lochenberg, a Dutch man who had lived among the Africans in the area for more than twenty years. Nqetho's people got wind of the Pondo attack in advance and ambushed them. Later, Nqetho met the English trader Francis Farewell, who was on his way to Zululand. Nqetho had him killed rather than allow the Zulu access to his goods. Thereafter Nqetho's people steered clear of the Amapondo but launched raids against their various neighbors, burning and pillaging as they went along. In the midst of this conflict, both sides insisted to local missionaries that they were at peace with each other.[66]

Finally, Faku ordered an attack on Nqetho's people along the Umzimvubu. This time the latter were routed and chased away to the territory of the Bhaca chief, Ncaphayi; Dingane's cattle ended up in Bhaca rather than Pondo hands.[67]

Accounts differ as to Nqetho's fate after the debacle on the Umzimvubu. The historian J. D. Omer-Cooper says Ncaphayi had Nqetho killed and that Dingane sent several expeditions to his territory to recover the cattle.[68] Stuart's informant Dinya says Nqetho was killed by the Bhele people near the Drakensberg.[69] The nineteenth-century colonial official Theophilus Shepstone, getting his information from African informants, said Nqetho returned to Natal, where his arrival was reported by a certain Baleni to Dingane, who ordered Nqetho's assassination.[70]

If Nqetho actually did end up being killed on Dingane's orders, then he would not have been the only Qwabe to be killed by Zulus during Dingane's reign. Shaka's repression of the Qwabe had led to one round of killings, but those were followed by a decade of peace. Nqetho's revolt in 1829 led to a second, even more deadly, round. The refugees under Nqetho were not the only ones to die. Many of Nqetho's followers who had stayed behind in Natal were also killed, albeit sometimes against Dingane's orders. Though most of the dead were subjects of the Qwabe chiefdom, many from other chiefdoms were killed merely for supporting Nqetho.[71]

By the time of Nqetho's death in the early 1830s, members of the Qwabe chiefdom were scattered all over southeastern Africa. Some remained with the Zulu, including returning refugees. Others stayed behind in Faku's territory, or gathered with other refugees around the European trading post at Port Natal. Most, however, lived just across the Thukela from Zululand, to be later joined by a large wave of refugees during the civil war between Mpande and Dinizulu.[72] While the Qwabe chiefdom was scattered, the institution of Qwabe chiefship was also in a parlous state. However, it was not entirely extinguished. It would soon be revived, and the stories of Malandela, Qwabe, Phakathwayo, and Nqetho would be revisited. As the testimony of James Stuart's informants reveals, precolonial Qwabe history would continue to be relevant to the conceptions and ideologies of history, loyalty, and community of Natal Africans throughout the colonial era.

The Qwabe flight also prompted Dingane to lash out against other chiefdoms. All it took for Dingane to attack Dube's Qadi was a rumor that the latter was considering fleeing Zululand just as Nqetho had, while Magaye and his people paid a similar price merely for allowing Nqetho and the rest of the Qwabe safe passage through their territory.[73]

It is true that Dingane seems to have had political reasons for all the violence he perpetrated, unlike Shaka, who sometimes called for killings out of nothing more than a desire for personal revenge.[74] But the victims of Dingane's violence, no less than the victims of Shaka's, may be forgiven for not seeing Dingane's actions as rational or justified. Qadi traditions, for example, highlight not only their loyalty to Dingane before he acted against them, but also the extreme severity and totality of the resulting violence.[75] As under Shaka, any member of a targeted chiefdom was fair game, including women and children, regardless of their complicity in crimes of disloyalty, real or (very often) imagined.

White supremacists in South Africa have long used the alleged brutality of Shaka and Dingane to justify white racial domination. Since the 1960s, scholars have worked hard to show that neither Shaka nor Dingane was as violent, or as dependent on violence, as white supremacists had argued. Neither Shaka nor Dingane had the power to have anything close to one million people killed, as has often been alleged. Nor did they have much influence on territories farther afield, including even the borderlands of present-day KwaZulu-Natal province. But the violence they perpetrated closer to the Zulu heartland was real enough, and the resulting animosity among Natal Africans, especially refugees from the Zulu kingdom, lingered for decades. This violence, and, perhaps more important, the memories of it, helps to explain the very muted opposition to, and sometimes even support for, the Europeans who invaded and conquered Natal from the 1820s onward. As Heather Hughes puts it, following John Lonsdale and Bruce Berman, it was the Africans who suffered most under the precolonial political and social orders who offered the least resistance to European imperialism.[76] However, although this principle might be true for the first few decades of European colonialism in Natal, it would prove much less applicable later on.

CONCLUSION

The power of the Zulu kingdom was ephemeral, at least in Natal proper, that part of KwaZulu-Natal south of the Thukela River that bisects the province. It lasted just over twenty years, and even during that period it was limited. Contrary to Zulu ethnic nationalist historiography, before 1838 the Zulu kingdom never claimed sovereignty over all of Natal proper, and Zulu rule was not firmly established in many of the areas where it did claim sovereignty. If these factors limited the ethnic incorporation of Natal's population into the Zulu ethnic group, that incorporation was also limited by the Zulu ruling class itself, which preferred to exclude many of their conquered subjects and identify them as a distinct people. Many of those that the Zulu ruling class did try to ethnically incorporate, such as the Qwabe, strenuously resisted incorporation. The Zulu kings' violent responses to that resistance only served to further alienate large segments of the population. Finally, the European conquest of Natal, in 1838, ended the short period of Zulu power in that area and confined the Zulu kingdom to Zululand, north of the Thukela.

Hardly any Natal Africans called themselves Zulu during this period, preferring to call themselves Qwabe, Thembu, Chunu, and so on, demonstrating that their allegiance to their chiefdoms had outlasted the challenge of the Zulu kings. While the Zulu kingdom and Zulu ethnicity were not able to set down roots in Natal before 1838, the other forms of categorization that had predated the rise of the Zulu kingdom proved to be much hardier. The ideas of lineage and chiefdom, closely related to one another, survived the Zulu interlude more or less unchanged, as strong as ever. Not only were those ideas older and more established than anything to do with the Zulus, but they were also founded on social phenomena that had even deeper roots in the area: patriarchy and the homestead. Patriarchy and lineage were linked because one's lineage was determined by the lineage to which one's father belonged, and married couples customarily lived among the husband's people. Patriarchy and the chiefdom were linked because the patriarch of each individual homestead formed the lowest level of the chain of command that had the chief at its top, and also because the chiefdom as a whole was modeled on the structure of the individual homestead. The fact that almost everyone could become at least somebody's elder someday ensured that even women and youths bought into the whole interlocking system, although they may have challenged specific chiefs, elders, and homestead heads from time to time. Thus when Shaka and Dingane tried to appropriate the powers of chiefs, elders, and homestead heads—for example the power to order, allow, or prevent marriages, as well as the power to control bridewealth—the Zulu kings' popularity took a severe beating.

Nevertheless, the reigns of Shaka and Dingane had helped to establish the idea that self-identification as "Zulu" was a possibility, when and if anybody found it desirable. This potential could feed off the linguistic and cultural similarities throughout the region that made Zulu language and culture at least somewhat familiar to everybody. Similarly, people's mobility allowed members of different chiefdoms from different locales to become each other's familiars, not only figuratively, but also literally through the bonds of matrimony in a society where the principle of exogamy made mates from beyond one's immediate neighborhood more attractive. Also, the fact that both Shaka and Dingane, as well as many of their successors, had come into conflict with Europeans would lend Zulu ethnicity a certain cachet as European dominance in the region became more obvious and more burdensome, and the less attractive aspects of Zulu rule became an ever more distant memory. Already in the 1930s, the anthropologist Max Gluckman noted that "this opposition [between Africans and Whites] has heightened allegiance to the chiefs, and especially the Zulu kingship. The sentiment about the king grows, helped by his lack of power, for he has no power to abuse."[77]

2

A ZULU KING TOO STRONG TO LOVE, A COLONIAL
STATE TOO WEAK TO HATE, 1838–1879

The European conquest of Natal proceeded in three stages. First, in 1824, a small group of mainly British traders established a small trading outpost in Port Natal, which eventually became Durban, the largest city in KwaZulu-Natal. Second, from 1837 onward, Boer trekkers streamed into Natal and ultimately waged war against Dingane, securing the land south of the Thukela and creating an independent republic called Natalia there. Finally, from 1842, the British gradually asserted control over Natalia, transforming it into the British colony of Natal. From then until the Anglo-Zulu War of 1879, Natal colony and the Zulu kingdom existed side by side, divided by the Thukela River.

The actions during this period of those Africans living in Natal indicate that they most emphatically did not identify with the Zulu kings, but rather with their various chiefdoms. When Europeans and Zulus came into conflict, few Natal Africans sided with the Zulus. Many stayed aloof from the conflict, while many more actually left Zulu territory for European territory, and some even went so far as to fight on the European side. In explaining their actions, they often discussed their fear of and resentment toward the Zulu kings. Many Zulus, meanwhile, spoke disparagingly of Natal Africans as *amaKhafula*, those "spat out" from the kingdom, a term which merged with the Europeans' derogatory name for blacks, "Kaffirs."[1] For their part, many Natal Europeans insisted on a distinction between Zulus and "Natal Natives," and encouraged Natal Africans to identify with their chiefdoms so as to prevent the emergence of black racial unity.

Of course, there were countervailing trends. The colonial partition along the Thukela River could not erase the common history, language, and culture of the people on both sides. Even after the river became a border, Africans continued to shuttle back and forth across it, so that grazing lands, homesteads, and marital and familial relationships often straddled it. But political separation often led to conflict, forcing people to choose sides. This would continue to be the case as long as the two territories remained separate and as long as the Zulu king had real power that could be used to victimize people, as had happened so often in the past, at least as far as many Natal Africans were concerned.

The unattractiveness of Zulu ethnicity and political allegiance to the Zulu king also depended on the relative attractiveness of the alternative, namely identification with one's chiefdom. As long as chiefs, headmen, and homestead heads could provide their followers with peace and prosperity, then their followers would continue to identify with them and the chiefdoms they represented. Of course, the actions of European settlers, missionaries, and colonial officials had an even bigger role in determining Africans' peace and prosperity, and therefore the legitimacy of the indigenous African elite. Natal Europeans had their own desires, which would ultimately prove to be incompatible with Natal Africans' well-being, but in these early decades of white rule the colonizers were too weak to fulfill many of those desires, and Natal Africans flourished as a result. Given all these factors, it is no wonder that being Zulu had little appeal to Africans in early colonial Natal.

THE EUROPEAN CONQUEST OF NATAL

In 1824, six British traders, led by Francis Farewell and Henry Francis Fynn, arrived at what is today Durban harbor, hoping to trade with the Zulus and neighboring peoples. They called their outpost Port Natal. This location was on the very outer limits of effective Zulu authority. From the first, Shaka seems to have realized that the traders could undermine his rule or bolster it and that they therefore had to be managed carefully. Rather than turn them away, he allowed them to occupy, administer, and trade on the small parcel of land occupied by the outpost, in exchange for recognizing his authority over them and their obligation to render him unspecified service. Shaka also decreed that the Port Natal traders could only trade with him and his representatives and not directly with ordinary Zulu subjects of their own accord.[2]

But Shaka's opponents found it no less profitable than he did to work with these Europeans. Shaka's wars in the coastal region around Port Natal had been particularly destructive. Many people had been killed, others driven from their homes. Food production had been disrupted and hunger was widespread. Shaka had given the Port Natal traders generous gifts of cattle, some of which they gave to the very people Shaka had been waging war against. The traders then used the cattle to induce people in the area to come settle at Port Natal.[3] The Africans who did so set up their own farms and began selling the traders a portion of their crops, and some even worked for the traders as wage laborers.[4]

The African population at Port Natal grew rapidly, totaling some three to four hundred by 1826. At first, they comprised those who either had never been Shaka's subjects or had fled from Shaka before the Europeans arrived. Shaka soon became concerned that Port Natal would serve as a haven for his enemies and sought to prevent his own subjects from settling there. But in 1826 the traders, with their horses and guns and armed African retainers, fought on Shaka's side against the Ndwandwe and did the same against a branch of the Khumalo under Bheje in 1827. In 1826, as well, Shaka established his new capital, KwaDukuza, just south of the Thukela, less than one hundred kilometers north of Port Natal, apparently in order to consolidate his hold over his southernmost territories and to distance himself from the increasingly restive northern sections of the kingdom. Convinced of the loyalty of the Port Natal traders, and relatively secure in his rule over the neighboring areas, Shaka lifted restrictions against refugees from his kingdom living with the traders.[5] But Shaka's situation was not as secure as he thought it was, and he was assassinated soon thereafter, in 1828.

Dingane's early purges of Shaka's favorites caused the flow of refugees into Port Natal to increase, especially from among Nqetho's Qwabe and Magaye's Cele, a development which Dingane saw as a grave threat to his position. Even more disturbing for Dingane were the defections from within the ruling class, such as Dingane's headman Ngqojana, and a whole regiment of the Zulu army that fled to Port Natal in 1834. As a result, Dingane decided to establish a buffer zone between the kingdom and Port Natal by evacuating his subjects from the coastal regions south of the Thukela River, which he did in 1832. Still the refugee flow continued, so that by 1835 some 2,500 refugees now lived in Port Natal. That year, Dingane and the missionary Gardiner reached an agreement whereby the Port Natal settlers would no longer accept refugees from the Zulu kingdom, but British traders violated that agreement before the year was over. Dingane's response was to suspend trade with Port Natal, but the fact was that he was increasingly dependent on that trade, and he was forced to lift the ban in 1836.[6] This did not solve the problem of Dingane's growing political insecurity, which caused him to lash out violently at more and more of his subjects, such as the Qadi in 1837, producing ever more refugees, which only further increased his insecurity.

Dingane's fear of the Port Natal settlers and the refugees living among them proved to be well founded, for they played a crucial role in helping the Boers defeat Dingane after 1837. Boer trekkers arrived in Natal during the latter part of 1837, as part of what has become known retrospectively as the Great Trek, the exodus of some 15,000 Boers from the Cape Colony to Natal, the Transvaal, and the Orange Free State during the late 1830s and 1840s. By May 1838, there were some 3,600 Boers in Natal.[7] Right from the beginning, the leader of the group that came to Natal, Piet Retief, tried to persuade Dingane to cede them the territory south of the Thukela, even though the Zulu kingdom only effectively ruled the coastal strip from the river to Port Natal. Dingane came to the conclusion that the Boers posed a threat to his supremacy and decided to proceed against them preemptively. In February 1838, he had Retief and his fellow negotiators killed at one of the conferences at the royal homestead uMgungundlovu, then had his army attack Retief's encampment, killing about 380 Boer settlers and 250 of their "Coloured" servants from the Cape.[8]

In the ensuing war between the Boers and the Zulus, thousands of Natal Africans fought on the Boer side. About 3,400 African men (out of a total African population at Port Natal of 10,000) took up arms under the command of the Port Natal settlers. According to the missionary Francis Owen, these Africans were "carried forward with the hopes of plunder and of thus retrieving the losses they have sustained from the Zoolus, who at different periods have subdued the various tribes to which they originally belonged."[9] One raid, in late March and early April of 1838, had attacked Zulu territory near present-day Kranskop, just on the Natal side of the Thukela. With no Zulu soldiers there, the raiders easily stole some 4,000 head of cattle and kidnapped some 500 women and children. But the Zulus were prepared when the Port Natal raiders attacked again later in April, this time fielding an army of 10,000 to counter the 3,000 from Port Natal. It did not help that the Port Natal raiders were increasingly divided. A running feud had broken out earlier between those Africans under the command of the trader Ogle and those under the trader Cane. At a decisive moment in the battle with the Zulus, Ogle's followers not only refused to follow Cane's orders, but also fled, enabling the Zulus to rout the Port Natal side. The Zulus then pressed onward to Port Natal, burning several African homesteads and killing dozens of Africans along the way. When they finally got to the settlement, they sacked it.[10]

However, the upper hand that the Zulus apparently enjoyed at this point was only temporary. Late in 1838, Andries Pretorius assumed the leadership of the Natal Boers and led an army which engaged between 8,000 and 10,000 Zulu soldiers at the Ncome River on 16 December. Though massively outnumbered, the Boers enjoyed some advantages. Most notably, they had rifles, while their adversaries did not, and they occupied a secure, well-fortified defensive position in the *laager* (encampment) they had formed by circling their wagons and covering them with thorny branches. For their part, the Zulus, under the command of Dingane's headmen Dambuza and Ndlela ka Sompisi, were committed to massed assaults on open land, which worked very well with similarly armed opponents, but was suicide against firearms. A thousand Zulu soldiers died in the plain surrounding the laager. Another 2,000 were killed while retreating, as the Boers relentlessly hunted down the Zulus who hid in rivers and ditches. The Boer forces, numbering some 600 men, included 3 Port Natal settlers and 120 of their African followers.[11]

Nine months after this battle, which Europeans would come to know as Blood River, large numbers of Dingane's subjects defected from the Zulu kingdom, which Zulus would later call "the breaking of the rope that held the nation together." In September 1839, Dingane's half-brother Mpande fled across the Thukela River along with 17,000 supporters and made an alliance with the Boers. Mpande seems to have decided to defect after he learned that Dingane, who had long questioned his loyalty and had killed all their father's other sons, had finally decided to kill him as well. But other aspects of this particular exodus attest to the continued sense of independence nurtured by Africans south of the Thukela. The emigrants were for the most part former inhabitants of the coastal areas between Port Natal and the Zulu heartland, Lala and Qwabe in particular. For example, one of the most prominent emigrants besides Mpande was Zulu ka Nogandaya, the Qwabe soldier who had been one of Shaka's favorites. Many of these people accompanied Mpande because they wanted to return to their former homes. Moreover, Mpande himself had become, under Dingane, a sort of governor of those parts of the kingdom both south of the Thukela (to which so many of his followers wanted to return) and immediately north of the Thukela (to which so many had been banished by both Shaka and Dingane).[12] Perhaps he had come to empathize with the Natal Africans over whom he ruled.

Neither the Battle of Ncome nor Mpande's defection had put an end to Dingane's kingship, let alone to the Zulu state and the army that maintained it. After the battle, in March 1839, Dingane agreed to cede to the Boers the territory south of the Thukela. But Mpande's defection and the growing security of their position emboldened the Boers. They struck an agreement with Mpande, promising to support him in an invasion of the Zulu kingdom, the overthrow of Dingane, and his own installation as Zulu king. In return, Mpande ceded to the Boers even some of the land north of the Thukela and promised to deliver cattle that the Boers claimed Dingane owed them. The Boers also used this failed cattle raid to justify their invasion of what was left of the Zulu kingdom north of the Thukela, which finally took place in 1839. The decisive engagement this time around occurred at Maqongqo Hills, where five thousand of Mpande's African supporters fought a similar number of Dingane's, and won. Dingane was killed by Swazi forces as he fled northward. Mpande then began the task of consolidating his rule as Zulu king, a task he never entirely accomplished.[13]

The Boers' rule in Natal only lasted a few years. By 1842, the British government had decided to intervene. The Boers' harsh reprisals against Africans accused of stock theft, and especially the Boers' increasing military activity against Africans south of Natal, in Pondoland, threatened to destabilize the whole region as far as the British-ruled Cape. The British government at the Cape sent an army to invade Natal in May 1842 and, after some initial reverses, they defeated the Boers by the end of June. In December 1842 the British colonial secretary agreed to the annexation of Natal. However, it is indicative of the low priority that the British accorded to this particular area that the process of annexation took some years. The Boer government continued to function, albeit now subject to the veto power of the British commandant resident in Natal. Another British government proclamation, on 12 May 1843, only declared the Crown's intention to annex. It was another year until the British formally annexed Natal and made it a district of the Cape Colony, on 31 May 1844. A British colonial administration for Natal was not established until December 1845. The vast majority of Boers in Natal preferred to trek again to the remaining independent Boer republics in the interior rather than accept British colonial rule, which they had trekked to get away from in the first place. As a result, the Boer population of Natal dwindled to about 350 in 1850, to be replaced by a British settler population that had surpassed 5,000 by 1852. Natal's African population at the time was about 100,000 and would never constitute less than 75 percent of the total, despite continued immigration by Europeans and, from 1860 to 1911, Indians.[14]

THE RECONSTITUTION OF AFRICAN CHIEFDOMS IN COLONIAL NATAL

The British annexation of Natal brought an end to several decades of upheaval. The challenges facing Africans trying to resume their previous lives varied quite a bit. For those who had not lost their places of residence, their sustenance, or their political independence, the transition was minor. For others it was more difficult. The Qwabes, for example, had seen their chiefdom destroyed, their chiefs killed, and had been scattered over a wide territory stretching from southeasternmost Zululand in the north, through the coastal regions of northern and southern Natal proper, down into Pondoland, in what is today the Eastern Cape. Less than a half-century later, the Qwabe chiefdom was one of the largest, most prosperous, and most powerful chiefdoms in the colony of Natal. And their story was by no means unique: the Qwabe chiefdom was just one of an elite group of chiefdoms in Natal that managed to withstand, and even flourish in the face of, colonialism. By 1881–82, Musi's Qwabe, some 10,000 in number, were the third largest chiefdom out of 173 existing in Natal at the time. The two larger chiefdoms, Mnganu's Thembu and Silwane's Chunu, had been broken up and scattered during the wars of Shaka and Dingane, much as the Qwabe had. The same was true of other large chiefdoms such as the Ngwane and the Mthethwa.[15]

The scattered Qwabe began to reconstitute their chiefdom in the early 1840s, a few years after their last chief, Nqetho, had defied Dingane and left the Zulu kingdom with his subjects, only to be killed shortly thereafter. Sometime between Dingane's defeat and murder in 1840 and the gradual extension of British rule over Natal from 1842 to 1845, the Qwabe at Port Natal began to look for a chief.[16] These people lived at the confluence of the Illovo and Amanzimtoti rivers. There, Nkomiyaphi, a close relative of Nqetho's who had come to Natal with him, built a new homestead and named it Emthandeni, which had been the name of the Qwabe chiefly homestead under Chief Phakathwayo before he was defeated and died during the wars against Shaka. Odwini, the main chiefly homestead of Khondlo, Phakathwayo's father and predecessor as chief, was similarly revived at Port Natal. Rather than claim the Qwabe chiefship for himself, Nkomiyaphi took part in the search for the rightful heir. Nkomiyaphi's refusal, or perhaps inability, to assume the position of chief suggests that there were limits to how far chiefship could be manipulated. This ideology was so powerful that to violate its rules would be to forfeit any claims to political legitimacy.

Having decided to search for a successor to Phakathwayo, the Port Natal Qwabe first had to determine who his rightful heir was, then locate that person and bring him (in this case) to the chiefdom's new home. Phakathwayo died with a daughter, Hetshepi, as his only child. All of his many brothers died in the course of conflicts with Shaka and Dingane. Godolozi was one of Phakathwayo's brothers, and after Godolozi was killed at Dingane's behest, his wife, Cobela, and his sons, Fokazi and Musi, went into hiding. Cobela, Fokazi, and Musi lived in Zululand at the homestead of Cobela's father, Mbokazi. After Mpande succeeded Dingane, they came out of hiding. The Qwabe at Port Natal heard of this and sent a deputation to Zululand to fetch Musi, bring him back, and prepare him to assume the Qwabe chiefship. This deputation was led by Mkhonto, a member of the Zulu royal family who had fled to Port Natal and become induna of the Africans there. Because Musi was still a boy, he could only serve as heir apparent, so his uncle Matiwane served as regent of the Qwabe chiefdom until Musi's adulthood.

A few years after bringing young Musi in from Zululand to prepare him to assume the Qwabe chiefship, members of the chiefdom came to the conclusion that Musi's uncle and regent, Matiwane, was scheming to usurp the chiefship from Musi permanently. They ended Matiwane's regency and appointed Musi chief.[17] In the late 1840s, a large group of Qwabe refugees left Zululand for Natal, settled in a broad swath from the Tongati-Mona confluence to the middle reaches of the Umvoti River, and appealed to Musi to settle among them and act as their chief.[18] It is indicative of the power of the Qwabe chiefship that members of the chiefdom would hold out for some fifteen years after the death of their last chief and then call on a youth from another district to come rule over them.

Between 1849 and 1856, Musi's control over the Qwabe chiefship would be challenged by his cousin Mamfongonyana. Mamfongonyana was the son of Godide, who also happened to be Musi's uncle and Phakathwayo's brother. He entered Natal in 1849 with another wave of Qwabe refugees. When Mamfongonyana and his party came to Natal, the government allowed them to settle on the land of a settler named Williams. Mamfongonyana then began to dispute Musi's claim to the Qwabe chiefship.[19]

Succession disputes have occurred frequently throughout Qwabe history, from the precolonial era to the present. In Musi's and Mamfongonyana's case, however, unlike with previous succession disputes, officials from an alien, colonial government were there to intervene. The official who arbitrated the dispute between Musi and Mamfongonyana was Theophilus Shepstone, Natal's secretary for native affairs (SNA) from 1849 to 1875. Shepstone had been born and raised in the Eastern Cape, which was dominated by the Xhosa, an ethnic group from the same Nguni cultural family as Natal Africans. Shepstone was fluent not only in the Xhosa language, closely related to the native languages of Natal Africans, but also in Xhosa political culture. He knew how chiefs, headmen, homestead heads, and others acted, and how they expected to be treated. He was thus able to avoid making the sorts of faux pas that most other Natal Europeans made so frequently in their dealings with Natal Africans. The demand for his skills was so great, and the supply so small, that Shepstone rapidly rose through the hierarchy of colonial officialdom and was effectively in charge of Natal's administration while still in his twenties, maintaining that position into his fifties and beyond.

What became known as "the Shepstone system" applied to virtually all Natal Africans. Each Natal African was in theory the subject of a particular chief, who had indunas to help him. (The Hlongwa chief Mhlazi was the only woman to serve as chief after the European conquest, and the phenomenon of female chiefship in Natal died with her. Nevertheless, though there were two other female chiefs in the immediate pre-conquest era in Natal, female chiefship was rare even then.)[20] The dozens of chiefdoms in Natal and the hierarchy of chiefs and indunas were carryovers from the precolonial era that were recognized under the Shepstone system. But now the chiefs were answerable to resident magistrates who administered each district in the colony, and the resident magistrates, in turn, were answerable to the SNA. The governor of the colony enjoyed the title of supreme chief, but in practice the governor virtually always followed Shepstone's advice. Indeed, in his dealings with Africans, Shepstone comported himself like an African inkosi and was treated as such by his subjects. Thus, for all intents and purposes, it was Shepstone, not the governor, who served as the supreme chief. The laws of the colony and of the British empire only sketched the barest outlines of the Shepstone system, giving Shepstone even more latitude. For example, colonial customary law, or Native Law, was not even codified until 1878. Until then it was largely what Shepstone said it was.

More than forty years after the dispute between Musi and Mamfongonyana, Shepstone would recall it as one of his first and most important official acts. It was, he said, "the first case in which the Government had been approached on a question of creating rank." His primary concern in this case was "that the natives should as early as possible be made aware of the position which the Government occupied and intended to carry out in regard to such questions." Though Musi and Mamfongonyana were actually Phakathwayo's nephews, both claimed to have ritually assumed the status of son (and therefore of heir) to him. After interviewing numerous African authorities on the subject, Shepstone found for Musi and ruled "that in so far as the members of the Qwabi tribe then or thereafter in Natal were concerned, Musi was to be the son of Pakatwayo." Although Shepstone also recognized Mamfongonyana as chief, his decision drew a crucial distinction in the status of the two Qwabe chiefs. Musi inherited his status as part of the precolonial legacy of the Qwabe chiefdom and was therefore a "hereditary" chief. Mamfongonyana, on the other hand, officially owed his status entirely to Shepstone's action and was therefore merely an "appointed" chief.[21]

Shepstone's appeal to African tradition, however, was not totally convincing to the Africans involved in the dispute. The arguments of the two sides hinged on their interpretations of the struggle between Nomo and Phakathwayo over the Qwabe succession just a few decades earlier. Though both Musi and Mamfongonyana claimed to be heirs to Phakathwayo, Mamfongonyana also claimed to have inherited the chiefship from Nomo, with whom Mamfongonyana's father had had a close relationship. Mamfongonyana therefore defended Nomo, while Musi sided with Phakathwayo. Shepstone's decision thus required a thorough familiarity not only with African law, but also with precolonial history. On the other hand, it made the disappointment of both sides that much greater when a government decision supposedly based on African law in fact failed to either conform to African law or satisfy the wishes of the interested parties. Shepstone told the Qwabe that they could choose which of the two chiefs they would pledge their loyalty to, provided that all who chose Mamfongonyana leave the reserves and live on private or Crown lands only. Years later, many of the Qwabe continued to consider such a division, and the weakening of the hereditary principle in Mamfongonyana's case, a flagrant violation of African law and precedent.[22]

Although Shepstone's intervention in the Qwabe succession dispute divided the chiefdom, it also put an end to questions about Musi's legitimacy and put the power of the colonial state behind him. After several decades of succession disputes within the chiefdom and warfare with its neighbors, of short-lived chiefs with contested legitimacy, of frequent migration through land plagued by violence and famine, the Qwabe chiefdom entered a long period of peace and stability. Musi would rule for another forty-three years, until 1892, and he and his subjects would consolidate the chiefdom in their permanent home in the Lower Tugela district.

THE WEAKNESS OF THE COLONIAL STATE AND SETTLER SOCIETY

The reconstitution in early colonial Natal of precolonial chiefdoms like the Qwabe is evidence of the hold they had on the popular imagination of Natal Africans. Chiefdoms continued to be, as they had been during the precolonial era, the main unit of social and political organization in local African society. People's ethnic identification would remain with their chiefdoms. That situation would not change as long as the colonial state and settler society were too weak to impose a new identity on Natal Africans, or, as would later happen, provoke Natal Africans into embracing a new identity as a defensive reaction to colonialism. Instead, colonial weakness created numerous opportunities for chiefs to strengthen themselves and their chiefdoms and maintain their popularity in the eyes of their subjects.

What were the alternative identities available to Natal Africans at this point? Fear, hostility, and rejection—not identification or sympathy—characterized Natal Africans' attitudes toward Zulus. The Zulus' use of the derogatory name amaKhafula to refer to Natal Africans indicates that the feeling of antagonism and lack of identification was mutual. The opinions of Natal

Europeans on this matter are crucial. On the one hand, as amateur ethnographers they were able to collect evidence on Natal Africans' identities, both assigned and asserted. On the other hand, Natal Europeans had the power not just to record this social reality but to help create it as well, through their conventional wisdom that developed around the topic, through official policy, and through dictionaries and other written works. However, Natal Europeans were themselves inconsistent in their terminology. Some Europeans would refer to Natal Africans as "Zulus," while others, or even the same individuals, would elsewhere insist on a distinction between the "Zulus" of the Zulu kingdom and the "Natal natives" or "Natal Kaffirs" of the colony across the Thukela.[23]

Natal Europeans also often identified Natal Africans racially as "blacks," and occasionally even as British subjects. For their part, Natal Africans could at times identify themselves as members of these categories, calling themselves *abantu abanyama* (black people) or even just *abantu* (people) in contrast to the *abelungu* (white people) and the Indians, who were variously referred to as *amaNdiya*, *abakwamnanayi*, or, derogatorily, *amaKula* (coolies). African converts to mission Christianity were particularly prone to identify themselves as black and as British subjects, especially in their appeals to whites. At the same time, they emphasized their rejection of Zulu identity. So, for example, in 1863 a delegate at a meeting of black Christians in Edendale said,

> We have left the race of our forefathers; we have left the black race and have clung to the white. We imitate them in everything we can. We feel we are in the midst of a civilised people, and that when we became converts to their faith we belonged to them. It was as a stone thrown into the water, impossible to return. . . . [W]e have all been well received—not as dogs, but as people. We have been protected since, and are happy. One thing alone detracts from our security. The law by which our cases are decided is only fit to be eaten by vultures. Who will say Kafir law is good, when we see thousands flying every day from it to the refuge of the wings of the Englishman? The question for us to decide is—whether we will have Kafir or English law? We have left the black race—it is impossible to return. We are under the wing of the Queen, let us ask her for her law. . . . Let us represent this evil to our superiors. Let us tell them we have left the black race, and belong to them. Will they send us back to barbarity? They may send our bodies, but, our spirits they cannot send.[24]

Another group of African Christians in Natal made a similar statement in 1875, again in relation to their desire to be subject to Roman-Dutch law and not customary law: "We fled the Zulu country because of fearing Kaffir Law and came to place ourselves under the Dutch Government, but their treatment to us was bad. And when the English Government arrived, we placed ourselves under it, and the missionaries taught us, so we rejoiced. But now the Government wishes to drive us back again by saying that we ought to serve our old law which drove us from Zululand through fear."[25] However, this kind of rhetoric was not common among Natal Africans, and in any event Natal Europeans were not keen to encourage it. As much as Natal Europeans talked about their civilizing mission, they had little desire to create a class of "black Englishmen" fully assimilated into European culture and socially and politically equal to them. And as much as white racial superiority was an explicit part of official policy and informal social convention alike, Natal Europeans worried that black racial consciousness among Natal Africans would lead them to unify in rebellion against their colonial masters. The solution was to encourage them to continue to identify with their chiefdoms, sometimes explicitly and self-consciously as part of a policy of "divide and rule."[26] Shepstone himself maintained that "tribal distinctions that obtain among them are highly useful in managing them in detail, and those are sufficiently preserved by their tribal heads. . . . [T]he cohesive power of one acknowledged ruling head, supreme over all subordinate authorities, is wanting amongst them. They form a republic of petty clans, without a federal head; and must therefore exist in a state of political weakness."[27]

Ironically, therefore, despite the powerful and frequently expressed desire of officials, settlers, and missionaries in early colonial Natal to do away with chiefship, the colonial state recognized it and incorporated it into its system of governance. The reason was simple: the early colonial state was in no position to transform the social and political landscape of Natal. Natal's first rural police had to be disbanded in 1851, after only three years of existence, because of budgetary concerns.[28] Natal was then without a rural police force until 1874, relying in the meantime on irregular levies of African soldiers.[29] As late as 1879, one official argued, in words reminiscent of those of another colonial official serving in colonial Kenya a quarter-century later, that "it is almost absurd even to suppose that one European and eight native constables, who form the police establishment at this Magistracy, and stationed in the centre of an extensive Division, containing a population of about 35,000 souls, can have much effect in deterring from the commission of crime."[30] And this was in Umgeni division, which contained the city of Pietermaritzburg and was a concentrated node of both white settlement and colonial state power in general. The state was even weaker in more outlying districts. Surveillance was severely limited as well: it was only in 1874 that colonial officials were empowered to employ African detectives to prevent and investigate cases of cattle stealing and stabbing, a high priority from the point of view of settlers.[31] The lack of roads was yet another factor making it difficult for the state to broadcast its authority. Until the 1870s, the only decent rural road in the colony was the one between Durban and Pietermaritzburg; the others were just ruts left by horse-drawn wagons and became quagmires when it rained. In most of the colony there were hardly any bad roads, let alone good ones, until the 1890s.[32]

Neither were missionaries able to challenge the authority of chiefs, even though missionaries generally opposed chiefship, especially after most chiefs refused to convert to Christianity or help the missionaries. On the one hand, in 1880 the secretary of the American Board of Commissioners claimed that in Natal the ratio of missionaries to the total population was "greater than in any other community on the globe two or three times over." But that year the African Christian population in Natal was less than 10,000 —about 3 percent of the colony's total African population of some 300,000 souls—despite a half-century's worth of proselytization. At the same time, only about 3,000 African students attended mission schools, and very few of them became the European-style Christians that the missionaries desired.[33] The vast majority of Natal Africans were therefore virtually immune to missionary influence at this early stage.

Mission Christianity figured somewhat more prominently in the history of the Qwabe chiefdom, but it was still peripheral to the lives of most Qwabe. As a youth in the 1840s, the Qwabe chief Musi studied under the missionary Newton Adams, of the congregationalist American Zulu Mission (AZM), in that organization's school at Umlazi Drift, near Port Natal, but he never converted to Christianity.[34] At the mission school, Musi learned to read a little, and was able to recite the Lord's Prayer from memory more than twenty years later.[35] The AZM set up stations near the Qwabe chiefdom as early as 1850. In 1863, Musi refused to let an African preacher for the AZM work among his people, but three years later he changed his mind, citing his fond memories of Adams and the relative prosperity of African Christians.

But only a small minority of the people in Musi's chiefdom and neighboring areas converted or had their children attend mission schools. And in this part of Natal, as in many others, relationships between Christians and "traditionalists" were often characterized by hostility and conflict. Many Christians left their pagan chiefs and placed themselves under Christian chiefs, or tried to be exempt from customary law entirely.[36]

Instead of trying to abolish chiefship outright, Shepstone tried to undermine it, but the chiefs and their subjects thwarted him. The case of Musi and Mamfongonyana was just one of many in which he took advantage of succession disputes to divide large chiefdoms, and classified certain chiefs as "appointed" rather than "hereditary" so as to make them more directly answerable to him. Shepstone even "invented" new chiefdoms and appointed commoners to serve as chiefs over both old and new chiefdoms. Nevertheless, the extent of this intervention could be exaggerated all too easily. There were many instances in which Shepstone deposed a chief and appointed his replacement, only to have the chief's subjects reject the government-appointed replacement and force the government to reinstate the original chief. Other "invented" chiefdoms could flourish for a while, but then disintegrate quickly. The classic example of this was Shepstone's own induna and court favorite, Ngoza ka Ludaba. Shepstone appointed Ngoza as chief of the Qamu chiefdom which Shepstone himself had created. Shepstone made a habit of assigning "chiefless" Natal Africans and incoming refugees to newly created chiefdoms like the Qamu, with the result that it was the largest chiefdom in Natal by 1869. But Ngoza died that year and his chiefdom was rapidly reduced by a welter of succession disputes and defections by his subjects.[37] Despite government policy favoring appointed chiefs and headmen and aiming for the gradual replacement of hereditary by appointed chiefs, appointed chiefs and headmen did a poor job of attracting or retaining subjects. By 1881–82, 57 percent of the chiefs were hereditary, but 70 percent of the people were subject to hereditary chiefs. Natal's 99 hereditary chiefs had an average of 646 huts under them, while appointed chiefs and headmen averaged only 376.[38] At this point the ten largest chiefdoms in Natal were all hereditary.[39] Government officials found it next to impossible to limit the ability of homestead heads, at least, to choose the chiefs under whom they would serve, and these people tended to prefer being subjects of hereditary chiefs.[40]

Shepstone occasionally used military force to crack down on chiefs who tried to exercise broader powers than even Shepstone was willing to allow. He thus called for armed expeditions against Chief Fodo in 1846–47, Chiefs Sidoyi and Matshana in 1857, and, most notably, Chief Langalibalele in 1873. These chiefs' "crimes" were varied: Fodo and his subjects launched a low-level war against a neighboring chiefdom, as did Sidoyi a decade later. Matshana had supposedly allowed the killing of one of his subjects who had been accused of witchcraft. Langalibalele's subjects failed to register their guns as they had been ordered to do by the local colonial official. Matshana and Langalibalele exacerbated their situations by fleeing rather than obeying orders to appear before government authorities. In each case, armed hostilities began only when Africans were attacked by colonial forces, usually including large numbers of Africans themselves: Langalibalele's men were among the colonial "native levies" sent to apprehend Matshana, sixteen years before they, in turn, would be similarly attacked.[41]

At first glance, the power of the colonial state against these chiefs was overwhelming and decisive. About two hundred of Langalibalele's followers were killed in the fighting, about fifteen of Matshana's followers were killed, and a few of Fodo's and Sidoyi's followers were killed. In some cases large numbers of livestock were confiscated and the chiefdoms were broken up. In every case the chief in question was deposed. After the incident with Fodo, Shepstone said the government's crackdown had "produced a very great effect upon the minds of the Native population, they saw in it what might have taken years to show them so clearly by other means, that the Government intended to be supreme in its own territory, and that all independent action on the part of Chiefs and Tribes would be prohibited and punished."[42] He added, "The tenor of the complimentary messages received from the several chiefs within the district on the subject of Fodo's affair has been such as to satisfy me that they are at present fully sensible of the danger of setting the Government at defiance."[43] Similarly, after the crackdowns on Matshana and Sidoyi, colonial officials claimed that on at least two occasions immediately thereafter they were able to bring disobedient chiefs in line simply by mentioning the names Matshana and Sidoyi.[44]

But the very frequency of incidents like these showed that many other chiefs and their subjects were not intimidated. Fodo's example did not prevent three chiefdoms in 1849 alone, one of them Langalibalele's, from being so recalcitrant that Shepstone had to send colonial forces against them.[45] In 1851, popular resistance to a proposed cattle census, troop levies for a war against the neighboring Sotho king Moshoeshoe, forced labor call-ups, and hut tax collection produced what Shepstone would later call "the most dangerous crisis it [Natal] has ever seen as regards the native popula-tion."[46] In 1854, Shepstone cracked down harshly on a chief accused of cattle stealing, saying "I am quite convinced that if the Government does not take decisive action in this the first instance of such a serious crime, there will soon be no chance of any white man keeping his cattle."[47] And yet another three years later, in 1857, Shepstone had to crack down on Matshana and Sidoyi. Then, in 1869, Shepstone was quite surprised and shaken by the confrontational manner in which some chiefs protested the marriage law that was introduced that year. Shepstone stood his ground and responded with veiled threats, causing the chiefs to back down, make profuse apolo-gies, and bestow him with gifts. Shepstone smugly assured his readers that as a result he had "succeeded in placing it [the peace of the Colony] on a firmer basis than it was before, for in such encounters, one side or the other must always permanently lose ground and strength too, it depends much on the skill with which you play your game, in this instance I won, they lost."[48] Four years after this "victory" came the Langalibalele affair.

In many confrontations, chiefs and their subjects even won out over colonial officials. This was most notably the case with Fodo himself. In 1852, the refusal of Fodo's former subjects to accept his government-appointed replacement forced Shepstone to reinstate Fodo. Far from being chastened by the episode, Fodo continued to act in a defiant manner toward the government, for example by refusing his magistrate's orders to pay hut tax in 1854 and by failing to put a stop to cattle rustling by his subjects a decade later.[49] Indeed, low-level but widespread resistance often enabled Natal Afri-cans to wrangle concessions from the colonial government. In 1850–51, popular resistance was such that officials had to suspend the cattle census and forced labor in order to get Africans to comply with the state's highest priority at the time, namely its troop levies.[50] Forced labor, and hut tax as well, on more than one occasion provoked such strong resistance that offi-cials had to suspend enforcement of those obligations. This was particularly true during 1853 and 1854. As early as 1853 Shepstone was endorsing some chiefs' complaints that their subjects were unable to pay hut tax.[51] Around the same time, chiefs Langalibalele and Phakade refused to compel their subjects to comply with either forced labor or hut tax requirements.[52] The situation got so bad that from 1854 to 1858 forced labor was put on hiatus

out of a fear that its continued use was about to provoke an armed rebellion.[53] Even in 1874, after colonial forces had crushed those of Langalibalele's
chiefdom, Shepstone still urged that forced labor be phased out on the
grounds that the labor thus procured was not worth the resentment and
resistance it produced.[54]

Most of the time, however, most chiefs were more subtle in their assertive-
ness. A major bone of contention between chiefs and officials was the ban on
chiefs acting as judges in criminal cases, as they had done during the precolonial era. Not surprisingly, many chiefs ignored government regulations
and continued to claim judicial authority in criminal cases. It was difficult for
officials to detect, let alone prevent, these activities unless, as sometimes
happened, the losing party appealed the chief's decision to the magistrate.[55]
For his part, the Qwabe chief Musi was not so defiant as to provoke military
action against him, but neither did he meekly accept the supremacy of
colonial officials. In 1852, the local resident magistrate Mesham ordered all
the chiefs in his district to locate a chiefly homestead in the vicinity of the
magistrate's office. Not only had Musi failed to do this, but he had also sent to
Mesham a message that Mesham considered insubordinate and impertinent,
and had moreover sent a delegation to the government's offices in Pietermaritzburg to complain about Mesham. When called to accounts by his
superiors, Mesham said, "Umusi bears the character amongst the natives of
being a proud, capricious, overbearing, and self-conceited man. . . . [H]e
doubtless thought that by being the first to complain, he could with the aid of
that flattery, shrewdness, cunning, ingenuity, qualities so peculiarly pre-
dominant in the Native character, succeed in exciting sympathy on his behalf
and procuring the condemnation of the innocent."[56]

But Musi's charisma, as well as the prestige he gained by being the
hereditary chief of a chiefdom as large and as storied as the Qwabe, made
him popular with many Natal Africans, as the steady growth in the number
of his subjects demonstrated. This growth occurred not only through natural increase, but also through the migration of people from one chiefdom to
another, in spite of official efforts to prevent or at least regulate such movement.[57] Of course, part of the attraction of being one of Musi's Qwabe was
not just his charisma or even the chiefdom's prestige, but also the plentiful
and fertile land that the Qwabe controlled.

On paper, at least, the land situation was dire for Natal Africans. By 1879
the state had officially expropriated 80 percent of the land for use by settlers

and the government itself, and most of the government-owned land, or "Crown" land, eventually ended up in the hands of European settlers as well. Natal Africans were therefore in theory confined to 20 percent of Natal's land area, an allotment consisting mostly of what were called "reserves" or "locations," land set aside specifically for Africans, much like the "reservations" of North American Indians. In the reserves, land was held in trust by the government, who allotted land to chiefs, who in turn allotted land to their subjects. Reserve land was owned by no one and could not be bought or sold or used as collateral. Instead it was held under what is known as "communal land tenure," according to which land is community property, not private property, and thus belongs to everyone. Chiefdoms controlled specific tracts of land, and within chiefdoms individual households had their own parcels, but rather than owning the land, they controlled access to the land and the fruits that sprang from it. Only a small number of Africans ever obtained enough money to buy land outright and to "own" it, in the European sense of freehold tenure. The problem for Africans was not only that they controlled, through communal land tenure or occasionally freehold tenure, a disproportionately small amount of land compared to what Europeans controlled; it was also that African-controlled land tended to be drier and more rugged than the land reserved for Europeans.

But most of the impact of this massive land expropriation was delayed until the 1880s because, until then, most Natal Africans continued living on settler and Crown lands just as they had done before. The oft-repeated claim that Shepstone "practically unaided, and with little money, . . . supervised the movement of nearly 80,000 Natal Africans during 1846 and 1847 into locations he had demarcated for their occupation" is simply not true.[58] In fact, the government was still too weak to do such a thing. For their part, Natal's European landowners also lacked the ability, and to some extent even the desire, to expel Africans from their lands wholesale. The government and the settlers needed time to establish and entrench themselves before they could overcome Africans' numerical preponderance and rootedness. Indeed, in the early colonial period, Natal Africans were more productive farmers than Natal Europeans were. In addition, the urbanized population throughout southern Africa was still quite small and transportation was still expensive, so the markets for agricultural goods produced in Natal were also small. It made more sense for Natal European landowners, many of whom were absentee landowners in any case, to rent their land to

African tenants. Until the 1880s, Natal Africans produced more food and more tax revenue than Natal Europeans did. At the same time, Natal Africans continued to live in the same places, and in much the same way, as they had done before conquest.[59] In short, the worst effects of European land expropriation were delayed for about four decades after the European conquest of Natal. This situation would later change quite dramatically, and Natal Africans would suffer enormously as a result.

The Qwabe chiefdom's new home was on land that Natal's government assigned to Inanda and Lower Tugela divisions, two coastal divisions along Natal's north coast between Durban and the Thukela River border with the Zulu kingdom. These two neighboring divisions had similar geographies. Both divisions had a coastal belt of fertile, well-watered, gently rolling land, and a hinterland strip (about half the total area in both cases) consisting of dry, rugged land. The relatively infertile hinterland was set aside as communal tenure African reserves. The coastal strip, meanwhile, was given to European landowners outright, or to the British Crown, which eventually put up the land for sale itself. In this way, Europeans secured the ownership of more than half the land in both Inanda and Lower Tugela, and the best land in both districts, at that. However, in practice there was little difference between the coast and the hinterland in terms of population or land use. As was the case in other parts of Natal, the Crown waited to sell its land until it could fetch higher prices, most European farmers sold their land to absentee landlords, and even those farmers who kept their land farmed only a small portion of it. The government, absentee landlords, and farmers all initially chose the tack of charging the Africans who lived on their land rent instead of expelling them. Though no Africans could live on their land without permission, in practice landlords of all varieties let Africans decide among themselves who would live on the land and where, as long as the Africans paid rent. Instead of being confined to the reserves, as the government had hoped, chiefly authority over land allotment extended to Crown and private land. These patterns were particularly evident in Inanda and Lower Tugela, where Crown lands were sold earlier than was the case elsewhere in Natal, much of it bought up by the Natal Land and Colonization Company, headquartered in London. The company and the other landowners in the area only used a small portion of the land for food and cash crops —notably sugar—and rented the rest to Africans.[60]

Farming and grazing land in the Qwabe chiefdom was therefore of relatively high quality compared to the land of other chiefdoms. It was also plentiful, because the sheer numbers of Qwabe allowed members of the chiefdom to stake out more land than other chiefdoms could during the chaotic years of the 1840s. The colonial government and private landowners only gradually intervened to officially demarcate the land allotted to individual chiefdoms, usually only if severe disputes arose and the state had the capacity to resolve them. As long as Natal was sparsely populated and the position of Europeans was relatively weak, Natal Africans were left to sort out territorial disputes among themselves, and this was a struggle in which the largest and most cohesive chiefdoms, like the Qwabe, had a great advantage.

While numbers allowed the Qwabe chiefdom to accumulate land, land also allowed the chiefdom to accumulate more members. We have already seen how chiefdom numbers fluctuated as much during the colonial period as they did during the precolonial period, with the old hereditary chiefdoms winning out over the new, government-created chiefdoms with government-appointed chiefs. The mechanism through which this was achieved was still what it had been during the precolonial period: khonza, or formally pledging allegiance to a chief. The motivations for changing chiefdom allegiances were also the same. Land was perhaps the main attraction, but dissatisfaction with one's old chief was another reason for moving, giving subjects some leverage in what could otherwise be an autocratic political system. Chiefdom membership also offered protections against the depredations of the state and, perhaps more important, incorporated otherwise isolated people into communities which could provide them with material benefits. Immigrants from Zululand, for example, typically entered Natal without a chiefdom they could call their own, and without land or property to speak of. Once in the colony, they found themselves subject to laws that forced most refugees into indentured labor. Those laws proved largely ineffectual, however, in the face of a "network of 'intertribal' solidarity" that entitled any African who had pledged allegiance to a chief to hospitality and protection, even from people belonging to other chiefdoms. As one official complained,

> If any duty approaches in character and influence that of a sacred obligation in the Kafir's mind it is hospitality and so strongly is this felt among the natives generally, that, I believe, there is a mutual compact among all tribes to defeat in every way not openly hostile any attempt to apprehend the refugee, *after he has once demanded and obtained the protection of a chief*. Any informer would be abhorred among them and at once cast out of the tribe.[61]

Continued access to plentiful, fertile land helped not only Musi and other chiefs, but also the whole system of patriarchy that was so closely interwoven with chiefship. The colonial state supported homestead heads directly by giving them sweeping powers under the colonial interpretation of African customary law. Indirectly, colonialism also created an environment in which homestead heads were able to amass substantial wealth, which gave them even more power. African agricultural production and, more crucial for patriarchal power, livestock herds increased steadily during the early colonial period. So, too, did the bridewealth that fathers were able to demand from their daughters' grooms. Immediately before and after European conquest, bridewealth payments were relatively small and often made in agricultural produce or in implements like hoes. Over the course of the 1840s, 1850s, and 1860s, however, going bridewealth rates rose substantially, and cattle came to be the most common form in which that payment was made. The result was that older and wealthier men came to dominate the marriage market, and polygyny became more common, as well. Growing complaints about this from young men, coupled with the general moral revulsion that Europeans felt toward polygyny, led to the passage of a new marriage law in 1869, which limited the bridewealth that commoners could charge to ten head of cattle. Polygyny declined in Natal over the years that followed, but homestead heads still held decisive power within their households. They had the power to determine what would be done with the agricultural produce, mainly grown by the women in their families, and with the livestock, most often tended by the young men. Through their control over household wealth, homestead heads were also able to determine when their sons could marry and become full-fledged homestead heads themselves. Young men's complaints about the high cost of bridewealth were one indication that the moral compact between them and their fathers was coming under strain. But the marriage law relieved this strain somewhat, and the general prosperity that Africans enjoyed at the time, not to mention young men's relative certainty that they would eventually become homestead heads, kept generational conflict to a minimum during this period.[62] When the situation changed in later decades, it would have important implications not only for household dynamics, but also for chiefdom politics and broader forms of ethnic and political identification.

NATAL AFRICANS' NEGATIVE ATTITUDES TOWARD
THE ZULU KINGS

In contrast, as long as the negative feelings that so many Natal Africans felt toward the Zulu kings during the precolonial period endured, Natal Africans would not be inclined to identify themselves ethnically and politically as Zulus. Memories of Shaka's and Dingane's depredations against various groups of Natal Africans lingered throughout the colonial period and to the present. But many Natal Africans continued to live in fear of the Zulus even after Shaka and Dingane had been killed. One historical episode is particularly illustrative of Natal Africans' fear of and animosity toward the Zulu kings, how colonial officials were able to exploit that fear, and how these ideas were linked to chiefdom and homestead politics. In 1869, Shepstone promulgated the marriage law that limited bridewealth for commoners to an assembly of chiefs and headmen. Though these representatives of the African elite were exempt from the new law, their fortunes were sufficiently tied up with those of homestead heads that they still responded bitterly to the law, which was intended, at least in part, to make it easier for young men to marry. Shepstone was unusually frank about how threatened he felt at this moment. In his telling, he was only able to defuse the situation by reminding the other men that the alternative to colonial rule was Zulu rule.

> It was necessary to preserve my own dignity and the prestige of the Government at such a moment. . . . I told them that the way to the Zulu Country was short and was open to them, and I would even prepare their way by sending a messenger to announce their intentions to the Zulu Authorities, that the Government wished no discontented subjects to live under its rule and that they might depart in peace, but that those who did live under it must obey its laws. I said that I had never had such words uttered to me before, and I desired them to go home and think over what they had said, and what they had heard from me, and meet me the next day to discuss what I saw they did not as yet understand. This of course broke up the meeting and during the night they seem to have taken in, more or less, the particulars of my explanation, for before the time of meeting next morning, messengers came with profuse and abject apologies for the intemperate and wayward language they had used in my presence the day before, they said they wished to be assured of my forgive-

ness before the public conference began. . . . They presented peace offerings, which of course I did not receive; so the conference was resumed, new light seemed to have broken in upon them. They were keenly inquisitive into the details of the measure, which after a time they completely mastered, and they came to the conclusion that it was not such a bad measure as they had supposed it to be. . . . At the conclusion, I said, that if I had felt obliged to take notice of their language, it must have been in a very serious way, that I overlooked it, because I saw that they regretted it, and had not meant all that their words conveyed; they thanked me heartily. The great men belonging to my train were enriched by sundry half crowns put into their hands as thank offerings which however they did not receive until they had asked my permission to do so. The meeting broke up with a hearty salute to me and all left in great good spirits.[63]

Of course, Shepstone stood to gain by emphasizing how effective he was at turning African dissent into cheerful compliance. But it would be difficult to dismiss as a figment of his imagination the Natal Africans' reaction to his reference to the Zulus, mainly because these sorts of feelings crop up time and again in the historical record. During the first decade of British rule, in particular, Natal Africans frequently expressed a deep concern about the possibility of Zulu attacks.[64] Some Africans even believed that the Zulu king Mpande was waging constant war against them by means of medicine.[65] When, in 1853, African workers in Pietermaritzburg began leaving the city en masse because of rumors of an imminent invasion from the Zulu kingdom, the city police had to use threats of arrest to keep them on the job.[66] One of the Qwabe chiefs, Mamfongonyana, in an interview with a colonial official, described the fundamental conflict between the immigrants and the Zulu kings.

Q: Did you leave any land in Zululand?
A: We had land there, but Chaka drove the tribe out.
Q: You came from Zululand to have your lives saved?
A: Yes. . . .
Q: How long is it since you came from Zululand?
A: About 1849. . . .
Q: Why did you leave the Zulu country?
A: Chaka killed our Chief. One night an assegai was thrown at Chaka which struck him on the arm. It was said this assegai belonged to our tribe; and Chaka wiped us out, and we had to run.[67]

Shaka could not have been the proximate reason for Mamfongonyana's Qwabe leaving the Zulu kingdom in 1849, because Shaka had died twenty years before. Mpande had been the Zulu king in 1849, but in this Qwabe's account all the different Zulu kings, and the Qwabes' conflicts with them, were conflated.

Immigration from the Zulu kingdom to the Natal colony was significant enough to keep the African proportion of the colony's population constant in the face of European immigration. The African population of Natal grew from about 113,000 in 1852 to 362,000 in 1880, while the European population grew from 8,000 to 25,000 over the same period.[68] The immigrants were also a major source of potential new subjects for chiefs in Natal, especially in border regions like Lower Tugela, where most of the Qwabe lived. The exact volume of the migration is difficult to determine. In 1864, Shepstone estimated that an average of about 600 Africans entered Natal from Zululand every year. In 1882, John C. Walton, a member of the Natal Native Commission, reported that official figures put the total number of African immigrants into Natal from 1856 to 1881 at 10,978, or about 400 a year. This number was almost certainly too low. With laws in place forcing such immigrants to surrender their cattle to the government and enter into wage labor for a period of three years, they had every reason not to report to the authorities. The government, moreover, was unable to prevent widespread flouting of these laws. Even Walton admitted that the government's totals excluded one of Natal's six counties, as well as several large groups that had entered Natal en masse since 1856.[69] One of these groups, the supporters of Prince Mbulazi, who in 1856 lost a war with Prince Cetshwayo for the position of heir to Mpande's Zulu kingship, numbered about 4,000.[70] While statistics for the early colonial period are hard to come by, it is significant that in every year after 1879 more Africans from Zululand entered Lower Tugela than entered any other division in Natal. Between 1881 and 1883, for example, no fewer than 6,057 Africans entered Lower Tugela from Zululand each year.[71]

The net migration of Africans *from* Zululand *into* Natal, despite the colonial government's desire to stop them and even to expel those who were already there, also suggests a certain antipathy toward the Zulu kings and a widespread refusal to identify as Zulu. People's stated reasons for leaving the Zulu kingdom and coming to Natal varied. Often those reasons could be personal. Many young women in the Zulu kingdom's female regiments refused to accept the marriages arranged for them by the king. The punishment for this refusal was death, so they fled to Natal either alone or with the lovers that they did want to marry. Similarly, some men fled to escape death sentences for impregnating young women out of wedlock or for committing one of many other capital crimes. One man even fled the Zulu kingdom shortly before Mpande's death because he was Mpande's bodyguard and by custom was to be killed and buried with him.[72]

Many others migrated because they supported members of the Zulu Royal House who were in conflict with whoever was Zulu king at any given time. In 1839, some 17,000 people accompanied Mpande when he broke with Dingane and sided with the Boers. Then, when Mpande returned to Zululand and took over the Zulu throne, many of Dingane's supporters fled to Natal themselves. In 1843, Mpande's aunt Mawa fled the kingdom with two to three thousand people, after Mpande started to purge those of his own relatives whom he saw as potential threats to his rule. In 1856, Mpande's sons Cetshwayo and Mbulazi fought a battle at Ndondakusuka over who would be first in line to the Zulu kingship, and after the war some four thousand of Mbulazi's supporters escaped to Natal.[73]

But most who migrated were the supporters of conquered chiefs who were trying to reestablish the independence of their chiefdoms from Zulu overrule. The Qwabe chief Mamfongonyana was said to have left the Zulu kingdom because of the indignities to which Mpande subjected him. The Cube chief Sigananda left because "he refused to go and konza to the Zulu king, for he too was a chief. Mpande ordered him to pay tribute and konza to him, but he refused. The king then sent a force to kill him, upon which he fled with many of his Cube people towards the Mzimkulu river." The Hlubi chief Phuthini also came to Natal when Mpande tried to kill him. Even many of those who fled with dissident members of the Zulu Royal House belonged to other chiefdoms. For example, the Qwabe headman Nguluzane was part of Mawa's party, but once in Natal he joined the Qwabe chiefdom.[74] While a handful of Natal chiefdoms consisting of migrants from the Zulu kingdom—such as those of Mkhonto, Thimuni, and Mzwili, in Lower Tugela—identified themselves as "Zulu," the vast majority did not.[75]

THE ANGLO-ZULU WAR

When the colonial government of Natal declared war on the Zulu kingdom in 1879, Natal Africans' opposition to the Zulu kings—a key factor preventing Natal Africans' self-identification as Zulus—was thrown into stark relief. For this reason it is worth examining Natal Africans' allegiances during the war in some detail. One might think that colonial sources would exaggerate Natal Africans' opposition to the Zulu kings, but in fact the reverse was actually the case. Natal Europeans lived in constant fear of a "concerted uprising" and even periodically imagined lurid scenarios in which they would all be killed simultaneously in their beds by their African domestic servants. Given the actual lack of anticolonial violence in early colonial Natal, such fears amounted to a paranoia reminiscent of the anticommunist "Red under every bed" scares in the Cold War–era West. This paranoia became particularly intense during the 1870s. The decade started with a racist and entirely unfounded rape scare among Natal Europeans.[76] The situation only got worse as war broke out, in the later part of the decade, between Europeans and Africans in both the Eastern Cape and the Transvaal. For example, the Norwegian missionary Schreuder, whose mission station lay in the heart of an African reserve on the border with the Zulu kingdom, told the government that it was "an open question, whether you could trust the loyalty of all your Natal Natives generally in case of any reverse." He attributed this situation to "bad reports from the frontier Kafir war (as the sympathy of race has a great effect on the mind of these kindred Natives)" and to "the opinion that for a good while has been abroad amongst the Natives, viz., that the Govt.'s power is not prominent in Natal."[77]

Even colonial officials commented on the paranoid hysteria of Natal's settlers. In 1878, the SNA said he found Natal Europeans more susceptible to war scares than were Africans.[78] In fact, officials often worried that unrest was being caused by whites' glib talk to or in the presence of Africans, or, conversely, by the failure of the government to tell Africans the reasons for troop movements through their districts.[79] However, some of the very officials who complained about settler overreactions could overreact on occasion themselves. For example, in September 1878, one of the government's border agents, F. B. Fynney, anxiously reported what seemed to be Zulu troop movements and reconnaissance missions along the Thukela River border. When government investigations revealed that the "armed Zulus" had only been a hunting party, both the SNA and Lieutenant Governor Bulwer reprimanded Fynney for his haste and panic in this case.[80] Bulwer told the SNA, "I hope you have reason to think that Mr. Fynney can be trusted for discretion and coolness. He seems to me to have been rather too apt of late to become excited by reports, and not to have shewn the discretion in dealing with reports that I was led to hope from him."[81]

Given Natal Europeans' hypersensitivity to the slightest hint of African resistance, it is very telling that the colonial sources give only occasional indications that Natal Africans were "disloyal" in any way. To the contrary, the overwhelming preponderance of the evidence suggests that the vast majority of Natal Africans had little sympathy for the Zulu side. This was already apparent before the war. Early in 1878, government officials sent out African spies among the people living on the Thukela River border with the Zulu kingdom, in order to ascertain the general mood of Africans, and especially chiefs, on the Natal side of the river. The spies found that most chiefs preferred colonial rule to that of the Zulu king, but nevertheless hoped that the impending war could be avoided.[82] The situation did not change in the course of the following year, even though the Natal government seemed increasingly set on war and doubled the hut tax at the same time. Not only did hut tax collections in 1878 proceed without incident, but Africans even seemed to be at pains to assure officials of their "loyalty." The resident magistrate of one border district found the demeanor of the Qwabe chiefdom, the largest in that district, to have been "highly satisfactory" during hut tax collections.[83]

As war became more of a certainty, many Natal Africans, too, came to believe that the Zulus might invade. These rumors suggest that, far from viewing the Zulus as potential liberators, Natal Africans tended to regard the potential invasion as negatively as Natal Europeans did. Concrete Zulu actions fed these rumors: the Zulus fully exploited their intimidating reputation. For example, in November 1878, men from the Zulu kingdom kidnapped a Natal African to enforce a bridewealth payment. One Ngabeni reported that four Zulus came to his homestead while he was away and took his son Filepu. The leader of the contingent, Mvabula, allegedly claimed that Ngabeni still owed him bridewealth for Filepu's mother, Nongazi. Mvabula therefore kidnapped Filepu in order to force Ngabeni to pay the money.[84] Groups of Zulus, often armed, made random forays across the river, usually without any apparent purpose, causing much concern among Natal Africans. The impression became widespread in Natal that Zulu soldiers would have no compunctions about obeying orders to kill Natal Africans who opposed them.[85] Before the crisis started, Africans from both sides had freely crossed the river and intermingled, trading with each other, marrying each other, herding livestock on both sides of the river, and sometimes even maintaining homesteads on both sides of the river.[86] By the latter months of

1878, however, the two groups were becoming overtly hostile toward one another. For example, in October 1878, two Natal Africans named Nyathi and Luji complained to the government of having been attacked while visiting Zululand to sell some cattle. On several occasions Zulus told them to return to Natal because there were several units of Zulu soldiers assembling, and they would most certainly kill any Natal Africans that they might encounter. Nyathi and Luji finally did run into some Zulu soldiers, but one of the soldiers recognized them and just told them to return immediately to Natal. Nyathi and Luji did so, but on the way they ran into another group of Zulu soldiers who chased them back across the river.[87]

Once the war actually started, with Lord Chelmsford's invasion of the Zulu kingdom on 11 January 1879, the rumors of a Zulu invasion became even more pervasive, and the unease of Natal Africans, especially those living along the river border, increased.[88] As had been the case before the war started, minor incidents seemed to confirm these fears. Various chiefs along the Natal side of the Thukela reported being regularly threatened verbally by Zulu soldiers just across the river.[89] Minor long-range shooting skirmishes erupted across the river from time to time. As the war progressed, the Zulus began burning the grass and bush on their side of the Thukela, a mysterious action that led many Natal Africans to conclude that an invasion was imminent.[90]

The closest thing to a Zulu "invasion" of Natal was the battle at Rorke's Drift, a ford right on the Thukela River, on 22–23 January 1879. The Zulu command itself chided the Zulu army detachments involved for having gotten themselves into such an unplanned and meaningless skirmish. Though the Zulu forces at Rorke's Drift numbered as many as 4,000, this was small compared to the 24,000 who slaughtered the British at Isandlwana on 22 January. Only 600 Zulus died in the Rorke's Drift battle (compared to 1,000 in their victory at Isandlwana), and a third of them were actually wounded soldiers who were killed one by one by British forces after the fighting was over. The fame of Rorke's Drift owes more to British propagandizing, eager as the British were both to justify their invasion of Zululand and to gloss over their debacle at Isandlwana, than to the battle's actual importance to the war.[91] More typical were tiny incursions like one that occurred in the lower Thukela valley in May. A detachment of the Frontier Police came across a small group of Zulu soldiers crossing the river and preparing an ambush. A brief fight ensued and the Zulus were chased back to the other side of the river.[92] Even though Natal Africans' fears of a Zulu invasion turned out to be unfounded, those fears were real enough as long as the war lasted to prompt them to take drastic measures to protect themselves. It was common practice during times of war for Africans to sleep in the wilderness instead of in their huts, and those living on the border did so frequently in 1879.[93]

Another indication of Natal Africans' opposition to the Zulus during the war was the relative lack of defections by Natal Africans to the Zulu side. Even before the war, Cetshwayo let it be known that he would heartily welcome any potential allies from Natal who might want to enter Zululand and join him.[94] Very few Natal Africans responded positively. The two most notable defections were those by Bheje and Mhadu, both of whom lived in the Thukela valley.

Bheje was a brother and subject of the Ngcolosi chief Hlangabeza. In 1878, the missionary Schreuder reported rumors that Cetshwayo had been trying to win over Bheje and had invited him to the Zulu capital.[95] Shortly thereafter, R. Robertson, a missionary stationed in the Zulu kingdom itself, reported that Bheje had come to Cetshwayo's court and received a gift of five to twenty head of cattle. Robertson said, "It is just possible that I, after having lived so many years among a suspicious and treacherous people, may see daggers where others see only knives and forks; but from all I know of the niggardly character of the King, I cannot bring myself to believe that these cattle are given without an object."[96] The secretary for native affairs called Bheje to his office to respond to these accusations. Bheje denied being in any sort of conspiracy or in continual contact with Cetshwayo, claiming to have visited him only the one time. The SNA concluded that Robertson was just being panicky. Toward the end of the year, Bheje and five of Hlangabeza's other headmen, including four relatives of Hlangabeza, left Natal and settled in Zululand without government permission, taking their families and cattle with them. All told, these refugees from Natal totaled about one hundred and seventy people.[97] During the war, Bheje fought on the Zulu side, only to be captured by the British. He was brought before the Native High Court and convicted of treason.[98]

Mhadu was a headman of Chief Mkhonto. Though Mkhonto himself was a member of the Zulu royal family, he and many of his subjects were Zulu refugees who had entered Natal during Dingane's reign. In September 1878, Mhadu and three other headmen of Mkhonto crossed into Zululand with their families and property.[99] Mhadu had been in regular conflict with Mkhonto, and after he left he was frequently reported to be heard shouting threats from across the river, such as threats to burn down people's homesteads.[100]

Both Bheje's and Mhadu's defections prompted officials to question the loyalty of their chiefs, Hlangabeza and Mkhonto. One of Hlangabeza's subjects even formally accused him of being in league with Cetshwayo.[101] However, far from turning to the Zulu, Hlangabeza's people were victimized by them. In the middle of the war, one of his subjects was shot dead while bathing in the Thukela. Rumors circulated to the effect that he had been shot by one of Hlangabeza's subjects who had gone over to the Zulu side, and that the killing was in retaliation for the killing of some Zulus in Natal.[102] A Zulu force attacked the subjects of Hlangabeza and two other Natal chiefs, Homoyi and Mzileni, on 25 June 1879. Of Hlangabeza's subjects alone, 13 people were killed, 13 women and children were taken captive, 31 homesteads were burned, 226 head of cattle and 341 goats taken, and £20 17s. 9d. in cash stolen.[103]

Similarly, during the war Mkhonto's own brother, Phakade, accused him of "disloyalty" before colonial authorities.[104] In late February, a group of Zulu men came to the banks of the Thukela and called on the people to relay a message from Cetshwayo to Mkhonto. According to the message, Cetshwayo wanted Natal Africans to know that his fight was not with them, but with the whites. Officials were concerned not only about the contents of the message, but also because the Natal Africans allowed the Zulus to cross the river, which was strictly against regulations.[105] When Mkhonto failed to report either this or other messages from Cetshwayo, officials became even more suspicious of him.[106] Finally, Captain Lucas, the commanding officer of the Border Guard, accused Mkhonto's subjects of persistent insubordination and Mkhonto of not having done enough to ensure their loyalty.

But closer examination of Mkhonto's case reveals dissatisfaction with his and his subjects' treatment at the hands of the colonial government rather than any sympathy with Cetshwayo. After all, shortly after the war started, one of Mkhonto's subjects was fired on by Zulus from across the river.[107] Mkhonto personally led border patrols despite his age and poor health.[108] Captain Lucas's treatment of Mkhonto and his subjects was particularly unfair. Early in the war and of his own initiative, Mkhonto assembled a force of 700 volunteers and marched them to Captain Lucas so they could serve in the Border Guard. Lucas told Mkhonto they already had a large enough contingent. Mkhonto pleaded with him, and finally Lucas agreed to let Mkhonto's men patrol the nearby stretch of river. When Captain Lucas replaced the force's headman with one of his own men, Heathcote, Mkhonto's men began to complain, saying "We are not Government men, but belong to Umkonto. We have no badges, no pots to cook our food, no guns, no blankets." When questioned by officials, the men said that they were "not meaning that we are not Children of the Government, but that we (Umkonto's people) did not belong to the force placed under Mr. Heathcote at the drift." One of Mkhonto's subjects told officials, "We are contented and have not two faces and want no other land, but our hearts were sore when we saw we were looked upon with suspicion. . . . We do not know what we have done. You sent us out to mind the river and we have done so by night and day and have not slept." He added, "We are all children of the Government. . . . Most of us have grown up in this land and we know no other Chief than Rulumeni (His Excellency the Lieutenant Governor)." Mkhonto was even briefly detained, but while in detention he expressed a desire to return to his people to facilitate hut tax collection. In the light of his loyal service in executing the border patrols, among other duties, he was allowed to do so.[109]

That neither Hlangabeza, nor Mkhonto, nor any but a handful of their subjects proved "disloyal" despite official fears that this was so, and despite intense, almost paranoid, scrutiny, is indicative of their loyalty to the British, or at least their opposition to Cetshwayo. That the vast majority of other chiefs and their subjects failed to arouse even false suspicions, on the other hand, is indicative of an even greater loyalty.

But perhaps the clearest evidence of where Natal Africans' allegiances lay during the war is to be found in their active participation on the British side. For example, on 15 January 1879, agent Fynney held a conference with the chiefs and headmen of the Lower Tugela district to gauge their support for the British war effort and their willingness to supply African soldiers to the British army. He found the chiefs and headmen "unanimous and unswerving in their loyalty to and support for the Government in its conflict with Cetshwayo, and all condemn his conduct and have enthusiastically complied with the requests for Native levies."[110] Some 16,000 Natal Africans served on the British side during the Anglo-Zulu War. About half of these were soldiers in the Natal Native Contingent, and the other half were military laborers, carriers, and the like.[111] The soldiers were organized into three regiments, the second and third of which actually received more men than the government had requisitioned. There were some Africans who dodged the draft or who deserted after they had been enlisted, but the same was true even of Natal Europeans. Indeed, much of the resistance to African conscription came not from Natal Africans themselves, but rather from the Europeans who employed them and refused to release them for military service.[112]

The pattern of African responses to conscription is telling. All of the districts in Natal that were most consistently in arrears when it came to wartime mobilization were in central or southern Natal, the parts of Natal farthest from the Zulu Kingdom. The government had the least difficulty procuring men in divisions situated along the border with Zululand.[113] These were the districts that had had the most intimate contact with the Zulu kingdom: They were the only districts in Natal that had actually been under direct Zulu rule before the Boers invaded, and most of the Zulu emigrants to Natal over the decades had settled in these border areas. This suggests that Natal Africans' participation on the British side had more to do with revenge against the Zulu king than with loyalty to the British queen. Such animosity survived most particularly among members of the Qwabe chiefdom. Years after the war, one of James Stuart's informants told of how Cetshwayo met some Qwabe soldiers after his capture on 28 August 1879: "During the Zulu war Qwabe people were recruited and took part. After his capture Cetshwayo saw them and said, 'And you too, Qwabe, do you take part against us? Are you still harbouring feelings of revenge against us?' [T]he Qwabes in question were actually present when the capture was effected. The ancient quarrel was therefore being kept still alive by the Qwabes."[114] The biggest irony was that the same people, or rather their children or grandchildren, would rebel against the British in the name of the Zulu king twenty-seven years later.

When Natal Africans did on occasion dodge the draft or desert, it did not necessarily mean that they were siding with the Zulu king. More often than not, they were willing to fight for the British, but chafed at the unequal and often humiliating treatment they received from the European officers placed in charge of them. After the British army's crushing defeat at the hands of the Zulu army at Isandlwana in January, British forces retreated to Natal. As soon as they reentered the colony, many of the African soldiers dispersed against their commanding officers' orders. They complained to officials that they had been treated like "women," because the British re-fused to give them guns, even though some of the Zulu soldiers whom they had to face had guns. They also complained that their officers simply or-dered them about and refused to listen to what they had to say.[115] Later, when faced with the problem of distinguishing Natal Africans from Zulus in the field, the British officers proposed that Natal Africans lay down their arms or sit down when they saw British forces approaching. Many Africans refused to do this, however, because they found it degrading.[116] A group of chiefs and headmen told agent Fynney they would do everything in their power to help the government, but Natal Africans would not attack the Zulus on their own ground as long as the government refused to give its African soldiers guns, or at least to send them out with European troops armed with guns.[117]

Nevertheless, Natal Europeans were enormously satisfied with the actions of Natal Africans during the war. In December 1879, the settler-dominated Legislative Council of Natal passed a resolution expressing their "high appre-ciation of the loyalty shewn and services rendered by the Natives of this Colony during the recent war in Zululand."[118] What a striking contrast with the white paranoia that preceded the war and would soon return!

Natal Africans' own assessment of the war was very different. They agreed that they had been "loyal," but had begun to wonder why. Shortly after the war ended, the SNA held a conference with the chiefs and headmen of Inanda district, at which he thanked them for their loyal support during the war. However, one of the chiefs complained at length.

> Never more will I fight for the white man. Why should I? I was called out with my people to help in the punishment of a common and dangerous enemy. Here have I, the son of Dabeju, of royal race, been lying in ditches and in mud, ripped by frost by night, drenched by rain and scorched by noon-day marches. I have stood out in the fight with my men; I have seen my favourite councilors, my relatives, my head men and my young men drop by my side shot by men whose whole life is evil. I have accepted the dispensation of the spirits, thinking I was assisting in removing the in-cubus of generations and felling the tree saturated with the blood of my fathers and my people's fathers, and now I find that we have been fighting for nothing, for a shadow. We are wholly losers by the campaign; the Zulus are wholly gainers. Nothing has been done to show them they are punished or conquered; not a head of cattle taken. I come out of the fight

unrequited in any sense. Well, so be it. You are not human beings, you white men, but phenomena. Your missionaries talk platitudes about a man giving his left cheek to be smitten by the man who has already hit his right. It is all very well as a platitude, but it won't do well with us black people, Zulu or no Zulu. My heart is angry, and never again will I respond to the call of your Government.[119]

In the years that followed the war, this sense of betrayal would only deepen. In one meeting that Stuart had with his African informants, Dlozi, Nduk-wana, and Mkando some twenty years after the war, all expressed in great detail their anger that their loyalty to the colonial state during the Anglo-Zulu War had gone unrewarded. If anything, the government's treatment of Natal Africans had gotten worse. Mkando said,

You make a law; we obey it. Again you make a law and we accept it and obey it. Over and over again you promulgate fresh laws and we abide by them cheerfully, and this sort of thing has continued until we have become old and greyheaded, and not even now, advanced in years as we are, do we know the meaning of your policy. We cut away the wild forests for sugar plantations and towns; we dig your roads. When will this digging of roads cease? We are made to live on farms and pay rent, and are imprisoned if we cannot pay. You chase our wives out of our homes by facilitating divorce. How is it you come to treat us thus, seeing we are your people? ... Why are individuals able to oust government subjects from the soil? ... We have to go out leaving no one in charge of our homes and children behind. Where shall we run to? When we went to fight Cetshwayo, you called us to help; we did so, and marched off with you to fight as allies. Had you called on us in the late war [the South African, or Anglo-Boer, War of 1899–1902] to fight we would readily have done so, but no demand was made for our services. How can you tell that we do not belong to you? What is it that bars and negatives our belonging to you?[120]

CONCLUSION

It might be argued that so many Natal Africans sided with the British not out of any fundamental antipathy toward the Zulu kings, but rather out of an appreciation of the British army's overwhelming military superiority. But the antipathy predated British rule, and Natal Africans continued to express their own fear of and hatred for the Zulu kings right through to the end of the

Anglo-Zulu War. As long as this antipathy lasted, Natal Africans would not identify themselves as Zulus. Instead they identified with their chiefdoms, which had survived Shaka and Dingane's reigns and European conquest only to emerge stronger than ever. But the Anglo-Zulu War changed the situation fundamentally, creating a situation in which new patterns of identification might develop. The war and its aftermath, including the gradual absorption of Zululand into Natal, undermined the distinction between the two territories. The Zulu king was no longer a real king who could alienate some of his subjects, but rather a blank canvas on which Natal Africans could cast their hopes and fantasies. He was no longer too powerful to love. The European community in Natal came out of the war stronger than ever and was able to create a situation progressively more advantageous for itself and disadvantageous for Natal Africans. The colonial state was no longer too weak to hate. As a result, life in the colony of Natal ceased to seem preferable to life in the Zulu kingdom as far as Natal Africans were concerned. The growing power of the colonial state and the immiseration of Natal Africans also undermined the age-old solidarity and cohesiveness of chiefdoms like the Qwabe, leaving Natal Africans to look for new forms of identification that would bind them together.

3

INCREASING CONFLICT AMONG
NATAL AFRICANS, 1879–1906

In order for Zulu ethnic consciousness to take root among Natal Africans, certain factors had to change. The most obvious of these were the meanings associated with the Zulu kings and all things Zulu. Less obviously, Zulu ethnicity's main competition in the arena of self-identification, namely the chiefdom, had to be weakened, creating needs that Zulu ethnicity might be able to fulfill. In other words, being Qwabe or Mthethwa had to become less attractive before being Zulu could start to seem more attractive. We have seen how hegemonic the notion of chiefship was for Natal Africans, how it was so deep-rooted that neither war nor conquest nor migration nor even European colonialism could undermine it, at least before 1879. Indeed, African chiefship was so hegemonic that the European colonial state came to rely on it in order to rule, not only by incorporating chiefs, customary law, and communal land tenure into colonial governance, but also by having European colonial officials comport themselves like African chiefs. This hegemony relied on a moral economy, a shared sense of mutual rights and obligations that bound together chiefs and subjects, elders and youths, men and women, and even colonizers and colonized, despite the social order's manifestly unequal and conflict-ridden nature. But once certain people became unable or unwilling to fulfill their obligations under this moral economy, the chiefdom—and the general structures of gender and generational power so closely intertwined with it—began to unravel. As a result, people from all segments of society began looking for new ways to legitimate their visions of the way things should be, and that search would bring changes in their ethnic self-identification as well.

Chiefship would also run into problems because of its inability to deal with increasing conflict between chiefdoms, which led to an epidemic of feuding from the 1880s onward. The very colonial government that had created artificial land hunger among Africans also banned fighting between chiefdoms over the little land left to them. Chiefs thus found themselves caught between a colonial state that could depose them and subjects who could rebel against them. More important, though, interchiefdom feuding created a need for some sort of identity that could unite Africans beyond the boundaries of their chiefdom identities. Unity through Zulu ethnic identification would ultimately become a solution for endemic violence within many different Natal African communities. Thus, in order to understand the increasing attractiveness of Zulu ethnicity to Natal Africans later on, one must also understand the depths of the conflicts that were tearing Natal African society apart.

THE MINERAL REVOLUTION AND AFRICAN POVERTY

Perhaps the fundamental economic conflict in Natal colony before 1879 was between indigenous Africans who wanted to pursue prosperity and independence through farming and herding, and European settlers who wanted to do the same, as Natal's economy long depended on the sale of various agricultural goods, from maize to cattle to sugar. Not only did African farmers at first outcompete their European rivals, in doing so they also managed to avoid having to rely on nonagricultural income, which could mainly be earned by working for Europeans, in order to survive. As a result, European employers suffered from chronic shortages of cheap labor, and struggled to find ways to get Africans to work for Europeans instead of on their own farms. African wage labor in Natal had existed from the beginning of colonialism, but the supply was rarely large enough or cheap enough to satisfy employers. From 1865, *togt* labor, a form of casual day labor, began to emerge, particularly in Natal's cities. During the 1870s, the proportion of African workers operating under the togt system increased enormously as Africans more and more refused to engage in monthly contracts. This gave African workers still more leverage by allowing them to play different employers off one another, or to simply return to their farms on any given day if wages were too low.

In response, settler employers relied ever more heavily on legislation and imported labor to discipline the workforce to their liking. Natal's first Masters and Servants Law, Ordinance no. 2 of 1850, made contract-breaking a criminal offense, but Africans often got around this law by refusing to engage in contracts for periods longer than one day. Settler employers managed to pressure Natal's government into passing several more Masters and Servants Laws throughout the colonial era. As a result of these laws, Africans in certain areas could no longer legally refuse work when it was offered to them, and even doing work improperly became subject to criminal sanction. Punishments for these crimes included imprisonment and spare diet, but also cash fines and hard labor, both of which pushed Africans into the labor market: wage labor was one of the only ways to earn cash, and the state often hired convict laborers out to private employers. Prosecutions boomed from fewer than 100 a year to between 800 and 900 annually between 1870 and 1875. Barracks and police surveillance were introduced in the cities, as were pass laws that required workers to work if they were offered a minimum wage for the day. Another important form of state intervention in the labor market was a compulsory tax to be paid in labor, or *isibhalo*, which colonial officials justified to Africans as being merely a continuation of the precolonial labor requisitions that had been the prerogative of chiefs and kings. Although isibhalo laborers, like convicts, were sometimes hired out to private employers, they were much more likely to be used for public-works projects such as road building (remember Mkando's lament: "When will this digging of roads cease?"). Imported labor from India and Tongaland (a region straddling the border between northern Zululand and southern Mozambique) was also intended to give employers more leverage over labor. The primary value of imported labor was not that it lowered labor costs—it did not—but that it made the supply more continuous and reliable. More than 40 percent of the non-European labor force in Natal in the 1870s was either Indian or Tonga, even though both populations were vastly outnumbered by Natal-born Africans. Legislation and other government interventions managed to keep wages down for a while. Where the average worker in Durban earned 8s. a month and a *muid* of ground maize (then and now the staple of the African diet) cost 6s. in 1870, by 1878 the wage was 20s. and the muid of ground maize cost 32s. The Anglo-Zulu War, however, led to a boom and an increased demand for labor, reversing many of the employers' gains. By the 1880s, wages for togt workers on the Durban docks were almost equal to those of casual day laborers on the London docks.[1]

Although the economic boom of the 1870s led to a rise in African wages at first, in the long run the forces behind the boom would create a labor situation more favorable for employers. As long as homestead agriculture continued to give Natal Africans the independence and standard of living they wanted, the attraction of wage labor would be limited. This was why it took boom periods, such as occurred in Natal during the 1870s, to bring substantial numbers of Natal Africans into the labor pool. During the 1870s, the diamond rush at Kimberley, in the interior, and the Anglo-Zulu War both increased the traffic at Durban harbor and led to an infusion of capital into the colony. The rise of the gold industry on the Witwatersrand after 1886 achieved similar, but more dramatic, results. Only events such as these could make wages high enough to draw Natal Africans away from their homesteads.

At the same time, however, the mineral revolution also brought to Natal the capital and the demand necessary to finally make large-scale settler agriculture profitable. Settlers were now in a better position than ever before to evict African tenants from their lands. This was also a period when the British government devolved ever more power to the locally elected Natal legislature, a transition which culminated, in 1893, in the granting of "responsible government," that is, internal self-government and a cabinet chosen by the Natal legislature, not the British government. The qualification process for obtaining voting rights was so skewed that virtually all the voters in colonial Natal were white: by 1905, the government had given only three Africans the right to vote, and none had obtained this right before 1875.[2] As a result, local self-government in fact meant white (male) settler self-government. European employers in Natal, and especially farmers, gained the political clout to obtain even more favorable legislation. The settler-dominated government made it more difficult for Africans to buy land outside the reserves or to choose not to work for European employers, and it facilitated the eviction of Africans from both government-owned and private land. Many things that hurt rural Africans increased: population densities, prices, rents, taxes, and fines for the growing catalogue of newly criminalized acts. The decline of homestead agriculture also made it increasingly difficult for homestead heads to meet their various needs. To make up the difference, they either pressured their young men to go out and work for wages, or caved in to demands from the young men themselves to be allowed to do so. More than anything else, however, it was a "crisis in

African production"—especially during and after the five-year drought from 1888 to 1893—that forced Africans of all classes to migrate in search of wage labor.[3]

The boom on the Witwatersrand also attracted large numbers of Natal Africans, especially after 1894, but the consequences of such long-distance migration were much more severe than those resulting from labor migration within Natal. African agricultural production soared after 1880, but the African population was increasing even faster, placing stress on the land and making migrant labor ever more attractive. At the same time, employers on the Witwatersrand, desperate for cheap labor, began to recruit Africans in Natal, the most densely populated region in southern Africa. Those employers competed successfully with Natal employers by offering high wages and efficient transport to the Rand. Heavily capitalized, Rand employers were able to offer higher wages than their Natal counterparts could. More important, by the 1894 the mining industry had set up an efficient labor procurement system that relied on roving labor recruiting agents in rural Natal and on new railways to transport Natal Africans to the Rand. As a result, labor migration from Natal to the Rand increased dramatically that year. At the same time, migration to the Rand kept young males away longer, giving them more time to be influenced by the more alien culture there, and giving their families more time to be affected by their absence. Because of the greater cultural alienation, geographical distance, and time away, migrants to Johannesburg tended to remit a smaller portion of their wages back home than did migrants within Natal.[4]

It was precisely those parts of Natal which were hardest hit by the economic reverses of the 1880s and 1890s that would become the centers of rebellion in 1906: the districts of Umsinga, Krantzkop, Mapumulo, and Lower Tugela, all on the Natal side of the Thukela River valley. These districts were home to some of the largest African reserves, which became in essence dumping grounds to which Africans were sent after they were evicted from settler farms. By 1894 the reserve lands of Lower Tugela district had a higher population density than did those of any other division in Natal.[5]

With homestead agriculture already weakened, the ecological crisis between 1896 and 1898 sealed African dependence on migrant labor, particularly in the Thukela Valley reserves. In a matter of two to three years, drought, rinderpest, and locusts decimated crops and, more important, cattle herds. Since cattle served more as currency than as foodstuff for

Africans in Natal generally, the cattle losses effectively wiped out their savings. Mapumulo was particularly hard-hit, as the rinderpest epidemic of 1897 killed 97 percent of the cattle there.[6] By 1904, if not earlier, the Thukela Valley districts had together become the greatest labor-exporting area in Natal. Mapumulo and Lower Tugela, where the second and largest phase of the 1906 rebellion took place, ranked second and fourth among all Natal districts in the total number of migrant workers they sent out each year. And they ranked first and third, respectively, in the percentage of adult males absent, more than 40 percent in both cases.[7]

POVERTY AND CONFLICT WITHIN AFRICAN SOCIETY

It is not hard to see this growing poverty as the root cause of the 1906 Poll Tax Rebellion. As John Lambert has put it, "Ultimately, it would appear that most Africans who rose against white domination in 1906 were driven to rebel by a sense of desperation and frustration. Faced with discriminatory legislation, overcrowding, insecurity of tenure on private lands, poor wages, debts, and with increasing demands for taxes and rents, many Africans in reserves and on private lands alike were driven into rebellion in a desperate attempt to save themselves."[8] Similarly, Shula Marks, the foremost authority on the rebellion, has argued that "the causes of the Bambatha uprising are to be sought in the intolerable pressures which colonial society was exerting upon the peasant communities of Natal."[9] Material grievances were clearly the main motivation for the rebels of 1906. But material grievances were not sufficient to provoke Natal Africans into anticolonial rebellion; before 1906, poverty had indeed caused Natal Africans to lash out, often violently, but not at the settlers and colonial officials who were so clearly behind their distress. Instead, the vast majority of the overt conflict and violence in late colonial Natal—the 1906 rebellion excepted—took place between different groups of Africans.

The axes of conflict within African society were numerous. Above all, they threatened the most fundamental and integrative institution in Africans' lives, namely patriarchy, which brought together both the chiefdom and the household. In the late 1800s, chiefs increasingly fought with their subjects, elders with youths, and men with women. Another variety of conflict occurred between members of different chiefdoms, most notably in the form of feuds over land. An important subset of interchiefdom conflict was that between Christians and, for lack of a better word, traditionalists.

These tensions were particularly pronounced when Christians were new-comers to certain areas, or renounced their chiefs and either sought exemption from customary law entirely or subjected themselves to Christian chiefs or headmen. But the line between interchiefdom conflict and intrachief-dom conflict was often hazy precisely because subjects could change their allegiance from one chief to another, and succession disputes often turned one chiefdom into two or more. Moreover, in order to maintain its monopoly on force, the state prohibited armed conflict between chiefdoms, so chiefs had to walk a fine line between pleasing the state and pleasing their subjects who wanted to fight to defend themselves against people from other chiefdoms. In short, the chiefdom's effectiveness as an integrative institution was tested during the late 1800s and found wanting, which motivated many Africans to search for other, broader forms of social identification and categorization, like Zulu ethnicity.

Another broader form of social identification and categorization was Christianity, but throughout the 1800s, conversion created more division than unity. Many Africans, especially chiefs and elders, would have agreed with Chief Ndlovu ka Thimuni (a neighbor of the Qwabe in Mapumulo) when he said that African Christians were "corrupted by new-comers from England and elsewhere who know nothing of the native. . . . To become a Christian is to lose one's way."[10] African traditionalists were critical of Christian pretensions to high status, and were insulted that Christians often called them "ignorant people." More than anything else, however, African patriarchs disliked Christianity because it threatened the power that they derived from being intermediaries between the living and the ancestors. One man from Mapumulo claimed that the spirits of the ancestors disappeared when he crossed the Thukela River from Zululand into Natal, where missionary activity was far greater.[11]

Part of the problem was that religious conflict in Natal came to coincide with gender and generational conflict. African women and children were more in favor of Christianity, in part, perhaps, because of the leverage it gave them in their struggles with African men. Those men in the Qwabe chiefdom who were opposed to mission education and evangelism in the 1860s worried that their daughters might run away to the Christians in order to get out of arranged marriages.[12] This is in fact precisely what happened, and with some frequency, too. Responding to complaints from traditionalist men, colonial officials often intervened to force the return of these runaways to their families.[13] By the 1890s missionaries said that the

Qwabe chief Meseni was "anxious for schools among his people, the children are eager to learn, and the mothers interested and willing, but the men are either indifferent or bitterly opposed."[14] It is therefore not surprising that females outnumbered males among both church members and mission school pupils.[15]

Like gender and generation, land was another factor behind much of the conflict in late colonial Natal, and on occasion religion intersected with it, as well. One reason for this was the increasing number of African Christians after about 1880. That year only about 3 percent of Natal's Africans were Christian, but by 1905 even a frontier district like Mapumulo was about 10 percent Christian. The American Board Mission, the largest in the colony, reported a fivefold increase in membership during the same period.[16] Another reason for the intersection between land conflict and religious conflict was that African Christians were relatively privileged when it came to reserve land. About a sixth of the land reserved for Africans in Natal was administered by various Christian missions, not by chiefs. These mission reserves were supposed to serve as a sort of enticement for Africans to convert, but from the beginning most Africans who lived on the mission reserves refused to do so, and the missions could not expel them. Meanwhile, there was a growing number of Christians who lived far from any mission reserve and faced the dilemma of pledging allegiance either to a "heathen" chief or to a Christian but relatively weak chief or headman in the same area. Even if their traditionalist chief controlled a large body of land, Christians often found that those chiefs tended to side with traditionalists and against Christians in local land disputes. Christians had little more leverage on many mission reserves, where traditionalist chiefs and their subjects were in practice able to control land more effectively than were the missionaries and Christian chiefs or headmen who were legally in charge. In general, land conflict and religious conflict fed into one another, sharpening the cleavage between African Christians and traditionalists.[17]

GENERATIONAL CONFLICT . . . AND INTRAGENERATIONAL CONFLICT

Christianity, however, was a minor factor in most gender and generational conflict, which was becoming an epidemic in Natal African society in the late 1800s and early 1900s. This particular variety of inter-African conflict threatened African patriarchy, specifically the power of male homestead heads (*abanumzana*) over women and youths. One of the most striking things about the available evidence on African daily life in late colonial Natal is the near-constant reference by colonial officials, missionaries, and, above all, African elders to gender and generational conflict, which they tended to call "insubordination." As John Lambert and Benedict Carton have shown, this "insubordination" had everything to do with the immiseration Natal Africans were experiencing at the time. African elders had less and less land and fewer cattle which they could reward their sons with or, conversely, withhold from their sons as a form of punishment or control. At the same time, the migrant labor option took young African men out of the orbit of their fathers' control for months at a time, and provided the young migrants with alternative sources of wealth that they could spend as they wished without having to curry favor with their fathers.[18]

Thus, especially after 1880, African elders and their sons struggled with each other for control over the young men's wealth, labor, and marriage. Migrancy meant that the productive labor that young men engaged in was not directly overseen by the homestead head for the benefit of the whole family. When a son was away, that meant that there was one less person available at the homestead to maintain the herds, the crops, and the physical condition of the homestead itself. And even when migrant workers returned home, they increasingly refused to fulfill their customary labor obligations for those purposes. Before 1880, when the wealth earned from migrant labor had been minimal or nonexistent, the relatively plentiful wealth of the homestead took the form of cattle, crops, and land, all of which were controlled by the homestead head. After 1800, many homestead heads insisted that they controlled their sons' wages, but young men tended to resist these claims. They often remitted little or none of their wages back to their families, choosing instead to spend their money on themselves or to put it into their own savings. Back home, many young men would refuse to give their fathers control of the money, and on occasion even refused to help pay the family's rent or taxes or to buy them food. Most did contribute at least to some degree, but in an amount and a manner of their own choosing. In a society where marriage required the groom's family to give the bride's family a small portion of its wealth, and in which marriage turned young men into full-fledged homestead heads themselves, control over wealth meant control over access to patriarchal power itself. As long as the main form of bridewealth was the cattle that the father owned, then the authority of homestead heads was rather secure. But migrancy enabled young men to buy their own cattle, marry, and become homestead heads without their fathers' permission. It is easy to see why so many African elders protested that migrant labor made them irrelevant.[19]

Women, too, sought the advantages that came with leaving the homestead, but in this case African men and the colonial state joined forces to keep them from doing so. The government's codification of African customary law in 1891, done by white government officials in consultation with African elder men, confined women to perpetual minority status. Married women were subject to their husbands, and unmarried women (including women or divorcees) were subject to their fathers, brothers, or brothers-in-law. No woman could own property in her own name or leave her homestead without the permission of her male guardian. Of course, these laws could not keep thousands of women from absconding anyway, the most common destinations being mission stations and towns. In these nodes of European culture and colonial power in Africa, women were still subject to patriarchy, albeit of a new and different kind, but one that many apparently preferred to live with. However, for those women left behind on rural homesteads, the migration of both men and other women made their own burdens that much greater. Migrancy increased the share of labor each woman was expected to perform and, by thus increasing their husbands' and fathers' dependence on that labor, made men in general more determined to keep them at home.[20]

As important as intergenerational conflict was, it is no less important to note that women and young men were often in conflict with each other, not just their patriarchs. It is true that young men and women of all ages to some extent shared an interest in challenging the patriarchal authority of homestead heads. For example, as Carton notes, the phenomenon of mothers giving their sons some of the household's wealth was such a common and threatening phenomenon for African elders that such transactions were specifically outlawed by the 1891 Native Law Code.[21] Women and men also engaged in illicit sexual practices. Adultery and seduction, the crime of a man having sex with an unmarried woman, were both outlawed and became common "crimes" during this period. Clearly many married women were chafing at the restrictions of a legal order that subjected them so thoroughly to their husbands. Unmarried men and women, for their part, were to some extent challenging their fathers' ability to determine when they could get married and therefore legally have sexual intercourse. Indeed, by having intercourse, and especially if pregnancy resulted, the couple could force their fathers to let them marry whom they wanted when they wanted.[22]

But not all the sexual "immorality" that horrified colonial officials and African elders was consensual: nonconsensual sex was an important form of conflict between men and women of the same generation. Arrests for rape more than doubled between 1893 and 1896, while those for "indecent assault" (coerced sexual activity other than vaginal intercourse) more than doubled between 1894 and 1904. It is true that the figures were nevertheless small: 25 rape arrests in 1897, 219 indecent assault arrests in 1904, in a population of just under one million in 1904.[23] However, given the minimal police presence in Natal at the time, especially in predominantly African areas, and given the sexual double standard that existed among both blacks and whites, these numbers should be taken with a grain of salt. Indeed, both African elders and colonial officials accused both African and European police of using their positions to seduce or even rape African women with impunity.[24]

Moreover, there is every reason to believe that many cases of seduction, which supposedly involved consensual (albeit illicitly premarital) intercourse, were actually cases of rape. Consider, for example, the following case.

Charge: Seduction, in that on or about June 25th 1894 he [the defendant] wrongfully and unlawfully seduced one Nolaga, the unmarried daughter of Kapu. Judgement: Guilty. Sentence: To be imprisoned with hard labor for two months and to receive a private whipping of fifteen lashes. Facts: Defendant was present at a marriage ceremony with the girl Nolaga, who is his sweetheart. In the evening they left together and when in the "veld," Defendant detained the girl for the purpose of having "Hlobonga" [external sexual intercourse] with her, but when in the act he went further and penetrated her vagina, but with the girl's consent, *as she did not resist him.* The girl on getting home reported what had taken place to her parents and her father reported it to his District Headman, who brought the Defendant before the Court.[25]

Note that the court judged that Nolaga had consented merely because she did not resist her boyfriend, and yet she was clearly sufficiently disturbed by the incident to tell her parents and to have her father report her boyfriend to the authorities. In the same vein, one official felt compelled to argue that "cases of hlobonga where the girl is not a consenting party should be dealt with as cases of indecent assault," which suggests that not all officials felt that way or acted accordingly.[26] Indeed, another official felt that seductions usually did *not* involve the active consent of the woman: "In my experience seductions occur more frequently in the manner described [in Nolaga's case] than they do with the girls' deliberate concurrence. The act brings shame only upon her, and in general she will resist it until, overcome (probably) by the heat engendered by the filthy practice referred to, she yields to the importunities of the man."[27] Seduction was an exceedingly common crime in late colonial Natal. As one official put it, "It is to be regretted, but is none the less true, that fines for seduction form quite, if not more than half the revenue of this dept."[28] Given the frequency with which seduction occurred, and given the evidence that seduction cases were often actually rape cases, sexual violence was undoubtedly far more common than official arrest statistics might indicate.

There were also other ways in which young men's sexual self-assertion actually involved the victimization of women. As the historian Julie Parle has pointed out, sexual coercion was not always so obviously physical. Both men and women used love medicines in order to make others fall in love with them. But men's love medicines were much more powerful and controlling than women's, and women risked social opprobrium if they used such medicines, while men did not.[29] Moreover, even if premarital sexual intercourse *was* consensual, the young women in such cases ran the risk not only of getting pregnant, but also of being abandoned by their lovers and being forced to bear the burden of raising the children by themselves. One African elder complained to the 1906–7 Natal Native Affairs Commission that "A boy might lobolo, or begin to lobolo, a particular girl, and when he had continued paying for her for some time, he would throw her over, take the cattle that had been set apart for her lobolo, and proceed to repeat this performance in regard to some other girl. This took place even where the father was quite willing that the marriage should take place."[30] As one official noted in 1904, "Illegitimacy is very prevalent and seems to become more so in succeeding years. Severe punishments are inflicted, but without, so far, perceptible effect."[31] This led to the common situation described in 1968 by the South African legal scholar H. J. Simons: "An obligation to maintain the child falls in common law on its natural father and mother, and can be enforced by order of court and statutory sanctions. But men easily evade their obligations, and this irresponsibility is a significant cause of the high rate of illegitimacy in contemporary society."[32]

Intragenerational conflict could not only set young men against young women, but also set young men against each other. For example, in late colonial Natal seduction proceedings against young men were often initiated, not by their lovers' fathers, but by their lovers' brothers. After all, one possible source of bridewealth for a young man from a household barely getting by would be the bridewealth earned by his own sister. Brothers would often therefore take a very keen interest in negotiations around their sisters' marriages, serving as the main representatives for their families and taking charge of the relevant cattle.[33] Brothers might also try to secure their future father-in-law's permission for marriage by pledging the bridewealth to be paid for their sisters in the future.[34] Therefore brothers were perhaps even less willing than their fathers to see young women enter into sexual relationships without having any bridewealth paid for them at all. Such brothers then put themselves in the rather odd position of punishing their sisters for consensual relationships and of punishing young men of their own generation.[35]

"Faction Fighting"

But perhaps the most notorious form of intragenerational conflict in late colonial Natal was the "faction fight." Here groups of young men from different chiefdoms would lash out violently, not at the colonial state, or even at their elders, but rather at each other, in the name of their respective chiefs. Calling these fights "faction fights" is somewhat controversial because in South Africa the term has acquired connotations of mindless, irrational, and inevitable conflict between blacks stemming from age-old hatreds and a racial proclivity to violence. These connotations not only are racist, but also obscure the role of whites in creating conditions which encourage "black-on-black violence" (to use another, similarly loaded term). Instead, I will call individual outbreaks of violence "fights," and long-running conflicts between particular groups "feuds."

It would be difficult to identify a "typical" fight since dozens occurred every year, since every district—urban or rural—played host to its share, and since the particulars varied enormously from fight to fight. However, by way of illustration, consider that which took place in 1887 in Alfred district in southern Natal, between subjects of Chief Mtshiwa and subjects of the chiefs Duka Fynn and Tom Fynn (these chiefs were two of the many descendants of the early Port Natal trader Henry Francis Fynn and his African wives).[36] One of Chief Duka's subjects was holding an engagement feast for his daughter, at which cattle would be slaughtered and fed to the guests, homemade beer would be provided, and singing and dancing would occur. Hundreds of guests showed up, as was often the case, particularly when the host was prominent and wealthy. Many of the guests were both uninvited and unexpected, although this was also typical, and the host of such a party risked severe censure from his neighbors if he did not provide plenty of beef and beer to all comers. But a large proportion of the guests at this particular feast were subjects of Chief Mtshiwa, who claimed some of the land occupied by Duka's subjects, including the land that was the site of the party. As a result, there was considerable tension between the two groups even before the party. Men from both sides showed up with spears, clubs, and shields, which in itself was not unusual, but in these circumstances the presence of weapons only further raised the tension. After Mtshiwa's subjects arrived, Duka asked them to go to two neighboring homesteads, where they would be served away from his own people. As they proceeded through the open veld toward the homesteads, a huge fight broke out between the two groups, with some of Tom Fynn's subjects joining in on the side of Duka's. Nobody was killed—even the worst fights in late colonial Natal had no more than seven deaths—but the number of participants was massive: afterward, government authorities charged 208 men with participating in the fight, and 106 of the accused pleaded guilty.[37] The European judge who tried the case assigned collective responsibility to the young men of both sides, fining all of the accused regardless of whether they had actually participated or not. However, the fine for Mtshiwa's subjects was £5 per person, while that for Duka's subjects was only £3 a head. The reason for this was that the judge concluded that Mtshiwa's subjects had been the aggressors, partly for the simple fact that they had showed up armed at a household on the land of their enemies, but partly also because the evidence seemed to indicate that it was one of Mtshiwa's people who had actually started the fighting.

Fights like this have been common for a long time in what is today KwaZulu-Natal. Indeed, many South Africans, both black and white, associate "faction fights" with KwaZulu-Natal in much the same way that they associate ritual murders and witch killings with Limpopo province, even though these phenomena occur throughout the country and elsewhere, too. Chiefdoms in KwaZulu-Natal have on occasion fought wars with one another since pre-Shakan times, as have neighboring polities all over the world throughout history. And they continue to this day, although they have subsided greatly since peaking in the 1980s and early 1990s, when hundreds died every year in the low-level civil war then plaguing KwaZulu-Natal. The scope of this violence was greatly exacerbated by the struggles between various political parties for primacy in the anti-apartheid movement and in post-apartheid politics, as well as active intervention by agents of the apartheid regime.[38]

During the colonial period, and apparently also afterward, the incidence of fighting was rather cyclical, but a wide range of statistics suggest that it generally increased from the 1880s to the 1900s. There is evidence of colonial-era fighting as far back as the 1850s, if not earlier, although the low levels of government surveillance before 1879 makes it hard to gauge the extent of such violence.[39] In the early 1880s, several magistrates noted a decline in fighting.[40] Even then, though, in 1881, 190 of the 192 convictions involving Africans in the Inanda district resident magistrate's court involved fighting, and throughout the 1880s the Native High Court alone dealt with an average of 30 cases of fighting a year, involving 900 people.[41] Such statistical information as exists for the late colonial period is incomplete, scattered across different jurisdictions and obscured by changing legal definitions. Until 1897, for example, fighting was prosecuted under the heading of "riot and breaches of peace," but after that date "faction fighting" became a separate category of crime. Similarly, trials stemming from fights occurred at all levels of the judicial hierarchy, from the resident magistrates' courts to the Native High Court. Statistics on riot convictions before 1895 only exist for the Native High Court, which naturally tried only a small fraction of the total number of cases. These indicate that the highest numbers of convictions came in 1884, 1886, and 1887, the latter in which they peaked at 937. Thereafter convictions declined to a low of 77. Between 1895 and 1898, at least 3,000 Africans were arrested every year for rioting, with the peak coming in 1897, when 6,785 Africans were charged with this particular offense. Between 1898 and 1905, convictions for "faction fighting" in the resident magistrates' courts ranged from a low of 710 in 1903 to a high of 3,212 in 1905. By the latter date, it was the second most prosecuted crime in Natal, accounting for more than a sixth of Africans convicted.[42]

THE BEER PARTY

What was the cause of all this violence? As far as most white officials at the time were concerned, the cause was beer parties. While such an explanation is clearly somewhat reductionist (and the more thoughtful white observers at the time had more nuanced understandings of the factors at work), there is some truth in it. Most fights, such as the one described above, were closely connected with beer parties. And it would be difficult to exaggerate the importance of the beer party in rural Natal, then or now.[43] It was quite simply the main form of entertainment and leisure-time socializing (in all the senses of that word) in rural Natal during this period. Beer parties were held on numerous occasions, most notably at marriage dances (*imisindo* or *imicanguza*), but also at puberty dances (known variously as *imigonqo*, *amacamba*, or *ukomulisa*).[44] A homestead head would also throw a beer party for his neighbors if they had provided him with labor for some major task, such as house building, harvesting, or corn shucking. Indeed, he could be ostracized if he did not.[45] The beer party offered the host an opportunity to enhance his prestige by acquiring a reputation not only for wealth, but also for generosity. It also offered poorer members of the community an opportunity to demand limited access to the wealth of their richer neighbors: according to African rules of hospitality, no visitor could be turned away, not even a stranger.[46] Failure to comply could even lead to violent retribution.[47] On the other hand, if someone offered hospitality incommensurate with his status in the community, local elites might criticize him for his presumptuousness.[48]

By the 1880s, colonial officials in Natal had come to identify the beer party as the root of many different evils. These included, in the order of prominence that officials assigned to them, fighting, stock theft (though even several officials questioned this particular link), illicit sex, and a decline in the quality and quantity of labor that Africans provided to white employers.[49] For officials, the problem was that beer parties were becoming so frequent, either because wages were too high or because harvests were too plentiful; indeed, a bad harvest of sorghum (*amabele*) could lead to a decline in the production of African homemade beer (*utshwala*) and thus also to a fall in the number of beer parties.[50] As the historian Paul La Hausse pointed out, official opposition to African liquor consumption reflected the frustration on the part of both colonial officials and settler employers over their inability to get Africans to work for them at the wages the Europeans wanted to pay them.[51] However, officials themselves clearly saw fighting, stock theft, and illicit sex as more significant consequences of drinking than what they called "the labor question."

Moreover, officials were not the only ones to express substantial concern about youths and drinking: African elders did, too. They maintained that, until recently, beer parties had been regulated by a certain amount of decorum and involved certain sacred rituals, such as the pouring of libations for the ancestors. Patriarchs ran the show, and women and youths were to obey their orders. The patriarchy of the beer party was symbolized by the fact that elder men were to be served first and given pride of place in a central location reserved for them. Attendees were to avoid excessive drunkenness, and women were strictly segregated from the men, if they were allowed to attend at all. Now, however, young men elbowed their way past their elders to get at the beer and "engag[ed] in sexual adventuring" such as "flirting with young women" and even "court[ing] married women." For their part, both married and unmarried women also flouted convention, by mingling with the men and drinking inordinate amounts out of turn. Small wonder that so many of the cases of adultery and seduction were alleged to have taken place at beer parties.[52] As one African elder said, "At the time Sir T. Shepstone governed [before 1875] the boys did not drink beer, only the men drank the beer, the boys stood on one side. But now the beer is drunk by the boys."[53] It is no surprise, then, that in response the colonial state drafted new drinking regulations that included the following provision.

Young men (Izinsizwa) who may be allowed or invited to attend a beer drinking party, and who shall fail or neglect to recognise and to respect the superior position and rank of their elders or the men present (Amadoda) [sic] shall be guilty of an offence. Any young man or men who shall sit down to drink beer in the company of the men (amadoda) as aforesaid, unless specifically invited so to do by the principal man of the hut, with the approval of the other men present, shall also be guilty of an offence.[54]

Young men also tried to circumvent both custom and law by turning to new concoctions that had no protocols associated with them. One of these was a newly invented drink called isishimiyana, a mixture of sugarcane spirits and beer. The potency and novelty of the new beverage made its consumption even more subversive than that of beer from the point of view of colonial officials. It was the young who dominated the consumption and production of isishimiyana, and they constantly frustrated government attempts to crack down on them.

> Very few cases of "isitshimiyana" have been brought to light, and it appears to be a matter of great difficulty to run the delinquents to earth. The liquor is almost universally drunk in this Division. Regular "isitshimiyana" parties are got up. The invitation is by means of a white flag suspended to a bamboo or other long pole placed in the most commanding position near the festive kraal. The effect is magical. Young men and girls now drink to the exclusion of the elders. The idea is that an "mtimba" (bride's) party has arrived. These young people enter the hut, drink is handed round, and revelry reigns supreme—the older people being actually denied admission, thus an instance of the growing power of the young men in defiance of the authority of the older generation.[55]

The African elders consulted by colonial officials therefore blamed the fighting not just on beer parties, but also largely (though not entirely) on young men. Young men were drinking more now partly because, the elders alleged, the state had usurped the punitive powers of everybody from chiefs to homestead heads. Without those punitive powers, elders who tried to rein in young men were merely laughed at. The latitude accorded to youth was also supposedly among the reasons why fights were more common: elders were powerless to stop them. And the alcohol, which the young men did not know how to handle, also lowered their inhibitions about fighting. The only answer was for the state to give elders more authority, which it did in the 1891 Native Law Code and the 1903 beer-drinking regulations.[56]

For African elders to blame fighting almost entirely on young men and beer was not only self-serving, but also disingenuous. Nevertheless, the vast majority of participants were indeed young men. Moreover, faction fighting as a social institution was closely connected with ideologies of masculinity, and with the masculinity of young men, in particular. Jonathan Clegg, in his incarnation as a sociologist (before he became a famous musician), attributed the rise of fighting over the course of KwaZulu-Natal's history to a crisis of masculinity. The economic decline experienced by Africans made it increasingly difficult for young men to achieve the prestigious position of homestead head, and white racism excluded them from newer positions of prestigious manhood. At the same time, there occurred a decline in the older institutions of male socialization, which affirmed young men's masculinity in many different ways, including by providing safe outlets in which they could assert their masculinity through stick-fighting. Instead, manhood in many rural areas became increasingly associated with an ideology of vengeance: *ukubuyisa isidumbu*, "bringing back the body." With few other available alternative means of gaining such affirmation, fighting picked up much of the slack.[57]

Arguments that attribute internecine violence to the dysfunctional masculinity of underclass blacks are troubling and not entirely satisfying, partly because they start us on the slippery slope toward blaming the victim. On the other hand, Clegg places front and center the victimization of young black men through racism and the poverty it produces, as do other arguments which emphasize the role of masculinity, such as Carton's. And many, even most, men—throughout history and all over the world, across boundaries of class—have (at least at times) linked their own dignity with masculinity and violence: warfare, murder, and rape, as well as fighting, have always been overwhelmingly male activities. In the case of fighting in rural colonial Natal, however, Clegg's and Carton's arguments falter because they talk about masculinity without linking it with women and sexuality. Young, unmarried men (*izinsizwa*) needed wives before they could become full-fledged men (*amadoda*), with all the rights, privileges, and prestige such a role entailed. And even though land disputes were frequently at the root of the ongoing wars between chiefdoms in colonial Natal, young men also needed wives before they could have access to land.

The connection between masculinity, women, sexuality, and fighting comes out clearly when one considers that many fights were attributed to romantic conflicts: two groups of men might fight because of their competition over certain women, or a jilted lover might try to regain his honor by declaring war on her people.[58] Note also that weddings were one of the most common occasions for the beer parties that so often seemed to lead to young men fighting. Several elders even identified this as the main cause of fights, such as the chief who said, "The fighting is chiefly caused by the presence on these occasions of young girls which creates jealousy between the groups of young men from different localities, each group wishing to obtain preference from the girls to do so by dancing and jumping (gwiya) to please the girls."[59] Many young men who lost these dancing competitions felt humiliation and "jealousy on account of the girls not dancing with them, or that others have been preferred before them."[60] Some of the men who were rejected in this way would then do a dance (called *gwiya* or *giya*) that Natal Africans considered an act of defiance so humiliating for the person toward whom the dance was directed that to ignore it would be to call one's own masculinity into question: an official compared this act to "the traditional trailing of a coat at an Irish faction fight."[61] In other cases, "a rejected lover is said to go to a marriage dance he has nothing to do with and repeatedly giya in the face of the bride in such a defiant manner that a fight ensues."[62]

Other scholars, too, have traced in some detail how violence is often caused by a loss of dignity and the sense of shame that results. For example, James Gilligan, in a wide-ranging examination of diverse forms of violence, time and again finds shame and a loss of dignity to be the psychological triggers for violence. Of course, poverty and political and social subordination are leading causes of such shame.[63] In a similar vein, the political scientist James Scott adds that that same political and social subordination also prevents its victims from finding catharsis by asserting themselves against those who dominate them.

> We may capture the existential dilemma at work here by contrasting it briefly with Hegel's analysis of the duelist. A person challenges another to a duel because he judges that his honor and standing (including often that of his family) to have been mortally insulted. He demands an apology or retraction, failing which his honor can be satisfied only by a duel to the death. What the challenge to a duel says, symbolically, is that to accept this insult is to lose standing, without which life is not worth living (the ideal code, seldom rigorously followed, of the warrior aristocrat). Who wins the duel is symbolically irrelevant; it is the challenge that restores honor. If the challenger loses, he paradoxically wins his point by demonstrating that he was willing to wager his physical life in order to preserve his honor, his name. The very logic of the duel makes its status as an ideal apparent; any code that preaches the assertion of standing and honor at the expense of life itself is likely to have many lukewarm adherents in a pinch. For most bondsmen through history, whether untouchables, slaves, serfs, captives, minorities held in contempt, the trick to survival, not always mastered by any means, has been to swallow one's bile, choke back one's rage, and conquer the impulse to physical violence.[64]

But while the bondsman might not be able to challenge a member of the elite to a duel, he may be able to issue such a challenge to another bondsman. Might not the not-acted-on, pent-up rage and impulse to physical violence produced in one context be released in the other? Perhaps this might help to explain the great increase in fighting among Africans at the same time as their racial subordination was becoming more intense and consequential. Of course, there were other, possibly more important, factors at work, as well.

THE ROLE OF CHIEFS IN FIGHTING

It would not do to see fighting strictly as the work of young men, sexually frustrated, drunk, lashing out as much against the elders who try to restrain them as against the young men of the opposing faction, even if this was what some elders told colonial officials. Actually, such claims should be treated with suspicion *especially* because they were made by elders before colonial officials. Elders, too, had an interest not only in waging these small-scale wars, but also in concealing their involvement from prying officials. Elders were virtually the only Africans that government officials ever consulted, and the elders consistently used such opportunities to lobby for increased power over and against both women and youths. The lobbying worked, for, as John Lambert and others have shown, "throughout [those] years and until the end of the colonial period, the thrust of official policy in Natal remained the preservation of the hierarchical and patriarchal nature of African society."[65]

Evidence of specific cases of young men and their elders coming to blows over fighting is sparse and unreliable. Take, for example, the long-running feud between the Mabaso under Chief Tulwana and the Thembu under Chief Mabizela and, later, his successor Ngqamuzana. The Thembu and Mabaso are two neighboring chiefdoms located in Umsinga district, which was during the colonial era one of the most densely populated in Natal. It was also the district where Jonathan Clegg did his research on the ideology of vengeance. Land disputes between the two chiefdoms seem to date back at least to the 1880s, and prompted the government in 1897 to draw an official boundary separating them.[66] Though the Thembu chiefdom was ten times bigger than the Mabaso, and therefore both in need of more land and better able to enforce its claims militarily, the Mabaso chief Tulwana felt shortchanged by the new boundary. Between 1902 and 1905, armed conflict between the two chiefdoms broke out on several occasions. The largest battle was on 23 November 1905, when five men were killed, numerous homesteads burned or destroyed, and large amounts of livestock looted. It could have been worse, for three large neighboring chiefdoms had made alliances with one or the other of the antagonists and were about to intervene militarily themselves, until the police stepped in. The resident magistrate maintained that, if it had not been for the police, the battle could have turned into the largest in the history of the colony.[67]

The chiefs and other elders involved in the Thembu-Mabaso feud claimed that the young men of both chiefdoms had fought in flagrant defiance of their orders. The Thembu chief Mabizela, for example, said,

> When I heard of the fight I said to Ndabazibona [one of his headmen], why have my orders been disobeyed, I issued orders that none of my men were to go to the dance, except Sikopela and his daughter. I was very angry because my men went to the dance in defiance of my order and had I not been afraid of the Magistrate, I should have killed them. I sent to my headman, Zixuku, who lives on the Umsinga Mountain on Saturday and Sunday to tell him to order all men living under him to remain quietly at their kraals and not to go about the country carrying shields.[68]

Similarly, the opposing chief, Tulwana, claimed that neither the presence of the police nor the remonstrations of chiefdom elders were sufficient to keep their youths from engaging the invading *impi* (army) militarily.

> As the police were about to go up the hill to question the impi, it came down from the hill towards the kraal of Magadhlela where my people were. My men then said, "as they are coming down the hill, they will reach the kraal and kill us," the boys (abafana) saying "we shall not allow them to come to our kraal." The men (amadoda) did not succeed in keeping the boys back and they went to meet the approaching impi.[69]

But, on closer examination, it becomes apparent that Mabizela, at least, was far from the pacifist he claimed to be. For example, in 1902, four of Tulwana's headmen accused Mabizela of threatening to have his forces destroy the Mabaso chiefdom in one day, leaving the bodies of men and women stacked on each other just like at Isandlwana, where the Zulu army had routed the British. The undersecretary for native affairs (USNA) doubted the accusations, partly because Tulwana's men may have had ulterior motives in making them, namely to discredit Mabizela and thus to win a better hearing from the government in their ongoing land dispute. But the USNA also doubted the accusations because Tulwana's headmen claimed "that Mabizela was sober when he made threats which a man of his position would not for a moment dare to make in public, especially after the serious warning you gave him in February of this year."[70] Such a "serious warning" might make a chief refrain from making war on his neighbors, but if he was really determined, threats of government action would only make him more circumspect.

In fact, when whites were not present, chiefs and elders sang a very different tune. Evidence for this comes from the confidential reports of Africans hired by the state to work as spies from 1897 onward. Chiefs who claimed to be cooperative pacifists in their meetings with officials were belligerent in other settings. For example, one spy quoted Mabizela as saying that "if he were not afraid of the Government he would wipe out the tribe of Kula."[71] A common theme in these reports is the lengths to which chiefs and other elders would go in order to participate in fights without being detected. Thus the same spy also alleged that a certain Chief Deliweyo had said "that when he heard that the two tribes [his own and Chief Swayimana's Nyuswa] were likely to fight, he would go to his kraal near to the Indwedwe, so that he could report to the Magistrate that there had been a fight, and in this manner, clear himself." The spy claimed to have been present at an assembly where Deliweyo's opponent, Swayimana, told his subjects how to proceed against other neighboring chiefdoms: "When there was a wedding in Ngangezwe's tribe they were to join in the dance and not to go as on-lookers, so that if there were a fight with Mdepa's men they would not be so harshly dealt with when the evidence showed that they were partakers in the festivities and not on-lookers only."[72] The spies told of many other chiefs offering up similar strategies. Chief Silwane, for example, told his soldiers to wrap their spears in cloth and go to a wedding with a large group of people from the chiefdom. Those on the outside of the crowd would be unarmed and would thus further conceal the armed soldiers in the center. He would also make sure that the magistrate had given him and his people permission to attend the wedding, as such permission had proven to be good grounds for defense in faction fight trials.[73] There were many reports of chiefs making alliances with one another. In one case, Chief Tshutshutshu told his allied chiefs not to be present at the fight, the better to avoid being implicated when the authorities investigated.[74] "Native Intelligence Officer No. 1" concluded one of his intelligence reports by saying, "Everywhere I hear the men saying that they are not afraid of the authorities, because the Lawyers will get them off if they fight. This is the talk at beer drinks. At beer drinks everyone talks of fighting, even the chiefs."[75] The very fact that the spies made such blanket accusations suggests a lack of bias on their part, for they did not single out any particular individual or group for praise or blame when it came to fighting.

Doubtless such reports made resident magistrates increasingly skeptical about chiefs' protestations of innocence. In the conferences that took place in the mid-1880s regarding the "evils of beer-drinking," officials tended to accept the chiefs' attribution of fighting to out-of-control youths. Even during the 1880s and 1890s, the government did little to clamp down on chiefs like Sawoti and Thetheleku, who tried to take land from neighboring chiefdoms, and in some cases even allowed those chiefs to wage war with impunity.[76] After about 1900, however, the state's attitude toward chiefs started to change. Officials became more suspicious of individual chiefs and more receptive to accusations of fighting made against chiefs by their rivals or by African spies. Thus, in 1903, one resident magistrate accused Chief Ndlovu ka Thimuni of having orchestrated a fight by his subjects, and even of having fined those who refused to participate.[77] That same year, the chiefdom of Chief Lewis "Tim" Ogle, also known as Ntembo, another Eurafrican descendant of an early Port Natal trader, was involved in several large fights. The resident magistrate of Ogle's district, who presided over the trial of Ogle's subjects, concluded that, despite Ogle's own testimony otherwise, "the evidence showed that Ogle actually urged his men to fight."[78] In 1905, one chief, Gobosi, was deposed for having worked with his headmen to cover up the involvement of some of his subjects in fighting, while the next year another chief, Bhambatha, was deposed for having actively participated in a fight.[79] Of all these chiefs, Bhambatha and Ndlovu would be two of the three most prominent leaders of the rebellion in 1906.

THE QWABE SUCCESSION DISPUTE

It is something of a truism to say that chiefs in colonial Africa were stuck between a rock and a hard place: between an increasingly powerful and despotic colonial state and increasingly impoverished subjects who blamed the colonial state for their misfortune. The ambiguous evidence about chiefs' attitudes toward fighting reflects the untenable position that they occupied, having to please two powerful constituencies with conflicting demands. But the colonial state also undermined the very institution of chiefship in more direct ways, especially as European settlers in Natal gained more control over the colonial government. They aimed to do what Shepstone had up to this point prevented them from doing: abolishing the pillars of African governance, namely chiefship, customary law, and communal land tenure. The historian Martin Chanock's generalization about the effects of colonialism on African society in Central Africa applies equally well to Natal: the colonizers' efforts to remake the African political and legal order sharpened conflicts instead of lessening them.[80]

The Qwabe succession dispute of the 1890s and early 1900s, perhaps more than any other incident, illustrates how colonialism undermined the hegemony of chiefship in the minds of Natal Africans. The Qwabe succession dispute was important for several reasons. First, it was the largest, longest, bloodiest, most intractable intrachiefdom conflict in colonial Natal, leading to persistent fighting and dozens of deaths over a period of fifteen years. Second, it had an enormous influence on colonial policy. Third, the leader of the largest outbreak of the 1906 rebellion was Meseni, the Qwabe chief (and not Bhambatha, whose role in the rebellion has been greatly exaggerated by posterity). This case study is therefore very helpful in understanding the evolving relationship between chiefs and their subjects, as well as that between chiefs and the colonial state, and how those relationships contributed, in some cases, to rebellion.

Succession disputes were hardly unique to the colonial era of Qwabe history, let alone the colonial era in the history of many other chiefdoms in KwaZulu-Natal. The first four Zulu kings—Shaka, Dingane, Mpande, and Cetshwayo—had all come to power through succession disputes; the first peaceful and orderly succession to the Zulu kingship only came, ironically, after the Anglo-Zulu War of 1879. Indeed, the founding myth of both the Zulu and the Qwabe chiefdoms involved a succession dispute, that between Zulu and Qwabe over their father Malandela's chiefship. Even the roots of the Qwabe succession dispute of the 1890s and 1900s must be traced back to the times of Shaka and Dingane, more than fifty years earlier. Not long before the Qwabe came into conflict with the Zulu under Shaka, there had been a succession dispute between Phakathwayo and Nomo. The resulting lack of unity doubtless contributed to the Zulu conquest, but it was also exacerbated by it. Phakathwayo and Nomo both died, and Shaka appointed Nqetho to be the new chief. But not everybody within the chiefdom accepted Nqetho's appointment, and Nqetho himself was killed in southern Natal or Pondoland after he and his followers had escaped Dingane, fearing for their lives. At Nqetho's death, the Qwabe chiefdom was scattered in a broad band from Pondoland to Zululand, with groups all along the Natal coast. Besides those claimants to the chiefship already mentioned, others had died as well, or were soon to do so, such as Godolozi and Godide.

The wars of Shaka and Dingane, as well as the Boer conquest, created a discontinuity in chiefly succession that paved the way for succession disputes in the Qwabe chiefdom as well as in many other chiefdoms in colonial Natal. In many important respects, the story of Musi's accession to the chiefship is typical of that of other chiefs in early colonial Natal. Indeed, in some ways it is identical to that of both Matshana and Sidoyi, who were both deposed as "rebels" in 1857. All three became chiefs as minors in the 1840s, when elders tried to reconstitute their chiefdoms in Natal after the wars of the period had scattered the chiefdom's subjects and killed off not only the previous chiefs, but also all possible adult successors. In all three cases a succession dispute resulted, the outcome of which was decided by Shepstone, although conflict continued thereafter.[81] In the Qwabe case, an early succession dispute in 1849 resulted in the division of the chiefdom, with Musi being made head of one branch and Mamfongonyana of the other. But even within Musi's branch there was still debate, with him and some of his subjects seeing him as a chief in his own right, while others thought that he was only "raising seed" for Phakathwayo, that is, acting as chief until Phakathwayo's true heir, Musi's son Meseni, became chief.[82] The dispute was exacerbated when, in 1869, Musi appointed another son, Mmiso, as his successor, and Meseni, for his part, began arrogating for himself the powers of the chiefship, including the "right" to collect taxes and compulsory laborers for the government. It was around this time, the early 1890s, that the first fights resulting from the succession dispute occurred. Musi's faction was called the Inkwenkwezi (locative Enkwenkwezini) after the homestead of Mmiso's mother, while Meseni's faction was called Emthandeni, after his own mother's homestead, which was also named after Phakathwayo's.[83]

If the Qwabe chiefdom was not unified, neither was the colonial government. This became apparent during the government's deliberations in choosing a successor to Musi after his death, in 1892. On the one hand it is clear that the European colonial officials took customary law very seriously. They held several hearings on the succession, calling numerous African witnesses to those hearings and questioned them at length, with opinions on that testimony and the facts of the case being sought from seven African assessors—four chiefs and three headmen—and three European assessors. The resident magistrate, S. O. Samuelson, also contributed a long and highly detailed opinion, likewise based on customary law. Samuelson and most of the assessors, both African and European, thought Mmiso was the rightful heir. On the other hand, some high-ranking officials made it clear that the only customary law that mattered was the one that supposedly provided for an office of an all-powerful Supreme Chief who was above the law. In colonial Natal, the Supreme Chief was the governor of the colony. Even when Musi had first complained to the government about Meseni's insubordination, officials had reminded him that, ultimately, the succession was the Supreme Chief's (that is, the governor's) decision, not Musi's. After Musi's death, both the acting secretary for native affairs, H. C. Shepstone, a son of Theophilus, and the governor, Sir Charles Mitchell, emphasized practical concerns: which heir was the most qualified and would attract the most support, and so on. Both Shepstone and Mitchell saw this as an opportunity to divide the Qwabe chiefdom, which was the third largest in the colony, with more than 10,000 subjects. As Mitchell put it, "I don't like these very large tribes: some day they will give trouble. For political reasons I should prefer to divide the tribe. 'Divide et impera' is a good maxim that has held good for two thousand years."[84] And yet neither Shepstone nor Mitchell wanted to act rashly. Finally they consulted Theophilus Shepstone himself. As one of his last acts, he drew up an opinion on the case, but did not complete it before his death, in 1893. He left behind his opinion, in favor of Meseni, but not the reasoning for it. This was enough for Mitchell, however, and he named Meseni chief of the whole chiefdom.[85]

The Inkwenkwezi refused to accept this decision against them, and in response they effectively exploited the divisions among Europeans. They hired a lawyer, S. O. Samuelson's brother, R. C. A. Samuelson, who would later gain notoriety as the Zulu king Dinuzulu's defense counsel at the king's trial for allegedly having participated in, and even instigated and led, the 1906 rebellion. The Inkwenkwezi soon found that they had no legal right to appeal a decision of the Supreme Chief pertaining to chiefly succession. However, Samuelson found a loophole in the law that *did* give them a right to appeal the Supreme Chief's decision regarding the inheritance of property. Even so, Samuelson and the Inkwenkwezi had to overcome various obstacles. For one thing, Samuelson's brother, S. O. Samuelson, was now undersecretary for native affairs and regularly resisted the Inkwenkwezi's efforts to gain access to government documents pertaining to their case, with coldly hostile language doubtless directed toward R. C. A. For another, the Native High Court judge assigned to their case was none other than J. W. Shepstone, brother of Theophilus and uncle of H. C., who promptly dismissed the Inkwenkwezi's complaint on the grounds that the 1891 Native Law Code provided for no appeal of a decision by the Supreme Chief. The Inkwenkwezi then appealed to the Supreme Court, who found in their favor. The subtext beneath this decision was that the Supreme Court was made up of settler appointees who, like most settlers in Natal at the time, were keen to make the Native Affairs Department subordinate to the settler-dominated government. The Supreme Court's legal reasoning was that the Native Law Code had, indeed, only barred appeal to the Supreme Chief's decisions regarding succession, not to his decisions regarding a chief's property. Furthermore, several laws passed since 1875 had progressively stripped the Supreme Chief of all his judicial powers and subjected legal decisions by both him and the Native High Court to review by the Supreme Court. Lawyers for the Supreme Chief argued that, in the Native Law Code, his powers were absolute, and therefore his decisions were final. The Supreme Court justices, on the other hand, were deeply troubled by the suggestion that the Supreme Chief's decisions could not be reviewed, even when they were in blatant conflict with the other provisions of the Native Law Code. The case was sent back to the Native High Court, where a new judge found for the Inkwenkwezi, giving Mmiso's heir Siziba ownership of Musi's property, Mmiso having died.[86]

Giving Musi's property to the child Siziba while Meseni still controlled the chiefship was a recipe for disaster. The Inkwenkwezi continued to appeal to the government to divide the chiefdom, and when that failed, fighting between the Inkwenkwezi and Emthandeni sections of the Qwabe chiefdom only got more intense. For most of the 1890s, the Native Affairs Department refused to divide the chiefdom on the grounds that to do so would send two dangerous messages: that the government could be pressured to change its decisions; and that such pressure was perhaps most effective when it was violent. In 1898, however, the sugar planter James Liege Hulett enjoyed a short tenure as prime minister, and he was willing to compromise. That year he separated the Qwabe chiefdom again (Theophilus Shepstone having already separated it once by dividing it between Musi and Mamfongonyana in 1849). Hulett appointed the young Siziba as chief of the Inkwenkwezi Qwabe chiefdom, under a regent to be named later. He also ordered the partial, but not complete, spatial separation of the Inkwenkwezi and Em-thandeni, allotting specific lands to specific factions and forcing some of the people to move.[87] Fighting between the two sections continued nevertheless, but this could hardly be ascribed to a government policy of divide and rule, as the Inkwenkwezi had fought so hard for the division in the face of a government that had, until Hulett, fought so hard *against* that division.

Finally, in 1900, the settlers in the Legislative Assembly decided to close the loophole that the Inkwenkwezi had exploited in 1894 in gaining control over Musi's property. As Shula Marks and David Welsh both note, the Qwabe succession dispute was the most important factor instigating the legislation. Welsh goes further, arguing that the aim of the legislation was to shore up the colonial governor's powers as Supreme Chief over Natal's Africans. In this way, Act No. 1 of 1900, or the Native Code Amendment Law, was just one factor in the consolidation of the Supreme Chief's power between 1893 and 1910.[88] More than this, however, it also betokened a turn-about in settler attitudes toward not only Shepstonism, but also the idea of a despotic Supreme Chief supposedly modeled on the Zulu kings.

The legislation closed the troubling loophole by empowering the Supreme Chief to determine the heir to a chief's property, and not just to appoint a chief's successor. Two justifications for the act came up time and again in the legislative debates. The first was to spare the Africans the immense costs of litigation—£1,200 in the Qwabe case—and to protect them from the wiles of unscrupulous lawyers. The legislators alleged that it was the prestige of the chiefship, not the property, that was so valuable to Africans that they would commit financial suicide in order to get it. This act would prevent Africans from engaging in such self-destructive behavior. Some were troubled by the fact that the act deprived Africans of the right of appeal in such cases, but these voices went unheeded. The more important reason for the legislation, however, was that the right of appeal undermined the Supreme Chief's authority. This was not only injurious to the mainte-nance of colonial domination, but also, some legislators maintained, to the Africans' own peace of mind. Africans, it was alleged, had a deep psychological need for a firm authority above them. If the Supreme Chief was not to be that authority, the Africans would find some presumably less palatable alternative. The legislators also expressed a great nostalgia for Theophilus Shepstone's African despotism. The image of "Somtsewu" holding *izindaba* (consultations) in Zulu with African leaders under a tree was referred to more than once with affection. The comparison with the limited authority and alienation from African society of the contemporary secretaries for native affairs was not flattering for the latter.[89]

S. O. Samuelson said as much in his comments on the legislation. Though he had opposed what he considered Meseni's usurpations in the very beginning of the dispute, since then Samuelson had done everything in his power to shore up the sort of powers that had allowed the Supreme Chief to make Meseni chief. Without the intervention of a despotic Supreme Chief, Musi would have been able to secure the succession of Siziba. As a true believer in the cult of Shepstonism, Samuelson emphasized the legitimacy and authenticity of this action in the eyes of Africans as well, the degree to which even chiefs supported the increase in the Supreme Chief's powers.

> Chiefs who have been informed of [the law's] provisions said that if this was the only thing that has been done for the Native Tribes by the Government, they would have enough for which to be ever grateful and thankful, because it saves both the families of Chiefs and the people from ruinous expense, because it establishes the Supreme Chief's authority as the sole arbiter of these matters, and secures the hearing of these cases in a manner agreeable and acceptable to the natives themselves.[90]

For the actual members of the Qwabe chiefdom, it was perhaps inevitable that neither side would be satisfied with the government's decisions. Indeed, this was one of the only things that the two sides in the dispute had in common. The government's handling of the dispute could certainly help to explain why Meseni would later rebel against the government, but it does not explain why the Enkwenkwezini joined him, rather than acting separately, as many other chiefdoms did. Meseni's own complaints reveal how tightly interwoven his dissatisfaction with the government was with his conflict with the Enkwenkwezini. Meseni and his supporters were particularly inclined to identify the government with the Enkwenkwezini, and vice versa, from 1901 onward, when the resident magistrate of Lower Tugela division, Frank Parry Shuter, was named regent for the young Siziba after the death of the previous regent. Shortly before the government made the decision to appoint Shuter to that position, Meseni complained to the government about its failure to evict Enkwenkwezini from his lands.

> I have come to complain that the land is with blood, when the people were separated from me, it was said we were not to shed blood, I say the Government must right the matter by removing the people, who are at fault. Other chiefs have been assisted, and those who caused the quarreling have been removed. Had I been informed at the meeting at Goble's that the land was theirs, I should have made reply thereto. I was never told that the land was theirs. I do not know the cause of shedding of blood. They first took the inheritance, now they take the Chieftainship, now they have taken the land as theirs and we are evicted. I ask that my complaint should be made right by the Government. I have done no wrong. I say that the Magistrate Stanger [Shuter, whose office was in the town of Stanger, in Lower Tugela division] knows their "impi." The doings of their "impi" is written in the Court books. The "impi" has done many things. I have repeatedly told my people to keep quiet. I am much grieved and would pay even £2, or £5, or £10, to prosecute my case against them. I am without pleasure. Other chiefs are happy. I am unhappy because blood is shed in the land. My people are evicted up with them. I was given hope when I was appointed chief. It was said the person who defied me would be driven away, but my hope has now turned to darkness because those people have, for years, spilt blood. I rely upon the help of God to restrain my people from retaliating. When we were divided, word was given by the Great [the government] that that which we were grieved about we were to bring to the Great. There my complaint ends. We have not been properly divided. I desire that they shall be removed from my people. . . . I do not know another chief who is situated as me. I am sat upon by another Chief.[91]

Clearly, Meseni was concerned that his authority was being undermined by large numbers of discontented subjects in his territory. Some of these were Enkwenkwezini, but some were Emthandeni who were pressuring Meseni to be more assertive against both the Enkwenkwezini and the government. Issues like generational conflict, land hunger, and faction fighting were already leading to conflict between chiefs and subjects; with the Qwabe succession dispute, Meseni's position was even more insecure than that of the average Natal chief.

But the Enkwenkwezini elite's position was no less insecure. They had preferred that Malumbo, another half-brother to Meseni, who had fallen out with him and become a leader of the Enkwenkwezini, be made regent for Siziba. But the government felt that Malumbo was too bellicose and refused to accept him.[92] On numerous occasions thereafter, Emthandeni partisans mocked the Enkwenkwezini for having "only a whiteman for their Chief."[93] The Enkwenkwezini were clearly sensitive to such criticisms, and also resentful of the government for its refusal to appoint Malumbo. In 1905, for example, the Enkwenkwezini headman Valindlela asked Shuter to tell the government, "We kraalheads of the Nkwenkwezi say we have no Chief. It is true that a whiteman is called our Chief but our Chief is the child Siziba." But, perhaps aware of which side his bread was buttered on, Valindlela added, "We were thankful when the Government placed Mr. Shuter to be over us as our Chief. We swear by him."[94] In an environment in which chiefs and headmen commonly found themselves torn by the demands of their subjects on the one side and their chiefs on the other, the situation of the Qwabe elite was especially difficult.

CONCLUSION

Succession disputes, feuding, warfare, and the division of chiefdoms were all common in the precolonial era as well as the colonial era. What had changed was that now the colonial government had the final say in all disputes. This power was not absolute, as is clear when we see how African collective passive resistance forced colonial officials to reinstate the "rebellious" colonial chief Fodo, or how persistent fighting forced them to divide Meseni's Qwabe in 1898. But the state was able to affect the outcome of disputes among Africans. It is impossible to say whether the Qwabe succession dispute would have turned out differently, or how it might have done so, had it not been for colonialism. Nevertheless, it is clear that the power of the colonial state allowed, even forced, chiefs to pursue policies that were not supported by their subjects. At the same time, the state's land policies made it harder for chiefs to attract subjects, and the crackdown on fighting made it harder for chiefs to gain more land. In Meseni's case, he had to deal with additional burdens, such as the government's 1898 prohibition against his subjects moving from reserve lands onto privately owned lands unless they renounced their allegiance to him and khonza'd (pledged allegiance to) another chief. Moreover, any Africans who lived on private lands and wanted to transfer their allegiance to Meseni no longer could. Meseni's subjects were thus forced to choose between allegiance to him, which would result in continued residence on the increasingly scarce and infertile location lands, and to another chief, which would result in new residence on private lands. The government also lifted the requirement that Meseni's subjects who transferred to the Enkwenkwezini chiefdom pay him the customary *valelisa* fee for leaving his rule. Meseni was thus not only less able to retain and attract subjects, he was also deprived of the profit he might have gained by losing subjects, profit that he could use to attract more subjects.[95]

Of course, many aspects of government policy toward chiefs undermined the authority of all chiefs, not just Meseni. The government whittled away at the chiefs' few remaining judicial powers, and cracked down more effectively when chiefs tried to exercise those powers anyway. Colonial officials, private landowners, and employers all acquired many of the powers that chiefs had once enjoyed, including the ability to appoint headmen (izinduna) themselves, instead of having to work through headmen appointed by their respective chiefs. At the same time, officials steadily increased the burdens they placed on Natal Africans, such as isibhalo labor and the growing number of taxes and fines, while still expecting chiefs to help enforce those obligations.[96]

Finally, the undermining of the patriarchal power of homestead heads (abanumzana) also undermined the power of chiefs, since the two were so closely tied together in a unitary social and political power hierarchy. After all, homestead heads were obligated to enforce the will of the state and the chiefs as well as their own will on the women and youths under them. The same lack of land and cattle that gave homestead heads less leverage in their disputes with youths also weakened homestead heads' abilities to act as effective proxies for chiefs. Youths' migration to cities not only gave them access to wealth independent of the rural patriarchy, it also took them beyond the spatial and geographical reach of rural patriarchal authority.

But while older patriarchal structures were under threat and were changing as a result, they were far from dead. The sexual conflicts between young men and women showed just how much the men were still invested in patriarchy. The same was true of the culture of fighting, which was over access to the main pillars of patriarchal power in rural colonial Natal: land, women, and masculine pride. The fact that much of the fighting was organized on the basis of chiefdom belonging demonstrates the continued hege-mony of chiefship: young men were not rejecting the social and political hierarchies prevailing in their home areas—they were trying to improve their positions within them. Despite all their conflicts with one another, indeed perhaps because of those conflicts, chiefs as well as all Natal Africans shared a desire to find a solution to their problems that would preserve the cohesion of their society. Zulu ethnicity could serve such a function.

4

THE ROLE OF MIGRANT LABOR IN THE SPREAD OF
ZULU ETHNICITY, 1886–1906

During the 1880s and 1890s, more and more Natal Africans overcame their long history of deep animosity toward the Zulus and
began to use Zulu ethnicity as a tool to overcome the many conflicts plaguing
their society, and to challenge the colonial state, at least rhetorically. This
dramatic turnaround started not in Natal, but in the gold boomtown of
Johannesburg that sprang up suddenly, in 1886, hundreds of miles away, in
the South African interior. A rapidly increasing number of the young men
who had been coming into conflict with their elders, and who constituted the
vast majority of participants in the endemic fighting in Natal, were also
migrant workers who went to Johannesburg. The same migrant labor that
gave young men more social leverage also promoted a new ethnic consciousness among those men, which they then took back with them to Natal.

Zulu ethnic consciousness was not the only broader sense of "groupness"
that emerged among migrants to cities in the late 1800s and early 1900s, only
to be brought back by the migrants to their home areas. The same thing was
happening all over the world as technology and economic change were
producing huge population shifts. The contexts in which such a process has
taken place have been diverse: urbanizing peasants learned to be French in
the growing cities of nineteenth-century France; Jews, Irish, and Poles in the
Progressive-era United States played a major role in the creation and spread
of Zionism and Irish and Polish nationalism; the new urban proletariat in
early-twentieth-century Egypt served as conduits for the spread of Egyptian
nationalism from the elites to the masses. Similar processes are happening
even today among "Third World" immigrants in the contemporary "First
World."[1] The similarities between the Hawaiian sugar plantations from 1870

to 1930 and Johannesburg during the same era are particularly striking: In Hawaii, for example, Ilocano, Cebuano, and Tagalog speakers learned to be Filipinos in contrast to the Japanese and Chinese workers with whom they lived and labored, much like Qwabe, Thembu, and Chunu learned to be Zulus in contrast to the Sotho, Shangaan, and Xhosa.[2]

In the case of sub-Saharan Africa, one still encounters the persistent (but erroneous) idea that urban migrants merely reproduce the "traditional" and "tribal" identities and cultures that they bring with them from their rural homes. Rather than becoming fully "urbanized," Africans in the cities are still essentially rural in outlook and way of life.[3] But already in the 1950s and 1960s, Africanist scholars were showing that urban ethnicity was something very new, neither "traditional" nor "tribal," and very different from what prevailed in rural areas. Whether it was Bisa mineworkers on the Zambian Copperbelt, or Hausa traders in southwestern Nigeria, alien migrants in urban industrial settings in Africa, just as in the rest of the world, discovered that their internal differences were trivial, and they learned to think of themselves as one people in ways they had not done before.[4] One could even synthesize Ferdinand Tönnies and Benedict Anderson and argue that, by destroying the organic solidarities of community and replacing them with the anonymity of large-scale society, it was urbanization itself that created a need for the "imagined communities" of ethnicity and nation in the first place.[5]

One of my aims here is to show how significant labor migration and urbanization were for the development of Zulu ethnicity, as well.[6] More than this, however, I would like to argue that the relationship between urbanization and ethnicity varies according to the social geography of the particular city in which the migrants have come to live, and of the rural areas from which they originate. The two main destinations for Zulu migrants have been Durban and Johannesburg. Migrant experiences in those two towns have been similar: they have tended to live together in the same part of town; migrants from the same area have tended to monopolize particular jobs; and intra-African conflict and violence tended to follow the dividing lines of ethnicity, language, and regional origin. But in Durban, the dividing lines coincided with the districts and chiefdoms from which the migrants came, replicating rural divisions and keeping Natal Africans from uniting. In Johannesburg, on the other hand, Africans from Natal and Zululand united for the first time *as Zulus*, all too often against the other emerging ethnic groups of southern Africa. Natal African migrants then brought this new Zulu ethnic consciousness home with them, where it would form the basis for the 1906 rebellion and, more important, for the sense of ethnolinguistic unity that even politically divided Zulus share today.

MIGRANT LABOR IN DURBAN

Durban was the largest single destination for migrant workers in Natal, especially after the mineral revolution led to vastly increased traffic through Durban's harbor, from the 1870s onward. The number of Africans employed in Durban grew from 1,777 in 1871 to 18,653 (of whom only 693 were women) in 1904.[7] Many, perhaps even most, of these workers were togt workers, or day laborers, of whom most worked on the Durban docks. A large proportion of the togt workers were also employed in various forms of overland transport of goods, such as porterage and cartage. These men (for the great majority of the togt workers were men) successfully resisted their employers' efforts to force them into more regular employment and longer-term contracts (ironic given South African labor's current fight against the casualization of employment). The flexibility of day labor enabled workers to play different employers off against one another, with the result that their wages were high even by world standards. For example, in the late 1880s the wages for Durban dockworkers were almost the same as they were for their London counterparts.[8] The largest groups of workers on more extended contracts were rickshaw pullers, policemen, and, largest of all, domestic servants. In stark contrast to the present situation, the vast majority of domestic servants in colonial Durban were young men, mainly because there were so few African women living there at the time. Many African men in colonial Durban were self-employed hawkers (especially of firewood) and clothes washers (known in Natal as the *AmaWasha*). African women were also street hawkers, but more often worked as independent beer brewers out of their own homes, which served as shebeens for their largely male clientele. Finally, on the margins of law there were the gangsters (*amalaita* or *izigebengu*) and prostitutes.[9]

Far from being treated as, or asserting themselves as, primarily Zulus or even Natal Africans, African workers in Durban organized themselves on the basis of the chiefdoms and districts from which they came. The rickshaw-pullers came mostly from Mahlabatini district, the sanitary workers were largely Bhaca from southern Natal, and the Qwabe among the togt laborers tended to act as a group in securing access to specific jobs. The Qwabe and other Africans from Mapumulo also virtually monopolized the borough police.[10] The Qwabe dominance of the Durban police force can be seen even in the Zulu word for "police," *amaphoyisa*. This word, borrowed from the English word "police," demonstrates the "y" for "l" substitution that distinguishes the Qwabe thefula dialect from most other varieties of Zulu.[11]

In 1906, all 300 of the borough police came from precisely those chiefdoms that rebelled in Mapumulo and Lower Tugela.[12] This is rather ironic when one considers that the borough police were mainly involved in actions against the rest of the African workforce in Durban, enforcing the plethora of laws against "desertion" (i.e., quitting a job without the permission of one's employer) or "insubordination" (often merely agitating for better pay and working conditions). In 1905, the superintendent of the Durban police estimated that about 40 percent of the Africans living in Durban were arrested each year.[13] For this reason, there was an enormous amount of tension between the African police and the rest of the African population in Durban.

This tension reached its climax in the famous Point Riot of 1902, when some 227 African laborers took on the borough police in one of the largest fights of the colonial period.[14] These Africans were living on the Durban Point (a small extension of land separating Durban harbor from the Indian Ocean) in private barracks built to meet the demand for housing from African workers. One day, when some African constables tried to arrest one of the barracks residents for drunkenness, some twenty of his fellow residents attacked and overpowered the constables, releasing their friend. More constables were called in, and the fight between the barracks residents and the police escalated from there. The Point Riot was not just about urban life; it also pointed up the ways that rural patterns of affiliation continued to matter even in Durban. For example, one of the men accused of leading the workers' side in the Point Riot had come from the same district as one of the policemen, and, according to a newspaper account of the incident, the two had been "rivals in sweethearting affairs. The ill-feeling had existed over two years."[15] Thus, for at least some of the participants in the Point Riot, this fight was a continuation of particular feuds being waged in rural Natal. Indeed, fighting was fairly common in Durban as well as in the countryside, and urban fighting fueled rural conflicts as much as the other way around.[16]

Some of these even pitted different segments of the police against one another, not surprising considering that the district of Mapumulo from which so many of them came was a major center of fighting, as well as the home of the Qwabe chiefdom then embroiled in its bitter feud with itself.[17]

Besides the labor market and fighting, food and lodging were another aspect of urban life in which rural affiliations were affirmed. Affordable housing was scarce in Durban; few workers besides domestic servants were given housing as well as wages. Therefore, domestic servants became the most important purveyors of housing for Africans in the city, as they played host to friends and relatives from the same rural district or chiefdom. In the garden cottages and backyards of fine, white-owned homes, the domestic servants and their associates formed "kitchen associations." Much like the "homeboy" associations of other parts of Africa, the kitchen associations provided the social space necessary for cementing group loyalties and planning collective action, including not only fights, but also competition with other Africans for jobs and protests against their employers. Information about employers and goings-on back home, as well as mutual aid in case of death or disability, were also obtained through these associations. Employers who objected to their premises being used in this way risked not only losing their servants, but also finding themselves unable to hire replacements, so universal and important was this practice for urban Africans.[18]

Europeans in Durban, and employers in particular, were quick to realize the close connection between lodging and the leverage that workers enjoyed in the labor market. Thus, in addition to all the laws governing relations between employers and employees, Europeans in Durban also tried to get Africans to live in barracks or compounds built, owned, and managed by the municipal government, rather than in the servants' quarters of the Europeans' own homes. The first such barracks were built in 1878, and no inducement was offered for Africans to move there other than the fact that no rent was charged. There were very few takers. In 1902, the colonial government passed a law forcing togt laborers to register and live in either the municipal compounds or in private ones licensed by the municipality. The effort was not entirely successful, owing to massive noncompliance not only from African workers but also from many of their employers.[19] It was clear to the superintendent of the Durban police why such a system was doomed to failure.

When the community found themselves burdened with the support of their servants' friends and relatives, including about 7,000 day labourers, they complained, and the council, to relieve the pressure, had erected at the Point large barracks, to accommodate about 2,000 of these day labourers, who very naturally preferred the freedom and comfort with their relatives in town. This in fact is the whole secret. Natives, like other human beings, who have not the privilege of reading the news, will collect at the largest centre of their fellow-men to hear it. The town, at present, being the largest centre, forms the greatest attraction to which they gravitate; apart from this, the natives who are born and brought up in small huts, with their friends and relatives, detest the idea of occupying large barracks with strangers, which appears to them more like a gaol than a home.[20]

Policemen had been just as likely as their fellows to live in domestic servants' quarters, but from 1899 they, too, were forced into special housing, on police premises. The police took up this housing by and large, but let their friends and relatives stay there as well. (The housing shortage was so acute that even many homeless Europeans sought shelter in the police stations.)[21] Even though an ever greater proportion of Durban's African workers took up residence in hostels run by their employers or by the municipal government, the workers divided the beds and rooms in those hostels on the basis of the chiefdoms to which they belonged.[22] In this way their bedfellows or roommates were more likely to be "homeboys" than total strangers from a different chiefdom or district. In short, neither urbanization nor direct state action could destroy the rural affiliations that migrant workers brought with them to Durban.

There were, of course, countervailing tendencies at work. For example, while a large proportion of African workers in Durban came from Mapumulo, many also came from the districts of southern Zululand, the heart of the former Zulu kingdom.[23] These Zulu migrants could have helped spread Zulu ethnic consciousness to their neighbors in the city. In order to do this, however, there would have had to have been some basis for African unity across the boundaries of chiefdom affiliation. Given the ethnic fragmentation of African society in Durban at this time, such unity was hard to come by.

Racial consciousness was one factor that could create the sort of African unity necessary for Zulu ethnic consciousness to spread, and racial consciousness was certainly more pronounced in the cities. Given how the categories of "black" and "Zulu" have come to overlap almost completely in KwaZulu-Natal, the spread of black racial consciousness could help to facilitate the spread of Zulu ethnic consciousness. But as long as interchiefdom conflict loomed so large in the lives of Natal Africans, their racial ties as blacks would not have much meaning for them. Nor would they be inclined to consider themselves Zulus. Colonial racism had the potential to change all that, and it would in the long term. Until the late 1800s, however, the delayed impact of colonialism, conflict with the Zulu kingdom, the colonizers' divide-and-rule tactics, the deep resonance of chiefdom affiliation in Natal Africans' hearts and minds, and their lack of experience with cosmopolitan urban settings prevented black racial consciousness from becoming significant.

We have seen how all these factors were changing as the nineteenth century reached its end, but a new factor was emerging that would in time promote both black racial consciousness and Zulu ethnic consciousness, namely the growing presence of Indian immigrants in Natal. Although Indian immigration to Natal began in 1860, an economic recession in the late 1860s and the Indian colonial government's concern about Natal's treatment of the migrants meant that the number of newcomers remained fairly low until the 1880s. In other words, the peak of Indian immigration to Natal during the 1880s and 1890s coincided with the large-scale expulsion of Africans from white-owned lands, the decline of African agriculture, and Africans' growing participation in the wage labor force. It also coincided with shifts in both the formal and informal racial orders created by the European colonial officials and settlers in Natal. The state's reaction to the Qwabe succession dispute demonstrated Natal Europeans' inclination to disregard the protocols of African political culture and indeed to dismantle chiefship, customary law, and communal land tenure. At the same time, Natal Europeans went from treating Indian and African laborers essentially the same in the 1860s and early 1870s to privileging Indian laborers over Africans from the late 1870s onward and allowing an Indian middle class of professionals and especially merchants to lord it over their African customers. Although in the 1890s Natal Europeans came to see Indians as an alien threat that had to be contained or even eliminated, they never changed Indians' privileged place over Africans in Natal's racial hierarchy.[24]

The result for Africans was a new catalogue of racial grievances and a new variety of racial conflict, this time with Indians. The grievances and the conflict were particularly pronounced in Natal's Sugar Belt, along the coast from Durban north to the Thukela River. The sugar industry was the largest employer of Indian immigrants during the colonial era, but it also employed many Africans from neighboring reserve areas like Mapumulo. (For example, in the early 1890s, a Lower Tugela sugar planter named Saunders complained that assemblies and ceremonies called by the Qwabe chief caused absenteeism among his workers.)[25] The very rationale behind Indian immigration in the first place, that Indian workers would work for lower wages than Africans would, was only the first source of conflict between the two groups. Later, as Indians acquired certain legal privileges and, more important, as European landowners started giving Indian small farmers preferential access to land, Natal Africans' resentment only grew. The situation worsened as Natal African agriculture declined and blacks became more dependent on Indian market gardeners and merchants from whom they could buy the food and other necessities that blacks could not grow or make themselves. Indeed, it was during this period that the figure of the exploitative Indian merchant became established in popular African consciousness, both as a stereotype and as a source of racial animus, a situation that continues to this day. And as alcoholism became more and more of a problem for Natal Africans, they became more inclined to blame the Indian merchants from whom they purchased the liquor, often illegally. European (and American) missionaries encouraged their Natal African converts to view Natal Indians as the very epitome of wickedness and the cause of many of the evils plaguing Natal African society. One of those converts, John Langalibalele Dube, was one of the earliest and most prominent political activists on behalf of his race, encouraging self-help and mastery of the ways of European civilization. Dube shared each of these attributes with his contemporary and fellow Natal Sugar Belt resident Mohandas Gandhi, but the two never collaborated or even had much if anything to say about each other. Instead, both men blamed the other race, as well as whites, for the problems that they and their followers faced.[26]

Natal Africans' grievances toward Natal Indians sometimes led to open conflict, especially in urban areas where the two groups competed for jobs. In 1890, for example, there was a fight between large groups of Indian and African workers at the barracks of the Natal Government Railways in Pietermaritzburg. Six years later, white merchants in Durban managed to get an armed body of Natal Africans to mass on the waterfront and protest the arrival of Indian immigrants there.[27]

In the end, though, the contribution of Natal Indians to the spread of Zulu ethnicity was minimal, far less than that of Natal Europeans. While Africans' and Indians' lives intersected on occasion, they were still highly marginal to each other's experiences. Thus, in his discussion of the Natal Indian working class, the historian Bill Freund could say, "In a number of texts rich in memory of life in peripheral Durban, I have been surprised at the complete non-appearance of Africans."[28] The same could be said of the lack of reference to Indians in the large volume of African testimony in the colonial archive recorded by Stuart and others. In the Natal native administration's confidential intelligence files, the largest compendium of information on African popular consciousness during the late colonial period, there is copious testimony by Africans relating to all manner of rumors and collective actions, to the Zulu king and numerous chiefs, to the politics of various chiefdoms, and to white people and Africans' thoughts about them. But I have not been able to find a single reference to Indians in the twenty volumes that make up that collection.[29]

MIGRANT LABOR IN JOHANNESBURG

While urban migration to Durban merely reinforced chiefdom ties among Natal Africans, the urban migration to Johannesburg that began in 1886 promoted a common Zulu ethnic consciousness among them. This was mainly because the migrant population in Johannesburg was far larger and more diverse than the one in Durban. The year 1886 saw the beginning of a gold rush on the Witwatersrand in the Transvaal, then also known as the South African Republic. Out of this gold rush would emerge Johannesburg, which with startling rapidity became the largest city in South Africa. This was the second of the two major mineral rushes in South African history, the first—a diamond rush—having begun in Kimberley in 1867. Although there was much that was similar about the two rushes, there were also some crucial differences. In Kimberley there was a long digger phase, in which hundreds of small-time miners dug for their fortunes in hundreds of small claims. On the Witwatersrand, however, the surface pickings were quickly exhausted, and the subsurface ore was buried so far underground and was of such low grade that almost from the beginning only large-scale concerns with access to large amounts of capital and machinery could compete. In Kimberley, the diamond diggings were monopolized by Cecil Rhodes's company, De Beers, by 1889, whereas on the Witwatersrand there emerged an oligopoly of a handful of large corporations that alternately competed and cooperated with one another. Kimberley was situated in a disputed frontier area that was quickly annexed by the British empire. The Witwatersrand, on the other hand, was situated in the very heart of the independent Boer South African Republic, only some fifty miles south of the republic's capital, Pretoria. Thus the gold mines were British-owned but Boer-ruled, a contradiction that would lead to the outbreak of war, the South African War, between the Boers and the British by 1899.

Nevertheless, the Witwatersrand operations drew on the organizational precedents, as well as the capital and infrastructure, established at Kimberley, if not even earlier at Cape Town and Durban and other South African towns. One of these organizational precedents was the migrant labor system, which had its benefits for both employers and African laborers. Most African workers, many of them young, unmarried men in societies practicing bridewealth exchange, only wanted to stay long enough to earn a certain amount of money and then return home. Many, though by no means all, employers were happy to oblige, for migrant labor kept them from having to provide for women and children, and for old or disabled workers. Migrant labor was also an effective safety valve for worker discontent: disgruntled workers were often more likely to leave than to agitate for better pay and working conditions. Another was the pass system, which required Africans to be employed in order to receive a pass which gave them permission to reside in the town. But the most notorious development of all at Kimberley was the compound system, whereby the mineowners, from 1885 onward, managed to force their employees to reside in hostels on company grounds, where the workers would be under the constant surveillance and control of their employers.

As with migrant labor itself, other aspects of the system reflected worker input and were not just imposed on them by the mineowners. The mineowners, after all, had the upper hand in terms of power, but this power was never total, and could even be enhanced through compromises that bought off a certain amount of worker discontent without seriously undermining the mineowners' dominance. For example, workers from the same polity or region often preferred to be recruited together, migrate together, and work and live together. Rural structures of authority were replicated or maintained both during the journey and at the destination. For their part, the mineowners accepted and incorporated these structures into their developing paternalism, which became based increasingly on a certain, not always accurate, understanding of what the whites called "tradition" and "tribe." The compounds themselves became "tribes," with white managers as their "chiefs," and the leaders of different groups of Africans as their "headmen."

Each subgroup of workers was also a "tribe." For example, Patrick Harries has shown how the migrant labor experience was a major factor in the creation of the ethnic group known variously today as Tonga (or Thonga), Shangaan, or Gaza, whose members live mainly in southernmost Mozambique and the adjacent borderlands of South Africa. They were, of course, the same Tonga who were such a large proportion of the wage labor force in much of Natal throughout the nineteenth century. In Kimberley, they became known as "Portuguese Zulus" or Shangaans. Harries's description of the process is worth quoting at length.

> On the coastal plain [from whence the Tonga came] political identity was rooted in the chiefdom, although ties of obligation and assistance extended to kinsmen living as clients of other chiefs. The putative nature of kinship and the *kondza* system [similar to the khonza system in Natal and Zululand] allowed the integration of outsiders into these bounded groups, whose membership was ascribed and delineated by various cultural traits, including an often pronounced antipathy to other kin groups. Allegiance to the kin group did not diminish loyalty to the wider chiefdom, and people found a political identity in both institutions. But in the cosmopolitan society of the diamond fields, these political identities were too narrow and restrictive to function effectively, and, gradually, the fictive element in kinship was extended to include a wider community in which the chief was replaced by culture as the focus of loyalty. At the same time, a society that accepted fictive kinship could easily extend this belief into a putative ethnicity built on the use of familial terms, such as "brother" or "uncle," to describe the relations between the workers. Ethnicity, like kinship, was based on myths of origin, ascriptive and putative belonging, as well as relations of reciprocity.[30]

Harries's description of the interrelationship between chiefdom, kinship, and ethnicity in Tongaland is clearly similar to what I have described with regard to Natal and Zululand. His description of migrant labor and ethnogenesis also finds strong echoes in the Zulu experience. In fact, Harries refers briefly to recurring fights between "Sotho" and "Zulu," first at the railway camps of the Cape in the 1870s, and later at Kimberley itself.[31] By 1906 there was a "Cape Town and District Zulu Association" for migrants in Cape Town.[32]

But Kimberley and the rest of the Cape Colony never attracted anywhere near as many Natal Africans as did Johannesburg, partly because Johannesburg was much closer to Natal than were Kimberley or any of the other major towns in the Cape. Another factor was that both the demand for migrant workers and the capacity of the system designed to recruit, transport, and employ migrants was still relatively small and primitive in the first couple decades of the diamond fields. Already in 1889, the Natal government issued 3,667 passes to Africans migrating to the Transvaal in the first four months alone. By 1894, the number had peaked at 30,675.[33] Of these, the largest number came from the districts that would be the centers of rebellion in 1906, especially Mapumulo and Lower Tugela, and from the Qwabe chiefdom in particular. Very few came from Zululand proper, north of the Thukela. In 1897, for example, the Qwabe chiefs Meseni and Zidumo ranked second and third respectively among all the chiefs in Natal in the amount of money remitted to the colony by their subjects on the Rand.[34] In October of that year, remittances from the Rand to Natal totaled £857 1s. 6d., while those to Zululand totaled only £46 7s. 6d.[35] On assuming his post in 1896 as the Natal government's official agent on the Rand, J. S. Marwick said that the Natal migrants came "chiefly from the north coast [the region between Durban and the Thukela River, including Mapumulo and Lower Tugela] and the Umsinga division [the home district of many of Bhambatha's followers in 1906]," both areas south of the Thukela.[36] Marwick told the *Standard and Diggers' News* that the Natal Africans who came to the Rand were "of the Zulu race, although called Natal Kafirs, and are chiefly refugees to Natal from the former Zulu regime."[37] The chief attraction of Johannesburg was undoubtedly financial. The wages there were simply higher there than they were in Natal. For example, the average monthly pay for an African working for the Johannesburg Scavenging Department was £2 18s. 10d., more than that for work in Pietermaritzburg (£2 16s.) or at the Durban harbor (£2 6s.).[38]

As in Durban, there was a pronounced ethnic division of labor. Most notably, Natal Africans were *not*, by and large, mineworkers, certainly not to the degree that other ethnic groups were. In 1903, for example, 73 percent of the Africans working on the mines were Shangaans, while only 2 percent were from Natal and Zululand. Conversely, 20 percent of the non-mining African labor force on the Rand came from Natal and Zululand, while only 11 percent were Shangaans. In total, Natal and Zululand contributed about 10 percent of the Rand's African labor force; only Mozambique, the Transvaal, and the Cape contributed more. Outside the mines, however, Natal Africans were outnumbered only by Cape Africans.[39] The proportion of Natal African women was even smaller in Johannesburg than it was in Durban: 5,173 men versus 119 women in 1896.[40]

The jobs that Natal Africans tended to take up on the Rand were also very similar to those they took up in Durban, namely domestic service, laundry, and police duties. Of these, the largest single group was probably the domestic servants. About half of the 7,500 or so domestic servants in Johannesburg in 1899, and an even larger proportion of the children's nurses as late as 1906, were from Natal or Zululand. In 1899, an African domestic servant in Johannesburg could earn 80 shillings a month, compared to 50 shillings a month for mine work. Unlike in Durban, domestic servants in Johannesburg either had in-house accommodations that were simply too small to house their friends as well, or joined their friends in renting rooms or even houses in the slums of Johannesburg or in the emerging "locations" designated for Africans.[41]

The other main group of Natal Africans outside of the mines was the AmaWasha. Keletso Atkins has shown that, contrary to conventional wisdom, the AmaWasha did *not* emerge in imitation of the Indian commercial washermen, known as Dhobis, who were among the earliest Indian migrants to Natal in the 1860s. Rather, they emerged in the 1850s, before Indian immigration, as a continuation of the old hide and skin dressing specialists, now transferred to an urban setting. The Natal government gave the Dhobis preferential treatment over the AmaWasha, leading to the decline of the AmaWasha in Natal and the migration of many of them to Johannesburg.[42] The Johannesburg AmaWasha, and perhaps those in Natal as well, were largely from the middle and upper Thukela River valleys, especially the Umsinga and Weenen districts, from which the rebel chief Bhambatha would draw most of his supporters in 1906. The numbers of AmaWasha in Johannesburg peaked at 1,222 in October 1896 and declined thereafter, having virtually disappeared by 1914. They were done in by a combination of several factors, including mechanization and government efforts to force them into locations far from their clientele.[43]

Finally, there were the Natal African mineworkers on the Rand: 1,485 workers out of a total of 11,530 Natal Africans on the Rand in 1903. Even here, however, many if not most of the Natal Africans working on the mines were "police" or "constables," actually what we would today call security guards. In one typical mining compound, despite a professed policy of having police drawn from every ethnic group represented, there was 1 Natal African police-man for every 22.9 Natal African workers, while the rest of the workforce was represented by 1 policeman for every 78.1 workers.[44] The vast majority of Natal Africans simply refused to work in mining itself.[45] Those who did work in mining preferred surface work—shoveling and tramming—to breaking ground or underground work. One recruiter estimated that two-thirds of Natal Africans employed by the mines worked on the surface.[46] There are many possible reasons why Natal Africans avoided underground work in favor of surface work, and avoided mine work in favor of domestic service and the like. One reason may be that they were simply not as desperate as Africans from elsewhere. As bad as the situation in Natal was for Africans living there, it may have been worse for Africans elsewhere, especially in less fertile parts of the subcontinent. Indeed, Natal Africans were also known for the unusually short periods for which they were willing to sign on, typically four months, and even today Africans from KwaZulu-Natal are more likely than other southern Africans to prefer migrant labor to permanent urban-ization, which suggests that reserve land in KwaZulu-Natal was better en-dowed relative to reserve land elsewhere.[47] Another factor may have been the Natal Africans' longer experience with wage labor compared to most other Africans in the region, with the exception of those from the Western Cape and the Ciskei. This experience might have made Natal Africans more aware of their options, more skilled at negotiating, and less willing to accept low pay or poor working conditions.

Natal Africans' dominance of police work on the mines and in the Trans-vaal government also had a lot to do with Europeans' stereotypes about different groups of Africans. Already in 1889, the Johannesburg magistrate's office specifically requested the recruitment of Zulus (and Swazis) as con-stables, even though Zulus were also already stereotyped as highway robbers that would prey on traveling migrants.[48] Two years later, the Johannesburg police commissioner ordered more "big" Zulu constables and called for an end to the recruitment of Sothos on the grounds that the latter were corrupt and prone to thievery.[49] To Europeans in Johannesburg, Africans from the

Cape were what a later generation of racists would call "uppity." According to one official,

> As a general principle it may be accepted that the Cape Native has had more civilising influences brought to bear on him than has any other Native of South Africa. His close association with European races has engendered in him a more independent and litigious sprit, has quickened his intellect and, I regret to say, has inculcated into his nature certain vices less prevalent in Natives from other Territories. These traits have a marked influence in his general happiness and comfort on the Mines. He is impatient of control and when brought to task exhibits a spirit ill calculated to secure the good opinion of those in authority over him. In his dealings with other aboriginal tribes he takes little pains to mask the contempt with which he regards their intelligence, and is domineering and insolent, while his tendencies to indulge in liquor and the smoking of hemp—which unfit him for work— bring him into conflict with those in authority.[50]

Another official called Xhosas "surly." Shangaans were supposedly ignorant but reliable, while Zulus were variously referred to as overbearing, autocratic, and domineering. One European even postulated a continuum of Africans on the basis of their care with money: the Pondos and Fingos of the Cape were supposedly the most frugal, while the Shangaans and Natal Africans were spendthrifts, and the Zulus "proper" were somewhere in between.[51]

Africans on the Rand frequently complained that "Zulus" were overrepresented among the police, while people from their own home areas and ethnic groups were underrepresented or not represented at all. This created a language barrier, leading to misunderstandings and the arrest of innocent people. Zulu police were also frequently accused of overreaching their authority by extorting fines, handcuffing, thrashing workers with *sjamboks*, and imprisoning workers on company premises.[52] In making these complaints, some of the Africans revealed their own stereotypes about the Zulu police. In 1907, the general secretary of the Transvaal Native Congress, J. M. Makhothe, told the Mining Industry Commission of Enquiry, "There are a good number of Zulu police who, by all appearances, are still savages to be placed in the position of police. For a man to assume the position of a constable he must first of all be a respectable man, he must know that he is in that position not to persecute, but to protect, the public. But these police are not like that, they are themselves not respectable. . . . The Zulu boys are very cruel."[53]

These kinds of ethnic divisions in Johannesburg led to fighting much like that occurring at the same time in Durban and rural Natal. Here, for the first time, we have fighting pitting "Zulus" against Africans from beyond Natal and Zululand. Moreover, in these fights there was no indication of divisions between Natal Africans and those from Zululand. There was, however, a new distinction between the Shangaans and the Zulus. At Kimberley and in the Cape railway camps of the 1870s, where Europeans categorized Shangaans as a subgroup of the Zulus known as "Portuguese Zulus," the two groups had usually allied in fights against other groups of Africans. The same happened in a fight in Johannesburg in 1892. Three years later, however, Zulus and Shangaans fought against one another in the largest fight ever to take place on the Witwatersrand, involving a total of two to three thousand men.[54] Another famous fight involving the Zulus in Johannesburg was the "Location Riot" of New Year's Day 1902, in which as many as two hundred Xhosa laborers specifically targeted Zulu policemen. On investigation, it became apparent that the Xhosa were motivated by the mistreatment they had regularly suffered at the hands of the Zulu police.[55]

Another negative consequence of these ethnic divisions was the difficulty workers often had in maintaining a united front in their various labor actions. In September 1896, the Transvaal government and organizations representing the management of the various mines agreed on a uniform, across-the-board wage reduction for their African mineworkers. The mine-owners also sent armed detachments into the compounds in the hopes of preempting rebellion. Instead, the interventions and the wage reductions provoked the workers into striking. The most militant workers were the Mozambicans, but their efforts to recruit other workers were not particularly successful, and many Sothos and Zulus refused to strike, effectively becoming "scabs." These difficulties in creating and maintaining worker solidarity were partly due to the ethnic division of labor. The Sothos were mostly shaft-sinkers and lashers, while, as we have seen, the Zulus were mostly compound police, shovelers, and trammers. These were all relatively privileged occupations and were not as adversely affected by the proposed wage cuts as were the underground jobs that the Mozambicans tended to hold. In addition, if the Zulus, Sothos, and others were disgruntled, they had the option of returning home, which many of them did. Indeed, the strike in 1896, as well as the simultaneous decline in the Zulu washermen's fortunes, marked a major turning point: the number of Natal Africans working on the Rand fell sharply after 1896, reaching 7,582 in 1899, on the eve of the South African War, down from its 1894 peak of over 30,000. Between 1899 and 1902, the South African War led to the emigration of virtually all those who remained. The Natal African population on the Rand recovered only slowly after the war.[56] In contrast, Mozambique at the time was plagued by such severe armed conflict and economic dislocation that most Mozambicans migrants preferred to stay on the Rand and make the best of a bad situation there.[57]

Many scholars have argued that ethnic conflict among labor forces on the Rand and elsewhere was created, or at least consciously promoted, by employers. For example, Peter Warwick, referring specifically to the Location Riot in 1892, but also making a point about management policy more generally, says, "The antagonism between Zulu and Xhosa workers was to a large extent the result of attempts by the mine owners to exercise greater control over the work force by 'divide and rule' tactics."[58] Similarly, Sean Moroney maintains that "inter-tribal jealousies were maintained through the compound 'police,' through separate housing, tribally composed work gangs and in day-to-day compound conflicts. The 'police' were no doubt the most effective agents of this strategy."[59] As with interchiefdom conflict in rural colonial Natal, there is plenty of evidence attesting to employers' self-conscious application of "divide and rule" policies. For example, in 1914, Henry Taberer, the director of the Government Native Labour Bureau, offered this solution to the danger of an African insurrection on the Rand: "As a last resource the inter-tribal differences between the natives themselves would enable us to turn, say, the Zulu on to the Basuto."[60]

On the other hand, many government officials who were quite sympathetic to the mineowners in general were nevertheless opposed to "divide-and-rule" policies and the destruction they wrought. Shortly after the Location Riot of 1902, a group of Zulus petitioned the commissioner for native affairs, Godfrey Lagden, to set aside a portion of the location for Zulus alone. The petition is worth citing at length, because it is one of the very few surviving pieces of evidence from Johannesburg during this period in which Zulus themselves speak, and specifically to the issue of ethnicity.

The petition of the undersigned . . . humbly sheweth:

1. That they are Zulus resident in the Johannesburg Native Location.
2. That at a meeting of Zulushwo at present reside in the Location your

petitioners were appointed a deputation to approach you with this their humble petition, and they now beg to submit the following facts for your favourable consideration.

3. It is undoubtedly well known to you that the Native Location here is inhabited by members of nearly every Native tribe in Africa.

4. Your petitioners humbly submit that the present moment must be regarded as a favourable one wherein to approach you with a view to enlisting your sympathy and assistance in their effort to be separated from those other tribes between whom and themselves there has ever existed a feeling of antagonism and which feeling must be regarded as distinctly prejudicial to the maintenance of peace and order.

5. Your petitioners are assured that there is ample space within the limits of the Location at the disposal of the authorities and therefore it is that they beg that they may be allowed to occupy a separate portion of the Location and would respectfully offer the following suggestions.

6. That the officer in charge of the Location be instructed to obtain (with your petitioners' assistance) a list of the names of all the Zulus whom we represent and who are willing to and anxious to be removed from immediate contact with other Natives (more particularly the Maxosa element) and that we then be allotted a section of the Location for our own sole use which section shall be defined by a line of demarcation either in the form of a street or by means of a wire fence.

7. Your petitioners feel satisfied that if this mode is adopted it will give the most satisfactory result and will tend to obviate any possibility of a conflict in the first instance, and will effectively remove our families from contact which we disapprove of and which we see will undoubtedly end in trouble to many who otherwise would remain true to the traditions of their race.

We beg your serious consideration of this our humble petition and we rest assured from our knowledge of your intimate acquaintance with the customs and feelings of the various tribes in this country that you will at least appreciate our effort to obtain the only relief possible through your direction.

We anticipate your early reply and your petitioners will ever, as in duty bound, pray. Signed, Levi Mapumulo, [etc.], Witness, D. Sheppard.[61]

This is striking not only because of the petitioners' active and explicit self-categorization as Zulus, but also because two of the petitioners' names—Mapumulo and Cele—suggest they came from Natal.[62]

It is also striking, and further evidence that Zulu "tribalism" did not come from whites' initiative, that Lagden refused, saying, "I don't consider it a good plan to divide the South African natives and give them separate locations. Experience has shown that it leads to fighting. They are all one Bantu family and should learn to live together."[63] In 1908, the colony's minister for native affairs addressed the subject of the underrepresentation of Transvaal Africans in Johannesburg's police force: "It has been urgently represented to me that the natives of this Colony, who contribute largely towards its revenues, should, as far as practicable, be employed by the Government in preference to natives from other parts of South Africa upon such duty or work as cannot be undertaken by white men. I am sure you will agree with me in thinking that the Transvaal natives are entitled to a reasonable claim for consideration in this respect."[64] In 1914, Commissioner Buckle, in charge of the Native Grievances Commission, concluded his report by saying, "I do not think that any attempt to prevent the natives from amalgamating is justifiable upon moral grounds. '*Divide et impera*' may be a good policy, but if the natives are inclined to substitute internal peace and mutual help for their practice of tribal quarrels, that is a movement towards civilisation, which we ought to encourage, not frustrate."[65] These officials realized almost a century ago the point that Patrick Harries has made only recently, that ethnic divisions are often *not* conducive either to management's control over labor or to capitalism more generally.[66]

More important, urban ethnic divisions were largely produced by Africans themselves. We have already seen how it was Zulus who petitioned for ethnically segregated locations, and it was the government that refused to oblige them. The same thing happened in compounds, where Africans complained bitterly if they were separated from those who came from the same region and spoke the same language.[67] Many Africans also complained, not just about an abusive police force, but specifically about abusive *Zulu* police, and the solution they proposed was a more *ethnically* representative police force. Similarly, it was Africans who insisted that they be treated by medical orderlies of the same ethnic group.[68] The ethnic division of labor was partly about white stereotypes of different groups of Africans, but also about Africans organizing themselves collectively on an ethnic basis to reject certain types of employment and monopolize others, such as when domestic servants, on preparing to return home, pressured their employers to replace them with their "homeboys" or "brothers."[69] Many fights were described as being organized along ethnic lines, but many others were specifically described as *not* being ethnic, but rather organized according to the different mining compounds where the protagonists lived.[70] This might seem to be an argument for the limits of ethnic self-categorization, but by no means do I intend to suggest that Africans only ever organized themselves ethnically. Surely it is by now a truism of identity studies that people identify themselves differently at different times and in different contexts—for example, variously as a man, a youth, a worker, a policeman, an African, a Zulu, or a Qwabe. My point is rather that when Europeans described certain forms of African collective behavior as ethnic, this was not a mere fantasy on their part, a result of their single-minded inability to see Africans as anything *other* than ethnic beings. Europeans could and did see Africans as organizing on other bases, as well.

When Africans organized themselves ethnically, it was in part because they wanted to reproduce the social structure of their home environments. Workers were usually recruited in batches in their home areas, from whence they traveled as a group. Once in Johannesburg, they often lived and worked as groups. In the mining compounds and in the police, European employers appointed group leaders, variously known as "boss boys," "headmen," or "indunas." The last title, of course, was the same as that for the middle tier of the Nguni aristocracy between the homestead heads (abanumzane) and chiefs (amakhosi). Although the vast majority of migrants in all cases were youths, there were some who were actually homestead heads or indunas or members of the chiefly and royal aristocracies back home, and it was these whom the employers tended to appoint as indunas on the Rand. One quantitatively inclined compound manager calculated that having an actual induna or homestead head as group leader increased efficiency by 35 to 40 percent.[71] Again, however, this was not just a case of the European "creation of tribalism," nor even "an accommodation of patriarchs" trying to maintain authority over youths. In fact, employers found that they faced worker resistance if they did *not* appoint headmen who occupied positions of prestige back home. If they did appoint headmen without such status, those headmen were not likely to be obeyed. As one compound manager complained, "They like to force their blue blooded chiefs on to you."[72] Another inveighed against the practice at some length.

Q: How do you account for the complaints?
A: I account for it chiefly through Zulu police boys. . . .
Q: These police are nominees of your predecessor I suppose?

A: Many of them are not. That is the pernicious practice that is in vogue at the present time. Many of the police in this compound and I believe elsewhere are recommended by recruiters. Many of these recruiters are unknown to the compound manager and very often he consents to a man saying "I will send you 20 boys if you will appoint one as police boy." These police boys come in and I could get rid of half of mine but we have to please the recruiters. If you happen to discharge or do anything to that police boy he goes back to his people and tells them a cock and bull story; they then report back to the recruiter, that recruiter reports to the NRC, the NRC reports to the management, and we are really as compound managers in the hands of the recruiters, who know nothing about the internal workings of the compound nor the behaviour of their police natives who are in many instances nothing more or less than spies. . . . [T]he majority of them have never been out before and here they expect to be pampered and looked up to and treated as they are in their own homes, forgetting altogether that they left their homes to come to work and not to sit down. It is a mistaken idea altogether that these chiefs and indunas should be allowed to be given these appointments.[73]

The induna system could also promote the spread of Zulu ethnicity, when, as occasionally happened, indunas were appointed who had connections with the Zulu Royal House. For example, at the Brakpan mine, one recruiter urged the mineowners to appoint "Franz a Zulu as a policeman. He is one of the Royal House and the mine has taken special steps to give him special housing accommodation with the result that the ordinary working Zulu is very well pleased with the treatment he is receiving, and they are coming forward in large numbers."[74]

Another indication that rural status distinctions were reproduced by Africans themselves and not imposed by Europeans is the presence of such distinctions in the "Regiment of the Hills" (Umkhosi Wezintaba).[75] Umkhosi Wezintaba was perhaps the largest criminal gang on the Rand between 1890 and 1920.[76] The name of the Zulu founder of the gang was Nkulunkulu or Nkulankula, which could have been derived from the word for "God" in Zulu.[77] A police report on the gang says that Nkulunkulu came from "Kwabe in Zululand," which may actually refer to Qwabe country in Natal. This would be ironic considering the association of the Qwabe and other Mapumulo Africans with the police, but at least one other prominent gang leader was also from Mapumulo, namely Msuluza Ngongoma of the amalaita gangs in Durban around 1906, which were influenced by Nkulunkulu's gang.[78] Moreover, many gang members were also members of the mine police, some of whom had been forced to join. Nkulunkulu's successor, Nongoloza, alias Jan Note, was also a Zulu from Natal proper, not Zululand. Indeed, though there were also Sothos, Xhosas, Shangaans, and Swazis in Nongoloza's gang, the vast majority were Zulus. While the gang's own legal system, with which it maintained its members' discipline, was patterned on colonial common-law courts and not native law courts, the gang's hierarchy was clearly based on the "traditional" hierarchy of Natal's indirect rule system. Thus Note himself was addressed as *inkos'enkulu*, which was the same title as both the Zulu kings and the colonial governor-general in his capacity as "Supreme Chief." Below him were the amakhosi (chiefs), again as in both the Zulu kingdom and colonial Natal. The rank-and-file members were styled "Mkehla," from the Zulu word for a married man. This seems to have been a sort of status aspiration, for very few labor migrants were married; after all, one of the major purposes of labor migration from the point of view of young men was to obtain money so as to buy cattle, pay lobola, and get married.[79]

Nevertheless, as the story of Nongoloza's gang indicates, the symbols, practices, and structures of rural Natal African culture were not simply reproduced on the Rand without change. As Sean Moroney puts it, "It is important to view ethnic solidarity in an industrial environment as a particular response to that environment, rather than a direct transfer of tribal values."[80] While some homestead heads and indunas came to the Rand, not all those who were styled "Mkehla" or "Induna" there actually had that title back home. But the changes went even further than this. Take, for example, the monthly parade held by the AmaWasha in Johannesburg from 1893 onward. In their hundreds, the men marched near a fire station, carrying sticks and formed into companies, "every company under the command of its own chief, in more than one case an induna of rank and comparative wealth" who recruited the men under him. Each company would perform dances and sing songs about "the former deeds of their tribe." Each company finished its performance with "the royal salute." Was this salute "Bayede!," which could be addressed to any chief or indeed any prominent person, or was it "Usuthu!," the particular salute of the Zulu kings from Cetshwayo onward, which was used by the rebels in Natal in 1906? In either case, the mere convening of all these people—who came from different Natal chiefdoms and who would not have had occasion to assemble together back home—would help to reinforce their sense of "imagined community."[81] Moroney has suggested that "it would be valuable to discover to what extent mass tribal action received its main impulse and cohesion via smaller, association-like, home groups."[82] The juxtaposition at the AmaWasha parade of small, regionally based "companies" led by local indunas with grand assemblies of "Zulus" is indicative of just such a link.

The AmaWasha parade was not the only occasion in which Natal Africans, referred to as Zulus, "performed" a new and broader sense of collective self-categorization. As in rural Natal, Africans on the Rand frequently engaged in dancing competitions which sometimes led to violence. Here, however, rather than being grouped according to their chiefdoms, they were now grouped as Zulus. In 1896, the Simmer and Jack mine put on a huge dancing spectacle with some 3,000 workers from its compound. They were grouped as "Zulus, Shangans, Mchopies, Zambesi boys, and Amabatka" and performed in those groups. There were

> rows of Zulus who were seated at two sides of the enclosure, waiting until it should be their turn to show their paces. . . . Several of the tribes were marched round the ring, intoning their peculiar musical chants and leaping and holding aloft their sticks, and several encounters resembling single-stick took place between pairs of opponents. In these much skill was shown, and the man who scored the first hit was rewarded with a small coin. There was also a concertina dance. Then there was a slight encounter, not in the programme, between natives of different tribes in a far corner of the compound. It was feared that an inter-tribal fight might occur.[83]

As at the AmaWasha parade, these dances used rural symbols and practices, but endowed them with new meaning. This mixture was symbolized by the often very Western clothing that the performers wore while doing their "traditional" dances, a juxtaposition that struck many European observers as comical.[84] But the very point of the dance was that it was reflecting new urban experiences, and not old rural ones. The ethnicity that the Zulus and Mozambicans (and perhaps others) performed on the Rand was not the same as that which they had experienced at home.

It might be argued that, since the evidence for Zulus' ethnic self-identification in this case comes to us from the testimony of whites, this evidence must also be considered evidence for the whites' role in "the creation of tribalism." But it is clear that, when it came to ethnic self-identification, Europeans on the Rand were merely recording a reality created by Africans, not creating that reality themselves. We have seen evidence of African initiative in this regard, often against European resistance, in everything from expressed desires to live in locations or labor hostels with fellow Zulus or to serve under Zulu overseers or work in "Zulu" jobs, to the organization of Nongoloza's gang. Moreover, Europeans on the Rand were inconsistent in their use of the terms *Zulu* and *Natal native*, as well as *Zululand* and *Natal*, sometimes suggesting a distinction between the two, sometimes using them interchangeably, sometimes doing both in the same passage. But as far as Natal Africans on the Rand were concerned, even though the vast majority of them came from the territory south of the river, the once politically charged distinction was fading from their memory. Two years before the 1906 rebellion, the missionary F. Suter said, "The native in Natal would be offended if you called him anything but a Zulu."[85]

GROWING RACIAL CONSCIOUSNESS

Zulu ethnic consciousness was not the only new and more inclusive identity to emerge on the Rand. As in Durban, black racial consciousness also spread among migrant workers, out of processes similar to those that were producing ethnic consciousness, and contributed to Zulu ethnic consciousness by promoting the idea that Natal Africans were one people. Black South Africans' racial self-identification did not begin on the Rand; it was also implicit in the very act of racial formation undertaken by whites, although being categorized as black and seeing oneself as black were not the same thing. But the spread of black racial consciousness depended on the diversity of the black population and on the lack of alternative forms of identification, like Zulu ethnicity in Natal, that could encompass every black person. Decades before Johannesburg even existed, South African black racial consciousness had emerged from time to time in the occasional alliances between different groups of Africans in other cosmopolitan centers like Kimberley and the Cape, as well as between different African polities in rural areas.[86] But as both the largest population concentration and the most cosmopolitan conurbation in South Africa, the Rand was throughout the twentieth century the center of self-consciously "black" or "Pan-African" political struggle. How did this situation come to be?

During the 1890s, when fights were at their most frequent, African unity was infrequently talked about and even less frequently acted on. As elsewhere in the region, such unity first had to be imagined, and rumor was the vehicle for such imagining. Another similarity with, say, Natal and Southern Rhodesia in the years leading up to the rebellions of 1906 and 1896, respectively, was that Africans seem to have drawn inspiration from the conflicts between Boers and the English. Thus, in late 1896, in the midst of the Shona and Ndebele uprisings in Southern Rhodesia and a year after the Jameson raid, a rumor circulated in Johannesburg that the Zulus and Swazis were conspiring to plan a concerted rebellion—with weapons supplied by the English—much like the actual rebellion that the English had undertaken in coordination with Jameson's raid.[87] Three years later, shortly before the South African War actually broke out, the deposed Zulu king Dinuzulu, by now a major figure in the black imaginary, was supposed to have called on his subjects on the Rand to return, for Jameson was allegedly planning another raid, and Natal Africans would have to join in fighting forces from the Transvaal.[88] By 1906, if not earlier, such rumors had coalesced in the famous "black peril" panic, according to which all the African kings and chiefs of southern Africa, as well as prominent black Christian ministers and politicians, were purportedly planning a joint uprising against white South Africans. The main link with the earlier rumors was that the conspiracy was sometimes alleged to include Boers resentful of their loss of independence, among them General Botha. Such rumors were propagated by both whites and blacks.[89] At the same time, as African workers became more united and more militant, many European observers suggested they were inspired by the example of the white labor unions, whose militancy culminated in virtual warfare with the authorities on a few occasions.[90]

Fights were the clearest indication that fantasies of African unity were mere fantasies. On the other hand, we have also seen how fighting could help cement broader ethnic unities. The same thing may have happened with race. The earliest indications of racial consciousness in the context of fighting are very tentative. For example, in an 1898 fight between workers from different mining compounds, when white police came to intervene and separate the fighters, the fighters "pranced about in wild and yelling joy, crying 'Kill the whites!' and other incentives to revolution."[91] Black racial consciousness emerged more clearly from 1904 onward, when the government sanctioned the introduction of Chinese migrant workers on the Rand, mainly to undercut black laborers who were enjoying increasing leverage in wage disputes. The black laborers' leverage was itself a function of their growing solidarity, but competition with Chinese migrant workers only increased that solidarity. As was the case before 1904, divisions within the labor force led to fighting, but now the fights were between different races, not different ethnic groups. The biggest such fight started on the Rose Deep Mine in May 1905. One of the Chinese workers there had died after being caned by the compound manager. The other Chinese workers at that compound then resolved to lodge a complaint with the authorities, and they left for the courthouse as a group, numbering about two hundred. In order to stop them, the compound manager turned out the compound's African police, who were joined by some two hundred African workers. More Chinese workers from the neighboring Simmer and Jack compound, thinking the Africans were attacking them, broke out of their compound and joined in the ensuing fight, in which twenty-six Chinese were injured.[92]

At the same time, fights among Africans were becoming less frequent. In 1910, for example, a fight broke out broke out at the Premier Diamond Mine between Sotho mineworkers and Zulu police, following a pattern typical of earlier years. Now, however, the director of the Government Native Labour Board insisted that "these troubles can hardly be said to be of frequent occurrence."[93] Three years later, the assistant magistrate of Johannesburg concurred.

I have been up here for ten years and ten months and one thing that has impressed itself upon me is the dissappearance [sic] of tribal feuds and riots amongst the various tribes of natives. Ten years ago tribal faction fights were quite prevalent on Sundays and Public Holidays. They sometimes assumed somewhat large dimensions. That sort of thing is practically extinct now. Natives of various tribes live on friendly terms in the same compound. They mix with one another and altogether the tribal barriers seem to me to be breaking down very fast. Just after the recent strike riots, I think on the 8th of July there was trouble in four compounds and it was very noticeable that all the natives in those four compounds were absolutely united in their demands and were acting apparently under a common leadership.[94]

Indeed, several commentators saw the strikes of July 1914 as a turning point. Commissioner Buckle noted that in the "strike there were Zulus, Basutos, Cape Colony natives of various tribes, Shangaans and other East Coast natives, and also Tropicals. They acted absolutely together." The strike occurred just two days after a strike by white workers, and Buckle felt that the black strikers might have been more successful if they had acted at the same time, while the security forces were otherwise occupied, rather than waiting. Buckle also commented on a recent fight between Sothos and Shangaans that quickly "developed into an attack by the Basutos upon the white compound guards and police and was followed by the looting of the compound store." He noted that "there is no doubt that deliberate attempts are being made among the natives to get rid of tribal distinctions and to unite the Bantu races for the purpose of obtaining better conditions from the Europeans," citing the African press and political organizations as evidence. But Buckle also saw this as "a perfectly legitimate movement."[95]

One of the reasons for the decline of fighting was alcohol. Several witnesses before the Buckle Commission in 1913–14 attributed the decline to the prohibition on the Rand of the sale of alcohol to Africans and of its consumption by them, as well as to increasingly effective police enforcement of the ban.[96] Indeed, like their colleagues in Natal, Europeans on the Rand had long tended to blame fighting largely on Africans' alcohol consumption. But there are also signs that alcohol may have played a more positive role in the development of African solidarity. Prohibition drove Africans to make their own liquor, giving it such names as *skokiana*, *kali*, and *skwaga*. One compound manager believed that conviviality led easily to solidarity.

Q: Do you see any signs that the tribes are coming together?

A: Yes, in my own personal experience. On Block "B" four or five years ago we had faction fights once a week regularly.

Q: Which were the tribes concerned?

A: Xosas and Basutos and the East Coast Boy generally joined with the side that he thought was getting the best of it.

Q: Have the Xosas and Basutos made up their quarrel then?

A: They seem to be much better towards each other than they have been. I think the skokiana or kali that they drink in their rooms brings them more together than anything else. The Xosas do not do that. They go into these different rooms and they sit round and talk.

Q: You mean all the tribes mix together?

A: Yes.

Q: Of course until quite recently you could practically count on them not joining together?

A: Yes.

Q: Do you think that state of affairs is changing?

A: It appears to me to be so.[97]

Even the African compound police participated in the subterfuge, smuggling liquor into the compounds and looking the other way when it was being produced or consumed.[98]

Another factor which contributed to this broader unity was the emergence of lingua francas, widely spoken second languages that enabled people who spoke different first languages to communicate with each other. Many Africans on the Rand complained that speaking different languages was a major factor in fostering misunderstanding and conflict between members of different ethnic groups. The two lingua francas that helped solve the problem were Fanakalo, a pidgin form of Zulu, and Tsotsitaal, a pidgin form of Afrikaans. These two languages had at least two things in common: both were highly simplified forms of the languages upon which they were based, and in neither case did the speakers of the base language predominate. After all, more Africans on the Rand spoke Sotho or Shangaan than Zulu, while most whites there preferred English to Afrikaans. The popularity of Zulu is doubly surprising given Zulu-speakers' close identification with the despised police forces and the substantial conflict that existed between Zulu-speakers and non-Zulus on the Rand. Similarly, Africans have long seen Afrikaans, even more than English, as the language of the oppressor.

The name "Fanakalo" comes from the phrase "enza fana ka lo," which means "do it like this" in Fanakalo (though not in Zulu). The name reveals the language's origins in conversations between employers (or managers or foremen) and employees.[99] The language itself emerged in the very earliest days of British colonialism in Natal, in the conversations between settlers and their African tenants or employees. With Indian immigration, it became a vehicle of communication not only between European employers and Indian workers, but also between Indian workers who spoke different languages. The variety of Fanakalo spoken by or with Indians became known as isiKula, derived from the derogatory word for an Asian laborer, *coolie*. After 1886, Fanakalo quickly spread to the Rand, as well. Here, despite its strongly negative associations for many Africans, it persisted for a long time on the mines and in the mining compounds. As recently as 1988, a survey found that it was the language of choice for most mineworkers in talking with their colleagues who spoke different languages, as well as with their supervisors.[100]

Ironically, even though Tsotsitaal was based largely on Afrikaans (the language of the majority of South African whites), it never acquired the negative associations that Fanakalo did, and it became widespread in the townships. Partly this was due to the fact that, unlike Fanakalo, Tsotsitaal did *not* emerge out of the master-servant relationship, but rather out of conversations between the African and Afrikaans-speaking "Coloured" migrants who often lived in the same areas on the Rand before apartheid. Tsotsitaal's popularity was also a function of its African component. Indeed, the language was originally known by an African name, *Shalambombo,* and after World War Two many Africans preferred to call it by another African name, *Isicamtho.* The name "Tsotsitaal" means literally "fly-language," *tsotsi* being a Sotho form of the Tswana word *tsetse,* referring to a kind of fly, and Tsotsitaal was also known as "Flaaitaal."[101] However, the names Shalambombo and Isicamtho were both probably derived from Zulu, and more Tsotsitaal words come from Zulu than from any other African language. Nevertheless, in an example of Tsotsitaal provided by Msimang, twenty-five of the words come from Afrikaans, nine from English, seven from Zulu, four from Sotho, and one from Portuguese. Moreover, the high-frequency basic function words are overwhelmingly Afrikaans.[102] Like Fanakalo, Tsotsitaal probably emerged very early in the Rand's history. Some sense of the age of Tsotsitaal can be gauged from the fact that many of the Zulu words in that language are archaic, no longer used in conventional speech by native Zulu speakers.[103] It was very probably these languages that enabled Africans from different ethnolinguistic groups to speak with one another in the first place. Without such linguistic vehicles it would have been impossible to forge the kinds of racial alliances that threatened whites so much.

Marwick's March

No single incident better illustrates the "Zulu-ization" and unification of Natal Africans than Marwick's March of 1899, in which thousands of Natal Africans walked from Johannesburg to Natal en masse to escape the onset of the war between the Boers and Britain. The Natal government's agent to the Rand from 1896 onward, J. S. Marwick, was a fluent Zulu-speaking white traditionalist-paternalist in the same mold as Theophilus Shepstone and James Stuart. Like Shepstone and Stuart, Marwick aroused both positive and negative feelings among the Africans who had to deal with him. He had two African names: Muhle ("the Good One") and Mubi ("the Bad One").[104] Marwick handled Natal Africans' remittances to their families back home and argued on their behalf when they came into conflict with their employers, creditors, or the Transvaal government, such as when they refused to pay hut tax in the Transvaal since they already paid it in Natal. Marwick was also the long arm of the Natal government, hunting down fugitives and tax cheats. For employers on the Rand, he was a sort of master labor recruiter. For the migrant workers' families back home, he was a medium of communication, particularly when, as was often the case, the migrants failed to return home or remitted an insufficient portion of their wages.[105] While Marwick essentially reproduced on the Rand Natal's system of indirect rule, there was a crucial difference: all Natal Africans went through him, regardless of the chiefdoms to which they belonged or the districts in which they lived. As such, Marwick and his office were yet another mechanism in the amalgamation of Natal Africans.

In 1899, in the early days of the South African War, a dramatic exodus of Natal Africans from the Rand both reflected and reinforced the new sense of Zulu ethnic consciousness that had developed there. In October 1899, Marwick led 7,000 Natal Africans on a 150-mile march from Johannesburg to Newcastle in northern Natal. As war between Britain and the South African Republic in the Transvaal became imminent that month, transportation lines became closed off. On 5 October, railway links between Natal and the Transvaal were shut down. This stranded in Johannesburg some 7,000 Natal Africans who, like their settler counterparts, had no desire to be "enemy aliens" there during wartime. The settlers, however, had managed to leave while the railways were still in operation, and Boer commandos at first refused to allow any more people to leave the Transvaal. At this point Marwick intervened, communicating with the Natal Africans on the Rand, Transvaal officials, and representatives of his own government. He assured the Natal Africans that he could negotiate their way out of the country without any threat to their safety from the settlers along the way. Conversely, to the officials of Natal and the Transvaal he vouched for the conduct of the Africans under his charge and vowed to prevent any loss of settler life or property at the hands of this, to settler eyes, threatening horde.[106] As the group was assembling in Johannesburg and preparing to leave, an African by the name of Hlobeni Buthelezi volunteered to be Marwick's chief induna for the march. Buthelezi said that he was a descendant of Madingula Buthelezi, prime minister for King Mpande, and that he was well known to all the Zulus on the Rand.

The group set out for Natal on 7 October.[107] The 7,000 Africans were almost entirely men, with the exception of a handful of women and children. When they reached Heidelberg, they found that one train would be going to Natal after all, but would only be able to accommodate about 120 people. Fifty women and children, as well as about seventy ill or wounded men, were put on the train. Over the seven days that the journey lasted, the marchers would cover an average of more than twenty miles a day. They would feed themselves with provisions purchased along the way with their own money, although the sellers, usually settlers, frequently engaged in profiteering or outright fraud. For example, at one stop Africans were sold tins allegedly containing food, but actually containing caustic soda. In any event, the food was never sufficient, and the people were on the verge of starvation by the time they reached Newcastle. Exposure was another problem, as it was late spring, when the nights were cool and rains frequent. Many men were so ill that they had to be carried by others. Marwick constantly circulated throughout the whole assembly, noting how its condition varied. The situation seemed quite positive in the front of the pack, where Africans were "marching thirty abreast with concertinas playing the most popular Native tunes." In the back, however, were the stragglers, often literally limping along, reaching camp at the end of the day after those at the front had already eaten and gone to sleep.

Besides the shortage of food, the threat posed by the elements, and the pure difficulty of the march, another peril was war. The marchers frequently encountered detachments of Boer militias who sometimes refused to let them pass, even though Marwick had secured permission from leading government and military officials in the South African Republic. At times it seemed that a massacre was imminent, as armed Boers nervously faced thousands of desperate Africans eager to return home. As the leader, Marwick himself was often threatened. One strategy that proved successful in averting disaster was for Marwick or one of his European assistants to tell the Boers that they were just doing their duty and "standing up for their country," much as the Boers themselves were doing. This sense of camaraderie in difference aroused a certain sympathy among the Boers for Marwick and the other marchers. Sometimes the relations between the Boers and British during the march were even quite light-hearted. For example, at one stop a Boer soldier showed off his marksmanship. One of Marwick's European assistants then earned the adulation of the Boers when he beat the Boer soldier in a shooting contest.

For all the incidents of camaraderie between Boers and Britons, they were still at war, a fact that could not help but to have been impressed on the minds of the African marchers. Despite belonging to the same race and sharing similar European-derived cultures, the Boers and Britons found themselves in a war that separated them according to their nationalities. Indeed, national belonging seemed to override any other concern, and at the same time drew begrudging admiration even from one's enemies. Moreover, the Africans were not entirely third parties to the conflict, but participants, since they, like the British colonialists, were subjects of the Great White Chief in Natal and his Queen overseas. They were on this march because of the consequences of that fact: the suddenly uncertain status of British subjects in Johannesburg, the shutting-down of transport links with British territories, and the intercession on their behalf of an officer of the British government.

Thus it is not surprising that Marwick's marchers applied to their relationships with other Africans lessons learned from the experiences of migrant labor and war. Over the first few days of the march, for example, there were several incidents in which the Natal Africans discovered "foreign" marchers in their midst: two groups of "Shangana" from Mozambique, as well as "a large number of Basutos and Cape Colony Natives." As soon as these interlopers were discovered, the marchers invariably expelled them from the group and forced them to turn back. Fittingly, the group disintegrated rapidly as it entered Natal, as, once more in their home territory, the marchers branched off and headed to their various destinations.

In many ways, Marwick's march was just an unusually grand example of the journey from Natal to the Rand that thousands of Natal Africans undertook every year, usually in groups under the leadership of some sort of induna. In other ways, Marwick's march was very different: Not only was it bigger, but it also brought together Natal Africans from every part of the colony. The only thing that brought them together was their Zulu-ness. The march also took place during a time of crisis, when two "nations" of Europeans were at war against each other. The example cannot have been lost on the marchers, and indeed it was not, as is clear in the ways that the marcher acted toward "non-Zulus." In the very act of distinguishing themselves from other Africans, the Natal Africans—"Zulus"?—marching with Marwick demonstrated a new sense of unity, centered around the legacy of the Zulu kings. It is perhaps no coincidence that it was during the South African War that rumors regarding the deposed Zulu king Dinuzulu began to circulate widely. These rumors varied, but they generally indicated that Dinuzulu was making preparations for the redemption of the Africans of Natal, and that he was calling on those Africans to prepare to follow him.

CONCLUSION

The Rand of the 1880s and 1890s was the first place where Natal Africans adopted Zulu ethnic consciousness to any significant degree. It is therefore not surprising that the earliest evidence of widespread Zulu ethnic consciousness among Natal Africans in Natal itself comes from the 1890s, or that it was especially associated with young men who had returned from the Rand, or that these ideas were most prevalent in those parts of Natal that had been the biggest labor exporters to the Rand. But the Rand was very different from Natal: it was ethnically diverse, overwhelmingly young and male, and far from the spheres of chiefly and patriarchal power. Zulu ethnic consciousness thus spread in a very different way in the two areas. We have seen how and why it spread in the Rand. It is now time to see how and why, and to what consequence, it spread in Natal.

5

NATAL AFRICANS' TURN TO DINUZULU, 1898–1905

As the young Natal Africans who migrated to Johannesburg for work beginning in 1886 started returning to Natal in the late 1880s and 1890s—at first in a trickle and then in the 7,000-man flood of Marwick's March in 1899—they brought with them the new Zulu ethnic consciousness they had learned on the Rand. In the years that followed, they acted as the main agents in the propagation of Zulu ethnic consciousness throughout the Natal African population. A new "imagined community" of Zulus emerged, or, rather, the older one that had been limited to the Zulu Kingdom north of the Thukela River expanded across the river into Natal proper. Natal Africans now became Zulus, in striking contrast to their animosity toward the Zulus during the precolonial and early colonial eras. Moreover, this was not the work of colonial officials, of Christian intellectuals black and white, or even of the chiefs. Zulu ethnicity was socially constructed, but not "from above" by elites such as these. Instead, it was socially constructed spontaneously and collectively "from below" by young, male migrant workers and then by their families and friends and acquaintances.

The new Zulu ethnicity of Natal Africans became a vehicle for two things: protest against the colonial state and reconciliation among the different groups of Natal Africans who had come into increasing conflict with one another. Being Zulu was a way to bring together elders and youths, chiefs and subjects, men and women, Christians and "heathens," and members of different chiefdoms who were at war with one another. The moral economy of mutual obligation that had mitigated conflict between colonizers and colonized broke down. Now more than ever, the colonial state, and whites in general, became an "other" that united blacks by giving them a shared target of resentment. The other moral economy, the one that bound African society together, was strengthened. Old ideas such as chiefship and patriarchy remained hegemonic, but they did not remain unchanged. They were infused with Zulu ethnicity and the symbols of it, and they gave young men a more powerful position in society, thus reflecting the changing economic realities resulting from migrant labor. At the same time, the new Zulu ethnicity continued to accord chiefs and elders a high status, just not as high as they had been used to. By melding change and tradition in this way, Zulu ethnicity made it easier for youths to persuade elders, made it easier for elders to accept the new situation, and helped heal the rifts in Natal African society, although never completely. The status of Natal Africans as Zulus has proved to be permanent and uncontroversial. However, a united and conflict-free Zulu body politic has been much harder to achieve and maintain.

THE RUMORS ABOUT DINUZULU

The bad situation that forced so many Natal Africans to go to Johannesburg in the 1880s was only getting worse as they were returning in the 1890s. This was, after all, a decade of drought, disease, and locusts that was capped off with the devastating rinderpest epidemic of 1896–97 that decimated African cattle herds. It was also a decade that saw the British government devolve more and more power to Natal's European settlers, allowing them to force Africans off white-owned land and into reserves while keeping the wages of African laborers low. Finally, the 1890s were a decade of increasing conflict between Africans. Besides the conflicts we have already examined between genders and generations, and between and within chiefdoms, there was also conflict between Christian and non-Christian Africans, which intensified as more and more Africans converted to Christianity.

The same growth in state power that helped create more misery for Natal Africans also gave colonial officials more access to Natal African public opinion than they had ever had. In the 1870s, Natal's rural police force consisted of 50 white officers and 150 African constables. By 1897 the total force had grown to 832, and there was an average of 22 white and 32 African policemen in each district, compared to just 4 African policemen per district just a decade earlier. Such a large force was not only able to better enforce laws, it was also able to subject the African population to much closer surveillance.[1] That same year, the government introduced a network of paid African government informants called "Native Intelligence Officers." The secretary for native affairs gave the following reasons for requesting such a system.

> Frequent reports of unrest and disquietude amongst the natives reach the Government and appear in the papers. There should be some means at the disposal of the Native Department for ascertaining quietly whether there is any foundation to such reports and, if so, the nature thereof. The employment of paid natives in different parts of the Colony to report to this office from time to time any matters which would be of interest and importance to the Government would I think beg undoubted utility. I have at present no means of knowing what is going on amongst the natives except through the Magistrates and Police from whom but little information is obtainable. . . . It would not be discreet to . . . [discuss] the same publicly because natives would ultimately get to know of it and the objects thereof would be frustrated.[2]

The resulting surveillance produced vast quantities of data on the ideas circulating within Natal African society. Much of it was rumor, gossip, and hearsay, and plainly fanciful. But it accurately recorded the rising tide of African discontent and, more important, demonstrated just how Africans understood their predicament.

Natal in the 1890s and 1900s was precisely the sort of place where rumors, and especially rumors articulating elaborate conspiracy theories, would proliferate. Natal lacked mass literacy, widespread basic education, true mass media, an effective government public-relations network, and a modern communications network. The colonial government worked hard to keep the public transparency of its actions to a minimum, especially when it came to letting Africans know what they were doing and why they were doing it. What was more, a deep linguistic and cultural chasm separated blacks and whites. Accurate information was hard to come by, and misunderstandings were hard to avoid.

If people do not know exactly how or why something is happening and cannot decisively determine whether or not a certain rumor is true, they often conclude that the mystery is intentional: various individuals are conspiring behind the scenes and trying to cover up their actions. These individuals could be government officials, aliens, communists, Freemasons, witches, or whatever group happens to be the bête noire of a particular society at a particular point in its history. At the same time, similarly anonymous and omnipotent agencies may also be conspiring on the side of good to save people from the evil conspirators. True or not, such conspiracy theories tell us a lot about how not just individuals but society as a whole sees itself and the world around it: who "we" are, who "they" are, what is good, what is evil, what is important. Conspiracy theories and other bodies of rumor often vary little from telling to telling and thus give us some indication of what the consensus is within a group of people. When different versions do vary, those differences can shed light on the implicit and explicit debates and conflicts in that same group.[3]

The returning migrants' Zulu ethnic consciousness, combined with the misery, conflict, and rampant rumor-making among Natal Africans, ensured that the reigning Zulu king Dinuzulu's return, in 1898, from a nine-year exile on the island of St. Helena, acquired enormous significance. Dinuzulu was the son of Cetshwayo, who had fought against the British in 1879 and lost. The British initially deposed and exiled Cetshwayo, but a concerted campaign led by the Anglican bishop of Natal, J. W. Colenso, led to Cetshwayo's return to Zululand in 1882, albeit as just one chief among many. Cetshwayo quickly became embroiled in a civil war with the other chiefs in Zululand, who had been given their positions by the British. He died in 1884 and was succeeded by Dinuzulu, who inherited the civil war as well as the Zulu kingship. Dinuzulu, the Zulu Royal House, and their supporters in the war became known as the Usuthu faction and the war cry "Usuthu!" was their signature. In 1888, the British intervened on behalf of their client chiefs, apprehended Dinuzulu, and sent him into exile on St. Helena the next year. Bishop Colenso's daughter Harriette then organized and led another campaign to pressure the British government to release Dinuzulu. Nine years of this activism, as well as the end of the Zulu Civil War, finally convinced the British to allow Dinuzulu back into Zululand.[4]

When news of Dinuzulu's return hit Natal in 1898, Dinuzulu immediately became the subject of a whole host of rumors, almost all of them untrue, which circulated throughout the colony until his death, in 1913. The first such rumor to come to the government's attention, in 1898, alleged that "Dinuzulu wished him [Mqhawe, the longtime Qadi chief] to be his Induna over all the tribes in Natal from the Tugela to the Umgeni [the river leading from Pietermaritzburg to Durban, which bisects Natal proper], and that Dinuzulu had said that that was the boundary of the land which belonged to him."[5]

This claim was rather astounding given the history of Mqhawe and the Qadi chiefdom. Mqhawe had ruled since about 1840 and was old enough to remember Dingane's massacre of large numbers of Qadi through subterfuge, rather than in combat. Even before that, the Qadi had been one of the largest Lala chiefdoms, which the Zulu kings had despised and relegated to second-class status.[6]

Why, then, did Dinuzulu become the vehicle for so many other people's dreams of redemption? One major reason was Dinuzulu's role in the Zulu Civil War. It was not lost on many Natal Africans that Dinuzulu's opponents in the civil war had been appointed by the British, or that on numerous occasions the British authorities punished Dinuzulu's participation in this intra-Zulu civil war as treason against the British Crown. The civil war spilled over into Natal proper, and especially the Thukela Valley chiefdoms such as the Qwabe, as refugees sought shelter there from the fighting. Just as before the war, Africans were fleeing to Natal to escape tyranny and bloodshed in Zululand, but now the violent despots were British-appointed chiefs, not the Zulu kings whose popularity in Natal was steadily rising.[7] The particular legacy of the Zululand civil war of the 1880s in the rumors and rebellion in Natal a decade or two later is very clear. As early as 1905, Dinuzulu's supporters in Natal were calling themselves not just Zulus, but also Usuthu and using the Usuthu war cry. Yet another name they applied to themselves was *umshokobezi* (pl. *abashokobezi*), which had also been applied to members of the Usuthu faction. They even wore the *ubushokobezi* war badges, which were the Usuthu insignia.[8] The noun *umshokobezi* also has the meaning of "a rebel," and there is a verb *ukushokobeza* meaning "to rebel." It is not clear whether the associations with rebellion or the associations with Dinuzulu came first, or whether the link was made before the Anglo-Zulu War, during the civil wars, or immediately before and during the 1906 rebellion.[9] In any event, at some point rebellion and allegiance to the Zulu king became literally synonymous.

The South African War (1899–1902), also known as the Anglo-Boer War, played a major role both in solidifying Natal Africans' support for Dinuzulu and in bringing about the notion among both blacks and whites of an impending race war. Both the Boers and the British had worried that Africans throughout the subcontinent would use the war as an opportunity to rebel against white rule while the whites were distracted and divided. Both sides pledged to avoid either targeting or enlisting Africans, but neither side completely lived up to that pledge. Moreover, while an all-out race war did not occur, Africans in many different areas, including some of the interior districts of Natal, did try to reassert their ownership of land that had been taken away from them.[10] The example of the war clearly made a profound impression on the consciousness of the Natal Africans returning from the Rand and on those who worked for the British army during the war. In 1901, before the war was even over, the resident magistrate of Weenen observed,

> No little pride is taken to themselves by those Natives who have seen service at the front. The stayers-at-home they contemptuously refer to as *amatinya* (a word of doubtful origin), *amavaka*, and *imisalisenga*, and several breaches of the peace have resulted from the opprobrious use of these epithets. A martial spirit has also characterised some of their faction fights. In one instance a witness graphically described the manner in which the one side had been ranged up in line, and the command given to "fayile" (fire), followed by a volley of sticks and stones.[11]

Still earlier, in August 1899, before the war had even started, the mere prospect of war had already become a virtual national obsession among Natal Africans, dominating their conversations with each other. As in the Anglo-Zulu War, many Natal Africans were eager to fight on the British side, partly in hopes that the British would reward their loyalty.[12] But not all Natal Africans were so loyal. One government informant claimed to have overheard a chief telling his headmen that he would welcome a Boer victory; the headmen remonstrated with the chief, telling him that he owed his position to the British and not to the Boers.[13] Moreover, Africans living in districts that had been occupied temporarily by the Boers in the early stages of the war faced reprisals during the occupation if they did not cooperate, and after the occupation if they testified against them at their trials on charges of treason.[14] The British also placed pressure on Natal Africans. The actual requisitions imposed on Natal Africans by British troops were burdensome enough: the Afrikaans word *commandeer* entered the English language during this war because both sides regularly confiscated civilian property. Still worse were the imagined requisitions. There were rumors that British troops would confiscate Natal Africans' cattle herds wholesale and kidnap and marry young Natal African women.[15]

Although there were no rumors that Dinuzulu himself had been "disloyal" during the war, there were rumors that he had been tempted, most notably by an alleged Boer promise to give him Zululand if he helped them defeat the British.[16] More telling was one government informant's description of how a Natal African named Timothy responded to the war. In 1900, many Natal Africans held meetings calling on their fellows to donate money for the British war effort. While attending one of those meetings, Timothy was reported to have "disapproved of their action very much and was of opinion that the money should be sent to Dinuzulu, whom he regarded as the head of the Natives. A man named Mfemfe told me [the government informant who overheard this statement] that this Timothy was very much against the English. He advised his friends to pray for Boer successes."[17]

Still, as late as 1902 there had been no reported rumors to the effect that Dinuzulu himself wanted to rebel against the British. In July of that year, after the war had ended, rumors began circulating that the British had asked Dinuzulu to give them Boer guns and cattle that he had obtained in a successful wartime raid in which a Zulu impi killed some fifty-six Boer soldiers.[18] In this particular case the rumor was true, but Dinuzulu had only eleven Boer guns, only three or four of which were in working order, and he promptly obeyed the order to return them.[19] But according to the rumors, Dinuzulu defied the British, and his defiance became more elaborate with each retelling. The first reported rumor that Dinuzulu planned to rebel against the British came in October 1902. A white girl was cleaning her father's revolver in the presence of one of her father's African servants, a fifteen year-old boy, who told her, "You had better take care of that as you will soon have occasion to use it." He said that three weeks from then, on a Sunday night, "all the natives employed were to murder their masters and that the general uprising would take place, that they had secured all the roads and that the Kafir emissaries were sent as far as Port Shepstone, that they were to march on to Durban and cut off the Port and take possession of Maritzburg, that they had spies in the fort and were well informed as to the movements of troops." When the authorities questioned the boy, he told them that he had heard the story from two Africans he had met on the street in Pietermaritzburg. The men had said that a great English soldier, who had been buried the previous Sunday, had been killed, along with several others, in a raid on Dinuzulu's homestead for the purpose of seizing the Boer cattle and guns. The boy said he told them, "I thought the War was all finished." They replied, "You know nothing. The English and the Boers are still fighting and now the English are fighting Dinuzulu as well. Do you think that war will be finished in this land?"[20] Other reports claimed that Dinuzulu had told the British he would return the cattle and guns only on the condition that "my people who were killed by the Boers be restored."[21]

Indeed, many Zulus believed that Dinuzulu's raid against the Boers had actually won the war for the British, and on several occasions, in reporting their grievances to the British authorities, Natal Africans pointed out the injustice of their loyalty during the war going unrewarded.[22] In December 1902 there was a mass exodus of African migrant workers from Durban to their homes in rural Natal, occasioned by one rumor that Dinuzulu was calling them out for war, and by another that the British were going to expel them from the city on Christmas.[23] The last reported rumor that Dinuzulu was rebelling because of the guns and cattle came in August 1903, at around the same time that chiefs in Natal were telling their subjects that Dinuzulu had agreed to return the guns without a problem.[24] But the Natal government during this period had a knack for stoking the fires of African discontent just as they were subsiding. The government's efforts to conduct a census in 1904, and its decision in 1905 to impose a poll tax to be collected the following year, gave new life to the rumors regarding Dinuzulu, which indeed would continue even after the 1906 rebellion had been crushed.

Unlike before and during the Anglo-Zulu War, in the 1890s and 1900s the Zulu king was a symbol, not an actual power-holder. He was a blank canvas upon which different Africans could paint their very different visions of the future and yet still believe that they were all united. The fact that Natal Africans made appeals to Dinuzulu, not just publicly but also in their most private moments, indicates how deep and sincere their loyalty to him was, and how hegemonic the idea of Zulu kingship was becoming, even in Natal.

NATAL AFRICANS INTO ZULUS

The rumors that circulated between 1898 and 1906 demonstrated a shift in Natal Africans' self-identification from non-Zulu to Zulu. In the process of embracing Dinuzulu as their leader, Natal Africans were also identifying themselves as members of the Zulu ethnic group. The line between political affiliation and ethnicity, and for that matter kinship, is a hazy one in the Zulu language. Historically, all subjects of any given king or chief were known by the name of that king's family. Thus the subjects of the Qwabe chief were known as amaQwabe ("Qwabes") and the subjects of the Zulu king were known as amaZulu ("Zulus"), which is also the name for people who are ethnically Zulu. These facts help us to appreciate the significance of seemingly innocuous events. For example, in 1902, an African spy reported his conversation with an African caretaker named Mazizi at a government office in Natal: "I addressed Mazizi by his correct surname Mnyandu, but he said that was not his correct surname, he was really a Zulu."[25] Mazizi was identifying himself as a Zulu, and the spy considered this act significant enough to be worthy of inclusion in his report to the government. Ties of culture, language, and kinship (through both marriage and birth) had always linked Natal Africans with Zulus. What was lacking was Natal Africans' self-identification as Zulus; instead there was active rejection. This changed after 1898.

Some Africans during this period were still making the old distinction between Zulus on the one hand and Natal Africans on the other. In 1903, one African government informant spoke of "we Natives of the Colony—of the old Colony of Natal," but referred to some of his interlocutors as "Natives of the Zululand Province," "these Zulus," or "you Zulus."[26] Other Natal Africans similarly used "Zulus" in a way that indicated that they did not consider themselves part of that category.[27] The Christian minister, journalist, and political activist John Dube once even allegedly told an audience of Natal Africans, "You are not like the Zulus," because they were too submissive in the face of their colonizers.[28] In distinguishing themselves from Zulus, Natal Africans typically referred to themselves as "Natives of the Colony" or "Natal Natives."[29] Of course, in these contexts *native* was an English term that was conventionally used to translate the Zulu word *umuntu/abantu* (person/people), which almost always referred to black people only, whites being called *umlungu/abelungu*.[30]

It is also clear that those Natal Africans who still distinguished themselves from Zulus did so because of persistent memories of historical conflict, which had been the case for many decades. For example, according to one rumor regarding Dinuzulu's supposed offer to make Mqhawe one of his induna, a prominent elder in the chiefdom expressed his opposition to the plan by arguing, "We assisted the English to destroy the Zulu power, and now the Zulu power wishes to bring us into subordination to it through our Chief."[31]

But alongside this continuity there was also change and innovation, and for the first time one finds extensive evidence of Natal Africans identifying themselves as Zulus. In some cases, as with Mazizi the caretaker, this self-identification was explicit. One African government informant reported a Natal African telling him that "their nation (the Zulu) was very wroth with the Government."[32] Another Natal African spoke of "our race, the Zulu race."[33] Other evidence is less explicit to varying degrees. For example, in 1903 a Natal European told authorities about a conversation he had had with a Natal African in which the latter had said that "the various factions of the Usutu races in Natal and Zululand were amalgamated by the Natal government," a reference to Dinuzulu's Usuthu faction, whose name also served as his royal salute.[34] This echoed the language of Dinuzulu's supporters in Zululand itself, such as the men who in 1903 allegedly told an anonymous government informant, "We are Usutus and we are not going to submit to ill-treatment by these white people."[35] Other informants repeated the rumor not only that Natal Africans and Zulus were merging, but that this merger was being effected by the colonial government itself.[36] In a "Zulu tribal history essay competition" held in 1912 (and later in 1942 and 1950), two of the Natal African contributors alluded to the shift in Natal Africans' self-identification. One, James Ludongwa, said, "Generally speaking the term 'Zulu' is now applied to all the natives," suggesting it had not always been. Another, Barnabas Sivetye, argued, "It is not reasonable at all to try and criticise the general use of the word Zulu, unless it is used with sense to include such people as Amaxosa with their subtribes, Damaras, etc."[37] Here Sivetye was clearly indicating that the new, broader definition of Zulus was a controversial issue, but it would seem that the broader definition of the word had won out.

Most commonly, though, evidence for a shift in Natal Africans' ethnic identification is to be found implicitly in their ubiquitous declarations of allegiance to Dinuzulu. Already in 1900, one Natal African was said to have "regarded [Dinuzulu] as the head of the natives."[38] Another spoke of "Dinuzulu, the head of our nation."[39] In 1904, an official reported that one of Chief Sobhuza's subjects declared at an assembly of chiefs and colonial officials that "they belong to the Kings of Zululand, mentioning Tshaka, Dingaan, and Cetwayo, and that this country, Natal, belonged to them (the natives) and that they were tired of the white people."[40]

Even more telling were all the rumors that said that Dinuzulu was "in league with" several prominent chiefs in Natal. In effect, those who propagated and those who believed the rumors were subordinating their own chiefs, the most legitimate political authority that Natal Africans recognized, to Dinuzulu, much as Shaka had subordinated the other chiefs to himself. Natal Africans were thereby accepting the Zulu conquest of the Natal region, which they had earlier resisted so strenuously. We saw how the very first rumor recorded by the government after Dinuzulu's return to Zululand said that Dinuzulu had made Mqhawe his induna and claimed all the people and territory as far south as the Umgeni River, halfway between the southern border of Natal proper and the Thukela River. Mqhawe was not the only chief rumored to be in league with Dinuzulu; others included the chiefs who would become the three main rebel leaders in 1906, namely Bhambatha, the Qwabe chief Meseni, and Ndlovu ka Thimuni, as well as Gobizembe, who was ousted before the rebellion owing to his subjects' refusal to pay the poll tax.[41] One rumor even went so far as to claim that "all the Chiefs in Natal were with Denizulu with the *exception* of Silwane who had refused to sing Denizulu's song."[42] Another rumor had it that "the Govt. across the sea told Denizulu that he was the King of all the Native Chiefs in Natal."[43] We have already seen how Meseni's Qwabe had been particularly victimized by Dinuzulu's predecessors and had fled the Zulu kingdom and fought for the British in 1879. Ndlovu was a distant cousin of Dinuzulu (they had the same great-great-grandfather) and therefore a member of the Zulu royal family, but his father Thimuni had had a falling out with Dinuzulu's grandfather King Mpande and had fled the kingdom as a result. Thimuni's and other branches of the Zulu royal family likewise fought for the British in 1879. When one of the government's African informers asked one rumor-monger, "Who is Dinuzulu and what can he do?" the man replied, "There are several of the big tribes near the Tugela that like him and will assist him."[44] While it was indeed "several of the big tribes near the Tugela" that rebelled in 1906, these were also the very chiefdoms—including most notably the Qwabe—that had suffered most at the hands of the Zulu kings and that had been most likely to fight on the British side in 1879.

BEING ZULU AS ANTICOLONIAL PROTEST

Despite what some of the rumors said, the government in colonial Natal most emphatically did *not* encourage Natal Africans' self-identification as Zulus, or, for that matter, as blacks, preferring to promote chiefdom identification instead. It was one thing to define Natal Africans as blacks and therefore subject to a host of discriminatory legislation. The danger was that Natal Africans would come to see themselves as blacks and therefore as united. The emergence of a broad sense of Zulu ethnic consciousness among Natal Africans could pose the same threat. Hence the importance of Natal's "Shepstone system" of indirect rule. Many Natal settlers had long been opposed to the government's recognition of chiefship and called for its abolition instead. In the first decade of the twentieth century, one official defended the system against such attacks by saying,

> I do not look for any general political movement, unless we give them [Africans in Natal] a common grievance. Natives, as a people, do not pull together, especially in Natal, where we have got them split up into the various tribes. There is a great deal of inter-tribal jealousy always existent. . . . I do not think the Native can lose his tribal instincts as long as we keep them alive. Until we do away with the tribal system the Native will always have in his mind that he is a member of a particular family or tribe.[45]

Without indirect rule, another official argued, a sense of racial unity would develop instead: "The really prudent and foreseeing policy was to preserve, whenever it could be done, the nationalities and characteristics of our natives. It was . . . a much safer and wiser course. Denationalisation was impolitic, suicidal, and destructive. . . . National and tribal disintegration would be followed by racial amalgamation."[46] Such sentiments had served as the foundation for "native administration" in Natal throughout the colonial period. While this policy had succeeded for decades, by the time these officials were speaking it had already come to break down in the face of Natal Africans' spontaneous self-"amalgamation" as both blacks and Zulus. As early as 1890, the colonial official John Bird argued that, while "the Natives of Natal" were emphatically not Zulus, this would change as colonialism became more burdensome to them. Bird presciently maintained that forcing Natal Africans off their land or raising taxes or rent would end the feuds between them, most notably with the Zulus, and lead to unity and even rebellion.[47]

Natal Africans' self-identification as Zulu was thus a rejection of the whole ideological apparatus of indirect rule in Natal. The colonizers liked to promote the idea that Natal Africans were subjects of the governor of the colony in his role as Supreme Chief, the Great White Chief who ruled his African subjects just like any African chief or king. Now Natal Africans were saying their king was actually the Zulu king. The colonizers encouraged chiefdom affiliation as a means to divide and rule. Now Natal Africans embraced Zuluness as a means of unifying themselves and protesting against the colonizers.

This shift was taking place at this time because the moral economy of colonialism, which up to now had ensured a measure of compliance on the part of Africans in their dealings with the colonial state, was unraveling. Many Natal Africans had never had much compunction about airing their grievances to white officials. From the 1880s onward, however, those complaints became much more frequent and numerous. In 1904 the resident magistrate of Mapumulo district, which would be the site of the largest outbreak of violence two years later, listed the most common grievances he had heard from blacks. The two biggest seemed to be isibhalo (the government tax to be paid in labor, usually by young men, for the purpose of public works) and the basic fact that the government passed laws without consulting Africans, much less obtaining consent from them. The constant racism they received from whites was no less burdensome. The resident magistrate of Mapumulo said "that it has been borne upon them that white men generally despise them, treat them, and look down upon them as being no better than dogs."[48]

Isibhalo, lack of government representation, and white racism had existed in Natal for decades and had up to this point provoked only complaints, not rumblings of rebellion. More specific recent government actions may have pushed Natal Africans over the line. Chief among these was the 1904 Zululand land settlement, which James Stuart's informant Socwatsha cited as one of the main causes of the rebellion, along with Dinuzulu's return, the epidemic of the cattle disease rinderpest also in the late 1890s, and of course the poll tax.[49] At first glance, the link may seem tenuous, for both the rumors and the rebellion took place mainly in Natal, not Zululand. But many Natal Africans had come to see migration to Zululand as a solution to the increasingly severe (and artificial) land shortage in Natal. The Natal Europeans who created Africans' land hunger through their policies of maldistribution of land at first also saw Zululand as a safety valve for Natal's "excess" African population, and to some extent encouraged Natal Africans' emigration. When the British government ceded Zululand to Natal, in 1897, at a time when the colonial state was stronger than ever, the Natal government began planning the expropriation of African-held land in Zululand. Though the expropriation in Zululand was not as severe as it had been in Natal—Africans retained 60 percent of the land in Zululand, compared to less than 20 percent in Natal—it caused no small amount of unrest and threats of rebellion in Zululand.[50] Nevertheless, there was no rebellion in Zululand until Bhambatha fled there in 1906, and even then few Zululanders joined in. Animosity toward the colonial state, and the willingness to rise up against it, was far greater in Natal than in Zululand.

Another government provocation from the Natal Africans' point of view was the census that was taken in 1904. When it was announced that the government would soon be counting Africans (and their possessions) for the census, rumors quickly circulated that many chiefs were planning on refusing to cooperate with the census-taking, and in some cases encouraging other chiefs to do so as well. As it happened, few if any of those rumors turned out to be true: officials encountered very little resistance regarding the census, least of all from the chiefs.[51] There was, however, an incident in Umvoti district that foreshadowed what was to come. When the resident magistrate originally announced the census-taking, the chiefs seemed to have no problem with it. Later, however, several chiefs and their followers became quite overt and confrontational in their opposition to the census. Many "openly refused to give the information" on the grounds that the census would be used as the basis for additional taxation. They usually backed down when the magistrate promised them that taxation was not the reason for the census. However, demonstrating some prescience, the future rebel leader Chief Bhambatha warned the magistrate that his followers "would be very angry if anything followed as a result of the census." And yet the magistrate considered Bhambatha and his followers to have been "civil notwithstanding what they had said." Chief Sobhuza and his followers came to the census-taking in a party some four hundred strong, armed with sticks and shields. The statement cited earlier from one of Chief Sobhuza's men was made at this assembly. It is worth quoting the magistrate's report of the man's speech in full.

One man in his speech said they had fought with the Boers but not with the English, and illustrated his remark by saying, "When I have a beast I can stab it and do what I like with it, and you (English) can do the same with us." He also stated that "if a person attacked another who has testicles he knew that he was attacking a man who was able to defend himself."

Further that "they belong to the Kings of Zululand, mentioning Tshaka, Dingaan, and Cetwayo, and that this country, Natal, belonged to them (the natives) and that they were tired of the white people." Also, in his abuse against the Government, he said the latter had broken faith with them by first introducing a hut tax of some shillings per annum, promising it would only last four years, but which was continued after the lapse of that period when a marriage license fee of £5 was imposed, but the Government finding that these marriage licenses did not bring in enough money abolished same and raised the hut tax to fourteen shillings per hut. Now they wanted something else. This man later on in the day went up to the table of my census clerks, Messrs. H. Hooper and W. W. Havemann, and addressing them said, "You white people need not talk to me as I have been to the Cape and England and know that you used to wear moutshas [loincloths] like we do, and the day is coming when we will have our guns to shoot you with," illustrating how they would do it by raising his stick to his shoulder in the position a gun is held and pointed it at Mr. Hooper.

Another of Sobhuza's men accused the government of "interfering with them and the lobolo of their girls," adding, "You came here and found us in occupation of this country, then keep on interfering with us by imposing your laws upon us, and we are tired of them." Again, despite these blandishments, the Africans at the assembly did not attack the officials. In fact, they provided the information asked of them, though one man was heard to say that he had lied when he told officials how many children he had.[52]

The incident at Umvoti, and specifically the talk of "broken faith," demonstrates that the moral economy that had existed between blacks and whites before was now stretched to the point of breaking. Theophilus Shepstone (unlike his successors) had allowed chiefs in Natal a good measure of the power and prestige they had enjoyed before colonialism, and went to great pains not only to promulgate new laws and taxes, but also to "sell" African patriarchs on the legitimacy of these new impositions. With very few exceptions, Natal Africans complied with the laws, paid the taxes, and even fought on the British side against the Zulus and the Boers. For Natal Africans, these actions undergirded a sort of social contract, according to which their loyalty would be repaid with government generosity, or at the very least the sort of benign neglect and non-interference that had characterized the early colonial period. Hence the depths of their outrage when the colonizers violated that contract, as in the case of both the Zululand land settlement and the 1904 census.[53] An awareness of this moral economy can also help us to understand some of the more opaque African grievances, such as "that they now no longer enjoy in undisturbed state the peace and quietness they did as formerly."[54] Natal Africans clearly felt that their loyalty to the colonial government was supposed to earn them, and indeed was premised upon, the government's fair treatment of them. Unable to seriously challenge colonial power at its core, Natal Africans tried instead to nibble away at its margins by establishing at least some boundaries, no matter how petty, that the colonial state could not cross.

Natal Africans' desire for a space of their own in some ways reflected, and was perhaps even a response to, Natal Europeans' racial segregationism. Sexual boundary-drawing lay very close to the heart of white segregationism, in South Africa as much as in the United States and the colonized world in general.[55] In Natal, despite repeated settler complaints and the occasional "black peril" rape scare, laws against interracial sex were only passed in 1903, and even then only for black men and white women: white men's sexual access to black women thus became both a racial and a gendered prerogative.[56] It is perhaps no surprise, then, that white men (especially policemen) having sex with black women was as prominent a grievance as any other for Natal Africans.[57] Most complaints along these lines came from African patriarchs, but not all of them did. For example, in 1898 one African mother protested her daughter's apparently consensual relationship with a white policeman with such vehemence that it actually got the mother arrested. Several neighbors wrote a petition on her behalf, saying, "We do not want them to spoil our daughters."[58] And Natal Africans were not just opposed to sex between black women and white men: in 1902, a Natal African in Johannesburg complained about white prostitutes soliciting black men there.[59]

Ironically, the Native Laws Amendment Act of 1900, through which the settlers hoped to increase the state's legitimacy in African eyes, only served to further undermine it. By the turn of the century, even Natal's settler legislators had become aware both of the value of Shepstone's traditionalism and of the costs—in growing African resistance to colonialism—of their own efforts to undermine it over the previous quarter century. Their solution was to recreate the position of an all-powerful white Supreme Chief, almost as independent as Shepstone had been of meddling from other branches of government, especially the courts. In practice, though, the act amounted to yet another factor limiting the state's accountability and allowing it to ride roughshod over its African subjects, in particular. Certainly there is no lack of evidence that Natal Africans were no longer "buying" colonial appropriations of their own political culture. For example, the salute "Bayede!" had once been limited to prominent amakhosi in the region. After Shaka became king, he and his followers tried to have the salute applicable to them alone. Since the central conceit of the Shepstone system was that Shepstone himself was just another inkosi like his African predecessors, it is no surprise that Shepstone insisted on being accorded the "Bayede!" salute as well. The 1891 Native Law Code mandated that Africans offer up the salute, not only to the "Supreme Chief" (the governor) and the secretary for native affairs, but also to "the Judges of the Court of Appeal and the Judge of the Native High Court," for the purpose of maintaining "Native good manners and respect to authority."[60] In practice, though, even petty officials insisted on the salute, and if they did not get it, they could arrest the "perpetrator" and take him to court, where, if convicted, he could be given a £5 fine or a month's imprisonment.[61] One man was flogged on the spot by his local administrator of native law, even though he had given the same official the salute on encountering him earlier in the day and thought that that was enough.[62] Indeed, such summary punishments were quite common. One African from Mapumulo district noted, "You cannot walk along the road without being knocked about by the police for not giving them the royal salute." In 1901, when the Duke and Duchess of Cornwall and York came on an official tour of Natal, the chiefs and headmen assembled to greet them refused to salute them with "Bayede!" They said that the salute "has been so much dragged in the mud, so degraded, that to offer it to these, whom we would delight to honour, would be nothing less than a gross insult, from which we shrink in horror. To greet these with *Bayete* would be to bracket them with a lot of empty headed boys, dogs in comparison."[63]

In short, the culture of Natal Africans helped to determine not only how people understood and responded to grievances, but also how things became grievances in the first place. During the twenty years leading up to the rebellion, Natal Africans experienced a seemingly endless series of disasters, both natural and man-made. But even the "natural" disasters were not necessarily perceived as such by Natal Africans, often with good reason: the rinderpest epidemic was caused by microorganisms, but its uneven impact was shaped by colonialism. The vast majority of the Natal government's relief aid went to the much smaller population of Europeans. Perhaps more important, Africans' deep mistrust of the government and of whites in general made them reluctant to inoculate their cattle against the disease, with the result that more than three-quarters of African-owned cattle died, compared to only about half of European-owned cattle.[64] According to Zulu beliefs, misfortune is often understood under the rubric of disease, even if the specific misfortune would not be considered a disease by Europeans. Moreover, this disease is often attributed to others' illegitimate use of power, or *ubuthakathi*, usually translated as "witchcraft" or "sorcery." Somebody who practices ubuthakathi is an *umthakathi*, a term usually translated as "witch," but perhaps better understood as "evil-doer." The umthakathi can inflict harm merely by mentioning the victim's name or casting a spell or endowing a familiar (an animal or strange beings akin to demons, such as the *tikoloshe*) with a certain power. Most often, though, the umthakathi acts by means of medicines (sing. *umuthi*, plur. *imithi*), and these actions are usually countered through other medicines or various kinds of emetics and purgatives.[65] Many Natal Africans not only blamed Europeans for the rinderpest epidemic, but thought the Europeans were actually witches themselves. The 1906 rebels thought that they had been beaten because the British had used "*umnyama* [evil; literally "black"] powers" on them.[66] One African informant's conversation with another African shows that Europeans had been seen as "witches" eight years earlier.

> I then got up and joined Sikumba. He said to me "you have heard us talking about these 'things' it is they who have brought sickness amongst our cattle." I said "how have they brought it?" Then he said "these 'things' travel all over the country and bring back diseases with them. They advised us to inoculate our cattle and then they put poison into our cattle and killed them all, and then they put the proper remedies into their own cattle and saved them."[67]

Sikumba's use of the word "things" to refer to *abelungu* (Europeans, white people) may reflect the taboo, common throughout the world, against invoking the name of something or someone that can do harm. Clearly such avoidance is the inverse of the evil-doer's need to invoke the name of the person targeted, without which his or her powers will not work.[68]

Perhaps the most famous rumor during this period was the one that emerged in November 1905, calling for Africans to kill their pigs and white-colored animals and destroy various kinds of objects. This rumor had two significant aspects: first, it included the warning that those who failed to heed the order would be struck by lightning, and second, it claimed that the antidote was to destroy animals and things that were white in color. Misfortune may be caused not only by human evil-doers, but also by one's ancestors (*amadlozi*) or by the Supreme Deity, the Lord of the Sky (iNkosi yapheZulu; remember that the word for sky is *Zulu*) in punishment for the people's failure to revere them correctly. The Lord of the Sky, in particular, is noted for inflicting such punishment in the form of lightning, and Zulu-speakers who hold these beliefs have often covered up or removed white-colored objects when a thunderstorm hits. This has led one historian to conclude that "the widespread killing of white animals, then, was probably not intended as a direct threat against white people, but rather as an attempt to set things right with the ancestors or to divert the lightning soon to be sent by the Lord of the Sky."[69]

But the preponderance of the evidence indicates that the killing of white animals was indeed a strike against white people. First, while some of the rumors attributed the order to the ancestors, other sources were much more commonly cited.[70] To begin with, there were more prosaic explanations, such as that it was harvest time and that the harvest had been an unusually bad one, so rather than use valuable grain to feed their pigs, many Africans were choosing instead to eat the grain themselves and to slaughter the pigs.[71] Some officials believed that the rumors were started by "ne'er-do-wells" who were simply looking for a cheap meal.[72] Finally, there were rumors that there was an epidemic of pig disease developing, that the pigs were supposed to be killed to stop the spread of the disease or to keep people from getting sick from diseased pork, and that the government would fine those who were caught keeping live pigs.[73] Indeed, earlier in 1905 the government had killed pigs infected with swine fever and cattle infected with East Coast fever in order to contain those diseases.[74] Most of the rumors said that the order had come from Dinuzulu or from the Sotho of the neighboring British colony of Basutoland. According to one rumor, the Sotho were about to launch an uprising against whites throughout the region, and any Natal Africans who failed to kill their pigs and white-colored goats, cattle, and fowls would be struck by lightning.[75] More common were the rumors that the order had come from Dinuzulu. The poll tax had already been announced, and Dinuzulu was allegedly calling on his followers not to pay. Some rumors went so far as to maintain that around the time of the coming *umkhosi*, or first fruits harvest festival (celebrated around the same time as Christmas each year), Dinuzulu was going to perform an *umlingo* ("unusual, strange, awe-inspiring or magical performance; trickery, conjuring, magic") "by which all the white people would be killed and the railways torn up and that any native having pigs or iron or any civilized clothing on that day, would be immediately killed."[76] Even the sun would disappear and the people would receive food miraculously.[77] The Sotho had supposedly told the Zulu that they would join them in any uprising provided that Natal Africans killed their pigs.[78]

Second, while it is true that, in Zulu symbolism, the color white (*mhlophe*) is not associated with white people (abelungu), there is no doubt that many Natal Africans at the time associated the things to be destroyed with white people. Unlike other livestock such as cattle, goats, sheep, and chickens, pigs had been introduced into the region by Europeans. Many Africans refused to raise or eat pigs because they were "smelly" and their meat was fatty, and in some quarters ritual prohibitions had emerged for pigs and their meat.[79] Moreover, the things to be removed, hidden, or destroyed were not only those that were white in color, but also "articles of European manufacture." At the time, Johannes Gwamanda, a Lutheran catechist and teacher, told officials of a conversation he had had with a Natal African passing through his district.

> He then said he was an Umsutu [a member of Dinuzulu's Usuthu faction or a Sotho; the meaning is ambiguous], and came from Dinuzulu in Zululand. He said he was one of five hundred men sent out by Dinuzulu to tell all the natives to kill their pigs, and to cease to inhabit houses resembling white men's houses. Those who had houses built like white men's were, he said, to be instructed to put a hut near by. All natives who were accustomed to wear clothes manufactured by the whites were to put on native clothes underneath—mutshas [loincloths] and prepuce covers, etc., and that the women who wore European clothing were to put on native petticoats underneath. Further, no native was to traverse an ordinary road, but to follow native footpaths. He said, also, that all articles of European manufacture, such as pots and pannikins, etc., were to be destroyed.[80]

Similarly, another rumor had it that "any Native remaining the possessor of a pig, European clothing, or iron cooking pots, or plank doors to their huts, will die with the Whites."[81] Even if the general order had only called for the destruction, concealment, or removal of white-colored objects and said nothing about pigs or "articles of European manufacture," we would still have to account for the connection between the rumors about white objects and those about the supposedly imminent expulsion or extermination of white people. These rumors were thus both calls to Natal Africans to show their allegiance to Dinuzulu, and subtle protests against colonial rule.

YOUNG, MALE MIGRANT WORKERS AND ZULU IDENTITY

The main agents behind the spread of these rumors and the new Zulu identity they spoke of were young men, and in particular young men who had returned from working in Johannesburg. This, in turn, tells us something about the implications of Zulu identity for unity and conflict within Natal African society. Mlibo, who compared the new rumors to those spread by Nongqawuse almost a half century earlier, was not the only Natal African to attribute the new ideas about all things Zulu to young men. Indeed, several witnesses said that the rumors were spread by wandering young men, alone or in groups, who were strangers and often claimed to be emissaries from Dinuzulu.[82] One government informant noted the conversation at one particular beer party: "It was stated that the young men had spoken freely of joining Dinuzulu against the English, because of the high rents which had been imposed. These remarks were only made after they had been drinking freely and was confined to the young men only, none of the older men being heard to speak in this spirit."[83] Those who were most likely to be reluctant to support Dinuzulu were often chiefs and elders who remembered the depredations of the Zulu kings.[84] Thus, the rumors were yet another arena in which the conflict between youths and elders was being worked out.

Other informants explicitly linked the rumors with young, male migrant workers who had been to Johannesburg. As one informant said,

> There seems to be quite an infatuation in the minds of a number of young people who are not kraal heads, so many of the old and more stable men have died out, and so many young men who go away to work out of the

Colony and in other places are left at the kraals, they talk about these matters when they are smoking their horns, and they pay no heed to any one who warns them to be careful and not to act in this way, the mothers of the young men people seem to favour what the young men are talking about, and there seems to be a good deal of earnestness in what is being said.[85]

Similarly, another informant attributed the rumors to "irresponsible people such as have come back penniless from the Gold Fields and other centres."[86] Still other Africans said some of the rumors had been spread by izigebengu and amalaita, that is, young gang members from Durban and Johannesburg.[87] The inescapable conclusion is that the widespread acceptance of Zulu ethnicity among Natal Africans on the Rand was being transmitted to and disseminated in Natal by those same young men on their return.

The function of these rumors was not only to unite Natal Africans as Zulus in protest against British colonialism, but also to allow men to renegotiate their status within Natal African society. I use the word *renegotiate* intentionally, to illustrate how closely conflict and cohesion were intertwined with one another in this process. Young men were asserting themselves vis-à-vis their elders, but they were doing so in a way that emphasized the commonality of their interests as both blacks and men. One historian, Benedict Carton, has argued that, through the rumors, the young men were also "direct[ing] the thrust of their aggression against African patriarchs who accommodated the colonialists." Carton maintains that "the broader purpose of rumour" was that "it allowed young African dissidents to criticize both homestead heads and colonial power without risking punishment for libel or sedition." In the case of the pig-killing in particular, Carton maintains that young men were seeking to punish their elders by forcing them to destroy their wealth in livestock and European-made wares.[88] But young men also bought cattle (some of it white-colored) for bridewealth, and they bought Western-style clothing as well. Indeed, young men with experience as migrant workers were *more* inclined than their elders to be culturally Westernized. There is in fact nothing in the evidence to suggest that the pig-killing rumors were a protest against patriarchy in the same way that they were a protest against colonialism. Certainly there is evidence that there was often debate between young and old in these matters, but to call that dissent "aggression" and the young men "dissidents" is to ignore the fact that those same men were promoting Zulu unity and endorsing pa-triarchy and chiefship.

After all, Zulu unity was not the only thing young men were promoting in the face of opposition from their elders. They were also asserting the right to drink beer when and how they wanted, to engage in premarital sex, to fight, and to go wherever they wanted. In general, these young men wanted more of a say in how their households and chiefdoms were run, especially when it came to spending the money the young men had earned working. But the young men did not reject patriarchy and chiefship outright. They still wanted to become patriarchs themselves, someday, and clearly sought to maintain a dominant position relative to women. When fighting, they organized themselves along the lines of the chiefdoms to which they be-longed, and they fought in the names of their chiefs. It is perhaps no coincidence that the rumors about Dinuzulu offered a solution not only to colonial oppression, but also to the main sources of division plaguing Natal African society, most notably divisions between chiefdoms (manifested most clearly in the epidemic of fighting) and between generations. The rumors had Dinuzulu uniting Natal's chiefdoms, but also promoting the young men's vision of the future while at the same time giving elders, and especially chiefs, a prominent place in that vision. Young men were recruit-ing their elders and pressuring them to join the fold, not attacking them.

It is true that numerous rumors portrayed chiefs resisting their young men's calls to support Dinuzulu. This was apparent in the very first reported rumor about Dinuzulu, the one about the son of a chief in Zululand and the son of a chief in Natal relaying a message purportedly from Dinuzulu to Mqhawe and another chief. The message was that Dinuzulu's rule extended into Natal and that Dinuzulu had supposedly appointed Chief Mqhawe to be headman over all his subjects between the Thukela and Umgeni rivers. When Mqhawe told this to the assembled men of his chiefdom, his chief headman said, "Look here, I am a grey man now. I was born under the English government, and I have lived until I am this age under the English Government, and I have never heard such a message from one chief to another, suggesting that a chief who was independent should become in-duna to another chief." Most of the men at the meeting thought Mqhawe should reject Dinuzulu's supposed offer, but most of the "dressed natives" (Westernized Christians) and young men favored it.[89] Mqhawe was not alone in this sentiment. Another informant reported hearing Chiefs Mehlokazulu and Mtonga tell one another "that if there was fighting they would lead the white people against him [Dinzulu], as his house had so ill-treated them in the past, and had killed so many of their relatives. They said they would attack him on one side and Sibebu would attack him on the other, and they would all avenge themselves for the cruelties that had been inflicted on them by his family."[90] Conversely, one of Mqhawe's subjects told a government informant that "the Chiefs were fools" for not supporting the anticipated uprising more actively, enthusiastically, and effectively.[91]

But even more rumors portrayed almost all the chiefs in Natal as being "in league with Dinuzulu." As one rumor had it, "besides these two Chiefs [Silwane and Swayimana ka Zipuku] there was not a Chief right away to the coast, and right through the country who had deserted the cause of Dinuzulu."[92] Chief Silwane was one of the very few chiefs rumored to be opposing Dinuzulu, but even in his case the evidence was ambiguous. In late 1905, Silwane was falsely rumored to have been killed in a lightning strike ordered by Dinuzulu in return for Silwane's supposed refusal to join the movement, and early the next year one of his children and four of his cattle actually *were* killed in a lightning strike.[93] But while some rumors claimed there was a bitter conflict between the two men and that Silwane had "deserted the cause of the Natives," other rumors painted a rather different picture.[94] One African government informant described a conversation he had with a man from a chiefdom neighboring that of Silwane, Sobantu, who claimed that Silwane was "in league with the Zulus": "I questioned the correctness of his statement that Silwane was with the Zulus saying that Silwane's father was killed by them. To this Sobantu replied that that was nothing; that in point of fact messengers were continually passing between the Zulus and Silwane. Silwane said he was on the Zulu side and did not support the English."[95] In fact, messengers *were* continually passing between Dinuzulu and Silwane because Silwane was planning to marry Dinuzulu's sister.[96] This was not unusual, for Dinuzulu had contracted diplomatic marriages for himself or for the women of the Zulu royal family with members of ruling families in Zululand, Natal, Swaziland, and the Transvaal.[97]

Much as the rumors preserved the status of chiefs and elders, they also gave women a role in the new order that was supposedly at hand. Although both the subjects and the propagators of rumors were overwhelmingly male, both could sometimes be female, as well. We have already referred to "women" and the "mothers of the young people" spreading rumors, and we have seen how the marriages of Dinuzulu's sisters figured in the rumors themselves. As propagators of the rumors, women were particularly important in two areas. First, as domestic servants, women played a major role in relaying the rumors to whites.[98] More important, among Africans, women could draw on their historical role as prophets, as Nongqawuse had done in the Xhosa cattle killing of 1856–57. The most notorious such incident in the run-up to the 1906 rebellion occurred in November 1905, when a young woman in Weenen district, which was to be one of the centers of rebellion just a few months later, quite publicly claimed that "at New Year, all the white people would be killed or driven into the sea."[99]

In terms of the content of the rumors, the most important woman to figure in those rumors by far was the Lovedu Rain Queen Modjadji. Although, like any inkosi in southern Africa, Dinuzulu had his own ritual specialists—diviners and healers—who helped him, he also obtained medicines from Modjadji, who lived on the borderlands of present-day Mpumalanga and Limpopo provinces, a few hundred miles north of KwaZulu-Natal. In the early 1890s, while Dinuzulu was in exile, representatives from the Zulu Royal House had visited Modjadji to ask for help in combating the locusts then plaguing Natal and Zululand.[100] Numerous rumors between 1903 and 1906 identified Modjadji as the source of Dinuzulu's powerful medicines. These medicines accomplished many things, *inter alia*, rendering it impossible for officials to lift from the ground the guns Dinuzulu had gotten from the Boers, protecting humans and oxen from bullets by turning the bullets into water, and, perhaps most important, promising to eliminate whites in Natal without a single African dying or even, it was often claimed, having to fight. Ironically, Dinuzulu was even blamed for the aphis blight that had struck Natal's sorghum crops in 1903. Supposedly, he wished thereby to toughen his people and protect them against bullets.[101]

Women and young people were more likely than chiefs and elders to become Christians.[102] It is therefore significant that the rumors also gave Christians a special place, for the rumors were thereby promoting a vision more in keeping with the sensibilities of women and young people than with those of chiefs and elders. The division between "traditionalists" (*amabhinca*) and Christians (*amakholwa*) was yet another axis of conflict between Africans that the rumors aimed to overcome. Indeed, throughout the colonial period there had been a degree of mutual suspicion and mutual rejection between amabhinca and amakholwa. And while many Natal Europeans believed that there was a Christian-led, Pan-African conspiracy to overthrow white rule, the notion was every bit as ludicrous as Natal Africans' beliefs in the same conspiracy. It is true that from the 1880s some African mission Christians broke away from the missionaries and set up independent churches that became known as "Ethiopian" churches, from Psalm 86:11: "Ethiopia shall soon stretch out its hands unto God." But southern African whites were quick to see *all* African Christians as real or potential Ethiopians. Even Africans who had only Westernized to the extent of wearing Western clothes and engaging in wage labor could be identified as Ethiopians. These Ethiopians, in turn, were seen as the cause of almost all African resistance to or even dissatisfaction with white rule, from servants' "cheekiness" to mass rebellion. If, as was often the case, the "restless" Africans could not be classed as "Ethiopians" in any sense of the term, then whites described them as being puppets in the hands of "Ethiopian" agitators. The implication, of course, was that Africans were normally contented with white supremacy and that it was only agitators who could make them feel otherwise.

At the same time that Natal Africans were circulating fantastic rumors about Dinuzulu, Natal Europeans were spreading similarly fantastic stories, mainly about "Ethiopian" Christians. As was the case with African rumors, these white rumors tell us far more about whites' collective worldview than they do about what was actually happening behind the scenes. A classic example of this was the elaborate conspiracy described in 1901 by a detective with the Johannesburg police. According to him, African mission Christians were conspiring not only to set up a new unified church independent of white missionary control, but also to launch a concerted uprising against white rule, bringing together African Christians of all types, as well as Dinuzulu, Modjadji, and the rulers of the Sotho, Swazi, Pondo, Xhosa, and Ndebele, and even Americans. The planned rebellion was to reach as far north as the equator, and the rebels would be armed with guns supposedly being smuggled into Mozambique in large quantities. The detective called the independent African church at the center of this conspiracy the "Sitopia."[103] In her examination of the 1906 rebellion and the events leading up to it, Marks concludes that "Ethiopians" played at best a minor role in the rebellion, and that by accusing Ethiopians of being agitators, whites were able to ignore the very real discontent that was actually spurring wide swaths of the population into protest.

At a time when Natal was even more obsessed than the rest of South Africa with the thought of the Ethiopian menace, it would be dangerous to accept without qualification white allegations as to the part played by "Ethiopians" in the disturbances. . . . [T]he influence of those [African Christians] who joined the rebels . . . would not appear to have been profound. In so far as there was a real rebellion, it was predominantly a tribal one, run as far as possible on traditional lines. The popular white belief that the Ethiopians had fomented the disturbances would appear to coincide with the official theory so familiar in South African and indeed colonial history of "agitator"-caused rebellions.[104]

Nevertheless, although Natal African Christians may not have played much of a role in the rebellion, they did evince a general identification with the Zulu king much like that of their non-Christian neighbors, and sometimes this identification extended to support of the rebellion that Dinuzulu was supposedly planning. Such attitudes toward the Zulu king, and toward the idea of supporting him against the British empire, stand in stark contrast to the prevailing attitudes of Natal African Christians before and during the Anglo-Zulu War. In 1905 and 1906, the prominent Christian activist John Dube, editor of the newspaper *Ilanga lase Natal*, regularly addressed his black, Christian, Natalian, and middle-class readers as *thina/nina maZulu* (we/you Zulus), especially in reference to the unrest surrounding the new poll tax.[105] Other prominent middle-class Christian politicians of the era such as Alfred Mangena and Mark Radebe identified themselves as Zulus, even though Radebe was Sotho and Mangena quite possibly a Xhosa.[106]

Many less prominent Natal African Christians, away from the intense government scrutiny that figures such as Dube labored under, went further and pledged their allegiance to Dinuzulu *instead of* the British monarch. In 1900, it had been a *kholwa* who had expressed disapproval at his fellow African Christians' drive to raise money for the British war effort, adding "that the money should be sent to Dinuzulu, whom he regarded as the head of the Natives."[107] Throughout the 1890s and 1900s, itinerant African Christian preachers crisscrossed Natal and indeed the whole of southern Africa, often spreading a message of black racial self-identification, racial uplift, and occasionally racial rebellion. One such figure was a preacher who called himself "John" and claimed to come from Egypt. John called the people in his audience "Egyptians" and presented them a classic vision of redemption through racial inversion. God would give them a new, black "Nkosi," and the government and land would be returned to black control. John called on people to pray, not to the God of Abraham and Isaac, but rather to the God of Ham and Neboheth, an allusion to the racist argument that blacks were the descendants of Ham and not of Ham's brother Shem, Noah's favored son and the ancestor of God's chosen people, the Israelites.[108] John even went so far as to argue that Africans were not Christians if they prayed for whites. Further echoing white racism, only this time on a cruder level, John referred to whites as *izinkawu*, monkeys. John seems to have confused his audience as much as anything else: many of them had not heard of Egypt and thought he was telling them that they were about to be conquered by yet another foreign power. In any event, "John" turned out to be an African Christian named Amos Khumalo from Ndwedwe district in Natal, although he claimed to have fought in Egypt on the Egyptian side against the English in 1885, perhaps referring to Gordon's operations that year in Khartoum.[109]

It was not only whites who were spreading rumors of an Ethiopian conspiracy involving Dinuzulu; some Natal African Christians were doing so as well. White rumor-mongers' typical claim that they received their information from Africans, and often Christian Africans, needs to be taken seriously. This is not to say that the rumors about an Ethiopian plot were not fantastic, but rather simply that the fantasy was shared by blacks as well as whites. In 1902, a government spy said that a man named Mzinyati had told him that the rumors about Dinuzulu had "come from native preachers" because, being literate, they had access to the knowledge being circulated in written documents. Mzinyati added that "the black preachers were known to be spreading the foregoing information and to be saying that the 'umbuso' (the kingdom, rule) would soon leave the white people and pass over to the black people."[110]

More significant still is the prominent role accorded to Natal African Christians in rumors spread by non-Christians. Already in the very first rumors in 1898, which alleged that Dinuzulu was trying to recruit Mqhawe to be his induna over Natal, it was said that "all the kraal natives were opposed to the acceptance, by Mqawe, of such a position under Dinuzulu, but the 'dressed natives' were in favour of it."[111] A 1902 rumor told of a united front that had been formed under Dinuzulu including Natal chiefs such as "Mqawe, Ngobizembe, Messeni, and Gayede" and "the Chief Sigcau in Pondoland and certain Abesuto Chiefs." While some prominent Natal

African Christians were excluded from this group, "all the other Native Christian communities are in the league, especially those belonging to the American Mission, who it is stated, are to be Dinuzulu's Indunas."[112] In real life, the most prominent Natal African Christian of them all, John Dube, was critical of various policies pursued by Natal's government, and many in the government identified him as a grave threat and kept him under close surveillance. But even government spies could not find evidence of Dube ever having publicly proclaimed his loyalty to Dinuzulu or having rejected the British monarch or having advocated rebellion. Dube was never punished with anything more than a stern reprimand or an obligation to issue a public apology or retraction.[113] In the rumors, on the other hand, Dube figured prominently as one of Dinuzulu's right-hand men.[114] The rumors articulated a vision for the future that was neither traditionalist nor anti-traditionalist, but rather a melding of the two.

THE QWABE AND MAPUMULO

Members of the Qwabe chiefdom and people from Mapumulo division, where most of the Qwabe lived, figured prominently in migrant labor to Johannesburg, where a new, broader sense of Zulu identity developed. The rebellion of 1906, in which the Qwabe and Mapumulo figured prominently, was also premised on this new Zulu identity. The rumors of the 1890s and 1900s serve to link the ideology of the Johannesburg migrants with the ideology of the rebels in Natal. It is therefore important to consider the role of the Qwabe and Mapumulo in the rumors, in terms of both the rumors' propagation and their content. In the Natal government's intelligence files concerning the rumors about Dinuzulu from 1898 to 1904, there are three reports from "Native Intelligence Officers" in Mapumulo, two reports from the resident magistrate of Mapumulo, and one report from Chief Swayimana of Mapumulo, all attesting to the presence of these rumors in that district.[115] The resident magistrate of Mapumulo concluded,

> [A] spirit exists of antagonism to the whites, and that racial dislike is becoming a factor which is not imaginary but real. . . . It is also stated that a combination of certain chiefs in this division, also others in Natal, has been entered into with Dinuzulu, having for its object the strengthening of the native position, and in case of necessity, also for using the forces

organised under this combination against the whites, and for the recognition of Dinuzulu as the supreme head, and that messengers are also stated to be passing frequently between them. [Chief Njengabantu is reputed to have said] that their forefathers had fought with the whites, and had got beaten, but that they the whites had not yet fought with them the natives of the present generation.[116]

The magistrate made this report in 1904, thus predicting the 1906 rebellion, its form and ideology, two years in advance.

It is not surprising that the name of the Qwabe chief Meseni occurs frequently in the reports of rumors, not least because his was one of the largest chiefdoms in the colony. What is particularly significant about the rumors regarding Meseni is their ambiguity. On the one hand, in 1902 an African government informant said he "was informed that the following Chiefs in Natal were all in communication and in league with Dinuzulu: Mqawe, Ngobizembe, Meseni, and Gayede."[117] On the other hand, two years later another African government informant reported rumors that Meseni had refused Dinuzulu's overtures.[118] Meseni himself expressed ambivalent attitudes toward the Zulu kings. A few years before the rebellion, in a conversation with James Stuart on Qwabe history, Meseni was keen to emphasize the more positive connections between the Qwabe and Zulu. For example, unlike some of Stuart's other informants, Meseni corroborated the story that Qwabe and Zulu were brothers, both sons of the ancient king Malandela. Meseni also denied the common stories that members of the Qwabe chiefdom were involved in Shaka's murder or in some attempts on Shaka's life. As proof, Meseni claimed that the Qwabe and Zulu were too friendly at the time for such a thing to have happened. Virtually alone among Stuart's informants, Meseni talked as if there had never been conflict between the Qwabe and Zulu. At the same time, though, Meseni insisted that "he [held] the highest rank among all the natives of Natal; he, moreover, [said] the Qwabe tribe is really of higher rank than the Zulu one, owing to Qwabe being senior to his brother, Zulu."[119] Meseni's claim suggests that he might have agreed with another chief who responded to rumors about Dinuzulu by asking his own subjects rhetorically, "Who is Dinuzulu? He is no bigger chief than I am."[120]

This ambiguity and ambivalence may very well have reflected Meseni's controversial place in the minds of both his Qwabe subjects and their

neighbors. Meseni, like all other chiefs in colonial Africa, often torn between the desires of his subjects to challenge the colonial state and the
reality that he could lose his position and possibly his life if he did so. Not
only did Meseni, like other chiefs in Natal at the time, have to arbitrate in
the pressing disputes between youths and elders. His position was particularly insecure because of the long and bitter Qwabe succession dispute that
had torn apart his chiefdom and impelled a steady stream of defectors to
neighboring chiefdoms. Meseni had to please both his most loyal subjects
and those who were considering defection. He somehow had to reconcile
the desire of some of his subjects to pursue war against other sections of the
Qwabe and neighboring chiefdoms with his need to placate government
officials. Thus Meseni was confrontational toward the government in the
Qwabe succession dispute, but bent over backward to avoid alienating the
government in other matters. When, in 1903, a group of Mapumulo chiefs
formed a delegation to file several grievances with the government, Meseni
at first agreed to come with them to Pietermaritzburg, and even signed their
letter of reference, only to refuse to participate at the last minute.[121] Meseni
did the same thing when the Mapumulo chiefs organized to protest the
government's ouster of Chief Njengabantu for "insubordination" in 1904,
and the government's raising of rents for African tenants on mission reserves in 1905.[122] It is thus not surprising that Natal Africans might wonder,
in the event of a war between Dinuzulu and the colonial government, whose
side Meseni might be on.

CONCLUSION

The rumors about Dinuzulu were an appeal for unity, but it is important to
bear in mind who the rumors came from and to what end the rumors were
directed. They came primarily from young men, and while they clearly
sought to heal the rifts within Zulu society by promoting Zulu ethnic consciousness, the rumors still revealed the young men's particular vision of an
ideal society. Chiefship and patriarchy would remain in the new dispensa-
tion, but now chiefs and homestead heads would be doing what young men
wanted. Even the talk of Christianity had a gendered and generational
component: given the greater resistance to Christianity from chiefs and
elders, and the greater support for it among youths and women, the latter
stood to gain from the proposed reconciliation between Christians and

traditionalists and the incorporation of Christians into the sociopolitical status hierarchy. With the introduction of the poll tax in 1905, young men only intensified their push for a new social order, but they did so in a way that gave other Natal Africans a place in that order, as well. Since chiefs and other elders were in many ways the main opponents to the young men's call for more power, the prominence and persistence of chiefship and patriarchy in the rumors no doubt made it easier for chiefs and elders to accept those calls.

6

THE POLL TAX PROTESTS AND REBELLION, 1905–1906

The rumors about Dinuzulu that spread throughout Natal from 1898 onward were an important phenomenon in the history of the region, for they demonstrated that a dramatic shift was taking place in Natal Africans' ethnic self-identification: they were becoming Zulus. The same was true of the protests and armed rebellion that followed the Natal government's introduction, in 1905, of a poll tax on all unmarried adult males in the colony. The protests and the rebellion followed many of the same patterns that the earlier rumors about Dinuzulu had done. Most obvious, the events of 1905–6 realized the predictions that the rumors had made. The active and collective resistance to the colonial state that Natal Africans had been talking about for so long finally occurred. More than this, the protests and rebellion were couched in the same trappings of Zulu ethnicity as the rumors had been: professed allegiance to the Zulu king Dinuzulu; the use of Usuthu, the name of Dinuzulu's faction in the Zulu Civil War and his royal salute; the use of ubushokobezi war badges and the name umshokobezi, both associated with the Usuthu faction; the use of intelezi, or medicine, obtained from Dinuzulu; and self-identification of Natal Africans as Zulus. Finally, Zulu ethnicity served the same purpose in the rebellions as it had in the rumors about Dinuzulu: it enabled youths to persuade chiefs and elders to accept the new order that the youth were calling for, and along the way heal rifts between members of different chiefdoms and between Christians and traditionalists. Thus it is important to pay attention not only to the prominent role of young men in the rebellion, but also to the precise nature of their relationship with chiefs and elders during this episode.

It is true that the rebellion occurred in only three isolated pockets, mostly in Natal proper and not in Zululand, and that the active rebels were only a tiny proportion of the total African population of the colony. But there is little doubt that many, if not most, Natal Africans sympathized with the rebels and believed many of the same things the rebels did, including that they were Zulus. This was apparent in the earlier rumors about Dinuzulu, but the same rumors persisted throughout the colony in 1905 and 1906. It is the very fact that rumors could be propagated behind a cloak of anonymity, while militant protest could and did incur the wrath of the colonial state, that helps to explain why the rebellion was less widespread than the rumors had been. But it is also striking that the rebels were precisely those Natal Africans, like the Qwabe, whose opposition to the Zulus had been greatest, and whose participation in migrant labor from Natal to Johannesburg had been most intense.

THE PROMULGATION OF THE POLL TAX AND THE FIRST PROTESTS AGAINST IT

The colonial government's first and most obvious mistake was to impose the poll tax in the first place. It did so because the end of the South African War and of the imperial government's wartime spending in the region had plunged Natal and the rest of the subcontinent into a rather severe recession. The debts incurred in fighting the war, and the need for reconstruction afterward, increased the Natal government's financial obligations. At the same time, however, the government's ability to meet those obligations was curtailed as financial aid from London decreased sharply and the recession ate into tax revenues. The government's chosen solution, in classic pre-Keynesian style, was to raise taxes and cut spending so as to balance the budget. From the government's point of view, the poll tax was a fair solution because it had to be paid by *all* unmarried adult males in the colony (except indentured laborers) regardless of race, and young men were supposedly not paying their fair share of taxes, from wage labor especially. The problem was that taxes were being increased precisely at a time when the people's ability to pay those taxes was declining. Moreover, the tax was punishingly regressive, as all young men had to pay the same amount despite huge differences in their earnings. Given the fact that blacks were, on average, much poorer than whites, the tax hit blacks much harder than it did whites.

At the same time, as the rumors of the previous years indicated, many blacks were on the verge of rebellion even before the tax was announced.

To make matters even worse, the tax was announced in a particularly ham-handed way. Natal Africans had long been expressing a certain nostalgia for Theophilus Shepstone's style of governance during his term as secretary for native affairs, but Natal Europeans had drawn the wrong conclusion from this. While Africans, and even many Europeans, emphasized Shepstone's consultative approach—symbolized by his open-air meetings with chiefs assembled under a tree—settler-legislators and officials focused on the absolute nature of his authority. One result was the Native Code Amendment Law, Act no. 1 of 1900, inspired by the Qwabe succession dispute, a law which severely curtailed the ability of the courts to act as a check on the Supreme Chief's powers. During the 1890s and 1900s, the whole hierarchy of "native administrators" from the governor in his role as Supreme Chief on down to the lowliest constable became even *more* arbitrary and *less* consultative. Thus, when in November 1905 the assistant magistrate of Durban, James Stuart, not only announced the poll tax to an assembly of African workers in the town, but also gave the reasons why the government had chosen to impose the tax and responded sympathetically to their complaints of economic hardship, he was severely criticized by both the settler press and certain other officials. They felt that Stuart should have done what the other magistrates had done: simply have told Africans to pay the tax without trying to justify it or listen to Africans' complaints about it. According to the Native High Court judge J. W. Shepstone—brother of Theophilus and former secretary for native affairs himself—Stuart had made a grave error: "It is the most impolitic speech I have ever heard of in dealing with an aboriginal people who, after all, are to be dealt with as children."[1] The editors of the African newspaper *Ilanga lase Natal* disagreed: "We maintain that it is Mr. Stuart who understands the natives far better than Mr. Shepstone does."[2]

From the first, African responses to the tax varied enormously depending on the nature of the forums in which they were acting. For example, Africans appearing before colonial officials emphasized their loyalty to the government even as they protested the tax. Between 21 December 1905 and 3 January 1906, thirteen chiefs from Lower Tugela either came before the resident magistrate in person or sent deputations to speak on their behalf. Their messages were remarkably similar. In each case, the chief had announced the poll tax to his subjects, only to have them tell him to inform the magistrate that they could not pay. Hut taxes and dog taxes were already burden enough, they said, as were the new £3 annual mission reserve rents and, worst of all, the steadily increasing rents on the private lands that covered virtually the entire division. If they fell behind in paying their rents, they either had to go to court or faced eviction and the demolition of their homesteads. But the people who came to speak before the resident magistrate did not voice distaste for colonial rule itself. Indeed, they were eager to impress on him what at least one man called their "love" for the government, even as they tried to convey the sense of betrayal they felt with regard to it.

> We say, do we not belong to the Government? If not to whom do we belong? Why has this thing been done? Is there anything which has been hidden by us from the Government? We contribute to the support of the Government. That which we were called upon to pay we have paid. . . . We say there is no Government, but that there is a person who has no consideration for us, who does not hear us. The Poll Tax has even stirred up the stupid person.[3]

While the rhetoric of formal encounters with colonial officials was plaintive and diplomatic, the rumors picked up through "official eavesdropping" revealed much more hostility. The rumors about Dinuzulu that had been so common over the previous seven years now became more common and more pointed: for example, it was during these months—from November 1905 to January 1906—that the pig-killing rumors emerged. In January, one settler employed by a coaling contractor at the Durban harbor to recruit African workers relayed a conversation he had had with one of his "old and trusted" headmen. According to the headman, the government's main misstep had not been so much in imposing the poll tax as in doing so without consulting Dinuzulu, without taking him "into their confidence," and without gaining "his co-operation regarding the payment of the Poll Tax." As a result, rebellion was now imminent.

Q: If Dinizulu ordered payment of the Poll Tax would they comply?[4]
A: Yes. There would be no means of getting out of it as they look to him for instructions as to their ruler.
Q: Unless you get instructions from Dinizulu do you mean to pay the Poll Tax?
A: No.
Q: Then what decision are you going to take?
A: We are watching the Government.

Q: How do you mean watching the Government?

A: We are going to see what action Government is going to take.

Q: You mean you are going to wait and see if you are arrested?

A: Yes.

Q: If arrested you go to gaol.

A: Yes.

Q: Now supposing Government holds your Chiefs and Headmen responsible for the collection of the Poll Tax and arrests them for non-payment, or seizes your stock, what then?

A: When that day dawns it is time for you to send your children away and go yourself.

Q: Why this?

A: Because we will never submit to this procedure.

Q: What do you mean?

A: That we mean to fight to the bitter end, although we know we shall be beaten still now we have nothing to live for.

Q: Now if trouble should come about what action are you natives in town going to take?

A: As soon as we hear that our Chiefs or Headmen are arrested, or our stock interfered with, we are going to request the Chief Magistrate [of Durban] to give us the road.

Q: If he refuses?

A: Then trouble starts at your doorstep.

Q: How are you advised of Dinizulu's intentions?

A: He has been here amongst us "invisible."[5]

This promise to refuse to pay the tax, and to fight, in the rural African reserves in particular, if their chiefs or headmen were arrested would be fulfilled by thousands of Natal Africans over the next six months, even though the vast majority would remain on the sidelines.

PROTESTS DURING THE COLLECTION OF THE TAX

It is therefore not surprising that, when government officials tried to collect the poll tax in late January and early February 1906, they were met with overt protests and, occasionally, violence. Indeed, the first bloodshed resulting from the poll tax protests occurred at this time, in Richmond in the Natal midlands. On 8 February, a detachment of mounted police went after a group of Africans who had refused to pay the tax. On encountering the group, which was illegally armed with spears, the police drew their weapons, leading the Africans to believe they were about to be attacked. When the police fell upon the Africans, one of the Africans grabbed the bridle of a policemen's horse, and the police started firing their guns. On this occasion, though, the Africans had the better of the fight, such that two Europeans were killed, while four Africans were merely wounded. The colonial government declared martial law the following day, and the Natal Field Forces were sent into the area. By 15 February, two Africans had been captured, summarily court-martialed, and shot; fifteen others were executed, after more trials were conducted, over the next two months.[6]

The Natal midlands was not the only area to witness large-scale antitax protests or even violence between government officials and Africans who refused to pay the tax. Both the middle and lower Thukela Valleys, where the two main outbreaks of rebellion would take place a few months later, saw their own protests, as did many other districts: antitax protests took place in 9 out of 25 districts in Natal proper, south of the Thukela, but only in 3 of 14 districts in Zululand, north of the river.[7] It is no accident that many of the districts that saw protests were also those districts where poverty and migrant labor were most extensive. However, the outbreak of antitax protests, and of violence associated with those protests, also depended on the actions of the different officials in charge of different districts. For example, Mapumulo and Lower Tugela were neighboring districts, in the lower Thukela Valley, that both had high rates of labor migration. Numerous chiefdoms also straddled the boundary between the two districts. Both districts saw antitax protests, but the protests in Mapumulo got out of hand, whereas those in Lower Tugela did not.

In Lower Tugela district, the resident magistrate was F. P. Shuter, who was also serving as regent of the Enkwenkwezini section of the Qwabe chiefdom during the minority of the heir to the chiefship, Siziba. Shuter's original plan was for Africans to come to his office, individually and of their own accord, to pay the poll tax, beginning on the official due date of 20 January. They largely failed to do so, however, and after interviewing the chiefs of the district he realized that the exactions of local landlords and moneylenders, in particular, were causing great hardship. Shuter told the chiefs that he would appeal to the government to address their concerns, and he did so, but Shuter's superiors insisted that the poll tax collection proceed. Shuter made sure that it did so, but only on a modest scale to begin with: he ordered chiefs to personally deliver their subjects to his office to pay the tax in groups of five or six at a time.[8] Shuter also made good on a request that many of the chiefs had made for a meeting with the minister for native affairs, in which they could air their complaints. The meeting took place on 9 February. Though the minister merely reiterated the chiefs' legal obligation to help enforce and collect the tax, he did listen to their complaints.[9] In the days and weeks that followed, few Africans in Lower Tugela failed to pay the tax, and no incidents of direct confrontation occurred.

In Mapumulo, on the other hand, the resident magistrate R. Ernst Dunn made a series of missteps that resulted in occasionally violent protests and a severe government crackdown. To begin with, when Dunn announced the tax to an assembly of the district's chiefs in October 1905, he reported, "Great opposition was raised to the measure, and some blustering statements were made, and all the Chiefs requested me to bring to the notice of the Government that each and all strongly protest against the act." Dunn was so lacking in judgment that, despite the evidence he himself had presented of a developing broad-based protest, he nevertheless concluded "that no difficulty will be experienced in collecting the Tax."[10]

Dunn's next mistake was to arrange a series of poll tax collection assemblies to which chiefs or headmen were to bring dozens, sometimes even hundreds, of their followers, in contrast to the small groups that Shuter received at any one time. The first such assembly was held for Chief Gobizembe's men on 22 January 1906.[11] Dunn arrived at Allan's Store with three European and six African policemen. Three hundred of Gobizembe's men came soon thereafter, split into two groups, and encircled Dunn and the policemen in a manner reminiscent of the "horns of the bull" maneuver associated with the armies of the Zulu kingdom. Each man carried a shield and a knobkerrie, or heavy fighting stick. Allan told Dunn and the others that he had heard Gobizembe's men say they would attack if a single one of them was accosted or arrested. They refused to carry out, and indeed shouted down, orders to give Dunn the customary salute, "Bayede!" They then also shouted down several attempts by Dunn himself to speak. As Dunn turned silent, Gobizembe's men began to giya, or dance in a manner intended to challenge or provoke others to fight, much as they would at dance competitions, beer parties, or faction fights. They withdrew two or three hundred yards away, lingered for a while, and slowly approached Dunn again, at which point he told Gobizembe to bring his men to heel.

Gobizembe asked them why they had refused to salute Dunn, but they did not answer. He ordered them to pay the tax, and they shouted, "We know nothing about the Poll Tax. We haven't the money." Gobizembe was failing to quiet the group's violent rumblings, and the police began to approach them. For whatever reason, the men turned and left en masse, shouting "Usuthu!"—the war cry of Dinuzulu's uSuthu faction—as they went.[12]

The five or so other poll tax collection ceremonies in Mapumulo turned out in a similar manner: men showed up armed, acted in a threatening manner imbued with symbolic allusions to the Zulu kingdom (such as when the Qwabe came wearing ubushokobezi, special war badges worn by members of Dinuzulu's uSuthu faction), and refused to pay the tax. Only three chiefdoms—those of Mdungwazwe, Swayimana, and Mahlubi—paid the tax, and in Swayimana's and Mahlubi's cases it was paid only for the sons of the chiefs and some of their headmen. Dunn started drinking so heavily that he was relieved of his duties on 14 February. On 27 February, the government gave Gobizembe six days to deliver the three hundred of his subjects who had been present at the poll tax collection assembly to the authorities for punishment. When six days had elapsed and he had only supplied twenty men, Gobizembe was arrested and his homestead shelled by artillery, and more than a thousand head of cattle, sheep, and goats were confiscated from him and his subjects. By the end of March, Gobizembe had been deposed. To escape such punishments, the chiefs and subjects of other chiefdoms became more forthcoming with their tax payments, but even then there was no small amount of foot-dragging.[13]

THE ROAD TO REBELLION FOR MESENI AND MAPUMULO

When poll tax protestors in the Natal midlands killed two white policemen in February 1906, it seemed to most Natalians, both white and black, that rebellion was imminent. But many Natal Africans did not look toward the midlands for the impending rebellion, but rather to Mapumulo and Lower Tugela. In February, government intelligence reports were "all pointing to the belief that something is to take place at Mapumulo and showing the existence of a very boastful spirit." One African informant told authorities that "all natives in the Mapumulo and Stanger [Lower Tugela] Districts were ready and waiting for the troops."[14]

Four months later, Mapumulo would indeed be the center of the largest outbreak of rebellion, but despite the poll tax protests (and perhaps because of the government's resulting crackdown there), the next outbreak occurred not in Mapumulo, but several miles farther inland, along the middle reaches of the Thukela, and was led by the recently deposed Zondi chief Bhambatha. On 5 April 1906, forces under Bhambatha attacked a detachment of police at Keate's Drift, on the border between Umvoti and Weenen divisions, more than thirty miles away from Mapumulo. This was the climax of a series of events that had begun in late February, when young men from Bhambatha's chiefdom headed off to a poll tax collection assembly in Greytown armed and intent on refusing to pay, much as had happened in Mapumulo in late January and early February. Bhambatha, however, refused to let those who planned to defy the poll tax attend the assembly, and he himself failed to attend. He disobeyed two orders to report to the magistrate of Umvoti division, and fled to Zululand when colonial troops came to apprehend him on 9 March. In Zululand, Bhambatha and his family stayed for a time at Dinuzulu's royal homestead, Osuthu. While Bhambatha was there, the government deposed him. He then recruited some men from Osuthu to return with him to Natal. Once back in his own chiefdom, Bhambatha took his government-appointed successor hostage, precipitating the confrontation at Keate's Drift. Bhambatha and his followers then escaped into Zululand again, this time to the Nkandla Forest, where one of Bhambatha's companions from Osuthu—Cakijana—convinced several people that the rebels had Dinuzulu's support. For one month—between 6 or 7 April and 5 May—there were no confrontations between the rebels and colonial troops in the Nkandla and Nqutu districts of Zululand, where the rebels were holed up. From 5 May to 10 June, however, the two sides met in a long string of minor skirmishes, culminating in the decisive battle of Mhome Gorge, in which large numbers of rebels—including Bhambatha—were killed and the rest scattered.[15]

On 19 June 1906, just nine days after Bhambatha's rebellion was crushed, rebels in Mapumulo attacked a European-owned store in Thring's Post and a detachment of colonial troops near the Otimati River. This rebellion was led by the Qwabe chief Meseni and involved hundreds, perhaps even thousands, of his subjects, but Meseni was an unlikely rebel leader. The rebellion was supposedly instigated by Dinuzulu and sought his restoration, but relations between the Qwabe and Zulu had been highly conflictual from earliest times to the Anglo-Zulu War just twenty-seven years before. And Meseni himself, though less antagonistic toward the Zulu kings than other Qwabe were, was still quite ambivalent about them. Meseni was also an unlikely rebel leader because he and his subjects had, over the previous fifteen years or so, been involved in repeated faction fights with almost all the neighboring chiefdoms, including those whose chiefs and subjects would ally with Meseni in 1906.[16]

Moreover, as it turned out, Meseni's actions—like those of the other chiefs in Mapumulo—were so far from being the actions of a rebel leader, that Shula Marks for one has characterized the rebellion as "reluctant," more a defensive response to the aggression of colonial forces than a premeditated uprising. As early as January and February, the Mapumulo chiefs Ntshingumuzi, Mlungwana, and Matshwili had held war-doctoring ceremonies for their subjects at their homesteads. This, combined with the confrontational behavior of the poll tax protestors around the same time, led many settlers to believe that rebellion in Mapumulo was imminent.[17] But, if rebellion was indeed imminent, Marks asks, why did it take another four months to happen? Why did so few Africans from Mapumulo join Bhambatha's forces? Why did Meseni not rebel during Bhambatha's uprising, when colonial forces were distracted and vulnerable? Why did Meseni wait until late June, *after* hostilities had already broken out in Mapumulo, to call on migrant workers from his chiefdom to return home? Marks suggests that it was rather the government's decision to move still more troops into Mapumulo in June that drove Meseni and some of the other Mapumulo chiefs to the conclusion that the government was about to attack them. Indeed, after the battle of Mhome Gorge there were rumors that the government was now going to do to the poll tax protestors in Mapumulo what they had done to Bhambatha and his followers.[18] There is still more evidence, above and beyond that cited by Marks, that the "rebellion" was "reluctant." On 23 June, one African government informant said, "As far as I could ascertain it was the intention of the Natives in revolt to wait somewhere until they were attacked by the white people."[19] Another quoted Meseni as saying, "I don't say I am going to Mapumulo [the Mapumulo magistrate's office, where colonial forces had reconnoitered] to fight the troops. I am waiting here for them to come down and attack me here and then I shall fight."[20]

But Meseni's own statement to the government eight days after his capture on 12 July, given while in custody to none other than James Stuart, suggests that his actions had been driven by more than the most recent activities of government forces in Mapumulo. On the one hand, Meseni said, in early June,

> [I] was in a state of unrest . . . for the Magistrate of Mapumulo had begun to regard me with suspicion, indeed he looked on me as if I were inimical towards the Government, which was not the case. . . . Major Maxwell, Magte. of Mapumulo, called some chiefs of this Division together and told them of Bambata's doings in Nkandhla forest, but he omitted to call or inform me, thereby showing he regarded me with suspicion; I, moreover, heard from those who had seen him that he looked on me as hostile and used the threat that he would cause an armed force to come and arrest me.[21]

On the other hand, Meseni reported how at the same time he had been visited by two groups of men who claimed to be emissaries from Dinuzulu. The first group relayed a supposed order from Dinuzulu that Meseni "was to arm and fight against the white people as they too had already armed for that purpose. If anyone refused to comply with this order the impi from Zululand would, whilst on its march towards Durban, pass through his country or location." The second group came with *iintelezi*, or medicines, supposedly from Dinuzulu, that would protect people from bullets. While Meseni said he did "not believe he [the visitor] ever had any izintelezi, his object having been merely to bring on a state of war," Meseni also said, "I believed that Dinuzulu would actually call the Zulus to arms against the white people, though I could not see how he could hope to meet with success."

Thus the actions of Meseni, and of the other "rebels" for that matter, cannot be isolated from the rumors of rebellion that had been circulating for years even before the poll tax was introduced, and which showed that many people believed that rebellion was imminent. As far back as 1902, Meseni had figured prominently in many of the rumors as supposedly being "in league with" Dinuzulu and party to the planned rebellion.[22] Such rumors were spread by young migrant laborers returning from Durban or Johannesburg who often claimed to be acting on behalf of chiefs, who were supposedly maintaining contact with one another by means of this secret network of undercover messengers.[23] In February 1906, these rumors had it that the chiefs in Mapumulo had agreed to join forces and support Gobizembe in the rebellion he was purportedly about to launch.[24] During Bhambatha's rebellion, from April to June, there were numerous rumors that

Bhambatha and Dinuzulu were not only in touch with each other, but were also sending messages to Meseni and other chiefs in Mapumulo and Lower Tugela to recruit them into the rebellion and plan coordinated actions. Meseni and his people were supposedly delaying action pending the receipt of evidence that Bhambatha was actually beating the British and that the anti-bullet medicine was actually working.[25]

Of course, the rumors that Meseni, Bhambatha, and Dinuzulu were jointly planning and, later, conducting the rebellion were false. But these rumors still had very real consequences, mainly because many Africans in Mapumulo and elsewhere believed that they were true and acted accordingly. Thus, even without a conspiracy among Natal chiefs and Dinuzulu, Natal Africans from widely separate districts were still able to protest the tax around the same time and in the same manner, clad in Dinuzulu's ubushokobezi war badges and shouting his war-cry, "Usuthu!" Moreover, those same people, acting on the basis of the rumors, could bring pressure to bear on their chiefs, calling on them to join the rebellion.

In the case of Meseni, it is clear that pressure from his subjects was decisive in pushing him to violence. Meseni was in a very insecure position. Recall that the legitimacy of his own claim to the chiefship was subject to debate, and for more than fifteen years his chiefdom had been literally torn apart by the resulting succession dispute and faction fighting. Many Qwabe deserted Meseni and joined the Enkwenkwezini branch of the chiefdom instead, even after Magistrate Shuter became its regent. The poll tax both laid bare and exacerbated Meseni's insecurity. On 18 February, several days after the Qwabe chiefdom's poll tax collection assembly, Meseni called another assembly of his subjects, this time at his homestead, for which he slaughtered a steer and provided "an abundance of beer." The meat and beer were perhaps intended in part to soften the blow, for Meseni took the occasion to tell his subjects that they had to pay the tax: as of 17 February, only one of his thousands of subjects had done so. The crowd replied angrily, "How much are you being paid by Government for this?"[26] The government threatened to punish Meseni as they had Gobizembe if he did not get more of his subjects to pay the tax and either turn over one hundred of his subjects who had been involved in protests at the poll tax collection assembly or pay a fine of two hundred head of cattle on their behalf.[27] In fact, Meseni was briefly imprisoned for a few days in late March and early April, but this was for failing to prevent faction fighting between his subjects and those of Swayimana, and not on account of the poll tax.[28] His subjects' compliance with the poll tax gradually improved, so that, by 7 April, 467 of them had paid the tax.[29] But this compliance cost Meseni the support of his subjects. As of 9 June government informants reported, "[Meseni] has lost power and authority over his people, and therefore he is no longer responsible for the actions of his tribesmen, that he himself is loyal but the Govt. must supervise his individual tribesmen who so far are quiet."[30]

Forced to choose between the government and his own subjects, Meseni gave in to the latter. Meseni certainly had his own reasons to rebel, but as far as government informants were concerned, Meseni's subjects, and the young men especially, were virtually dragging him into rebellion. On 23 June, in the midst of hostilities, one informant reported, "It was said that the cause of the revolt of the Natives was the Poll Tax which all the young people objected to, that they, ever since they had heard about it, had been urging their Chiefs to resist payment, and that the Chiefs have now, at last, been practically compelled to consent." The same informant said his father had counseled Meseni "not to become involved in what was being done by the young men, because they would only bring destruction on him and the people."[31] As another informant said of the rebellion in general, "This is not the doing of the Chiefs, it is the work of their men."[32]

ZULU ETHNICITY AS A UNIFYING, RATHER THAN DIVISIVE, FACTOR

The sense of unity that emerged before and during the rebellion—and that allowed rebels to overcome divisions of generation, chiefdom, and religion —was based on the Zulu ethnic consciousness that had finally and only recently been established in Natal, as a result of migrant labor and rumors. It was a complex ideology, involving not only loyalty to Dinuzulu, but also symbols and historical references evoking Dinuzulu and the other Zulu kings. The centerpieces of the rebellion were the ceremonies held beforehand at the homesteads of the rebel chiefs. During the ceremonies, the young men of the chiefdom would gather at the homestead of their chief. There they would be "doctored for war" by special war doctors and sprinkled with intelezi, a special medicine often consisting of the personal effects, effluvia, and even body parts of the enemy. These ceremonies were very old, pre-dating the era of Shaka, almost one hundred years before the rebellion. The ceremonies were central to the Shakan wars, and were also evident in the faction fights of the 1890s and 1900s, with which Natal Africans were so familiar. In this part of Natal, however, the enemy for whom the soldiers prepared had never been the colonial state. All that changed, if only in a modest way at first, with the promulgation of the poll tax. Early in 1906, when the young men of the Mapumulo and Lower Tugela began protesting the poll tax, those from the chiefdoms of Matshwili and Ntshingumuzi doctored themselves for war. Although there was little evidence that either chief had organized the ceremonies, the mere fact that they had occurred and were not, as was usually the case, directed toward other African chiefdoms prompted officials to reprimand both chiefs and fine them in cattle.[33]

Bhambatha's rebellion was significant as a model for the later rebellion in Mapumulo and Lower Tugela. Bhambatha's rebellion not only inspired others to rebel, but also suggested the form that other rebellions should take. In both cases, rebels—and especially their leaders—tapped into well-springs of popular sentiment toward Dinuzulu. Bhambatha had his followers use Dinuzulu's "Usuthu" war cry, ubushokobezi war badges, and intelezi, or medicine, which he had supposedly obtained from Dinuzulu. Just as rumors prior to the rebellion had said that Dinuzulu obtained magical powers from Basutoland war doctors and their medicines, Bhambatha also relied on a doctor from Basutoland, in this case to prepare his troops.[34] Just as the armies of the old Zulu kings had done, Bhambatha's rebels transformed the bodies of some of their dead opponents—such as Sgt. Brown, one of those killed at Keate's Drift—into protective intelezi. The rebels removed Brown's upper lip, forearm, and part of his intestine. Medicine made from the forearm was intended to improve the rebels' marksmanship with guns or spears, and medicine from the gastrointestinal tract was to cause enemies to feel internal upset. Those who assembled at Sigananda's chiefdom while Bhambatha was there during April and May took on the name abashokobezi (sing. umshokobezi), derived from the name for the Usuthu war badge, ubushokobezi. The semantic shift that abashokobezi underwent from "adherents of the Usuthu faction" to "rebels" was furthered by a specific conceptualization of the Zulu Civil War (1879–84). According to this notion, Cetshwayo and his followers were defying "the white people's law," while supporters of other chiefs who owed their positions to the intervention of the British Empire were amambuka, or traitors.

If the poll tax rebels more than twenty years later came to refer to themselves as abashokobezi, then their opponents became amambuka.[35]

The appeals to Dinuzulu emerged out of a negative reaction to colonial propaganda as much as out of any positive attraction to Dinuzulu himself. The Zulu kings had always been central to colonialist efforts to assume cultural hegemony over Natal Africans. According to this rhetoric, the Great White Chief of colonialism was a more just and humane ruler than the Zulu kings had been. At the same time, the Great White Chief and his agents appropriated various symbols of African kingship—especially titles and royal salutes—in an effort to tap into the reservoirs of legitimacy African kings had accumulated. The Great White Chief was therefore supposedly just another African king, but a superior king because of his superior civilization. Popular African rhetoric regarding Dinuzulu, on the other hand, seems to have been—in part, at least—a response to the ideological claims of the colonialists. James Stuart, for example, said that, in the beginning of April, when rebels captured Bhambatha's government-appointed successor, they taunted the latter, saying, "Where are your white friends now? We acknowledge, not a Natal king, but a black one."[36] Whatever else the rebellion may have been, it was also a rejection of efforts to legitimate colonialism through the appropriation of the trappings of African kingship.

In the event, the rebels put too much faith in Dinuzulu. He turned a deaf ear to Bhambatha's efforts to recruit him, a fact established, ironically, when colonial prosecutors failed to prove, in a colonial court of law, that Dinuzulu had either rebelled or instigated others to do so.[37] In addition, Dinuzulu's intelezi, which was supposed to turn bullets into water, failed to do so. As the tide began to turn against Bhambatha and his followers, in May and June, the deaths of so many of them caused the survivors to lose their faith in the intelezi as well.[38]

After Bhambatha's rebellion broke out, there were unconfirmed reports that more chiefs in Mapumulo and Lower Tugela—notably Meseni, Ndlovu ka Thimuni, and Matshwili—were holding war-doctoring ceremonies. European officials and Africans alike began to suspect that the chiefs were holding the ceremonies because they were conspiring with, or at least sympathized with, Dinuzulu and Bhambatha. Typically, however, the chiefs denied the rumors, and officials had difficulty corroborating them.[39] It was only after the rebellion that the government would discover just how reliable the rumors were.

Ultimately, Meseni and Ndlovu were both prompted to prepare for war by a combination of government action, pressure from their subjects, and orders brought by strange messengers allegedly from Dinuzulu. Ndlovu said, after hearing the message, that he told the messenger he was hesitant to comply. The messenger answered, "You remember your father having refused to comply with the King's order to put Piet Retief to death, well, bear such refusal in mind now just as Siteku does." This was a reference to the Zulu king Dingane's orders to have the leader of the Boer trekkers recently arrived in Natal put to death in 1838. Ndlovu's ancestors had failed to comply with the order, precipitating a break with Dingane that would lead to their flight to Natal. Ndlovu took the messenger's statement as a threat and assumed that Dinuzulu was behind the whole matter, even though the messenger had not said so explicitly. On the other hand, as Ndlovu stated, "The Magistrate of Mapumulo showed in several ways not only that he regarded me with suspicion, but as actively hostile. I felt, therefore, as if I was between two fires. I acted as I have done simply because I was afraid of the Native Authorities of Zululand."[40]

While Ndlovu was not the first chief in Mapumulo and Lower Tugela to ritually prepare his men for rebellion, he was the first to actually carry out the rebellion. When hostilities first broke out in Mapumulo, on 19 June, government intelligence linked the four hundred rebels involved in the attacks to Ndlovu's chiefdom. Statements taken during and after the rebellion indicated that doctoring for war had begun at Ndlovu's chiefdom as early as 16 June. Unlike the war-doctoring that typically preceded faction fights, the preparations for rebellion at Ndlovu's homestead attracted many men from other chiefdoms in Mapumulo and neighboring Krantzkop division. The doctoring did not end with the beginning of hostilities. The body of the European trooper killed during the attack was converted into intelezi with which to further prepare the rebels.[41]

The example of Bhambatha's rebellion was particularly important for Ndlovu and the rebels under him, many of whom believed that Bhambatha was still alive and would come with his army to assist the Mapumulo rebels. This is not surprising, given the fact that Ndlovu's subjects lived mainly in northwestern Mapumulo, that part of the division closest to where Bhambatha's rebellion had taken place. There were more rumors about men joining Bhambatha's rebellion from Ndlovu's chiefdom than from any other in Mapumulo, except Gobizembe's. During the Mapumulo rebellion, it was the rebels under Ndlovu who made reference to Bhambatha. For example, one informant claimed to have been captured by Ndlovu's men and then to have escaped. He asked them "to what chiefs this body of men belonged, and they replied, we are the people who went to assist Bambata."[42] However, only two days later came indications that Ndlovu's men were losing their faith in Bhambatha. That day, two men who said they were deserters from Ndlovu's army gave statements to the government. They reported that they had grown suspicious as many men from Mapumulo had gone off to join Bhambatha but had never returned. The rebels under Ndlovu had been told that Bhambatha and the others were not dead, but had invaded Natal and burned Greytown. The deserters had come to doubt this, "as they had not heard or seen anything of Bambata's impi, and they had not had the assistance they were promised."[43]

By far the greatest doctoring, however, took place in Meseni's chiefdom. The main ceremony was at Meseni's homestead Emthandeni, which had been founded by Phakathwayo almost a century earlier, but smaller ceremonies were also held at the homesteads of Meseni's most prominent headmen. Some two to five thousand people, many of them from chiefdoms besides Meseni's, came to Emthandeni, where they were attended to by war doctors, some of whom likewise came from other chiefdoms. The men from various chiefdoms going to or coming from Emthandeni were seen wearing Dinuzulu's ubushokobezi war badges.[44] However, the connection with Dinuzulu was more than just symbolic for the rebels, who were told, "Dinuzulu is at the bottom of the rebellion."[45] After government forces defeated and scattered the rebels at Emthandeni, between 3 and 5 July, the troops discovered the body of the postman Veal—converted into intelezi much like that of his colleague Powell—and 1,500 "war-huts" which the visiting rebels had occupied.[46]

The popular association of rebellion with Dinuzulu, present from the beginning, extended to the very end. After Meseni and Ndlovu were captured, rumors were rife that the two rebel leaders had escaped to Zululand because they had rebelled at Dinuzulu's behest and that they now wanted to report to him personally.[47] Even after the actual rebellion was crushed, rumors of rebellion continued. In September 1906, one settler reported being told "that the balance of Meseni's rebels still in the field are arming at the Hlangwini . . . and that Dinuzulu was going to cross the Tugela and kill off all the whites."[48] More than a year later, many Africans persisted in believing that Dinuzulu and Bhambatha would redeem them. In 1907, when the government ordered the branding of all cattle, a rumor spread throughout Lower Tugela that this was just the first step in the government's planned confiscation of whatever cattle Africans still had. Dinuzulu, not yet apprehended or put to trial, was supposed to have had his messengers broadcast a new message to his people.

> People, be ready with your weapons. I am at war with the white people. The white people want Bambata from me. I have told the white people I do not know where Bambata is, but as a matter of truth, Bambata is with me and I shall not deliver him up to the white people. The white people are now here seeking for Bambata. Sell off all your cattle to one another. The Government intend to take them from you (panga). I have my guards out to watch the movements of the Troops in search of Bambata.[49]

Officials in Mapumulo noted similar rumors. Just as before the rebellion, there were stories that Dinuzulu was in regular contact with the king of Basutoland, who had taught him magic and given him medicines. The passing of a comet through the skies above Natal was seen as a sign, as was an epidemic of cattle disease which apparently avoided European cattle, striking African cattle instead: "The cattle disease is also put down to the evil influence of the Europeans, who do not wish the natives to possess property." One commonly heard phrase was "Although we were killed, we are not dead." Faction fighting reemerged, and people struggled to remind each other of the lessons learned from the rebellion. When a group of Africans from one chiefdom got together to plan an attack on another, an elderly man said "that they must stop fighting amongst themselves. Did they not know that they were Tshaka's people, and that the impi that they were waiting for was drawing near?"[50] The old grievances about the depredations by Shaka and the other Zulu kings were now dead. Instead, people struggled to transcend their differences by uniting under the idea that they were all the people of the Zulu kings.

THE ROLE OF PATRIARCHY AND CHIEFSHIP IN THE REBELLION

One of the most important conflicts that the ideology of Zulu ethnicity was used to overcome was that between youths and elders. Much as was the case with the earlier rumors about Dinuzulu, the 1906 rebellion and the culture surrounding it was a forum in which young men used Zulu ethnicity to assert their power, but also to persuade chiefs and elders to join them, indeed, in leadership positions. Young men were challenging their elders, not rejecting the patriarchy that young men themselves benefitted from. Many aspects of the rebellion prompted observers then, as well as historians today, to characterize the events of 1906 as "youths rebel[ling] against compliant elders and colonial power."[51] But were the youths rebelling against these compliant elders because they were elders or because they were compliant? The evidence very strongly suggests that it was differing opinions about the poll tax protests, not differing generational positions, that set some Africans against each other during this episode. This is not to say that there had been no generational conflict in the period leading up to the rebellion. Such conflict did exist, and it was often quite bitter, sometimes seeming to outweigh other axes of conflict in African society. Nevertheless, before and during the rebellion young men did not attack their chiefs and elders. Rather, rebels both young and old attacked loyalists both young and old. Youths invariably tried to recruit chiefs and elders for their leadership and their ritual power. In this the young men often succeeded, but even when they failed the result was not "intergenerational civil war," for conflict between elders and youths, and between chiefs and subjects, was minimal, particularly when compared to that between the colonial state and the poll tax rebels. Far more important than the intergenerational conflict was the intergenerational collaboration.

Most chiefs did not rebel, even in Mapumulo and Lower Tugela, but this did not necessarily mean that the chiefs opposed the rebels. Officials singled out chiefs, holding them responsible for the actions of their subjects. As a result, many chiefs apparently tried to please their subjects by supporting the rebellion with a disingenuity and lack of obviousness sufficient to keep official suspicions from being aroused. That many, perhaps even most, chiefs were engaged in passive resistance during this episode can be seen in the occasional bits of intelligence that the government received from African informants about what was going on behind officials' backs. Gobizembe's brother told officials of a public meeting of the chiefdom's subjects in the days leading up to the poll tax collection assembly.

> Just after the Poll Tax Act was made known to us Chief Gobizembe gathered all his men together and told them that they had to pay the Poll Tax to the Government. His men (both young and elderly) said they would be

unable to pay this tax as they had difficulty in obtaining money to pay their hut tax and dog tax. Gobizembe, seeing his men were not inclined to pay the tax, wished to agree with them, when I said, no don't defy the Government. Pay their tax, but go down to Maritzburg to ask the Government to abolish the Dog Tax. Then they stated we refused to pay the Crown Forest Tax ("Imali ya Mahlati") and it was abolished. . . . Just before the Chief went with his men to Allen's [sic] store where the Poll Tax was being collected he again collected his men together and told them that the Government said they had to pay the tax. When his men refused to pay the tax and the Chief seeing they were against him sided with them.[52]

While it is true that government informants may lie for personal gain or revenge, the reliability of some such testimony can be confirmed nevertheless. In this particular case, Gobizembe's later actions seem to corroborate his brother's testimony. Gobizembe followed Dunn's orders at the assembly and called on his subjects to pay the tax, but it is significant that they attacked Dunn and not Gobizembe. Two days later, at another assembly in Mapumulo, Gobizembe and three other chiefs came to tell Dunn that their men could not pay the tax because they did not have the money.[53] Whether Gobizembe supported the poll tax protestors or not, Gobizembe's brother's testimony clearly states that elders in general were siding with youths on this issue.

There were those chiefs who were more total in their cooperation with the colonial authorities, but even their cases indicate the limits of a generational interpretation. Take, for example, Chief Swayimana of Mapumulo. He had his sons and the sons of his headmen pay the tax, beat his subjects with a whip at the poll tax collection assembly when they tried to approach Dunn, and afterward fined the transgessors of his own accord.[54] But it was Swayimana who attacked the young men at the assembly, not the other way around. He was later targeted for reprisals, but it is difficult to determine whether this was because he was an elder or because he was collaborating so closely with the state.[55] Indeed, when the rebellion did break out in Mapumulo, Swayimana was one of only three chiefs in the district (out of a total of twenty-one) to actively aid the government.

After the rebellion, the magistrates of Mapumulo and Lower Tugela evaluated the loyalty, or lack thereof, among the chiefs, or, in sections without chiefs, among district headmen. In Mapumulo, only five out of twenty-one were outright rebels, and in Lower Tugela only three of nineteen. However, the magistrates considered another five in Mapumulo and nine in Lower Tugela "suspicious." Typically, these suspicious chiefs had not proved particularly helpful to or communicative with government officials in the government's crackdown. Three of them—Ntshingumuzi, Xekwana, and Ngqokwana—ended up being deposed just as Meseni and Ndlovu had been.[56] In any event, failure to rebel did not necessarily indicate support for the state; it could just as likely have resulted from fear of the state. This fear proved to be well founded: during the rebellion between three and four thousand African rebels were killed, but only thirty Europeans and six African "loyalists."[57]

Crucially, those who deserted to the rebel side were rejecting individual patriarchs—homestead heads, headmen, and chiefs—and not patriarchy in general, for they sought the leadership and ritual power of elders instead of trying to go it alone. The unambiguously loyalist chiefs in Mapumulo and Lower Tugela—notably Swayimana, Mahlubi, and Nyakana—did not flee the area, but stayed, huddling during the violent week of 2–8 July 1906, in the protection of the magistrate's office "with the few loyal adherents they had." The "few loyal adherents" of these chiefs were exceptions, as their chiefdoms suffered massive desertions. Though the vast majority of those who left were young men, many were elders. In fact, elders from the two chiefdoms—among them relatives and headmen of both Swayimana and Mahlubi—played a prominent role in the exodus, recruiting, assembling, and leading of the rebels to Meseni's homestead, Emthandeni. One elder from Mahlubi's chiefdom was even "said to have had a hand in the preparation of the war medicines" there.[58] The men only left their chiefs because their chiefs refused to lead them into rebellion. Conversely, Meseni's attraction lay primarily in his willingness to assume the mantle that the young men were thrusting on him. As one government informant put it,

> I have heard that Swaimana's people have tried to get their Chief to join them, but that he refused; he said he was a man of the Government and would not be concerned in their matters, and that they all said, "Very well, as he is a white man at heart, we will have nothing more to do with him, we will go over to the Chief who is prepared to take action against the white people." . . . I heard that [the Enkwenkwezini Qwabe] said they had long been waiting for someone to appear who would be a leader against the white people, and now that Messeni had become a leader they were going to join him.[59]

If their own chiefs were not going to stand up to the colonial state, then the rebels—young and old alike—would find another chief who would.

For all their rebelliousness, young men in Mapumulo proved quite willing to cede control of the rebellion to their elders, once those elders had responded to the call to assume the rebellion's leadership. Swayimana and Mahlubi were not the only chiefs to see their headmen lead their young men to the rebel chiefs. Njubanjuba's Luthuli came to Emthandeni under the leadership of his headman Muntukaziwa.[60] Many young men among Xekwana's Nyuswa gathered at the homestead of Sikhotha—an elder in the chiefdom who had been jailed for failing to control the young men in his charge during their poll tax collection assembly in February—before heading off to join the rebels.[61] The Mbedu chief Ngqokwana's headman Mzwakili led men from that chiefdom to war-doctoring at the homestead of chief Ndlovu ka Thimuni, one of the main rebel leaders in Mapumulo besides Meseni.[62] With Gobizembe deposed, members of his Zulu-Ntuli chiefdom mobilized for rebellion under the leadership of his brother, the headman Sambela. Theirs was the last rebel detachment to be disposed of by government forces, eluding capture until 18 July 1906.[63] Enkwenkwezini Qwabe headmen allegedly coordinated rebel activity right under the nose of their chief, Magistrate Shuter of Lower Tugela.[64]

Once the rebels arrived at the homesteads of Meseni or Ndlovu for war-doctoring, the rebels found an operation likewise controlled by elders. Elders played a prominent role in the war-doctoring at Emthandeni, and one of Meseni's headmen was holding the same rituals at his own homestead.[65] Most important of all, Meseni and Ndlovu were themselves elders. Meseni was over fifty, and after the rebellion officials said both he and Ndlovu were suffering from "senile decay."[66] However much their people may have pushed them into it, for better or worse Meseni and Ndlovu *were* leaders. Both played a major role in inciting people, in their own chiefdom and in others, to join the rebellions and fight.

Elder participation in the 1906 rebellion was not confined to leadership positions. Of the more than 4,000 Natal Africans convicted and imprisoned for rebellion, 304 were released on account of sickness and old age, and some 400 were over fifty years old.[67] Of the 2,242 people convicted of rebellion in Mapumulo, Lower Tugela, and neighboring Ndwedwe division, 244 were over fifty.[68] That 10 percent of the captured rebels could be so old—and, it must be added, many below fifty years of age were hardly youths—is indicative of the broad cooperation between the generations and the sympathies that crossed the gulfs that otherwise separated them. Even European observers noted the significant number of "grey-headed kraal heads" and "middle-aged and older men" among the captives from Mapumulo and Ndwedwe. If youths nevertheless predominated among the rebels, this did not necessarily mean that the rebellion was a purely, or even overwhelmingly, youthful movement. The youths, after all, were the ones who were supposed to pay the poll tax. More important, however, the generational division of labor in late-twentieth and early-nineteenth-century Natal African society—or in virtually any society, for that matter—allotted warfare to young males.[69] In this respect, the 1906 rebellion was no different from any other war.

Many Natal Africans themselves blamed elders for acquiescing to youths' demands that they undertake what proved to be a futile and suicidal rebellion. In August 1906, in a letter to the editor of the African newspaper *Ilanga lase Natal*, one man said, "The country is dead, it was destroyed by the elders." He listed several reasons for believing this. First, "the first people who made evil suggestions to the young men were the elders." Second, the government explained the rationale behind the tax, "but even this the men would not accept, but assisted each other as the boys in objecting." Third, "their [the youths'] fathers drove them by permitting them; they encouraged their young men." The letter-writer concluded by saying, "It would be correct to say that the country was destroyed by the youths if, in this war, chiefs and elders had not been killed." That is, it would *not* be correct to say that the country was destroyed by youths, because the participation of the elders showed that the latter had forsaken their responsibility to control the youths.[70]

AN END TO FACTION FIGHTING

Zulu ethnicity and war-doctoring ceremonies with Dinuzulu's medicine healed rifts not only between young and old, but also between feuding chiefdoms. Over the previous twenty years, Meseni's Qwabe had been involved in faction fights with almost every other chiefdom in the area. For example, the cooperation of so many of Xekwana's Nyuswa with Meseni's Qwabe stood in stark contrast to the feuding that had prevailed between the two groups up to that time. Even many Nyuswa were unable to explain the turnabout to government officials.[71] The same was true of Swayimana's

Nyuswa and Ngqokwana's Mbedu. Observing that people from both chiefdoms attended the doctoring at Emthandeni, a government informant said,
"I cannot understand how it is that the people under Swaimana and Ngqokwana, who have been so unfriendly with Messeni's people, and have often
fought against them, should now be joined with them."[72] The headman who
led a detachment of Njubanjuba's Luthuli to Emthandeni presented Meseni
with Njubanjuba's spear and war badges as a gesture of reconciliation and a
sign that their chief supported them.[73]

Perhaps the most dramatic rapprochement, however, was that between
the various sections of the Qwabe chiefdom in Mapumulo and Lower Tugela:
the Emthandeni Qwabe under Meseni, the Enkwenkwezini Qwabe under the
resident magistrate Shuter in Lower Tugela, and the Qwabe section under
Mamfongonyana's successor, Ntshingumuzi. Even as late as April and May
1906, conflict between the different Qwabe sections seemed to outweigh and
preclude any threat of rebellion by them. The armed poll tax protests by
Meseni's subjects in early February coincided with continued fighting between members of the Emthandeni and Enkwenwkwezini.[74] In late May
there were rumors that "the Chief Messeni and Malumbo his brother [a
leading Enkwenkwezini headman] although at enmity on inter-tribal matters had arranged to allow mutual grievances to stand by, in order that they
and their people might watch and see how far the proceedings at Nkandhla
[Bhambatha's rebellion] went, and that it had been practically agreed between them that if the European forces suffered any reverse, then their people
were to join the revolt." Shuter reassured his colleagues, pointing out the
continued antagonism between the two sides. Although Malumbo and many
of his supporters had expressed some disappointment that Malumbo had
not been made regent for Siziba, this had not produced any conflict between
them and Shuter. According to Shuter, the Enkwenkwezini fully supported
his actions in excluding Meseni's jurisdiction from Lower Tugela, applauding
any move that deprived Meseni of a foothold there. They allegedly referred to
Meseni as an umthakathi, or witch, and testified against him in the trials
stemming from the feuds between Meseni's Qwabe and Swayimana's Nyuswa
chiefdom, which led to the government depriving Meseni of any authority
over or claim to subjects in Lower Tugela. In May 1906, Malumbo had even
informed against Meseni, accusing him of trying to send messengers to
Dinuzulu in Zululand. In sum, an alliance of the warring Qwabe factions
seemed out of the question.[75]

In June, before and during the rebellion in Mapumulo, government informants gave similarly conflicting reports. One rumor spoke of an alliance between the men of chiefs Cakijana (the Lower Tugela chief, not to be confused with Bhambatha's right-hand man) and Ntshingumuzi in Lower Tugela. These men were supposedly also "in communication with the people of Meseni and F. P. Shuter, with an eye toward the ideal unification of their peoples."[76] Another rumor had it that Meseni and his subjects had alternately threatened and courted two leading Enkwenkwezini headmen—Mabilwana and Meseni's brother Malumbo—but had failed to persuade them to join the rebellion.[77] According to another, Meseni was "waiting until the whole of the Qwabe tribe [had] collected, including those under Tshingamuzi [Ntshingumuzi]."[78] Yet another said that men from the other sections of the Qwabe chiefdom already were at Emthandeni.

> A number of that section of the Qwabe Tribe under Mr. Shuter had also arrived at Messeni's kraal. I heard that they said they had long been waiting for someone to appear who would be a leader against the white people, and now that Messeni had become a leader, they were going to join him. It was stated that more were coming. It was said that companies were also coming from the other section of the Qwabe Tribe under Tshingumuzi to Messeni's kraal.[79]

At first, officials saw no reason to doubt the loyalty of the Enkwenkwezini, and were even inclined to reward them accordingly. After all, magistrate Shuter in Lower Tugela had only convicted four Enkwenkwezini of rebellion, and Mabilwana had come to Shuter's office on 25 June to provide intelligence about the rebels. Even the government's own intelligence pointed to Enkwenkwezini loyalty. In the immediate aftermath of the rebellion, officials sent an African spy undercover to scout the Enkwenkwezini territory in Lower Tugela. The spy did so, even meeting Malumbo and another ranking Enkwenkwezini headman, Gadeni. Everybody seemed loyal and things were quiet. In fact, members of the chiefdom assumed the spy was a rebel and took him prisoner, freeing him only when he produced his badges. The Enkwenkwezini headmen told him they had searched the bush for rebels but had found none. They assured the spy that if they ever found any, they would immediately take them to the magistrate's office in Stanger. As the spy was leaving, the headmen told him to pledge allegiance on their behalf to the officers in charge of the police and militia. With all this evidence of Enkwenkwezini loyalty, the Compensation Board was inclined to look favorably on Enkwenkwezini appeals for compensation for livestock lost to government and rebel forces. Between July and October 1906, the board awarded 269 head of cattle to 27 Enkwenkwezini men, and 130 goats and 2 sheep to 13 members of that section.[80]

Government hearings held in October 1906, however, cast doubt on the loyalty of the Enkwenkwezini. Officials brought in twelve witnesses to testify that large numbers of Enkwenkwezini had rebelled. They had all seen Enkwenkwezini either at the doctoring at Emthandeni, or leaving for Mapumulo, armed, during the rebellion, or both. They not only accused Mabilwana and several Enkwenkwezini under him of participating in the rebellion, but also said that Mabilwana had actually worked for Meseni as a spy. Those residing in Lower Tugela also testified that Malumbo and Gadeni had received a message from Meseni calling for them to assemble their men and proceed to Emthandeni. Malumbo and Gadeni had done so, and even brought along a black bull to ritually slaughter to further cement the reconciliation between the two sections. On the way to Emthandeni, however, they ran into rebels fleeing the government crackdown that began on 3 July. Hearing of the debacle, the Enkwenkwezini promptly returned to their lands in Lower Tugela. The witnesses also accused the Enkwenkwezini of widely sheltering rebels, including subjects of Meseni, many of whom had come with their cattle to escape not only arrest, but the government's punitive cattle confiscations, as well.[81]

Further hearings in the first months of 1907 reversed virtually all the Compensation Board awards to the Enkwenkwezini. One witness against the Enkwenkwezini was Meseni himself. He testified that Mabilwana had come to Emthandeni "with a large contingent of armed rebels" from the Enkwenkwezini section. Mabilwana and another Enkwenkwezini headman "brought a black goat with them which they slaughtered and the contents of the bladder were sprinkled round me [Meseni]." Then the Enkwenkwezini under Mabilwana fought at Payana on 27 June. Mabilwana disappeared afterward. During Mabilwana's absence, Meseni heard that he had acted as a spy at the government offices in Stanger, telling magistrate Shuter that Meseni "was preparing to come down and burn up the place." When Mabilwana returned to Emthandeni, Meseni "rebuked him" and accused him of being a spy, a charge which Mabilwana denied. The government's star witness, however, was Meseni's subject Zwezinye, who had been present at Emthandeni during the "doctoring" there. Time and again, Zwezinye testified that certain individuals who had been awarded compensations had actually been at Emthandeni for the "doctoring" themselves. The usual result was that Shuter rescinded the awards those individuals had earlier been granted.[82]

At first glance it might seem that the charges against the Enkwenkwezini were fabricated, but on closer examination it becomes apparent that there is good reason for believing the testimony of their accusers. It is true that testimony such as this must be read with some caution, for, as Marks points out, there were numerous cases in which rebels tried to exact revenge on loyalists by accusing them of participation in the rebellion.[83] After all, Meseni and the other Emthandeni, after more than fifteen years of feuding, had every reason to bring the Enkwenkwezini down with them. However, it was not only Emthandeni testimony that cast doubt on Enkwenkwezini loyalty. Rumors of their disloyalty had predated the rebellion. After the rebellion, officials became suspicious when they noted that, during the initial rebel trials, testimony exonerating Enkwenkwezini suspected of rebellion usually came from Enkwenkwezini headmen. The officials also discovered that many Enkwenkwezini had withheld information during questioning, damaging the credibility of the testimony they had presented to exonerate themselves or other Enkwenkwezini.[84] Most damaging to the Enkwenkwezini case, however, was the testimony of the twelve witnesses at the hearing in October. Six of the witnesses, it is true, had been subjects of Meseni, but three were subjects of other chiefs, one was an Indian storekeeper living among the Enkwenkwezini in Lower Tugela, and two were even Enkwenkwezini themselves.[85]

Ultimately, the charges against the Enkwenkwezini were probably true precisely because officials had no other reason to side with the Enkwenkwezini's accusers. Marks herself concedes that while officials could often be duped into believing false charges of rebellion, there were also cases in which officials "saw through" such fabrications.[86] She also concludes that attempts to implicate loyalists in the rebellion "were most successful when their [the conspirators'] ambitions coincided with the desires of the magistrate and the European population."[87] The relationship between the Emthandeni and Magistrate Shuter, however, had been one of almost pure conflict. Shuter therefore had little reason to sympathize with the Emthandeni, lending even greater credibility to his judgment that many Enkwenkwezini had, in fact, rebelled.

The poll tax rebels used ritual to render the divisions of prevailing local politics irrelevant. The fact that people from so many different chiefdoms set aside their feuds with Meseni's Qwabe and united with them in rebellion provides dramatic counter-evidence against Marks's argument that, "at the level of final commitment to armed rebellion, it was the minutiae of local-level politics which seemed to tip the balance."[88] Njubanjuba's spear and badges, and the black goat that was ritually slaughtered, and even the contents of the slaughtered goat's bladder, which the Enkwenkwezini allegedly sprinkled around Meseni, all served to ritually cement a union between former enemies. In the process, the rebels managed to liberate themselves from the burden of the past and the social conflicts they had inherited.

TRADITIONALISTS AND CHRISTIANS DURING THE REBELLION

The final social conflict that the ideology of Zulu ethnic unity overcame, along with conflict between youth and elders and between feuding chiefdoms, was that between African traditionalists (amabhinca) and African Christians (amakholwa). Natal African Christians had always had, at best, an ambiguous relationship both with other Natal Africans and with the Zulu kings. Much as many African Christians had embraced the new Zulu ethnicity emerging around the rumors regarding Dinuzulu, many also embraced the 1906 rebellion, steeped as it was in Zulu ethnicity. Similarly, much as many of the earlier rumors accorded some African Christians a prominent place alongside traditionalists in Dinuzulu's new order, during the rebellion traditionalists did the same. But while some Natal Christian Africans embraced the rebellion, others went to great lengths to distance themselves from it and to impress the colonial state with their loyalty, although opposition to the rebellion did not necessarily translate into a lack of self-identification with the rebels, both politically and ethnically. And while some rebels brought Christians into their movement, others targeted them for attack.

In Mapumulo, during the months of maneuvering on both sides that preceded the rebellion's brief but violent denouement, there seemed to be both rebel and loyalist amakholwa. One African, who was both a Christian and a government informant, told officials, "The rebels say that we kolwas were the first to pay hut tax and poll tax and therefore we will be the first to be killed." Similarly, in late June 1906, John Hlonono, pastor of the Ameri-

can Zulu Mission (AZM) station at Emushane, in the heart of Qwabe country, reported being threatened by the rebels then assembling at Meseni's
homestead. On the other hand, another Christian African government informant reported that Meseni denied ordering the killing of Hlonono and
other amakholwa. Other informants said some amakholwa were not only
joining the rebels, but even leading some of their detachments.[89] During the
rebellion, one of its leaders, Chief Ndlovu ka Thimuni, the same man who
just a few years earlier had expressed rather negative feelings about Christianity, prevented his men from killing a Norwegian missionary. Afterward,
"he strongly urged his people and sons to become Christians and exhorted
them to acquire a Western education."[90]

Despite the months of waiting, the final conflagration came so unexpect-
edly and was over so quickly that it was difficult to determine just who had
rebelled and who had remained loyal. It was particularly difficult for the
AZM, for by 1906 not a single one of its stations in Mapumulo had a resident
American missionary. Early, garbled reports suggested that there had been
mass defections from the AZM stations to the rebel side, with only the
African preachers in charge and a handful of their followers remaining
loyal. Afterward, however, it became apparent that it only seemed that way
because so many people had fled their homes and sought refuge in the bush
on hearing that hostilities had broken out. The American missionaries
retracted their initial, panicked statements, which had received wide cir-
culation in the Natal press, and said the vast majority of AZM amakholwa
had, in fact, remained loyal. Settlers and colonial officials in Natal, however,
had developed a deep mistrust of the AZM even before the poll tax was
introduced. In particular, they doubted the loyalty of the republican Americans to the British monarch, and they disliked the organization's policy of
leaving so many of its stations without resident white missionaries. Natal's
settlers were not inclined to believe the AZM's retraction, and colonial officials conducted hearings into the matter.[91]

Numerous African witnesses, including both rebels and loyalists, who had
been in Mapumulo during the rebellion attested to the participation of
amakholwa in the rebellion. A loyalist chief contradicted the American
missionaries: "I say the Amakolwa did rebel." He named eight of his Christian subjects who fought government forces in one battle, four of whom had
died. One of the dead had been a pastor in a local independent African
Christian church: "[He] prayed with the impi [rebel force] . . . [and] died

with his Bible in his hand." Of the other seven, the chief said one belonged to the Church of England, called another an "Ethiopian" (a member of an African Christian church independent of missionary control), and noted that a third had a Bible in his pocket. Another witness, Elijah, the headman of the AZM station at Noodsberg, in Mapumulo, listed thirty-seven men from his station who had participated in the rebellion. Of these, twenty had been convicted of rebellion, two had been killed in battle, three were now at their homes, one was in prison untried, and eleven were still unaccounted for. John Hlonono was a third witness, and he told officials that twenty residents of his mission station at Emushane were rebels, of whom twelve had been sentenced and eight were still at large. The government's fourth witness, Billy Mkwanazi, testified to Christian participation at Esidumbini, the AZM's third station in Mapumulo. Unlike Elijah or Hlonono, Mkwanazi was subject to a chief, not a Christian headman. In fact, he was a high-ranking official in his chiefdom, despite being Christian. He named seventy-two Christian rebels from Esidumbini, including twenty-nine subjects of the Christian headman and forty-three subjects of traditionalist chiefs. Together, these four witnesses identified 137 Mapumulo amakholwa as rebels.[92]

The Qwabe chief Meseni, who had been the most prominent rebel leader, after being captured by government forces testified that, besides traditional healers and diviners, four African Christian preachers attended to the rebels under him. The chief preacher was Selby Msome, a Wesleyan subject of Meseni's who ran a church and a school in the chiefdom. It was because Msome was Wesleyan that the AZM, five years before, had refused Meseni's request for permission to let Msome use one of the AZM's abandoned school buildings. During the rebellion, Msome held Christian services early every morning at Meseni's homestead, where the rebels had gathered. A second preacher, named July, had earlier been a Wesleyan himself, but renounced missionary control, assumed the leadership of a group of "Ethiopians," and ran a large school. The third preacher working for Meseni during the rebellion also worked at July's school. The fourth preacher came from the American mission station at Esidumbini, situated, like the AZM's station at Emushane, in largely Qwabe territory.[93]

On 26 February 1907, Natal's minister for native affairs and undersecretary for native affairs held an interview with two American missionaries who presented the AZM's case. The Americans put forth evidence that only nine out of the forty-seven men on the church roll at Esidumbini were alleged to have rebelled, eight of forty-two at Noodsberg, one at Emushane, and none at Mapumulo. When asked to explain the discrepancy between these figures and those given by the other witnesses, including three AZM amakholwa, the missionaries argued that the witnesses' definition of "Christian" had been too broad. The witnesses had included in their testimony any men who had been involved with the AZM, and even some affiliated with other mission organizations or independent African churches. The missionaries, however, included only "communicants": men (in this case) who had been baptized by a recognized authority but had not violated church discipline or left the church, in other words the men listed on the AZM rolls as church members. As one missionary said, "We cannot hold ourselves responsible for every man who puts on trousers and who lives on the Station—only those who have joined the Church and thus show that they submit themselves to our teaching." The other added, "Two-thirds of those who live on the stations are heathen and live in kraals. . . . But is it fair that these impressions should go out regarding our Mission having these men, many of whom are heathen? We have no control over any who are not communicants."[94] Perhaps it was the missionaries' expressed insistence on a distinction between "communicants" and "adherents" that inspired somebody to go back to the translated testimony of one witness and replace the word "Amakolwas" with "adherents."[95]

When AZM missionaries and amakholwa revised the lists compiled by the government from the witnesses' testimony, they grouped the undifferentiated "Christians" into several categories, revealing the diversity of relations between Africans and the AZM. For example, of eighty-eight alleged Christian rebels from Esidumbini who were subjects of traditionalist chiefs, nineteen were polygamists. Another fourteen were not polygamists, but still dressed in an African manner. Twenty-one men dressed in a European manner, but had no schooling. One man had schooling, but was not a church member. Another belonged to the Wesleyan church, not the AZM. Only eleven of the eighty-eight were AZM church members. Of thirty-seven alleged Christian rebels from Noodsberg, only eleven were church members, including two who were later acquitted and one who was listed twice. Of the others, six were "dressed men" who never went to church, seven were "dressed men" who went to church but were not members (including one who had been expelled from the AZM "long ago"), six attended only irregularly, five belonged to independent African churches, and one was unclassified.[96]

Africans, both Christian and traditionalist, had a broader understanding of the term *amakholwa*, and therefore of Christian involvement, than the missionaries did. When government officials asked African witnesses to name the amakholwa who had rebelled, the Africans included in their lists everybody who worshipped Jesus Christ: mission church members, but also those more casually involved in mission Christianity, as well as "Ethiopians." It was the American missionaries, not the Africans, who insisted on making finer distinctions. Those finer distinctions were not irrelevant to Africans, but clearly both traditionalists and amakholwa were ecumenical enough to consider as Christians all who professed to be. The anti-poll tax movement in Mapumulo did not exclude the multifarious Christianity that had developed there, but incorporated every stream of it, including the mission variety.

CONCLUSION

The prominent place of both chiefship and Zulu ethnicity in the African responses to the poll tax should not be taken as an indication that African popular ideology at this point was simply "traditional." Shula Marks argues that the Natal Africans who protested the poll tax "were restorationist rather than 'revolutionary': they desired to 'recreate the past' rather than capture the future." The rebellion failed because of "the continuing validity of the earlier 'moral universe' of the peasantry: in Zululand . . . this was still tied to the hegemonic ideology of the Zulu royal family, and this was beginning to permeate Natal. In Natal itself, the Shepstone system which bolstered chiefly authority may have acted as a buffer against the acceptance of alternative ideologies, while in some sense paving the way for a recreation even in Natal of royal ideology."[97] Marks adds, "At the level of final commitment to armed rebellion, it was the minutiae of local-level politics which seemed to tip the balance."[98] And yet local-level politics had been characterized by feuding, whereas the rebellion and the protests that preceded it often united people who had been feuding months, even weeks, before. In the same way, local-level politics tells us why some Natal Africans were willing to fight on the British side in the Anglo-Zulu War of 1879, but not why some of those same people, or at least their children or grandchildren, were willing to rebel against the British in the name of the Zulu king twenty-seven years later. Far from limiting the spread of the rebellion throughout Natal, chiefship and Zulu royal ideology—both greatly changed over the

preceding years—united Africans throughout the colony. While both chiefship and Zulu ethnicity have come to be associated, often rightly, with
conservatism and acceptance of the status quo, this was one instance (there
would be others) where both ideas challenged prevailing power structures.

A close examination of the poll tax protests shows that the protestors'
ideology was actually very *un*-traditional, very new, and that the "earlier
moral universe" of Natal's African peasants had not survived unchanged.
The spread of Zulu ethnicity, for example, showed that Natal Africans'
attitudes toward the Zulu kings had changed dramatically. Similarly, the
young men who formed the bulk of the protestors, partly because it was
they who had to pay the new tax, rejected colonial rule but not wage labor
or mission Christianity. At the same time, while these young men exerted
tremendous pressure on their elders to support their protests, the young
men did not reject, much less attack, either chiefship or patriarchy in general. Thus Benedict Carton's argument that the rebellion was "an expression
of [young men's] rage" not only "against the poll or 'head' tax," but also
against "the prevailing exemplars of patriarchy"—in short, that the rebellion was an intergenerational civil war as much as it was an anticolonial
rebellion—is simply not supported by the evidence.[99] It is true that the tax
was imposed only on unmarried adult males, and that young men predominated in the collective reactions against it, and even that some conflict
occurred between African elders and youths. But a detailed examination of
the minutiae of local politics in the period from the promulgation of the
poll tax in August 1905 to the final quashing of the revolt in July 1906 reveals
extensive cooperation between elders and youths. In fact, intergenerational
cooperation—and indeed the young protestors' continued acceptance of
generational hierarchies even in the context of rebellion—was so widespread as to suggest that youths came into conflict with certain elders
because those elders were "loyalists" and not because they were elders.
Much as the generational interpretation fails to explain the phenomenon of
"faction fighting," in which African youths fought each other in the name of
their respective patriarchs, it also fails to explain why the young poll tax
rebels assembled at chiefly homesteads under the leadership of chiefs and
other elders. Indeed, as with the rumors about Dinuzulu, what is striking
about the protests against the poll tax is the degree to which so many of the
divisions and conflicts among Natal Africans—between different generations, classes, genders, chiefdoms, and religions—could be set aside, even if
only temporarily.

Close attention to both the ideology and the local politics surrounding the poll tax protests also helps to explain the patterns of participation. The content of the rumors that preceded the rebellion calls into question two common arguments about the rebellion itself: first, that it had the support of only a narrow section (geographically or generationally defined) of Natal's African population, and second, that it was a "reluctant" rebellion, and perhaps not even a rebellion at all. Yet Natal Africans of all walks of life throughout the colony spoke of the rebellion approvingly for years before the poll tax was even promulgated. Nevertheless, it is true that the protests, and especially the armed rebellion, were limited to a small minority. As James Scott and others have pointed out, what needs explaining is not the failure of most people to rebel, but rather the willingness of an always small minority to rebel in the face of the overwhelming might of the state.[100]

The problem is that, at first glance, the particular circumstances of the rebels would seem to have predisposed them *against* rebelling. There were three main outbreaks of violence: in Richmond in the Natal midlands, in the middle Thukela Valley, and in the lower Thukela Valley. The first outbreak was very small—involving only some twenty-seven Africans—and arguably provoked rather than planned. The second outbreak, under the leadership of the Zondi chief Bhambatha, has gained the most notoriety, partly because it was the first overt act of armed rebellion initiated by Africans themselves, and partly also because the rebels in this case managed to hold out against government forces for two months. Indeed, the rebellion is most commonly known as Bhambatha's rebellion, except among Zulu-speakers themselves, who referred to it then and continue to refer to it now as Impi yamaKhanda (War of the Heads, the poll tax being known in Zulu as a "head tax"). The alternative appellation suggests that the prominence that historians and others have attributed to this second outbreak of violence is misplaced. Bhambatha's rebellion never involved more than 2,000 soldiers, and Bhambatha was a minor chief in terms of both the size and the historical prestige of his chiefdom. In contrast, the third outbreak of violence involved as many as 8,000 soldiers, and its leaders, Meseni and Ndlovu, were chiefs of the highly prestigious Qwabe chiefdom and of a breakaway section of the Zulu royal family, respectively.[101] But all three rebellions were limited to Natal proper, with the exception of Bhambatha's brief excursion into Zululand. Moreover, the Qwabe in particular had a history of conflict with the Zulu kings, and it was the Thukela Valley chiefdoms that had furnished the most enthusiastic British recruits in the 1879 war against the Zulus. Finally, it was those same Thukela Valley chiefdoms that had seen the most faction fighting in the years leading up to the 1906 rebellion. On the face of it, it seemed highly unlikely that rebels from these chiefdoms could achieve even the smattering of unity they did achieve, and also unlikely that these people would come out in favor of Dinuzulu.

That so many people from the Thukela Valley chiefdoms in Natal *did* rebel in Dinuzulu's name can be put down to the unique interplay of geography, economics, and culture in this particular region. The Thukela Valley was relatively arid, infertile, remote from the colony's main markets, and yet at the same time relatively thickly populated by Africans. These factors made the area unattractive to Natal's European settlers and therefore ideal for being demarcated as reserve land for Natal's Africans. The Thukela Valley reserves became some of the most overcrowded in Natal, supplying the Africans there with an unusually thick catalogue of grievances. Those same geographical and economic realities pushed Thukela Valley Africans into migrant labor—especially in Johannesburg—to a larger extent than Africans from any other part of Natal. In Johannesburg, those who came from the middle Thukela Valley largely became watermen, while those from the lower Thukela Valley became policemen. More important, on the Rand these people became Zulus, and when they returned, they played a major role in circulating rumors of an imminent rebellion under Dinuzulu's leadership. Finally, in the lower Thukela Valley, as in few other parts of Natal and Zululand, those rumors actually came true, and the rebellion was larger there than anywhere else.[102]

EPILOGUE

Ever since the political unification of South Africa under white rule in 1910, ethnic politics (as opposed to racial politics) has been more popular among Zulus than among any other African ethnic group in the country. This would not have been the case had it not been for the transformation I have discussed here, what might be called the "Zuluization" of Natal Africans. Without these changes, appeals to Zulu ethnicity would not have resonated among Africans in Natal proper, the most heavily populated half of the province of Natal (now KwaZulu-Natal) and the home of the province's two main cities, Durban and Pietermaritzburg. And yet they have. But while the "grand tradition" of the Zulus has thrived to this day, what the historian Paul La Hausse has called the "little traditions" of the various Zulu chiefdoms, such as the Qwabe, have been repressed, though not entirely forgotten.[1] One is reminded of the Breton-French philosopher Ernest Renan's famous lecture "What Is a Nation?" in which he said, "The essential element of a nation is that all its individuals must have many things in common but it must also have forgotten many things." In the case of the French nation, Renan said it had to forget "things" such as the St. Bartholomew's Day Massacre of 1572, the thirteenth-century massacres in the South, and the decidedly mixed and un-Frankish ancestry of the French people.[2] In the case of the Zulus, Renan could have made the same points about Shaka's and Dingane's massacres of the Qwabe and others, not to mention the Zulus' own diverse origins. These traditions survive, barely, in the rural areas, but are not to be found in the Zulu history curriculum of primary and secondary schools. Nor are most Zulus even aware of this history, or at least willing to admit that it exists.

This is not to say that Zulu ethnic consciousness has entirely repressed conflicts among Zulus, though one could be forgiven for thinking so in the face of the relentless—and understandable—rhetoric of Zulu and indeed pan-African unity that one finds even in conversations with ordinary people. Zulu ethnicity is thus one of those hegemonic concepts that all Zulus accept. Indeed, almost every case of popular political mobilization in KwaZulu-Natal in the century since the Zulu rebellion of 1906 has involved heavy use of Zulu symbols. For an African in KwaZulu-Natal to reject Zulu ethnicity would be akin to an American burning the American flag: the blasphemy of the act is enough to repel even those who might be otherwise sympathetic to the motivations behind it.

As a hegemonic idea, Zulu ethnicity has meant many different things to many different people, but it has not been infinitely malleable. Most important, nobody has quite been able to disassociate Zulu ethnicity from support for age-old social and political hierarchies: king/chief and subject, elder and youth, man and woman. One of the main reasons for this is the continued relevance of the dynamic I have highlighted in this book: even those who have used Zulu ethnicity to challenge power hierarchies have at the same time reaffirmed them. This was certainly true of young men in the late nineteenth century and early twentieth, and it has continued to be true since. Even women, who played such a marginal role in the propagation of the new Zulu ethnicity in 1906 and before, have embraced Zulu ethnicity more and more in their collective political actions, but those actions have had highly ambiguous consequences for gender relations.

Perhaps it was precisely the strongly hierarchical and patriarchal implications of Zulu ethnicity that led to its being championed in the twentieth century by two groups of people once strongly opposed to it: middle-class African Christians (kholwa) and whites. We have already seen how, in the 1890s and early 1900s, more and more of the kholwa began to embrace Zulu ethnicity and traditionalism at the same time as whites began to question the value of the "civilizing mission" that was supposed to make "black English-men" out of the "natives." The creation of the white-dominated Union of South Africa, in 1910, was followed by a long string of segregationist legislation of ever-increasing severity. On a national level, the black Christian elite responded by organizing the South African Native National Congress, which later became the African National Congress (ANC). From the beginning, the congress was torn by a tension between militancy and conservatism, not least because the businessmen and professionals who made up its leadership had their own privileges that they wanted to maintain. This tendency was particularly strong in Natal, where prominent kholwa political leaders like John Dube and George Champion tried to secure the independence of the Natal branches of national organizations like the ANC and the Industrial and Commercial Workers Union (ICU). Dube played a major role in one of the earliest iterations of the Inkatha movement. The name "Inkatha" itself was significant, for it referred to the grass coil that was the symbol of both the Zulu king and the unity of the Zulu nation. In the process, Dube and other members of Natal's kholwa elite forged an alliance with the Zulu king Solomon ka Dinuzulu and the chiefs of Natal.

The kholwa alliance with the Zulu king was in many ways facilitated by changes in white political attitudes on both the national and local levels. Nationally, the first constitution of the Union of South Africa created a separate "Native Administration" with authority over Africans superseding that of other national ministries or provincial governments. It also made the governor-general of South Africa the "Supreme Chief" over all Africans. The 1927 Native Administration Act provided for official government recognition of chiefs and customary law. In effect, union led to the implementation of the Shepstone system on a national scale. Within Natal, prominent whites such as J. S. Marwick, Charles Wheelwright, G. Heaton Nicholls, G. Hulett, and William Campbell came to the conclusion that government recognition of the supremacy of the Zulu king over the other chiefs in Natal would ensure social stability. Each of these men straddled the boundaries between the national Native Affairs Department (NAD), national and provincial parliaments, and the sugar industry, one of the most important sectors of Natal's economy. They thus had both the motivation and means to go a long way toward realizing this goal, and Solomon and his successors certainly proved willing to cooperate. Though official recognition would only come in 1950, during the reign of Solomon's son Cyprian, NAD officials were effectively treating Solomon as Zulu king by the early 1930s, if not before. Many of these whites also encouraged and worked closely with the kholwa involved in the Inkatha movements.[3]

Other, lesser-known, kholwa activists and intellectuals also promoted Zulu ethnicity and were just as influential with the rank and file as were Dube and Champion and the like, but came from even more ambiguous social positions. After all, as privileged as Dube and Champion were, they were also victims of the racist social and political order. Some of their kholwa contemporaries, like Petros Lamula and Lymon Maling, were much poorer, so much so as to call into question the meaningfulness of categories like "middle class" and "elite" in their cases. They were literate Christians and in some ways and at certain points in their lives better off economically than the average black South African, but the difference was marginal and their alienation from other blacks minimal. Indeed, during their careers in the early twentieth century there was a seismic shift in Zulu society, as widespread conversion to Christianity enabled African Christians to gain parity with and ultimately outnumber "traditionalists." As Zulus became a majority Christian people, the distinctiveness of the kholwa class diminished. This both facilitated and was facilitated by the kholwa embrace and promotion of Zulu ethnicity. In effect, at the same time as Zulus became Christians, Christian Africans were becoming Zulus. Lamula, Maling, and other African Christians like them were missionaries of both Christianity and Zulu-ness, doing the sort of highly local meeting and greeting that was key to the success of their proselytizing. But while their attitudes toward authority, and especially white authority, were even more ambiguous than Dube's or Champion's, both Lamula's and Maling's visions of Zulu ethnicity and tradition affirmed the supremacy of the chief and the elder, the husband and the father.[4] Lamula's and Maling's careers could be seen as continuations of the kholwa embrace of Zulu ethnicity by poor, rural Christian adherents and ministers who strongly sympathized with, and in some cases even participated in, the rebellion of 1906.

In contrast to the kholwa, young African men in early-twentieth-century Natal did not leave behind copious and explicit statements about their attitudes toward Zulu ethnicity, chiefship, and patriarchy, but historical research has provided some hints. The activities of the Industrial and Commercial Workers' Union (ICU) in Natal from about 1925 to 1930 mobilized young African men politically to an extent not seen since the 1906 rebellion. Not surprisingly, the ICU-organized protests that occurred in Durban and elsewhere in 1929 and 1930 showed strong continuities with earlier protests. Not only did the protestors, mainly young men, refer directly and often to the 1906 rebellion, but they used many of the same symbols: the image of the Zulu king, the ubushokobezi war badges, the Usuthu war cry, and so on.[5] In addition to the evidence of a continued commitment to Zulu ethnicity in the context of popular protest, it is also clear that the gendered and generational conflicts of the late 1800s continued well into the twentieth century, and followed many of the same patterns.[6] But up to this point, historians studying these episodes have focused on conflict between youths and the colonial states and elders. They have not considered the degree to which young men might have continued to be invested in chiefship and patriarchy. Nevertheless, they have shown that the ICU's courting of chiefly support was very popular with the union's rank and file, and the young men's support for the union ebbed precisely when the Zulu king and the chiefs distanced themselves from the ICU, partly because of pressure from the government.[7] They have also shown that women's participation in the ICU was limited, sometimes actively so by men.[8] And even today it is quite common even for young, unmarried African men to justify their patriarchal relations with women by appeals to "Zulu tradition."[9]

Women's commitment to Zulu ethnicity, "tradition," patriarchy, and generational privilege, even while engaged in protest and "rebellious behavior," has been even more striking than young men's. Though women were distinctly marginalized within the ICU, many still joined the union, or at least its Women's Auxiliary. Their most notable involvement was in the 1929–30 beer boycott, of particular interest to women since they wanted to boycott beer sold at government-controlled beerhalls, which competed with African home brew, produced and sold largely by women. But for all the gender conflict that existed at the time between African men and African women, the women involved in the boycott went to great lengths to reassure African men of their own commitment to "traditional" patriarchy. As La Hausse has put it, "Inscribed within the radicalism of these women's beer protests lay a conservative impulse: an attempt to restitute imagined female roles in an older social order."[10] As the ICU started rapidly disintegrating in 1930, many women active in that movement switched their focus to stopping the epidemic of out-of-wedlock births among young women. The result was the Bantu Purity League, which steeped itself in the trappings of Zulu ethnicity and saw young women's salvation in a return to "traditional" morality, including obedience to patriarchal authority. At the same time, two of the League's most prominent figures, Sibusisiwe Violet Makhanya and Bertha Mkhize, were unmarried women who were not afraid to be confrontational in their dealings with African men.[11] The same combination of women's self-assertion with an affirmation of patriarchy and Zulu ethnicity is obvious today in the activities of the Inkatha Women's

Brigade and in Nomagugu Ngobese's Nomkhubulwane Culture and Youth Development Organisation, devoted to the worship of the Zulu goddess Nomkhubulwane, but also noted for its promotion of virginity testing.[12]

Many of the scholars who have studied the interplay of Zulu ethnic politics and Zulu women's movements have been keen to emphasize that acceptance or even promotion of patriarchy has coexisted with the same women's continued self-assertion. One might go further and suggest that the Zulu women involved in these movements have strategically used patriarchy and Zulu ethnicity as a way of selling men on women's exercise of authority, just as young men did in the period I have examined in this book. Further research into women's and men's attitudes on these issues would be very illuminating on this topic. One might also wonder whether young men have been using patriarchy and Zulu ethnicity for the same purposes more recently. There was, after all, a strong generational component in the conflict between Inkatha and the ANC during the 1980s and early 1990s, with elders being associated with Inkatha and youth with the ANC. As a result, the ANC worked very hard to establish its Zulu ethnic credentials while at the same time using CONTRALESA (the Congress of Traditional Leaders of South Africa) as a means of drawing chiefs away from Inkatha. This strategy certainly worked in two key arenas: electoral politics, which saw the ANC become the leading party even in KwaZulu-Natal, in 1999, and Zulu kingship, where King Goodwill Zwelethini has drifted away from Buthelezi and increasingly, though not entirely, into the orbit of the ANC.[13] Further research on popular political consciousness might show whether the same sorts of strategies were employed by the ANC's youthful supporters in their conflicts with elders who supported Inkatha. Certainly the writings of workers themselves have shown that a wide range of political positions have been articulated through reference to the symbols of Zulu ethnicity.[14] Indeed, one wonders whether it would be possible for political action to be successful in KwaZulu-Natal, even today, without a substantial appeal to Zulu-ness.

All this suggests not only that Zulu ethnicity continues to be highly hegemonic in popular political culture, but also that it will continue to be so for a long time to come. Being Zulu has done far better than has being Qwabe, Mthethwa, or what have you. Massive black urbanization, especially since the lifting of influx control in 1986, has led to the depopulation of the areas once known as reserves or locations, such as Mapumulo. The fact that so many South Africans prefer urban life, even at its most squalid, to rural life is indicative of the latter's extreme unattractiveness. Nevertheless, the more that Zulus and other black South Africans flee the rural areas, the more they seem to embrace rural life as a nostalgic ideal. In the urban areas, far from the sway of chiefs, this pastoral nostalgia tends to be linked with Zulu ethnicity. Identification with specific chiefdoms seems all but dead outside of the rural communal land tenure areas. Even there, though, it is open to debate how much legitimacy chiefs still have. They still have power, certainly, as arbiters in customary law proceedings and as administrators of land distribution within their chiefdoms, and they have fought hard to keep this power. As a result, a highly patriarchal and hierarchical political and legal regime continues to exist in communal land tenure areas, clashing quite glaringly with the democratic structure of South African government and law more generally. To the extent that the chiefs' subjects still support them, it is very difficult—even dangerous—for scholars or journalists to determine how much of that support derives from a fear of the chiefs' coercive power.[15]

In the end, though, it is clear that chiefship, and therefore chiefdom identification, in KwaZulu-Natal is gradually becoming irrelevant, as the chiefs lose more and more of their subjects to urban areas. African urbanization in KwaZulu-Natal has been around for well over a century. The difference is that now, with the decline of migrant labor, African urbanization —and the loss to the chiefs—is permanent. Most black South Africans no longer have to take chiefs into account in the micropolitics of their daily lives. The "little traditions" of the various chiefdoms are dying, so that to be "traditional" is now to be Zulu. Zulu's victory over Qwabe and the others is now almost complete.

Almost complete, but not entirely. In 2003, in response to various disputes between traditional leaders throughout South Africa, President Thabo Mbeki convened the Nhlapo Commission on Traditional Leadership Disputes and Claims. Among the issues to be resolved were the claims made by as many as twelve Zulu chiefs—most notably the Hlubi chief—that they were not subject to the Zulu king, and were in fact independent kings in their own rights. Several supporters of the Zulu king threatened violent action if such independence were ever established, either by the government or by the chiefs themselves. The commission's proceedings were highly contentious, and in late 2007, the commission's chair, Thandabantu Nhlapo, and two other academics, Jan Bekker and Jeff Peires, resigned, allegedly for personal reasons. On 30 April 2008, the commission released its findings. In the Zulu case, the commission maintained the status quo, concluding that Shaka had conquered all the chiefdoms of KwaZulu-Natal during his reign and that the Zulu kings had maintained authority over these territories ever since. The various events that had undermined Zulu supremacy—the Boer conquest of Natal, the British invasion of the Zulu kingdom and ouster of Cetshwayo, and later the British government's various legal actions against Dinuzulu—all were illegal according to the commission. The apartheid government's recognition, in 1950, of Cyprian as not only Zulu king but also as paramount chief over all the other chiefs of Natal, in the commission's opinion, nullified earlier actions by white-ruled governments that had said otherwise.[16] It remains to be seen whether this is indeed the end of the story.

৵৩৫

The Qwabe chiefly homestead Emthandeni still stands in Mapumulo, perched atop a tall hill overlooking a valley. Its cattle byre, however, is empty, and the overgrown grass and bushes inside indicate that the cattle are not merely out grazing: there have been no cattle at Emthandeni for a very long time. To the men who accompanied me on my visits to Emthandeni, that the head of such a large and prestigious chiefdom would have no cattle at his homestead could only mean one thing: that this chief was poor, indeed. The chief, a chubby man in his twenties named Makhosini ("the place of the kings"), had been recently nominated to succeed his father, but had not yet been formally installed. Though he said he knew very little about Qwabe history himself, he kindly arranged interviews with the senior Qwabe headman and a local schoolteacher, both of whom the chief considered authorities. From these men, I learned that Meseni's subjects had finally been able to wrest control and reestablish their independence from the Ngubane chief in the 1930s, after protracted appeals through the courts and the South African Native Administration. Meseni did not live to see the rebirth of his Qwabe chiefdom, however, because he died in exile on St. Helena in the 1910s. Unfortunately, the old divisions persisted, and there was still a plethora of Qwabe chiefdoms extending from Zululand to southern Natal, and the chiefs of some branches still claimed to be the rightful chiefs of others. Worse, there were indications that new divisions were emerging. I had to postpone my first trip to Emthandeni because the unresolved succession to the recently deceased chief might lead to fighting in the chiefdom.

NOTES

INTRODUCTION

1 Ranger, "The Invention of Tradition in Colonial Africa"; Ranger, "The Invention of Tradition Revisited"; Vail, *The Creation of Tribalism in Southern Africa*.

2 Weber, *Peasants into Frenchmen*.

3 For a large collection of short articles by numerous authors representing the broad scope of existing research on Zulu identity, see Carton, Laband, and Sithole, *Zulu Identities*.

4 Mzala, *Gatsha Buthelezi*; Maré and Hamilton, *An Appetite for Power*; Maré, *Ethnicity and Politics in South Africa*.

5 Marks, "Patriotism, Patriarchy, and Purity"; Marks, "Natal, the Zulu Royal Family, and the Ideology of Segregation"; Marks, *The Ambiguities of Dependence*; Cope, *To Bind the Nation*.

6 Sitas, "Class, Nation, Ethnicity in Natal's Black Working Class," 260–61.

7 La Hausse, *Restless Identities*, 6–7.

8 La Hausse, "The Message of the Warriors," esp. 30, 37; Bradford, *A Taste of Freedom*.

9 For the history of the nineteenth-century Zulu kingdom before and after the Anglo-Zulu War of 1879, see Jeff Guy's historical trilogy: *The Destruction of the Zulu Kingdom*; *The Heretic*; and *The View across the River*. More influential in my own conceptualization of the issues involved has been Guy, "Analysing the Pre-Capitalist Societies in Southern Africa." For more on internal disunity within the Zulu kingdom, see Laband, *Rope of Sand*; Laband, "The Cohesion of the Zulu Polity under the Impact of the Anglo-Zulu War."

10 See, among other writings, Hamilton, "Ideology, Oral Traditions, and the Struggle for Power in the Early Zulu Kingdom"; J. Wright, "The Dynamics of Power and Conflict in the Thukela-Mzimkhulu Region in the Late Eighteenth and Early Nineteenth Centuries"; Hamilton and Wright, "The Making of the AmaLala." Hamilton and Wright are currently working on a book that will synthesize their extensive research on precolonial KwaZulu-Natal.

11 Marks, *Reluctant Rebellion*.

12 Shula Marks, "Class, Ideology, and the Bambatha Rebellion"; Lambert, *Betrayed Trust*; Carton, *Blood from Your Children*; Guy, *The Maphumulo Uprising*.

13 Marks, "Class, Ideology, and the Bambatha Rebellion," 358. See also Marks, *Reluctant Rebellion*, 313–14.

14 Marks, "Class, Ideology, and the Bambatha Rebellion," 366–67.

15 Marks, "Patriotism, Patriarchy, and Purity"; Carton, *Blood from Your Children*; McClendon, *Genders and Generations Apart*; Bonnin, "Claiming Spaces, Changing Places"; Hassim, "Family, Motherhood, and Zulu Nationalism."

16 See the following works by Gluckman: *Analysis of a Social System in Modern Zululand*; "The Kingdom of the Zulu in South Africa"; *Custom and Conflict in Africa*; *Order and Rebellion in Tribal Africa*; and *Politics, Law, and Ritual in Tribal Society*. Similar ideas were developed by Victor Turner, who relied mainly on evidence from central Africa, as for example in *The Ritual Process*. In *Terror and Resistance*, a very interesting, though deeply flawed, analysis of the precolonial Zulu kingdom, E. V. Walter went so far as to argue that this was one case where high levels of both state violence and state legitimacy could coexist.

17 Wrong, *Power*; Kertzer, *Ritual, Politics, and Power*; Gramsci, *The Antonio Gramsci Reader*, esp. 190–209; Simon, *Gramsci's Political Thought*; Crehan, *Gramsci, Culture, and Anthropology*; Foucault, *The History of Sexuality*, 81–102.

18 Lonsdale, "The Moral Economy of Mau Mau: The Problem" and "The Moral Economy of Mau Mau: Wealth, Poverty, and Civic Virtue in Kikuyu Political Thought."

19 Marks and Engels, *Contesting Colonial Hegemony*.

20 Guha, *Dominance without Hegemony*.

21 The academic literature on colonizers' attempts to rule through the civilizing mission was particularly popular and influential during the 1980s and 1990s. Notable examples include Dirks, *Colonialism and Culture*; Comaroff and Comaroff, *Of Revelation and Revolution*; Hunt, *A Colonial Lexicon of Birth Ritual, Medicalization, and Mobility in the Congo*; T. Mitchell, *Colonising Egypt*; Conklin, *A Mission to Civilize*; Rabinow, *French Modern*; G. Wright, *The Politics of Design in French Colonial Urbanism*; Stoler, *Race and the Education of Desire*; Burke, *Lifebuoy Men, Lux Women*.

22 Fields, *Revival and Rebellion in Colonial Central Africa*, chaps. 1–2.

23 Cooper, "Conflict and Connection"; Larson, "'Capacities and Modes of Thinking.'"

24 Hamilton, *Terrific Majesty*; Mamdani, *Citizen and Subject*.

25 Mahoney, *The Zulu Past in the Present*.

26 Cobbing, "A Tainted Well."

27 Hamilton, *Terrific Majesty*, 51–69, 130–67.

28 Webb and Wright, *The James Stuart Archive*, 1:6, 103, 314.

29 Ibid., 2:248; 4:326, 364.

30 Ibid., 5:228.

31 Ibid., 1:93.

32 Ibid., 5:331.

33 Ibid., 1:331.

34 Ibid., 5:307.

35 Interviews with Jethros Gumede (18 August 1996), Mboneni Gumede (27 July 1997), and Tom Ntuli (27 July 1997), all conducted in Mapumulo district, KwaZulu-Natal Province, South Africa, with Thuthukani Cele as translator and interpreter.

36 Mofolo, *Chaka.*

37 Fuze, *The Black People and Whence They Came.* The book was first written in 1905 and first published in Zulu in 1922.

38 Atkins, *The Moon Is Dead! Give Us Our Money!* 5–6; Guha, *Elementary Aspects of Peasant Insurgency in Colonial India,* 14–17; Ginzburg, *The Cheese and the Worms,* xiv–xviii; Isaacman, "Peasants and Rural Social Protest in Africa," 222; Marks, "Class, Ideology, and the Bambatha Rebellion," 356–57.

1 FAILURE OF ZULU ETHNIC INTEGRATION

1 For some examples, see Webb and Wright, *The James Stuart Archive,* 1:208; 2:255; 3:195.

2 See, for example, KCAL Zulu Tribal History Essay Competition, Reginald Dludla, "The Qwabe Tribe." This essay was submitted for a competition in 1950.

3 Interview with Mboneni Gumede, with Thuthukani Cele as translator and interpreter, Mapumulo Magistracy, KwaZulu-Natal, South Africa, 27 July 1997. Gumede served as an authority on Qwabe history for Reggie Khumalo, who produced literature and radio programs on Zulu history. Nevertheless, Gumede took issue with some of Khumalo's accounts.

4 For the most thorough analysis of the Malandela story, see Hamilton, "Ideology, Oral Traditions, and the Struggle for Power in the Early Zulu Kingdom," 158–83.

5 Kubeka, "A Preliminary Survey of Zulu Dialects in Natal and Zululand." See also Ownby, "Early Nguni History"; J. Wright, "Politics, Ideology, and the Invention of the Nguni."

6 See the entries for all these English and Zulu terms in Doke et al., *English-Zulu Zulu-English Dictionary.*

7 For more on the distinction between chiefdom and lineage, see Hammond-Tooke, "In Search of the Lineage: The Cape Nguni Case," "Descent Groups, Chiefdoms and South African Historiography," "Who Worships Whom: Agnates and Ancestors among Nguni," and "Kinship Authority and Political Authority in Pre-colonial South Africa."

8 See the entries for *uhlanga, inkosi,* and *khonza* in Doke et al., *English-Zulu Zulu-English Dictionary.*

9 For just some examples among many from the precolonial era, see Webb and Wright, *The James Stuart Archive,* 2:112, 203, 251, 267.

10 Gluckman, *Analysis of a Social System in Modern Zululand;* "The Kingdom of

the Zulu in South Africa"; *Custom and Conflict in Africa*; *Order and Rebellion in Tribal Africa*; *Politics, Law, and Ritual in Tribal Society.*

11 Based on my own count from the Durban telephone book, not as labor-intensive a process as it might sound.

12 Huffman, "Archaeology and Ethnohistory in the African Iron Age" and "Archaeological Evidence and Conventional Explanations of Southern Bantu Settlement Patterns." Also see Kuper, "Symbolic Dimensions of the Southern Bantu Homestead," *Wives for Cattle*, "Lineage Theory," and "The 'House' and Zulu Political Structure." Finally, see Ownby, "Early Nguni History."

13 The equilibrium of social structures was a common theme in Gluckman's work. For his examinations of this issue within a Zulu context, see Gluckman, *Analysis of a Social System in Modern Zululand*, 29–30, and "The Kingdom of the Zulu of South Africa," 42.

14 The foremost scholarly authority on the Nguni household is Adam Kuper. For archaeological work into these subjects, see Huffman, "Archaeology and Ethnohistory in the African Iron Age" and "Archaeological Evidence and Conventional Explanations of Southern Bantu Settlement Patterns."

15 To some extent, cattle were used to serve the same purpose in European society as well. The word *cattle* is etymologically related to both *chattel* and *capital*, and the words *fee* and *pecuniary* are derived respectively from the Germanic and Latin words for cattle.

16 The earliest and most influential academic description of this phenomenon was by the great Africanist and African Americanist Melville J. Herskovits in "The Cattle Complex in East Africa." For a more recent and extremely insightful take, see Ferguson, "The Bovine Mystique."

17 The concept and the discussion that follows come from Guy, "Analysing Pre-Capitalist Societies in Southern Africa."

18 Guy, "Gender Oppression in Southern Africa's Precapitalist Societies," 45. For other work on gender in precolonial southeast African society, see J. Wright, "Control of Women's Labour in the Zulu Kingdom"; Hanretta, "Women, Marginality, and the Zulu State"; Weir, "'I Shall Need to Use Her to Rule.'"

19 Scott, *Domination and the Arts of Resistance*, 82–83. For more on generation in the specific context of precolonial southeastern Africa, see Guy, "Analysing Pre-Capitalist Societies," and Carton, *Blood from Your Children*, esp. chaps. 1–2.

20 Etherington, *Great Treks*, 23–24, 33–35; Gump, "Ecological Change and Pre-Shakan State Formation."

21 Wright and Hamilton, "Traditions and Transformations." For the most recent and authoritative account of slaving in this region during this period, see Eldredge, "Delagoa Bay and the Hinterland in the Early Nineteenth Century."

22 Hamilton, "Ideology, Oral Traditions, and the Struggle for Power in the Early Zulu Kingdom," chap. 2.

23 Wright and Hamilton, "Traditions and Transformations," 64–65.

24 Shaka's life story has been told many times, and sometimes quite well, by

popular authors, but the burst of academic investigations into precolonial Zulu history from the 1970s onward largely discredited these earlier biographies. Amazingly, the first book-length academic biography of Shaka came out only recently: Dan Wylie's *Myth of Iron*.

25 Hedges, "Trade and Politics," 175; Hamilton, "Ideology, Oral Traditions, and the Struggle for Power in the Early Zulu Kingdom," 172.

26 Webb and Wright, *The James Stuart Archive*, 4:226.

27 Hedges, "Trade and Politics," 177.

28 J. Wright, "The Dynamics of Power and Conflict in the Thukela-Mzimkhulu Region in the Late Eighteenth and Early Nineteenth Centuries," 164–66.

29 Webb and Wright, *The James Stuart Archive*, 3:26, 30, 35–36.

30 Ibid., 2:180, cited in Hamilton, "Ideology, Oral Traditions, and the Struggle for Power in the Early Zulu Kingdom," 175–81.

31 Hamilton, "Ideology, Oral Traditions, and the Struggle for Power in the Early Zulu Kingdom," 175–81.

32 Webb and Wright, *The James Stuart Archive*, 3:249.

33 Ibid., 1:115; 3:100.

34 Ibid., 1:210–11; 3:269–70.

35 Ibid., 1:190; 3:31.

36 Hamilton, "Ideology, Oral Traditions, and the Struggle for Power in the Early Zulu Kingdom," 175.

37 Ibid., 172–74.

38 J. Wright, "The Dynamics of Power and Conflict in the Thukela-Mzimkhulu Region in the Late Eighteenth and Early Nineteenth Centuries," 181–84.

39 Webb and Wright, *The James Stuart Archive*, 2:61.

40 Ibid., 2:247.

41 Interview with Mboneni Gumede, with Thuthukani Cele as translator and interpreter Mapumulo Magistracy, KwaZulu-Natal, South Africa, 27 July 1997. For accounts of this battle by Stuart's informants, see Webb and Wright, *The James Stuart Archive*, 1:182–83, 208–10; 2:168–69, 177–78; 3:240–45, 270–71. For Shepstone's account of the battle, see Bird, *The Annals of Natal*, 1:149–50. See also Kunene, *Emperor Shaka the Great*, and Bryant, *Olden Times in Zululand and Natal*.

42 J. Wright, "Political Transformations in the Thukela-Mzimkhulu Region in the Late Eighteenth and Early Nineteenth Centuries," 169.

43 Wright and Hamilton, "Traditions and Transformations," 67.

44 This is the main thesis of Hamilton, "Ideology, Oral Traditions, and the Struggle for Power in the Early Zulu Kingdom." See also Kubeka, "A Preliminary Survey of Zulu Dialects in Natal and Zululand"; Ownby, "Early Nguni History"; and Hamilton and Wright, "The Making of the *AmaLala*."

45 Hughes, "Politics and Society in Inanda, Natal," 73–74.

46 Hamilton, "Ideology, Oral Traditions, and the Struggle for Power in the Early Zulu Kingdom," chaps. 3–8; Hamilton and Wright, "The Making of the *AmaLala*."

47 Guy, "Analysing the Pre-Capitalist Societies in Southern Africa" and "Gender Oppression in Southern Africa's Precapitalist Societies."

48 Webb and Wright, *The James Stuart Archive*, 2:169. See also ibid., 1:194; 2:178.

49 Ibid., 1:194. For other accounts, see ibid., 1:209; 3:80; 5:39. Unlike Kambi and Melaphi and others, Ngidi and Jantshi argue that the people behind the assassination were probably not Qwabe, but rather more likely members of the Zulu Royal House, who succeeded in killing Shaka four years later.

50 Ibid., 1:8.

51 Ibid., 3:43. For still other references to Shaka's massacre of the Qwabe, see ibid., 1:16; 3:249.

52 Ibid., 2:107–8. For other accounts of Shaka's actions against the Langa, see ibid., 1:7, 11, 19, 191; 3:151; 5:30, 62–63, 73.

53 Ibid., 1:19; 5:130.

54 See, for example, ibid., 1:107–8, 7, 11, 19, 191, 285; 2:277; 3:151; 5:30, 62–63, 73, 117, 130, 339.

55 Ibid., 4:94.

56 Ibid., 3:114.

57 Ibid., 2:84, 250. Shaka also viewed doctors as threats to his rule and killed off many of them. Unlike Dingane, however, Shaka does not seem to have killed off ordinary people merely because they belonged to the same chiefdoms as did the doctors who had been slated for execution. For Shaka's actions against doctors, see ibid., 1:9, 195, 330–31; 4:177, 267, 342; 5:40–41.

58 Ibid., 3:7.

59 Ibid., 3:31, 36.

60 Ibid., 1:210; 3:88–89.

61 Ibid., 3:82–83.

62 Ibid., 2:70; 3:37, 82, 269.

63 Ibid., 3:36–38, 82–83.

64 Ibid., 3:37, 269.

65 Ibid., 1:104.

66 Omer-Cooper, *The Zulu Aftermath*, 159–60. Omer-Cooper's account of Nqetho's exploits in Pondoland is one of the only parts of the book based on archival sources. For the murder of Farewell, whose African name was Febana, Webb and Wright, *The James Stuart Archive*, 2:268; 3:27.

67 Omer-Cooper, *The Zulu Aftermath*, 161; Webb and Wright, *The James Stuart Archive*, 3:38, 269.

68 Omer-Cooper, *The Zulu Aftermath*, 161. This is one of the many points in the book for which no source citations are given. Typically, Omer-Cooper derives such points from the work of Nathaniel Isaacs, Henry Francis Fynn, or, most often, A. T. Bryant.

69 Webb and Wright, *The James Stuart Archive*, 1:105.

70 Bird, *The Annals of Natal*, 1:149–50.

71 Webb and Wright, *The James Stuart Archive*, 1:105–6; 2:70–71; 3:37, 82–83, 85.

72 Bird, *The Annals of Natal*, 149–50.

73 Webb and Wright, *The James Stuart Archive*, 1:106; 4:66–67.

74 Okoye, "Dingane."

75 Hughes, "Politics and Society in Inanda, Natal," 66.

76 Ibid., 75.

77 Gluckman, *Analysis of a Social System in Modern Zululand*, 44, quoted in Marks, *The Ambiguities of Dependence*, 111.

2 A ZULU KING TOO STRONG TO LOVE

1 Guy, *The Destruction of the Zulu Kingdom*, 18; Bryant, *A Zulu-English Dictionary*, 286.

2 Ballard, "Traders, Trekkers, and Colonists."

3 Stuart and Malcolm, *The Diary of Henry Francis Fynn*, 22–23.

4 Slater, "Transitions in the Political Economy of Southeast Africa before 1840," 334.

5 J. Wright, "The Dynamics of Power and Conflict in the Thukela-Mzimkhulu Region in the Late Eighteenth and Early Nineteenth Centuries: A Critical Reconstruction," 337–48.

6 Okoye, "Dingane"; Colenbrander, "The Zulu Kingdom, 1828–79," 89.

7 Liebenberg, *Andries Pretorius in Natal*, 11.

8 Laband, *The Rise and Fall of the Zulu Nation*, 81–91.

9 Cubbin, "Origins of the British Settlement at Port Natal, May 1824–July 1842," 150.

10 Ibid., 154–58.

11 Laband, *Rise and Fall of the Zulu Nation*, 98–101; Liebenberg, *Andries Pretorius in Natal*, 34–41.

12 Colenbrander, "The Zulu Kingdom, 1828–79," 93–96.

13 Laband, *Rise and Fall of the Zulu Nation*, 107–21.

14 Ballard, "Traders, Trekkers, and Colonists," 123–25; Welsh, *The Roots of Segregation*, 2–4, 9–14; Lambert, *Betrayed Trust*, 8–10.

15 Colony of Natal, *Report of the Natal Native Commission, 1881–2*, 40–46; Lambert, *Betrayed Trust*, 25.

16 See the following enclosures in Pietermaritzburg Archives Repository (PAR), SNA 1/1/277 3041/1897: 484a/1893 Statement of Hetshepi, 18 April 1893; 1369/1890 Statement of Musi, 19 November 1890; The Disputed Succession to Musi's Chieftainship, Theophilus Shepstone, n.d. [but probably June 1893]; Proceedings of the hearing into the succession to Musi's chieftainship, 20–28 February 1893, testimony of Fokazi, Bababa, Ngongolwana, and Mkhonto.

17 PAR, SNA 1/1/277 1369/1890 enc. in 3041/1897 Statement of Musi, 19 November 1890.

18 Evidence for the history of the Qwabe chiefdom during Musi's residence at the Tongati-Mona confluence (late 1840s to 1856) is to be found in the following

enclosures in PAR, SNA 1/1/277 3041/1897: 484a/1893 Statement of Hetshepi, 18 April 1893; 1369/1890 Statement of Musi, 19 November 1890; 392a/1893 Statement of Mvagazi, 28 March 1893; The Disputed Succession to Musi's Chieftainship, Theophilus Shepstone, n.d. [but probably June 1893]; Proceedings of the hearing into the succession to Musi's chieftainship, 20–28 February 1893, testimony of Fokazi, Bababa, Paga, Ngongolwana, Ntshwili, Ngotshane, Mdungazwe, Mnewabo, Ncaphayi, and Mhambi.

19 Colony of Natal, *Evidence Taken before the Natal Native Commission, 1881,* 216, evidence of Mamfongonyana's headman.

20 Colony of Natal, *Correspondence Relating to Granting to natives in Natal of documentary tribal titles to land* (1890), 99, 105.

21 PAR, SNA 1/1/277 3041/1897 The Disputed Succession to Musi's Chieftainship, Theophilus Shepstone, n.d. [but probably June 1893].

22 Webb and Wright, *The James Stuart Archive,* 3:242–43, 252, 257, 266–68; 4:163.

23 J. Wright, "Notes on the Politics of Being 'Zulu,' 1820–1920," 9–11.

24 Quoted in Welsh, *The Roots of Segregation,* 58.

25 Quoted in ibid., 235.

26 Mahoney, "Racial Formation and Ethnogenesis from Below."

27 Quoted in Welsh, *The Roots of Segregation,* 22.

28 PAR, Theophilus Shepstone Papers, vol. 82, Notes Explanatory of Returns, 1864, sec. 21.

29 PAR, SNA 1/1/24 25/1874 Comm. Police to SNA, 22 April 1874.

30 Colony of Natal, *Blue Book on Native Affairs* (1879), Report of RM Umgeni, 5. Compare with Richard Meinertzhagen, a British colonial official in Kenya, who in 1902 wrote in his diary, "Here we are, three white men in the heart of Africa, with 20 Nigger soldiers and 50 Nigger police, 68 miles from doctors or reinforcements, administering and policing a district inhabited by half a million well armed savages who have only quite recently come into touch with the white man . . . the position is most humourous to my mind." Quoted in Ranger, "African Reaction to the Imposition of Colonial Rule in East and Central Africa," 294.

31 PAR, SNA 1/1/24 71/1874 Minute paper, 1874.

32 Lambert, *Betrayed Trust,* 10–11, 80–81, 93, 107; Guest, "The New Economy," 304–7.

33 Etherington, *Preachers, Peasants, and Politics in Southeast Africa, 1835–1880,* 4, 24, 129.

34 Ibid., *Preachers, Peasants, and Politics in Southeast Africa, 1835–1880,* 3; Houghton Library, ABM vol. 6, no. 141, Abraham to Anderson, 22 June 1866; Houghton Library, ABM vol. 6, no. 300 A. Grout to Clark, 23 November 1866; Houghton Library, ABM vol. 7, no. 287, Tyler to Anderson, 14 June 1866; PAR, SNA 1/1/277 3041/1897 The Disputed Succession to Musi's Chieftainship, Theophilus Shepstone, n.d. [but probably June 1893].

35 PAR, SNA 1/1/277 1369/1890 enc. in 3041/1897 Statement of Musi, 19 November 1890.

36 Mahoney, "The Millennium Comes to Mapumulo."

37 Lambert, *Betrayed Trust*, 26–28.

38 Figures cited in Welsh, *The Roots of Segregation*, 14, 20, 114.

39 Colony of Natal, *Report of the Natal Native Commission, 1881–1882*, 40–46.

40 See, for example, the official comments on the subject in PAR, SNA 1/1/34 1652/1879 RM Umvoti to acting SNA, 29 July 1879.

41 For Fodo, Matshana, and Sidoyi, see Welsh, *The Roots of Segregation*, 19–20, 120–22; Lambert, *Betrayed Trust*, 26, 31. Published accounts of the "Langalibalele affair" are legion: J. Colenso, *Langalibalele and the Hlubi Tribe*; F. E. Colenso, *My Chief and I*; Rees, *F. S. Colenso*, 259; Brookes and Webb, *A History of Natal*, 113–21; Welsh, *The Roots of Segregation*, chap. 8; Pearse et al., *Langalibalele and the Natal Carbineers*; Guest, *Langalibalele*; Herd, *The Bent Pine*; Etherington, "Why Langalibalele Ran Away"; Wright and Manson, *The Hlubi Chiefdom in Zululand-Natal*; Guy, *The Heretic*.

42 Quoted in Welsh, *The Roots of Segregation*, 19–20.

43 Quoted in Guy, "An Accommodation of Patriarchs," 13.

44 Etherington, "The 'Shepstone System' in the Colony of Natal and beyond Its Borders," 179.

45 Lambert, *Betrayed Trust*, 26.

46 PAR, Theophilus Shepstone Papers, vol. 82, Notes Explanatory of Returns, 1864, section 26.

47 Quoted in Lambert, *Betrayed Trust*, 26.

48 PAR, SNA 1/1/19 120/1869 Memorandum, SNA, 2 September 1869.

49 *Natal Government Gazette Supplement*, 30 November 1852, evidence of Theophilus Shepstone. nos. 131–33; PAR, SNA 1/8/5 SNA to RM Upper Umkomanzi, 22 March 1854; SNA 1/3/10 166/1861 RM Richmond to SNA, 9 July 1861; SNA 1/3/10 192/1861 Field Cornet Umzimkulu to SNA, 21 August 1861.

50 Lambert, *Betrayed Trust*, 28–29. PAR, SNA 1/3/1 RM Inanda to SNA, 26 November 1850; RM Inanda to SNA, 30 January 1851; RM Inanda to Sec. to Govt., 21 July 1851.

51 PAR, SNA 1/7/2 66/1853 Report, SNA, 27 May 1853.

52 Lambert, *Betrayed Trust*, 31.

53 Welsh, *The Roots of Segregation*, 123.

54 Ibid., 126.

55 *Natal Government Gazette Supplement*, 8 March 1853, evidence of Lloyd Evans Mesham, RM Inanda.

56 PAR, NHC II/9/21 T. S. Mesham, RM Inanda, to Col. Sec., 12 February 1852, enc. in Siziba v. Meseni, 1894.

57 PAR, SNA 1/1/34 1652/1879 RM Umvoti to acting SNA, 29 July 1879. As an indication of the volume of such traffic, Umvoti county (one of six counties in Natal) in 1879 had ten homestead heads, representing forty-one huts, or about 160 people, apply for such transfer. Needless to say, this was only the legal traffic. It is impossible to say how many people moved without applying to the government.

58 Ballard, "Traders, Trekkers, and Colonists," 125. See also Welsh, *The Roots of Segregation*, 19.

59 Lambert, *Betrayed Trust*, 7–20. See also Etherington, "The 'Shepstone System' in the Colony of Natal and beyond Its Borders," 174–75; Bundy, *The Rise and Fall of the South African Peasantry*; Bradford, "Peasants, Historians, and Gender."

60 Lambert, *Betrayed Trust*, chaps. 1, 3, 5; Slater, "Land, Labour, and Capital in Natal."

61 Quoted in Atkins, *The Moon Is Dead! Give Us Our Money!* 23, emphasis added.

62 Lambert, *Betrayed Trust*, chaps. 1 and 3; Carton, *Blood from Your Children*, chap. 1.

63 PAR, SNA 1/1/19 120/1869 Memorandum, SNA, 2 September 1869.

64 PAR, SNA 1/1/1 no. 2 Affidavits, Umkumbeli, Macatshiso, Umceleni, 27 February 1846; SNA 1/1/1 no. 16 Donald Moodie to SNA, 4 April 1848; SNA 1/1/1 no. 18 SNA to Lt. Gov., 20 April 1848; SNA 1/8/1 SNA to Secretary to Government, 24 December 1846.

65 PAR, SNA 1/1/2 no. 62 D. Tookey to SNA, 13 September 1848.

66 PAR, SNA 1/8/5 SNA to RM Pietermaritzburg, 3 October 1853.

67 Colony of Natal, *Evidence before the Natal Native Affairs Commission, 1881–2*, 213–17.

68 Colony of Natal, *Statistical Year Book for the Year 1906*, 3.

69 Atkins, *The Moon Is Dead! Give Us Our Money!* 24–25.

70 Laband, *Rope of Sand*, 147.

71 Colony of Natal, *Blue Book on Native Affairs, 1884*, Report of John L. Knight, ANL and Border Agent, Lower Tugela. Colony of Natal, *Supplement to the Blue Book for the Colony of Natal: Departmental Reports, 1884*, Report of W. D. Wheelwright, RM Umvoti.

72 Webb and Wright, *The James Stuart Archive*, 3:261; 4:133, 180, 275.

73 For opposition to and defection from Mpande and Cetshwayo, see Mael, "The Problem of Political Integration in the Zulu Empire"; Phillip Kennedy, "The Fatal Diplomacy: Sir Theophilus Shepstone and the Zulu Kings, 1839–1879," (PhD dissertation, University of California, Los Angeles, 1976); Kennedy, "Mpande and the Zulu Kingship," 21–38; Laband, "The Cohesion of the Zulu Polity under the Impact of the Anglo-Zulu War"; Laban, *Rope of Sand*, chaps. 5–12.

74 Webb and Wright, *The James Stuart Archive*, 1:209; 2:27, 33, 227; 3:243.

75 Colony of Natal, *Report of the Natal Native Commission, 1881–2*, 37–46.

76 Etherington, "Natal's Black Rape Scare of the 1870s."

77 PAR, SNA 1/1/30 74/1878 W. Schreuder to acting SNA, 17 December 1877; 133/1878 W. Schreuder to acting SNA, 14 January 1878.

78 PAR, SNA 1/3/30 530/1878 Report of the acting SNA, 19 June 1878.

79 PAR, SNA 1/3/30 31/1878 Col. Durnford to acting SNA, 5 August 1878; 1/1/31 R1157/1878 Fynney to acting SNA, 3 September 1878.

80 PAR, SNA 1/1/31 1388/1878 Fynney to acting SNA, 18 October 1878.

81 PAR, SNA 1/1/31 42/1878 Bulwer to acting SNA, 20 September 1878.

82 PAR, SNA 1/1/30 74/1878 Confidential Report of the Acting SNA on the Native Chiefs and Tribes residing on and near the borders of the Zulu Country, 14 January 1878.

83 PAR, SNA 1/1/30 479/1878 RM Lower Tugela to acting SNA, 8 April 1878; 502/1878 RM Lower Tugela to acting SNA, 15 April 1878; 516/1878 RM Lower Tugela to acting SNA, 22 April 1878; 546/1878 RM Lower Tugela to acting SNA, 29 April 1878; 576/1878 RM Lower Tugela to acting SNA, 6 May 1878.

84 PAR, SNA 1/1/31 1530/1878 RM Umvoti to acting SNA, 26 November 1878.

85 PAR, SNA 1/1/31 R3277/1878 Fynney to acting SNA, 28 August 1878; 1/6/11 no. 4 Report by the acting SNA, 26 September 1878.

86 PAR, SNA 1/3/30 153/1878 RM Umvoti to acting SNA, 26 August 1878.

87 PAR, SNA 1/1/31 1390/1878 Statements, Nyathi and Luji, 23 October 1878.

88 PAR, SNA 1/1/33 277/1879 Fynney to acting SNA, 10 February 1879.

89 PAR, SNA 1/1/32 36/1879 Report by the acting SNA, 15 January 1879.

90 PAR, SNA 1/1/34 1124/1879 Fynney to acting SNA, 24 May 1879.

91 Laband, *Rope of Sand*, 231–41.

92 PAR, SNA 1/1/34 1153/1879 Fynney to acting SNA, 29 May 1879.

93 PAR, SNA 1/1/34 1319/1879 Maj. Gen. Clifford to Lt. Gov., 30 June 1879.

94 PAR, SNA 1/1/31 R3277/1878 Fynney to acting SNA, 28 August 1878; 1/6/11 no. 4 Report by the acting SNA, 26 September 1878.

95 PAR, SNA 1/1/30 16/1878 W. Schreuder to acting SNA, 2 January 1878.

96 PAR, SNA 1/1/30 528/1878 Rev. R. Robertson to acting SNA, 21 January 1879.

97 PAR, SNA 1/1/31 1474/1878 RM Umvoti to acting SNA, 13 November 1878.

98 PAR, NHC II/7/8 Riot and Homicide cases, Attorney General (pros.) vs. Beje et al., 1880; NHC II/8/4 Judge's Note Book of Riot and Homicide Cases (High Treason), Supreme Chief vs. Beje Majingolo et al., 1880.

99 PAR, SNA 1/1/30 41/1878 Fynney to acting SNA, 16 September 1878.

100 PAR, SNA 1/1/34 1557/1879 RM Lower Tugela to acting SNA, 28 August 1879.

101 PAR, SNA 1/1/31 1529/1878 RM Umvoti to acting SNA, 24 November 1878.

102 PAR, SNA 1/1/34 1020/1879 RM Umvoti to acting SNA, 11 May 1879.

103 PAR, SNA 1/1/34 1485/1879 J. E. Fannin, Special Border Agent Umovti, to acting SNA, 29 July 1879.

104 PAR, SNA 1/1/32 no. 42 Fourth report of the acting SNA on report of Border agent on conduct of Umkonto, n.d. [but probably ca. January 1879].

105 PAR, SNA 1/6/12 1325/1879 1325/1879 Capt. Lucas to Lt. Gov. Bulwer, 26 February 1879.

106 PAR, SNA 1/1/33 428/1879 Fynney to acting SNA, 28 February 1879.

107 PAR, SNA 1/1/33 91/1879 Fynney to acting SNA, 15 January 1879.

108 PAR, SNA 1/1/33 277/1879 Fynney to acting SNA, 10 February 1879.

109 PAR, SNA 1/1/33 15/1879 Fynney to acting SNA, 13 March 1879.

110 PAR, SNA 1/1/32 37/1879 Report by Fynney, 15 January 1879; 1/1/33 91/1879 Fynney to acting SNA, 15 January 1879.

111 Laband, *Rope of Sand*, 208.

112 Thompson, *The Natal Native Contingent in the Anglo-Zulu War, 1879*, chaps. 2–3.
113 PAR, SNA 1/6/13 545/1879 Further returns of native drivers, leaders, and special pioneers ordered to be furnished since 22 January 1879.
114 Webb and Wright, *The James Stuart Archive*, 2:255.
115 PAR, SNA 1/1/33 144/1879 RM Lower Tugela to acting SNA, 31 January 1879.
116 PAR, SNA 1/6/13 904/1879 Circular: Means of distinguishing friendly Natives in the field from Zulus, 11 February 1879.
117 PAR, SNA 1/1/33 18/1879 Fynney to acting SNA, 19 March 1879.
118 Text from a placard hanging in the halls of the Pietermaritzburg Archives Repository.
119 Quoted in Thompson, *The Natal Native Contingent in the Anglo-Zulu War, 1879*, 373.
120 Webb and Wright, *The James Stuart Archive*, 3:155, Mkando.

3 CONFLICT AMONG NATAL AFRICANS

1 Hemson, "Class Consciousness and Migrant Workers," 14–29; Atkins, *The Moon Is Dead! Give Us Our Money!* 100–114.
2 Welsh, *The Roots of Segregation*, esp. p. 243.
3 Lambert, *Betrayed Trust*, 71–72, 115, 118.
4 Carton, *Blood from Your Children*, 63–68.
5 Colony of Natal, *Blue Book on Native Affairs, 1894*, 7.
6 Marks, *Reluctant Rebellion*, 198.
7 Hemson, "Class Consciousness and Migrant Workers," 52, 56.
8 Lambert, *Betrayed Trust*, 189.
9 Marks, "Class, Ideology, and the Bambatha Rebellion," 355.
10 Webb and Wright, *The James Stuart Archive*, 4:201, 210.
11 Ibid., 3:155, 158, 171, 183; 4:54.
12 Houghton Library, Cambridge, Massachusetts, American Board Mission collection, vol. 7, no. 119, Report, Katie Lloyd, 1867.
13 Pietermaritzburg Archives Repository (PAR), AZM A/1/2 Minutes of the Semi-Annual Meeting, 1 February 1893, 421.
14 PAR, AZM A/3/41 Report of Esidumbini Mission Station, Laura Mellen, 13 June 1897.
15 Houghton Library, ABM, vol. 14, no. 31, Annual Tabular View, 1891; vol. 21, no. 129, Annual Tabular View, 1900.
16 Mahoney, "Millennium Comes to Mapumulo," 380, 386.
17 PAR, AZM A/2/10 Mfanefile Khuzwayo to Goodenough, 12 December 1899, Hlonono to Wilcox, 7 April 1898; Lambert, *Betrayed Trust*, 77–78, 83–84, 127; Les Switzer, "The Problems of an African Mission in a White-Dominated, Multi-Racial Society," 34, 111–14.
18 These arguments are conveyed most succinctly in Lambert, *Betrayed Trust*, 123, 179–80; and in Carton, *Blood from Your Children*, 67, 71–72, 76–77.

19 Lambert, *Betrayed Trust*, 123, 135, 179–80; Carton, *Blood from Your Children*, 55, 60, 64, 75–76, 111.

20 Lambert, *Betrayed Trust*, 52, 62, 135–38, 180; Carton, *Blood from Your Children*, 87–111. The most thorough and theoretically developed treatment of this subject for South Africa in general is Walker, "Gender and the Development of the Migrant Labour System, c. 1850–1930."

21 Carton, *Blood from Your Children*, 60.

22 Lambert, *Betrayed Trust*, 135–38; Carton, *Blood from Your Children*, 88–94, 105–10.

23 NCP 7/4/2 Colony of Natal, *Departmental Reports, 1894–5*, E6; NCP 7/4/4 Colony of Natal, *Departmental Reports 1897*, F31–32; Colony of Natal, *Blue Book on Native Affairs, 1904*, 177–78.

24 Colony of Natal, *Blue Book on Native Affairs, 1904*, 56, RM Bergville, 7 January 1905. Colony of Natal, *Native Affairs Commission 1906–7: Evidence*, testimony of Bekakupiwa, 790; testimony of Mafika Mhlongo, 820; testimony of John Hlonono, 849; and testimony of John L. Dube, 959.

25 PAR, SNA 1/1/270 2951/1897 Court of ANL Klip River, case no. 92/1894, Supreme Chief v. Mabande ka Mbadule Ch. Kwebane, 6 July 1894, emphasis added.

26 PAR, SNA 1/1/270 2951/1897 Court of ANL Klip River, case no. 92/1894, RM Umvoti, 22 September 1894.

27 PAR, SNA 1/1/270 2951/1897 Court of ANL Klip River, case no. 92/1894, RM Klip River, 18 September 1894.

28 PAR, SNA 1/1/270 2951/1897 Court of ANL Klip River, case no. 92/1894, RM Upper Tugela, 18 September 1894.

29 Parle, "States of Mind," 81–103, 180–228; Parle and Scorgie, "Bewitching Zulu Women"; Parle and Mahoney, "An Ambiguous Sexual Revolution," 134–51.

30 Quoted in Carton, *Blood from Your Children*, 105. Carton argues that young men at this time "were risktakers who were engaging in premarital sex, which led to pregnancy" (ibid., 176) But he does not consider how it was often young women, and not young men, who had to face the negative consequences of such "risktaking."

31 Colony of Natal, *Blue Book on Native Affairs, 1902* report, RM Estcourt, 12 January 1903, A13.

32 Simons, *African Women*, 228.

33 Colony of Natal, *Natal Native Affairs Commission, 1906–7: Evidence*, testimony of Mgodini, 731.

34 Colony of Natal, *Natal Native Affairs Commission, 1906–7: Evidence*, testimony of Tshonkweni, 812.

35 As, for example, in PAR, SNA 1/1/313 1974/1904 Rex vs. Umsindo ka Maqilimana, Estcourt Division, 17 September 1904.

36 The following account is based on PAR, SNA 1/1/103 1125/1887 Papers relating to the faction fight between the Amanyuswa tribe under Chief Umtshiwa and the Etsimbeni tribe under Chief Duka Fynn, 22 December 1887.

37 For two cases in which six fighters were killed, see PAR, SNA 1/1/212 1605/1895 SNA to RM Umlazi, 27 December 1895; SNA 1/1/328 2756/1905 Report, Tpr. Schonberg NP Glendale, 18 October 1905.

38 For an account of this most recent chapter in the history of collective violence in KwaZulu-Natal, see Jeffrey, *The Natal Story*.

39 PAR, SNA 1/3/1 RM Umvoti to SNA, 25 February 1851; SNA 1/3/6 RM Klip River to SNA, 10 August 1857.

40 Colony of Natal, *Blue Book for Native Affairs, 1879*, Report, RM Umgeni, 5; *Blue Book for Native Affairs, 1882*, Report, RM Klip River, 205; *Blue Book for Native Affairs, 1884*, Report, RM Newcastle, 13 March 1885, 13.

41 Colony of Natal, *Blue Book for Native Affairs, 1881*, Report, RM Inanda, 156. PAR, SNA 1/1/103 1125/1887 Master of the Supreme Court to SNA, 10 March 1888.

42 Statistics compiled from the following annual government publications for the relevant years: Colony of Natal, *Supplement to the Blue Book for the Colony of Natal: Departmental Reports*; *Blue Book for Native Affairs: Departmental Reports*.

43 Indeed, the beer party is a significant institution throughout Africa. For analyses of the beer party in other parts of the continent, see O'Laughlin, "Mbum Beer-Parties"; "Structures of Production and Exchange in an African Social Formation" (PhD dissertation, Yale University, 1973); La Hausse, *Brewers, Beerhalls, and Boycotts*; Crush and Ambler, *Liquor and Labour in Southern Africa*; Akyeampong, *Drink, Power, and Cultural Change*; McAllister, *Building the Homestead*; Willis, *Potent Brews*.

44 PAR, SNA 1/1/145 897/1891 RM Newcastle to SNA, 6 November 1884. Colony of Natal, *Blue Book on Native Affairs, 19032* B64–65: Rules for controlling and regulating the gathering of natives at different kraals or homes for the purpose of feasting or beer drinking [under the provisions and sanctioned by Act 5, 1898, sec. 2; promulgated 8 January 1903].

45 Colony of Natal, *Blue Book on Native Affairs, 1902*, A14, Report, RM Estcourt, 12 January 1903. PAR, SNA 1/1/302 2158/1903 Statement, Chief Mabojana, Amacele, Lower Umzimkulu, 25 June 1903.

46 PAR, SNA 1/1/145 897/1891 RM Umsinga, 23 October 1884; RM Upper Umkomanzi, 11 January 1887.

47 PAR, SNA 1/4/8 C106/1900 Report of Native Intelligence Officer no. 1, 10 September 1900; SNA 1/1/299 491/1903 Report, USNA, 10 February 1903.

48 PAR, SNA 1/1/145 897/1891 Transcript of the meeting between chiefs and officials at Verulam, Inanda, 10 December 1884, testimony of Ncaphayi.

49 This ranking is based on the frequency with which each factor was cited by the various officials questioned in PAR, SNA 1/1/145 897/1891 SNA Circular 1056/1886 to RM's and ANL's, 18 December 1886.

50 Colony of Natal, *Blue Book on Native Affairs, 1881* Report of RM Ixopo, 1880, 117; Report of RM Newcastle, 1881, 139; Report of RM Alexandra, 1881, 181; Report of RM Upper Tugela, 1881, 189; Report of RM Alexandra, 1882, 222. Colony of Natal, *Blue Book on Native Affairs, 1885* Report of RM Inanda, 18 May 1885, 27.

51 La Hausse, "The Struggle for the City," 15–16; "Drink and Cultural Innovation in Durban," 86–88.

52 Carton, *Blood from Your Children*, 72–73; Lambert, *Betrayed Trust*, 127.

53 PAR, SNA 1/1/145 897/1891 Meetings of Chiefs re Minute of SNA of 11 October 1884, Zwartkop Location, 6 November 1884, testimony of Suzindela.

54 Colony of Natal, *Blue Book on Native Affairs, 1903* B64–65, Rules for controlling and regulating the gathering of natives at different kraals or homes for the purpose of feasting or beer drinking [under the provisions and sanctioned by Act 5, 1898, sec. 2; promulgated 8 January 1903].

55 Colony of Natal, *Blue Book on Native Affairs, 1904*, Report, RM Ndwedwe, 3 January 1905, 36.

56 See the copious testimony to this effect from chiefs and headmen in PAR, SNA 1/1/145 897/1891 Replies to SNA Circular 1056/1886, 18 December 1886.

57 Clegg, "*Ukubuyisa isidumbu*—'Bringing Back the Body.'"

58 See, for example, PAR, SNA 1/4/5 C42/1898 Report of Native Intelligence Officer no. 2, 9 September 1898; SNA 1/1/306 3601/1903 RM Umsinga to USNA, 25 November 1903.

59 PAR, SNA 1/1/145 897/1891 Minutes of the meeting at Verulam, Inanda, 10 December 1884, testimony of Mananabukana, hereditary chief of the Ngwane.

60 PAR, SNA 1/1/145 897/1891 Meeting of Chiefs at Camperdown, 11 November 1884, testimony of Mngundane.

61 PAR, SNA 1/1/145 897/1891 RM Lower Tugela to SNA, 28 December 1886.

62 PAR, SNA 1/1/145 897/1891 ANL and BA Lower Tugela, 28 October 1884.

63 Gilligan, *Violence*.

64 Scott, *Domination and the Arts of Resistance*, 37.

65 Lambert, *Betrayed Trust*, 52.

66 Colony of Natal, *Blue Book for Native Affairs, 1897*, 36.

67 Colony of Natal, *Blue Book for Native Affairs, 1905*, Report, RM Umsinga, 2 January 1906, 3.

68 PAR, SNA 1/1/306 3601/1903 Statement, Mabizela, Thembu Chief, Umsinga, 16 November 1903.

69 PAR, SNA 1/1/306 3601/1903 Statement, Tulwana, Amabaso Chief, Umsinga, 16 November 1903.

70 PAR, SNA 1/1/297 2567/1902 USNA to SNA, 4 August 1902.

71 PAR, SNA 1/4/6 C36/1899 Report of Native Intelligence Officer no. 1, 3 August 1899.

72 PAR, SNA 1/4/6 C13/1899 Report of Native Intelligence Officer no. 1, 15 May 1899.

73 PAR, SNA 1/4/6 C36/1899 Report of Native Intelligence Officer no. 1, 3 August 1899.

74 PAR, SNA 1/4/9 C49/1901 Report of Native Intelligence Officer no. 1, 16 November 1901.

75 PAR, SNA 1/4/5 C34/1898 Report of Native Intelligence Officer no. 1, 7 November 1898.

76 Lambert, *Betrayed Trust*, 129.

77 PAR, SNA 1/1/299 289/1903 RM Lower Tugela to USNA, 23 January 1903.

78 PAR, SNA 1/1/302 2013/1903 RM Newcastle to RM Alexandra, 31 March 1903.

79 PAR, SNA 1/1/330 3117/1905 RM Ndwedwe reports unsatisfactory conduct of the Acting Chief Gobosi, Amanyuswa Tribe, 21 November 1905; SNA 1/1/333 78/1906 RM Umvoti, 8 January 1906.

80 Chanock, *Law, Custom, and Social Order*, 85–102.

81 For Matshana and Sidoyi, see chapter 2.

82 See the following enclosures in PAR, SNA 1/1/277 3041/1897: 484a/1893 Statement of Hetshepi, 18 April 1893; 1369/1890 Statement of Musi, 19 November 1890; 392a/1893 Statement of Mvagazi, 28 March 1893; The Disputed Succession to Musi's Chieftainship, Theophilus Shepstone, n.d. [but probably 1893]; Proceedings of the hearing into the succession to Musi's chieftainship, 20–28 February 1893, testimony of Fokazi, Bababa, Paga, Ngongolwana, Mkhonto, Ntshwili, Ngotshane, Mdungazwe, Mnewabo, Ncaphayi, and Mhambi.

83 See the following enclosures in PAR, SNA 1/1/277 3041/1897: 1369/1890 Affidavit of Chief Musi, 19 November 1890; SNA 1/1/133 1369/1890 SNA to Gov., 19 November 1890; SNA 1/1/133 1369/1890 Report by S. O. Samuelson, acting RM Lower Tugela, 28 February 1891.

84 PAR, SNA 1/1/277 2948/1897 enc. in 3041/1897 Gov. to SNA, 12 May 1893.

85 See the following enclosures in PAR, SNA 1/1/277 3041/1897: 392a/1893 Report, S. O. Samuelson, 1 March 1892; SNA to Gov., 14 October 1892; SNA to S. O. Samuelson, 18 November 1892; 261/1892 Report on the succession of the late Chief Musi Qwabe, S. O. Samuelson, 21 November 1892; Evidence taken in the matter of the Succession to the Chief Musi, 20–28 February 1893; Opinions of the assessors, 3–6 March 1893; RM's Rudolph, Fynn, and Chadwick to SNA, 2 May 1893; Memorandum on the succession to the chieftainship of the Qwabe tribe upon the death of the late chief Musi, by H. C. Shepstone, SNA, 12 May 1893; The Disputed Succession to Musi's Chieftainship, Theophilus Shepstone, n.d. [but probably between 3 and 23 June 1893]; Gov. to SNA, 12 July 1893; Appointment of Meseni to the Qwabe chieftainship, 31 July 1893.

86 PAR, SNA 1/1/277 1491/1893 enc. in 3041/1897 R. C. A. Samuelson to SNA, 20 December 1893; *Natal Witness*, 3 August 1894; PAR, NHC II/11/18 4125/1894 Rudolph to Col. Under-Secretary, 10 August 1894.

87 PAR, SNA 1/1/277 2956/1897 SNA to Col. Sec., 26 January 1898; SNA 1/1/277 2956/1897 Transcript of hearing into division of Musi's chiefdom, 28 February 1898.

88 Marks, *Reluctant Rebellion*, 228; Welsh, *The Roots of Segregation*, 287–93.

89 Colony of Natal, *Natal Legislative Assembly Debates*, 1900, v. 29, Debates over the Native Code Amendment Bill, no. 16, 1900, 4–13 June 1900, 141–44, 170, 185–89, 197–99; *Natal Legislative Council Debates*, 1900, v. 9, Debate on the Code of Native Law Amendment Bill, 14–5 June 1900, 45–61.

90 Colony of Natal, *Report of the Secretary for Native Affairs for the Years 1899–1900*, report of USNA, 3.

91 PAR, SNA 1/1/292 1754/1901 Statement of Chief Meseni to RM Lower Tugela, 29 July 1901.

92 PAR, SNA 1/1/292 1229/1901 Governor to Prime Minister, 27 September 1901.

93 PAR, SNA 1/1/329 2934/1905 Memorandum, RM Lower Tugela, 6 November 1905. See also, for example, SNA 1/4/14 C41/1905 Deposition by Sibankwa, 10 November 1905.

94 PAR, SNA 1/1/329 2934/1905 Statement of Valindlela, 14 November 1905.

95 PAR, SNA 1/1/280 561/1898 RM and ANL Mapumulo to SNA, 10 March 1898; SNA 1/1/285 862/1899 RM Mapumulo to SNA, 26 April 1899.

96 Lambert, *Betrayed Trust*, 123–24, 181–82; Welsh, *Roots of Segregation*, chap. 15.

4 THE ROLE OF MIGRANT LABOR

1 Weber, *Peasants into Frenchmen*; Jacobson, *Special Sorrows*; Lockman, "The Social Roots of Nationalism"; Abadan-Unat, "East-West vs. South-North Migration."

2 Takaki, *Pau Hana*.

3 See, for example, Kaplan, "The Coming Anarchy."

4 J. Mitchell, *The Kalela Dance*; Epstein, *Politics in an Urban African Community*; Wallerstein, "Ethnicity and National Integration in West Africa"; A. Cohen, *Custom and Politics in Urban Africa*.

5 Tönnies, *Community and Society*; Anderson, *Imagined Communities*.

6 This aspect of Zulu history has only received cursory treatment thus far, but I am nevertheless indebted to the historians who have done the spadework, for without it my own work would have been much more difficult. See especially J. Wright, "Notes on the Politics of Being 'Zulu,' 1820–1920," 10; Harries, "Imagery, Symbolism, and Tradition in a South African Bantustan," 110. I am likewise indebted to the social historians of the Rand who have traced the development of African ethnic self-organization for other ethnic groups there, namely Delius, "Sebatakgomo"; Breckenridge, "Migrancy, Crime, and Faction Fighting"; Beinart, "The Origins of the Indlavini"; Harries, *Work, Culture, and Identity*; Bonner, "African Urbanisation on the Rand between the 1930s and the 1960s."

7 Hemson, "Class Consciousness and Migrant Workers," 21, 58.

8 Ibid., 29. For extended examinations of togt labor, see ibid., chaps. 1–2, and Atkins, *The Moon Is Dead! Give Us Our Money!* chaps. 4–5.

9 Atkins, *The Moon Is Dead! Give Us Our Money!* 111–14, 129–40; La Hausse, "The Struggle for the City," 29–38.

10 La Hausse, "'The Cows of Nongoloza,'" 86.

11 See the entries under *phoyisa* and *thefula* in Doke et al., *English-Zulu Zulu-English Dictionary*, 672, 789.

12 Durban Archives Repository, 3/DBN 5/2/5/4/1 Report, Durban Superintendent of Police, 31 July 1906.

13 Hemson, "Class Consciousness and Migrant Workers," 99.

14 Colony of Natal, *Blue Book for Native Affairs, 1902*, Report, RM Durban, A53.

15 Article from the *Natal Advertiser*, 19 September 1902, enc. in Durban Archives Repository, 3/DBN 5/2/5/3/6 Report, Durban Superintendent of Police, 24 September 1902.

16 Durban Archives Repository, 3/DBN 5/2/5/3/6 Report, Durban Superintendent of Police, 7 June 1901; 3/DBN 5/2/5/4/1 Report, Durban Superintendent of Police, 1 January 1904; 3/DBN 5/2/5/4/1 Report, Durban Superintendent of Police, 2 May 1904; 3/DBN 5/2/5/4/1 Report, Durban Superintendent of Police, 4 April 1906. Lambert, *Betrayed Trust*, 185.

17 Durban Archives Repository, 3/DBN 5/2/5/3/6 Report, Durban Superintendent of Police, 24 March 1902; Report, Durban Superintendent of Police, 7 May 1902.

18 Atkins, *The Moon Is Dead! Give Us Our Money!* 120–29.

19 Hemson, "Class Consciousness and Migrant Workers," 28–38, 81–100.

20 Durban Archives Repository, 3/DBN 5/2/5/4/1 Report, Durban Superintendent of Police, 5 December 1904.

21 Durban Archives Repository, 3/DBN 5/2/5/3/6 Report, Durban Superintendent of Police, 6 March 1899; Report, Durban Superintendent of Police, 6 March 1901.

22 La Hausse, "'The Cows of Nongoloza,'" 86n30.

23 Ibid., 85, 86n29. I am indebted to one of my anonymous peer reviewers for pointing out the significance of this fact.

24 Devermont, "Refining Racial Identities on the South African Sugar Belt, 1851–1913."

25 Pietermaritzburg Archives Repository (PAR), SNA 1/1/277 3041/1897 Evidence taken in the matter of the Succession to the Chief Musi, Testimony of Ndungazwe, 27 February 1893.

26 Hughes, "'The Coolies Will Elbow Us Out of the Country.'"

27 Bhana and Vahed, *The Making of a Political Reformer*, 26, 34.

28 Freund, *Insiders and Outsiders*, 38.

29 See PAR, SNA 1/4/1–20 Confidential Papers, 1897–1910.

30 Harries, *Work, Culture, and Identity*, 64. For the factors contributing to Tonga ethnogenesis in Kimberley more generally, see ibid., chap. 3.

31 Ibid., 65.

32 Odendaal, *Vukani Bantu!* 62.

33 Lambert, *Betrayed Trust*, 96.

34 Colony of Natal, *Blue Book on Native Affairs, 1897*, Report by J. S. Marwick, Natal Agent in Johannesburg, 28 February 1898, 24, 27. For comparative labor outflows to the Transvaal from the various districts of Natal, see Colony of Natal, *Blue Book on Native Affairs* for the years 1894 to 1909 inclusive.

35 See PAR, SNA 1/1/265 2557/1897 Marwick to USNA, 13 November 1897.

36 *Johannesburg Star*, 25 October 1895.

37 *Standard and Diggers' News*, 28 October 1895.

38 Colony of the Transvaal, *Reports of the Transvaal Labour Commission: Minutes of Proceedings and Evidence* (1904), 76, 412–13.

39 Colony of the Transvaal, *Reports of the Transvaal Labour Commission: Minutes of Proceedings and Evidence* (1904), 109–111.

40 J. J. Fourie, "Die koms van die Bantoe na die Rand en hulle posisie aldaar, 1886–1899," 242.

41 Van Onselen, *New Babylon, New Nineveh*, 212–13, 237, 241–42.

42 Atkins, *The Moon Is Dead! Give Us Our Money!* 61–63, 129–40.

43 Van Onselen, *New Babylon, New Nineveh*, 275–308.

44 Transvaal Archives Repository, K 358–2 Native Grievances Commission, Evidence of Charles Lawrence Butlin, 5 February 1914.

45 "The Wash Boys' Parade," *Standard and Diggers News*, 2 July 1895. Colony of the Transvaal, *Reports of the Transvaal Labour Commission: Minutes of Proceedings and Evidence* (1904), testimony of Rev. F. Suter, 23, and testimony of Courtney Acutt, 257–58, 263. Transvaal Archives Repository, SNA 432 NA1825/1909 Director GNLB, Memorandum on the position of the Native Labour Supply in the Proclaimed Labour Districts of the Transvaal, as at 31st March 1909, June 1909.

46 Colony of the Transvaal, *Reports of the Transvaal Labour Commission: Minutes of Proceedings and Evidence* (1904), testimony of Thomas Maxwell, 29–32.

47 "The Wash Boys' Parade," *Standard and Diggers News*, 2 July 1895; Colony of the Transvaal, *Reports of the Transvaal Labour Commission: Minutes of Proceedings and Evidence* (1904), testimony of Thomas Maxwell, 30.

48 Compare Transvaal Archives Repository, SP 15 SPR1043/1889 Asst. Lanndrost Johannesburg to Staatsprocureur, 2 May 1889, with SP 16 SPR1110/1889 Publieke Aanklaager Johannesburg to Staatsprocureur, 14 May 1889.

49 Transvaal Archives Repository, SN 18 SR93/1891 Commandant van Polisie Johannesburg to Asst. Landdrost Johannesburg, 21 January 1891.

50 Transvaal Archives Repository, SNA 187 NA3069/1903 Acting Pass Commissioner Johannesburg, Memorandum on unpopularity among Cape Colony natives of service on the Rand, 17 December 1903.

51 Transvaal Archives Repository, TKP 267/2 MICE 1908, Evidence of Henry Melville Taberer, 14 October 1907, 1309; K 358–2 Evidence of Alfred Henry George Pigg, 5 February 1914; K 358–2 Evidence of Henry Melville Taberer, 6 February 1914.

52 Transvaal Archives Repository, SNA 166 NA1918/1903 Rex vs. Zulu and Bekile, Native Policemen, Sheba Gold Mine, for Extortion and Assault, 22 August 1903; SNA 184 NA2935/1903 Langden to Windham, 20 November 1903; SNA 187 NA3069/1903 Asst. Chief Magistrate Transkei to SNA Cape Town, 22 October 1903; TKP 241, 74, 86, 90, 94; TKP 267/2 MICE 1908, Evidence of H. L. Phooko, 19 September 1907; LD 1579 AG743/1908 SNA Transvaal to Sec. to the Law Department, 12 March 1908; SNA 465 NA1578/1910 Imperial Secretary, Johannesburg, to Secretary for Native Affairs, 12 May 1910; K 358–2 Testimony of Frank Page ("Cape Boy"), Rigger, New Rietfontein Mine, no. 609, 28 October 1913; K 358–2 Evidence of Levi Thomas Mvabaza, newspaper editor, 15 October 1913.

53 Transvaal Archives Repository, TKP 267/2 MICE 1908, 1442–43, 1446, Evidence

of J. M. Makhothe, General Secretary, Transvaal Native Congress, and Contractor, 29 October 1907.

54 Harries, *Work, Culture, and Identity*, 121–24.

55 Transvaal Archives Repository, LD 37 183/1902 Commissioner of Police, Johannesburg, to Secretary to the Law Department, 7 January 1902.

56 Based on data culled from the various editions of the *Blue Book on Native Affairs* for the years 1894 to 1909 inclusive, as well as TKP 204 Colony of the Transvaal, *Reports of the Transvaal Labour Commission: Minutes and Proceedings of Evidence* (1904), 109–11, 780.

57 This account of the 1896–97 labor disputes is based on Harries, *Work, Culture, and Identity*, 133–34.

58 Warwick, "Black Industrial Protest on the Witwatersrand," 24.

59 Sean Moroney, "Industrial Conflict in a Labour Repressive Economy," 45.

60 Transvaal Archives Repository, K 358–2 Evidence of Henry Melville Taberer, 6 February 1914.

61 Transvaal Archives Repository, SNA 26 NA819/1902 Petition, Levi Mapumulo, Philip Cela and Tibela Zwana, to Godfrey Lagden, Commissioner for Native Affairs, 9 April 1902.

62 For the Natalian origins of the Cele and Mapumulo, Theophilus Shepstone, "Inhabitants of the Territory (now the Colony of Natal), during the time of Jobe, father of Dingizwayo, before the extermination of native tribes by Chaka," Enclosure no. 1 in Lieutenant-Governor Scott's Despatch No. 12, 26 February 1864, reprinted in Bird, *The Annals of Natal*, 1:124–26, 149.

63 Transvaal Archives Repository, SNA 26 NA819/1902 Petition, Levi Mapumulo, Philip Cela, and Tibela Zwana, to Godfrey Lagden, Commissioner for Native Affairs, 9 April 1902.

64 Transvaal Archives Repository, LD 1579 AG743/1908 MNA to AG, 1 April 1908.

65 Transvaal Archives Repository, Union of South Africa, *Report of the Native Grievances Inquiry, 1913–14*, par. 510.

66 Harries, *Work, Culture, and Identity*, 224, 285n158. A similar point is made in Breckenridge, "Migrancy, Crime, and Faction Fighting," esp. 57.

67 Transvaal Archives Repository, SNA 126 NA1003/1903 Sansom to Lagden, 15 April 1903.

68 Transvaal Archives Repository, K 358–2 Evidence of Charles Walter Villiers, 3 March 1914.

69 "Kafir Domestics," *Standard and Diggers' News*, 25 October 1898.

70 Harries, *Work, Culture, and Identity*, 121–23; "Great Native Fight," *The Star*, 14 November 1892; "The Rand Battle," *Standard and Diggers' News*, 25 October 1898; "Exasperated Natives," *The Star*, 27 March 1899.

71 Transvaal Archives Repository, TKP 267/1 MICE 1908, Evidence of James Quarton Braidwood, 27 August 1907.

72 Transvaal Archives Repository, K 358–2 Native Grievances Commission, Testimony D. W. Robertson, 30 January 1914. See also Transvaal Archives Repository,

TKP 267/1 MICE 1908, Evidence of James Quarton Braidwood, 27 August 1907; K 358–2 Native Grievances Commission, Evidence of Charles Walter Villiers, 3 March 1914.

73 Transvaal Archives Repository, K 358–2 Native Grievances Commission, Evidence of Alfred Henry George Pigg, 5 February 1914.

74 Transvaal Archives Repository, K 358–2 Native Grievances Commission, Evidence of Charles Walter Villiers, 3 March 1914.

75 The translation of *umkhosi* as "regiment" is somewhat idiosyncratic. The more usual Zulu word for "regiment" is *ibutho* or *impi*, while *umkhosi* more typically refers to the first-fruits ceremony or to any festival or holiday. But *umkhosi* can also refer to a "cause of alarm, e.g. host, army." See Doke et al., *English-Zulu Zulu-English Dictionary*, 94–95, 405, 511.

76 The classic description and analysis of this gang is Van Onselen, "The Regiment of the Hills—*Umkosi Wezintaba*," revised and expanded in Van Onselen, *New Babylon, New Nineveh*, part 2, chap. 4.

77 Doke et al., *English-Zulu Zulu-English Dictionary*, 577–78.

78 La Hausse, "'The Cows of Nongoloza,'" 90.

79 The evidence for the history and structure of Nongoloza's gang comes from Transvaal Archives Repository, JUS 144 3/778/12 Secretary for Justice to the Chief Commissioner of Police Pretoria, 3 January 1913; Affidavit, Tomboek Umfanawenduku, 19 June 1912; Affidavit, Johnson Johannes, 19 June 1912; Affidavit, Jan Note, alias Nongoloza, 27 December 1912.

80 Moroney, "Industrial Conflict in a Labour Repressive Economy," 107.

81 For a detailed description of this ceremony, see "The Wash Boys' Parade," *Standard and Diggers' News*, 2 July 1895. For the importance of pilgrimage and assembly in promoting a sense of common identity among an otherwise disparate group of people, see Anderson, *Imagined Communities*.

82 Moroney, "Industrial Conflict in a Labour Repressive Economy," 110.

83 "Native Dances," *The Star*, 24 August 1896.

84 Compare J. Mitchell, *The Kalela Dance*. For more on African migrant workers' dancing on the Rand and elsewhere, see Harries, *Work, Culture, and Identity*, xiv, 58–59, 75, 79, 123–26, 209–13; and "Exasperated Natives" and "Native War Dance," *The Star*, 27 March 1899.

85 TKP 204 Colony of the Transvaal, *Reports of the Transvaal Labour Commission: Minutes and Proceedings of Evidence* (1904), 25. For examples of Europeans' use of the terms *Zulu, Zululand, Natal,* and *Natal native,* see Colony of the Transvaal, *Reports of the Transvaal Labour Commission: Minutes and Proceedings of Evidence* (1904), testimony of F. Suter, 23, 26; testimony of Thomas Maxwell, 29–33; testimony of Courtney Acutt, 257–58, 263; as well as Transvaal Archives Repository, K 358–2 Native Grievances Commission, Evidence of Henry Melville Taberer, 6 February 1914.

86 Andre Odendaal, *Vukani Bantu!*; Brett Cohen, "Something Like a Blowing Wind."

87 Transvaal Archives Repository, SSA 465 RA6060/96 Special Commissioner to SSA, 30 December 1896.

88 Transvaal Archives Repository, SP 885 GCPM 92/1899 Hoofd Detectief der ZAR aan Commissaris van Politie, 9 May 1899.

89 Transvaal Archives Repository, JUS 144 3/786/12 R. H. Swale to the Secretary of the Joint Native Affairs Committee, 29 May 1912. For more on the "black peril" scares on the Rand in particular, see Van Onselen, *New Babylon, New Nineveh*, 237–74.

90 Transvaal Archives Repository, Union of South Africa, *Report of the Native Grievances Inquiry, 1913–14*, par. 474.

91 "The Rand Battle," *Standard and Diggers' News*, 25 October 1898.

92 Transvaal Archives Repository, LD 1072 AG1998/05, Report from the Acting Deputy Commissioner of Police, Rand and Mounted, to the Commissioner of Police, 5 May 1905.

93 Transvaal Archives Repository, SNA 465 NA1578/1910 Director, GNLB, to SNA, 7 June 1910.

94 Transvaal Archives Repository, K 358–2 Native Grievances Commission, Evidence of Graham Cross, Asst. Mag. Johannesburg, 15 October 1913.

95 Transvaal Archives Repository, Union of South Africa, *Report of the Native Grievances Inquiry, 1913–14*, paras. 478–87. For more testimony emphasizing the significance of the July 1914 strikes as evidence of growing African unity, see Transvaal Archives Repository, K 358–2 Native Grievances Commission, Evidence of Henry Melville Taberer, 6 February 1914.

96 For example, Transvaal Archives Repository, K 358–2 Native Grievances Commission, Testimony D. W. Robertson, 30 January 1914; Testimony of Joseph Winter, 27 October 1913. For the road to prohibition on the Rand, see Van Onselen, "Randlords and Rotgut: The Role of Alcohol in the Development of European Imperialism and Southern African Capitalism, with Special Reference to Black Mineworkers in the Transvaal Republic," in *New Babylon, New Nineveh*, part 1, chap. 2.

97 Transvaal Archives Repository, K 358–2 Native Grievances Commission, Testimony of James Gray Millar, Compound Manager Block B Langlaagte Mine, 27 October 1913.

98 Transvaal Archives Repository, K 358–2 Native Grievances Commission, Testimony Theodora Williams, 15 October 1913.

99 Holm, *Pidgin and Creole Languages*, 2:555.

100 Mesthrie, "The Origins of Fanakalo."

101 Holm, *Pidgin and Creole Languages*, 2:350.

102 Msimang, "Impact of Zulu on Tsotsitaal," 83.

103 Ibid., 84–85.

104 For Marwick's later career in Natal and his relationship with Africans there, see La Hausse, *Restless Identities*.

105 PAR, SNA 1/1/216 272/1896 Marwick to USNA, 18 February 1896; SNA 1/1/216

204/1896 Circular No. 4, 1896, USNA to RM's, 12 February 1896; Marwick to USNA, 17 February 1896; SNA 1/1/211 1391/1895 Marwick to USNA, 7 November 1895; SNA 1/1/278 1611/1897 RM Lower Tugela to Marwick, 9 June 1897; *Standard and Diggers News,* 12 November 1897; SNA 1/1/265 Marwick to USNA, 13 November 1897.

106 For various accounts of the march, see the Killie Campbell Africana Library, Marwick Papers, 2567 Newspaper clipping, s.n., n.d.; Marwick Papers, 2569 J. S. Marwick to the editor, *Natal Mercury,* n.d.; Marwick Papers, 2570 Report on the March, n.d.; Marwick Papers, 2572 Newspaper clippings, s.n., n.d.; Marwick Papers, 2576 Marwick's Memorable March, written and compiled by Edith B. Clark, from records in her possession, 3 July 1945; Marwick Papers, 2577 "When the Anglo-Boer War Became Imminent: Exodus of the Zulus and Swazis from the Witwatersrand," s.n., n.d.; Marwick Papers, 2605 PM Natal to Marwick, 15 October 1899; Marwick Papers, 2607 Commandant General SAR to Marwick, 4 October 1899; Marwick Papers, 2746 "A March from Johannesburg," s.n., n.d.; Marwick Papers, 3071 Telegraphic correspondence re march, October–November 1899. See also McCord, *The Calling of Katie Makanya,* 142–43.

107 For the most thorough, and the only firsthand, account of the march, and the source for the following narrative, see PAR, SNA 1/1/284 255/1899 Report relative to the exodus of Natal Natives from the South African Republic, J. S. Marwick, 19 October 1899.

˙5 NATAL AFRICANS' TURN TO DINUZULU

1 Lambert, *Betrayed Trust,* 59, 186.

2 Pietermaritzburg Archives Repository (PAR), SNA 1/4/4 C82/1897 SNA to Col. Sec., 18 November 1897.

3 Many of the insights into conspiracy theories and the theory of rumor come from an extremely original and penetrating analysis of another body of rumor in colonial Africa, Luise White's *Speaking with Vampires,* esp. chaps. 1 and 2.

4 For the careers of Cetshwayo, Dinuzulu, and the Colensos, see Jeff Guy's important trilogy, consisting of *The Destruction of the Zulu Kingdom, The Heretic,* and *The View Across the River.*

5 PAR, SNA 1/4/5 C28/1898 Report of Native Intelligence Officer no. 1, 8 July 1898.

6 Hughes, "Politics and Society in Inanda, Natal," 64, 66, 73–75.

7 See Mahoney, "Between the Zulu King and the Great White Chief," 117–31.

8 PAR, SNA 1/4/14 C79/1905 RM Estcourt to USNA, 20 December 1905.

9 Doke et al., *English-Zulu Zulu-English Dictionary,* 744.

10 Warwick, *Black People and the South African War, 1899–1902*; Krikler, *Revolution from Above, Rebellion from Below.*

11 Colony of Natal, *Blue Book on Native Affairs, 1902,* B28, report, RM Weenen, 31 December 1901.

12 PAR, SNA 1/4/6 C58/1899 Enc. report from Native Intelligence Officer no. 4, 30 August 1899.

13 PAR, SNA 1/4/8 C75/1900 Report of Native Intelligence Officer no. 1, 8 May 1900.

14 PAR, SNA 1/4/8 C10/1900 SNA to PM, 19 January 1900; SNA 1/4/8 C10/1901 Papers relative to the eviction of Native Tenants on account of their having given evidence in Treason Cases, 4 January 1901.

15 PAR, SNA 1/4/6 C97/1899 Inspector Natal Native Trust to SNA, 12 October 1899; SNA 1/4/9 C4/1901 USNA to RM Ixopo, 11 January 1901.

16 PAR, SNA 1/4/7 Reply of RM Lion's River to Confidential Circular no. 51, 9 September 1899.

17 PAR, SNA 1/4/8 C63/1900 Report of Native Intelligence Officer no. 2, 31 March 1900.

18 PAR, SNA 1/4/10 C49/1902 SNA to Chief Magistrate and Civil Commissioner Eshowe, 19 July 1902.

19 PAR, SNA 1/4/10 C107/1902 CM and CC Eshowe to PM to Editor, Natal Witness, 16 December 1902.

20 PAR, SNA 1/4/10 C78/1902 P. Dangerfield to USNA, 22 October 1902.

21 PAR, SNA 1/4/10 C101/1902 Statement of Native Intelligence Officer no. 2, 25 November 1902. This alleged stipulation of Dinuzulu's was also reported in PAR, SNA 1/4/10 C102/1902 Report of Special no. 4, 25 November 1902.

22 PAR, SNA 1/4/10 C108/1902 Sgt. H. S. Smith, Natal Police Durban to Criminal Investigation Officer, 8 December 1902; SNA 1/4/13 C10/1904 Report RM Umvoti, 13 April 1904; Webb and Wright, *The James Stuart Archive*, 3:155.

23 PAR, SNA 1/4/10 C108/1902 Sgt. H. S. Smith, Natal Police Durban to Criminal Investigation Officer, 8 December 1902.

24 PAR, SNA 1/4/12 C89/1903 Report of Native Intelligence Officer no. 3, 13 August 1903; SNA 1/4/12 C87/1903 Report of Native Intelligence Officer no. 1, 9 August 1903.

25 PAR, SNA 1/4/10 C101/1902 Statement of Native Intelligence Officer no. 2, 25 November 1902.

26 PAR, SNA 1/4/12 C27/1903 Anonymous Statement, 31 March 1903.

27 PAR, SNA 1/4/10 C78/1902 USNA to SNA, 23 October 1902; SNA 1/4/12 C42/1903 USNA to SNA, 5 June 1903.

28 PAR, SNA 1/4/12 C6/1903 Report re "John Dube," of Inanda Mission Station, Chief Commissioner of Police, 13 December 1902.

29 PAR, SNA 1/4/12 C25/1903 USNA to SNA, 31 March 1903; SNA 1/4/13 C77/1904 Report of Intelligence Officer no. 2, November 1904.

30 Compare, for example, the Zulu originals and the English translations in the following: PAR, SNA 1/4/9 C2/1901 Translation of Extract from *Ipepa lo Hlanga*, 14 December 1900; SNA 1/4/9 C3/1901 Translation of a letter published in the *Ipepa lo Hlanga*, 11 January 1901; PAR, SNA 1/4/14 C22/1905 Extract from *Ilanga lase Natal*, 19 May 1905.

31 PAR, SNA 1/4/5 C28/1898 Report of Native Intelligence Officer no. 1, 8 July 1898.

32 PAR, SNA 1/4/10 C105/1902 Statement of Native Intelligence Officer no. 2, 25 November 1902.

33 PAR, SNA 1/4/12 C3/1903 Report of Intelligence Officer no. 2, n.d.

34 PAR, SNA 1/4/12 C77/1903 W. R. Wilson to Lt. Col. Lugg, Umvoti Mounted Rifles, 27 July 1903.

35 PAR, SNA 1/4/12 C27/1903 Anonymous Statement, 31 March 1903.

36 PAR, SNA 1/4/12 C83/1903 Statement, Vela, son of Mazibugwana, Chief Silwane, 30 July 1903.

37 Killie Campbell Africana Library, 97/8/13 Zulu Tribal History Essay Competition for year 1912, James Ludongwa, "The Zulus," n.d.; 97/8/7 Zulu Tribal History Essay Competition for year 1912, Barnabas Sivetye, "The Zulus."

38 PAR, SNA 1/4/8 C63/1900 Report of Native Intelligence Officer no. 2, 31 March 1900.

39 PAR, SNA 1/4/12 C48/1903 Statement Native Intelligence Officer no. 2, 17 June 1903.

40 PAR, SNA 1/4/13 C10/1904 Report RM Umvoti, 13 April 1904.

41 For Bhambatha's supposed alliance with Dinuzulu, see PAR, SNA 1/4/12 C77/1903 W. R. Wilson to Lt. Col. Lugg, Umvoti Mounted Rifles, 27 July 1903; SNA 1/4/12 C83/1903 Statement, Vela, son of Mazibugwana, Chief Silwane, 30 July 1903; SNA 1/4/12 C87/1903 Report of Native Intelligence Officer no. 1, 9 August 1903; SNA 1/4/12 C102/1903 Statement of Intelligence Officer no. 1, 4 November 1903. For rumors about Meseni, Gobizembe, and Dinuzulu, see PAR, SNA 1/4/12 C2/1903 Report of Secret Intelligence Officer no. 1, December 1902. For Ndlovu ka Thimuni, see PAR, SNA 1/4/13 C79/1904 Report of Intelligence Officer no. 2, 4 December 1904.

42 PAR, SNA 1/4/12 C83/1903 Statement, Vela, son of Mazibugwana, Chief Silwane, 30 July 1903, emphasis added.

43 PAR, SNA 1/4/12 C83/1903 Statement, Vela, son of Mazibugwana, Chief Silwane, 30 July 1903.

44 PAR, SNA 1/4/10 C102/1902 Report of Special no. 4, 25 November 1902.

45 Quoted in Welsh, *The Roots of Segregation*, 232.

46 Ibid., 233.

47 Bird, *Is the Kafir Population in Natal Alien or Aboriginal?* 24–28.

48 PAR, SNA 1/4/13 C19/1904 RM Mapumulo to SNA, 4 May 1904.

49 Killie Campbell Africana Library, Stuart Papers KCM 24361 Notes on the recent Rebellion per Socwatsha, 25 August 1907.

50 PAR, SNA 1/4/12 C42/1903 USNA to SNA, 5 June 1903.

51 PAR, SNA 1/4/13 C8/1904 RM Krantzkop to USNA, 20 May 1904; SNA 1/4/13 C13/1904 RM Umlazi to USNA, 7 June 1904; SNA 1/4/13 C18/1904 Report of Native Intelligence Officer no. 1, 1 May 1904; SNA 1/4/13 C19/1904 RM Mapumulo to SNA, 4 May 1904.

52 PAR, SNA 1/4/13 C10/1904 Report RM Umvoti, 13 April 1904.

53 Redding, "A Blood-Stained Tax," 36–42.

54 PAR, SNA 1/4/13 C19/1904 RM Mapumulo to SNA, 4 May 1904.

55 Stoler, *Race and the Education of Desire*.

56 Simons, *African Women*; Etherington, "Natal's Black Rape Scare of the 1870s"; Martens, "Settler Homes, Manhood, and 'Houseboys.'"

57 See the numerous statements to this effect in the evidence before the Natal Native Affairs Commission, 1906–7.

58 PAR, SNA 1/4/5 C80/1898 Mkutyane, Xibane, Ndabazelanga, Mfanefile Kuzwayo to SNA, 13 November 1898; SNA 1/4/5 C49/1898 Statement of Nomfula, widow of late Chief Mkonto, 30 December 1898.

59 PAR, SNA 1/4/10 C42/1902 Statement, Anonymous African Informant, 13 June 1902.

60 Quoted in Marks, *Reluctant Rebellion*, 37n5.

61 PAR, SNA 1/4/10 C7/1902 Cutting from the Natal Witness, letter to the editor dated 28 January 1902.

62 PAR, SNA 1/4/5 C7/1898 William Pearce to SNA, 3 February 1898.

63 The quotes are from Lambert, *Betrayed Trust*, 185–86.

64 Ibid., 148–53.

65 Berglund, *Zulu Thought-Patterns and Symbolism*, 266–95, 345–50.

66 Redding, "A Blood-Stained Tax," 47–48.

67 PAR, SNA 1/4/5 C37/1898 Report of Native Intelligence Officer no. 4, 16 November 1898.

68 Berglund, *Zulu Thought-Patterns and Symbolism*, 287–93.

69 Redding, "A Blood-Stained Tax," 42–43.

70 Carton, *Blood from Your Children*, 121.

71 PAR, SNA 1/4/14 C50/1905 USNA to RM's Newcastle and Dundee, 30 November 1905; SNA 1/4/14 C79/1905 RM Estcourt to USNA, 20 December 1905.

72 PAR, SNA 1/4/14 C65/1905 RM Umlazi to MNA, 10 December 1905; SNA 1/4/14 C71/1905 RM Pinetown to USNA, 14 December 1905.

73 PAR, SNA 1/4/14 C65/1905 RM Umlazi to MNA, 10 December 1905; SNA 1/4/14 C67/1905 RM Pinetown to USNA, 12 December 1905; SNA 1/4/14 C71/1905 RM Pinetown to USNA, 14 December 1905.

74 Marks, *Reluctant Rebellion*, 167.

75 PAR, SNA 1/4/14 C69/1905 James Peniston, Inspector Natal Native Trust, to Armstrong, Clerk Natal Native Trust, 13 December 1905; SNA 1/4/14 C71/1905 RM Pinetown to USNA, 14 December 1905.

76 For the significance of the umkhosi to Zulu kingship, see chapter 1. For the translation of *umlingo*, see Doke et al., *English-Zulu Zulu-English Dictionary*, 459.

77 PAR, SNA 1/4/14 C78/1905 RM Greytown to USNA, 20 December 1905; SNA 1/4/14 C79/1905 RM Estcourt to USNA, 20 December 1905; SNA 1/4/14 C86/1905 RM Weenen to Col. Sec., 29 November 1905; SNA 1/4/14 C87/1905 Statements of Johannes Gwamanda and Ncinyoni ka Nvunyelwa, 18 December 1905; SNA 1/4/14 C95/1905 RM Alexandra to USNA, 27 December 1905.

78 PAR, SNA 1/4/14 C86/1905 RM Weenen to Col. Sec., 29 November 1905.

79 Berglund, *Zulu Thought-Patterns and Symbolism*, 158, 180; Hlongwane, "An

Insight into the Causes and Events of the Zulu Rebellion of 1906 from the Black Point of View," 23–24.

80 PAR, SNA 1/4/14 C87/1905 Statement, Johannes Gwamanda, Chief Silwane, 18 December 1905. For similar rumors, see PAR, SNA 1/4/14 C79/1905 RM Estcourt to USNA, 20 December 1905; SNA 1/4/14 C86/1905 RM Weenen to Col. Sec., 29 November 1905.

81 PAR, SNA 1/4/14 C95/1905 RM Alexandra to USNA, 27 December 1905.

82 See, for example, PAR, SNA 1/4/12 C27/1903 Anonymous Statement, 31 March 1903; SNA 1/4/12 C83/1903 Statement, Vela, son of Mazibugwana, Chief Silwane, 30 July 1903; SNA 1/4/12 C54/1903 USNA to SNA, 20 June 1903; SNA 1/4/13 C21/1904 Statement, Chief Swaimana ka Zipuku, Mapumulo Division, 12 May 1904; SNA 1/4/14 C87/1905 Statement, Johannes Gwamanda, Chief Silwane, 18 December 1905.

83 PAR, SNA 1/4/14 C36/1905 Report of Intelligence Officer no. 2, 28 August 1905.

84 See also PAR, SNA 1/4/5 C28/1898 Report of Native Intelligence Officer no. 1, 8 July 1898; SNA 1/4/12 C23/1903 Report of Intelligence Officer no. 3, 9 March 1903.

85 PAR, SNA 1/4/13 C50/1904 Report of Native Intelligence Officer no. 1, 13 July 1904.

86 PAR, SNA 1/4/15 C54/1906 Report by James Umlaw, an exempted Native, 29 January 1906.

87 PAR, SNA 1/4/14 C65/1905 RM Umlazi to MNA 10 December 1905. For histories of these early gangs, see La Hausse, "'The Cows of Nongoloza'"; Van Onselen, "'The Regiment of the Hills'—Umkosi Wezintaba"; Van Onselen, "Crime and Total Institutions in the Making of Modern South Africa"; Van Onselen, The Small Matter of a Horse.

88 Carton, Blood from Your Children, 121–22.

89 PAR, SNA 1/4/5 C28/1898 Report of Native Intelligence Officer no. 1, 8 July 1898.

90 PAR, SNA 1/4/12 C23/1903 Report of Intelligence Officer no. 3, 9 March 1903.

91 PAR, SNA 1/4/12 C4/1903 Report of Native Intelligence Officer no. 2, 5 January 1903.

92 PAR, SNA 1/4/13 C50/1904 Report of Native Intelligence Officer no. 1, 13 July 1904.

93 PAR, SNA 1/4/14 C55/1905 F. D. Umpleby to Posselt, 13 December 1905; Carton, Blood from Your Children, 122.

94 Besides the rumors cited above, see also PAR, SNA 1/4/12 C72/1903 A. W. Wright Natal Police to Sub Inspector Banister Natal Police, 17 July 1903; SNA 1/4/12 C83/1903 Statement, Vela, son of Mazibugwana, Chief Silwane, 30 July 1903; SNA 1/4/13 C50/1904 Report of Native Intelligence Officer no. 1, 13 July 1904.

95 PAR, SNA 1/4/12 C3/1903 Report of Intelligence Officer no. 2, January 1903.

96 PAR, SNA 1/4/13 C79/1904 Report of Intelligence Officer no. 2, 4 December 1904; SNA 1/4/14 C1/1905 Statement of Intelligence Officer no. 2, 6 January 1905; SNA 1/4/14 C86/1905 RM Weenen to Col. Sec., 29 November 1905.

97 Marks, *Reluctant Rebellion*, 161–62.

98 See, for example, PAR, SNA 1/4/14 C77/1905 USNA to RM Estcourt, 20 December 1905; SNA 1/4/14 C79/1905 RM Estcourt to USNA, 20 December 1905.

99 PAR, SNA 1/4/14 C86/1905 RM Weenen to Col. Sec., 29 November 1905.

100 PAR, SNA 1/4/12 C55/1903 Native Commissioner Northern Division Transvaal to SNA, 5 June 1903. The classic academic description of the Rain Queen and her followers is Krige and Krige, *In the Realm of the Rain Queen*. The Rain Queen was also one of the models for the title character in H. Rider Haggard's popular turn-of-the-century novel *She*.

101 One or more of these themes crops up in each of the following reports: PAR, SNA 1/4/12 C23/1903 Report of Intelligence Officer no. 3, 9 March 1903; SNA 1/4/12 C77/1903 W. R. Wilson to Lt. Col. Lugg, Umvoti Mounted Rifles, 27 July 1903; SNA 1/4/12 C89/1903 Report of Native Intelligence Officer no. 3, 13 August 1903; SNA 1/4/13 C21/1904 Statement, Chief Swaimana ka Zipuku, Mapumulo Division, 12 May 1904; SNA 1/4/13 C50/1904 Report of Native Intelligence Officer no. 1, 13 July 1904.

102 Mahoney, "The Millennium Comes to Mapumulo."

103 PAR, SNA 1/4/12 C55/1903 Report, Detective R. H. Arnold, Johannesburg Police, 26 April 1901.

104 Marks, *Reluctant Rebellion*, 328, 335. See also ibid., 74–79, 308–10, and 326–35.

105 See, for example, articles on the poll tax and the rebellion in *Ilanga lase Natal*, 17 November 1905; 2 March 1906; 16 March 1906; 17 August 1906.

106 Marks, *Reluctant Rebellion*, 114–16, 363–64.

107 PAR, SNA 1/4/8 C63/1900 Report of Native Intelligence Officer no. 2, 31 March 1900.

108 I have not been able to find any other reference to the name "Neboheth," either in the Bible or elsewhere. However, "Heth" is the name of a son of Canaan and grandson of Ham. Isaac's wife Rebekah did not want her sons to marry descendants of Heth because they were not descendants of Abraham. Her favored son, Isaac, did not marry such a woman, while Esau, who lost his birthright to Jacob, married two (Genesis 26:34, 27:46, 36:2, 49:29). "Nebo" was the ancestor of several men who had to divorce their wives because those women were foreigners (Ezra 10:43). "Nebajoth" was the son of Ishmael, eldest son and legal heir to Abraham, who similarly lost his birthright to Isaac. Esau also married one of Nebajoth's sisters. It would seem that "John" was conflating these three figures, perhaps because they represented nativism and lost birthrights, biblical ideas that would resonate with Natal Africans dealing with land expropriation and both formal and informal racism. Thanks to Hope Stephenson, a Bible scholar at the Yale School of Divinity, for alerting me to the relevant Bible passages.

109 PAR, SNA 1/4/14 C54/1905 Rex vs. John alias Amos Kumalo, 20 December 1905.

110 PAR, SNA 1/4/10 C102/1902 Report of Special no. 4, 25 November 1902.

111 PAR, SNA 1/4/5 C28/1898 Report of Native Intelligence Officer no. 1, 8 July 1898.

112 PAR, SNA 1/4/12 C2/1903 Report of Secret Intelligence Officer no. 1, December 1902.

113 For an example of the cat-and-mouse game between Dube and the government in the years leading up to the rebellion, see PAR, SNA 1/4/12 C6/1903 Report re "John Dube," of Inanda Mission Station, Chief Commissioner of Police, 13 December 1902.

114 As, for example, in PAR, SNA 1/4/12 C67/1903 Report of Native Intelligence Officer no. 1, 4 July 1903.

115 PAR, SNA 1/4/10 C102/1902 Report of Special no. 4, 25 November 1902; SNA 1/4/12 C87/1903 Report of Native Intelligence Officer no. 1, 9 August 1903; SNA 1/4/12 C102/1903 Statement of Intelligence Officer no. 1, 4 November 1903; SNA 1/4/13 C7/1904 RM Mapumulo to USNA, 3 May 1904; SNA 1/4/13 C19/1904 RM Mapumulo to SNA, 4 May 1904; SNA 1/4/13 C21/1904 Statement, Chief Swaimana ka Zipuku, Mapumulo Division, 12 May 1904.

116 PAR, SNA 1/4/13 C19/1904 RM Mapumulo to SNA, 4 May 1904.

117 PAR, SNA 1/4/12 C2/1903 Report of Secret Intelligence Officer no. 1, December 1902.

118 PAR, SNA 1/4/13 C79/1904 Report of Intelligence Officer no. 2, 4 December 1904.

119 Webb and Wright, *The James Stuart Archive*, 3:100.

120 PAR, 1/MPO Add. 1/1/1 Natal Mounted Police Intelligence Book, Report of Trooper Isaac Sjoblom, 8 June 1906.

121 PAR, SNA 1/4/12 C102/1903 Statement of Intelligence Officer no. 1, 4 November 1903.

122 PAR, SNA 1/4/13 C69/1904 Report of Intelligence Officer no. 1, 12 November 1904; SNA 1/4/14 C11/05 Report of Intelligence Officer no. 1, 6 February 1905.

6 THE POLL TAX PROTESTS AND REBELLION

1 Pietermaritzburg Archives Repository (PAR), SNA 1/4/14 C43/1905 MNA to Chief Magistrate Durban, 13 November 1905; *Times of Natal*, 7 November 1905.

2 PAR, SNA 1/1/330 3220/1905 Political Reports, Translations of cuttings from *Ilanga lase Natal* dated 17 and 24 November 1905. In the original, the word translated as "Natives" was actually *abantu*, or "people."

3 PAR, SNA 1/4/15 C21/1906 Memoranda enc. in RM Lower Tugela to USNA, 3 January 1906.

4 *Dinuzulu* and *Dinizulu* are both common spellings and pronunciations of the name. About half of the mother-tongue Zulu speakers consulted chose each one. This "i-u" alternation in unstressed syllables is common in Zulu: for example, even in the standard language both *fishane* and *fushane* are acceptable alternatives for "short."

5 PAR, SNA 1/4/15 C37/1906 T. F. Baynes to Chief Magistrate Durban, 8 January 1906.

6 Marks, *Reluctant Rebellion*, 174–90.

7 Carton, *Blood from Your Children*, 123. Carton does not include the three districts in Zululand which had been annexed from the Transvaal after the South African War, all of which were quiet during this period.

8 PAR, SNA 1/1/335 372/1906 Report, RM Lower Tugela, 3 February 1906.

9 PAR, SNA 1/4/15 C42/1906 Minutes of a meeting between the RM Lower Tugela, USNA, MNA, and Lower Tugela chiefs, 9 February 1906.

10 PAR, SNA 1/1/328 2830/1905 RM Mapumulo to MNA, 23 October 1905.

11 Contemporary sources refer to this chief as both "Gobizembe" and "Ngobizembe." Marks and Carton both opt for the latter spelling, but native speakers consulted have uniformly responded that "Gobizembe" is, in fact, the correct version.

12 PAR, SNA 1/4/15 C48/1906 Sgt. E. W. L'Estrange NP to Sub-Insp. Clifton NP, 22 January 1906; 1/MPO 5/4 Statement, Nkomonopondo, 5 March 1906.

13 For a more detailed description of these events, see Mahoney, "Between the Zulu King and the Great White Chief," 252–75.

14 PAR, SNA 1/1/336 505/1906 RM Durban to SNA, 26 February 1906; Report, Detective R. H. Arnold, 26 February 1906.

15 For narratives of Bhambatha's rebellion, see Stuart, *A History of the Zulu Rebellion, 1906*, 155–317; and Marks, *Reluctant Rebellion*, 201–24.

16 See chapter 3.

17 Stuart, *A History of the Zulu Rebellion*, 347.

18 Marks, *Reluctant Rebellion*, 225–26, 229–30.

19 PAR, SNA 1/1/343 1897/1906 Statement, Mabeza, 23 June 1906.

20 PAR, 1/MPO Add. 1/1/1 Natal Mounted Rifles Intelligence Book, Report, Tom Khuzwayo, 26 June 1906.

21 PAR, AGO 1/7/52 Sp:277/1909 Statement, Meseni, 20 July 1906.

22 PAR, SNA 1/4/12 C2/1903 Report of Secret Intelligence Officer no. 1, December 1902.

23 PAR, SNA 1/4/15 C54/1906 Statement, James Umlaw, 29 January 1906. See also the discussion in chapter 5.

24 PAR, SNA 1/1/336 530/1906 Statement, James Umlaw, 16 February 1906.

25 PAR, 1/MPO Add. 1/1/1 Natal Mounted Rifles Intelligence Book, Report no. 22, R. Boyles, 18 May 1906; 1/MPO Add. 1/1/1 Natal Mounted Rifles Intelligence Book, Report Lt. Landsburg, 28 May 1906; 1/MPO Add. 1/1/1 Natal Mounted Rifles Intelligence Book, Report Ngabeni, 5 June 1906; 1/MPO Add. 1/1/1 Natal Mounted Police Intelligence Book, Report of James Umlaw, 11 June 1906; 1/MPO 5/4 Statement, Robert Boyles, 14 August 1906. Killie Campbell Africana Library, Stuart Papers KCM 24361 Notes on the recent Rebellion per Socwatsha, 23 and 25 August 1907.

26 PAR, SNA 1/1/337 612/1906 RM Mapumulo to SNA, 18 February 1906.

27 PAR, 1/MPO 5/4 Minutes of interview between Leuchars, Swayimana, and Meseni, 11 March 1906.

28 PAR, SNA 1/1/320 950/1906 Order of the Governor, 29 March 1906; SNA 1/1/339 1021/1906 RM Lower Tugela to USNA, 1 April 1906; CSO 1808 2635/1906 Advocate Foss to Col. Sec., 31 March 1906; CSO 1808 2635/1906 RM Mapumulo to USNA, 3 April 1906. For more on the faction fight between Meseni's and Swayimana's subjects, see chapter 3. Meseni was in prison for only a few days, not the six weeks claimed by Stuart and by Marks, who apparently bases her claim on Stuart's. See Stuart, *A History of the Zulu Rebellion*, 346; Marks, *Reluctant Rebellion*, 199.

29 PAR, SNA 1/1/336 549/1906 Return of poll tax collections, n.d.

30 PAR, 1/MPO Add. 1/1/1 Natal Mounted Rifles Intelligence Book, Report Lt. Landsburg, 9 June 1906.

31 PAR, SNA 1/1/343 1897/1906 Statement, Mabeza, 23 June 1906.

32 PAR, 1/MPO Add. 1/1/1 Natal Mounted Rifles Intelligence Book, Statement, Nowanyana, 22 June 1906.

33 Marks, *Reluctant Rebellion*, 225.

34 Ibid., 206–9.

35 Carton, "'Blood from Your Sons,'" 245–46, 250, 266–68. Carton repeats the error of various colonial officials in referring to the badges as *umtshokobezi*, when this word, in fact, refers to the individual who wears it ("tsh" reflects turn-of-the-century spelling and pronunciation; "sh" is the contemporary equivalent).

36 Stuart, *A History of the Zulu Rebellion*, 168, quoted in Marks, *Reluctant Rebellion*, 206.

37 Marks, *Reluctant Rebellion*, 205, 207–9, 212, 220, 249–304.

38 Ibid., 216–17; Carton, "'Blood from Your Sons,'" 273.

39 See, for example, PAR, 1/MPO Add. 1/1/1 Natal Mounted Rifles Intelligence Book, Report, Lt. Landsberg, 14 June 1906.

40 PAR, AGO 1/7/52 Sp:277/1909 Statement, Meseni, 20 July 1906; Statement, Ndlovu, 21 July 1906. James Stuart took down the statements. The third rebel chief, Matshwili, was not alive to give a statement, having been killed during the rebellion.

41 PAR, 1/MPO 5/4 Statement, Sifo, 21 July 1906; 1/MPO 5/4 Statement, Henry Hosking, Trooper NMR, 29 July 1906; 1/MPO 5/4 Statement, Bixa, 2 August 1906; 1/MPO 5/4 Statement, Thomas D. Oglesby, Sr., n.d.; 1/MPO Add. 1/1/1 Natal Mounted Rifles Intelligence Book, Report, John Hlonono, 25 June 1906; 1/MPO Add. 1/1/1 Natal Mounted Rifles Intelligence Book, Report, Tom Khuzwayo, 26 June 1906; GH 1471 112/1906 Gov. to Col. Sec., 19 June 1906.

42 PAR, 1/MPO Add. 1/1/1 Natal Mounted Rifles Intelligence Book, Statement, Mandlala, 25 June 1906.

43 PAR, 1/MPO Add. 1/1/1 Natal Mounted Rifles Intelligence Book, Statement, Nyamana and Sogwana, 27 June 1906.

44 PAR, SNA 1/1/343 1897/1906 Statement, Mabeza, 23 June 1906; GH 1550 7220/1907 RM Mapumulo to Col. Sec., 6 November 1907; 1/MPO Add. 1/1/1 Natal Mounted Rifles Intelligence Book, Report, Tshabalala, 21 June 1906; 1/MPO

Add. 1/1/1 Natal Mounted Rifles Intelligence Book, Report, Mantingwana, 21 June 1906; 1/MPO Add. 1/1/1 Natal Mounted Rifles Intelligence Book, Report, Tom Khuzwayo, 26 June 1906.

45 PAR, 1/MPO Add. 1/1/1 Natal Mounted Rifles Intelligence Book, Report, John Hlonono, 25 June 1906.

46 Marks, *Reluctant Rebellion*, 231–32.

47 PAR, 1/MPO 5/4 Statement, Sifo, 21 July 1906.

48 PAR, 1/MPO 5/4 Statement, Bennet Boyles, 11 September 1906.

49 PAR, SNA 1/4/18 C172/1907 RM Lower Tugela to USNA, 4 October 1907.

50 PAR, SNA 1/4/18 C172/1907 Report, Sub-Inspector Hulett, NP Mapumulo, 8 October 1907.

51 Carton, *Blood from Your Children*, 151. For contemporary accounts emphasizing the generational factor, see Marks, *Reluctant Rebellion*, 309.

52 PAR, 1/MPO 5/4 Statement, Isaac alias Duhla ka Mkhonto, 5 March 1906.

53 PAR, SNA 1/4/1/5 C48/1906 Report, RM Mapumulo, 25 January 1906.

54 PAR, SNA 1/1/335 400/1906 Report, RM Mapumulo, 5 February 1906; SNA 1/1/341 1426/1906 Statements, Swayimana and Sgt. Mhlazana NP, 19 March 1906; SNA 1/4/15 C67/1906 H. Carter to USNA, 31 January 1906; 1/MPO 5/4 Statement, Swayimana, 8 March 1906; 1/MPO 5/4 Statement, Sogwaqili, 1 March 1906.

55 PAR, 1/MPO 5/4 Statement, Swayimana, 9 March 1906.

56 PAR, SNA 1/1/345 2262/1906 RM Mapumulo to USNA, 31 August 1906; SNA 1/1/414 3263/1908 Report, RM Lower Tugela, 30 November 1906.

57 Marks, *Reluctant Rebellion*, 237.

58 PAR, SNA 1/1/349 2999/1906 RM Mapumulo to USNA, 23 December 1906; 1/MPO Add. 1/1/1 Natal Mounted Rifles Intelligence Book, Report, Mapumulo Native Constables Johi and Nsunsukwana, 2 July 1906; GH 1550 7220/1907 J. B. K. Farrer, RM Mapumulo, to Col. Sec., 6 November 1907.

59 PAR, SNA 1/1/343 1897/1906 Statement, Mabeza, 23 June 1906.

60 PAR, SNA 1/1/355 3763/1906 Report, RM Mapumulo, 10 December 1906; SNA 1/1/362 373/1907 Report, RM Mapumulo, with enclosures, 26 January 1907.

61 Webb and Wright, *The James Stuart Archive*, 4:51–58.

62 PAR, SNA 1/1/345 2262/1906 RM Mapumulo to USNA, 26 January 1907.

63 PAR, SNA 1/4/16 C207/1906 RM Mapumulo to SNA, 13 July 1906; Marks, *Reluctant Rebellion*, 232–33.

64 PAR, SNA 1/1/352 3440/1906 Depositions, Sambana ka Gunjini, et al., 16 October 1906; RM Lower Tugela to USNA, 16 October 1906 to 16 April 1907.

65 PAR, 1/MPO Add. 1/1/1 Natal Mounted Rifles Intelligence Book, Report, John Hlonono, 25 June 1906.

66 PAR, GH 1550 7220/1907 Enc. List of rebel prisoners over 50 years of age, n.d.

67 Benedict Carton, "'Blood from Your Sons,'" 264, 288.

68 PAR, SNA 1/1/372 1982/1907 RM Mapumulo to Col. Sec., 7 June 1907; GH 1549 381/1907 Return of Natives convicted and imprisoned for rebellion, enc. in Asst.

Commr. of Police to Min. Justice, 11 September 1907; GH 1549 7220/1907 Enc. List of rebel prisoners over 50 years of age, n.d.; CSO 2599 C147/1906 Appendix E, Return showing number of cases dealt with in the Magisterial Divisions by Magistrates authorized to try cases under Martial Law, n.d.

69 Marks, *Reluctant Rebellion*, 309, 311, 317.

70 PAR, SNA 1/1/348 2675/1906 Translation, W. J. M. to the editor, *Ilanga lase Natal*, 3 August 1906. Thanks are owed to an anonymous peer reviewer of this book who suggested that "'W.J.M' is almost certainly W.J. Mseleku a kholwa associated with the Zulu cultural revival" of the early twentieth century.

71 Marks, *Reluctant Rebellion*, 336n2.

72 PAR, SNA 1/1/343 1897/1906 Statement, Mabeza, 23 June 1906.

73 PAR, SNA 1/1/353 3482/1906 Report, RM Lower Tugela, 8 November 1906; SNA 1/1/399 1476/1908 Report, RM Lower Tugela, 12 April 1908; SNA 1/1/414 3263/1908 Report, RM Lower Tugela, 30 November 1906.

74 PAR, SNA 1/1/339 1021/1906 RM Lower Tugela to USNA, 1 April 1906 to 29 May 1906.

75 PAR, SNA 1/4/16 C167/1906 USNA, to RM Lower Tugela, 21 May 1906; Report RM Lower Tugela, 24 May 1906.

76 PAR, 1/MPO Add. 1/1/1 Natal Mounted Rifles Intelligence Book, Report, James Umlaw, 11 June 1906.

77 PAR, 1/MPO Add. 1/1/1 Natal Mounted Rifles Intelligence Book, Report, John Hlonono, 25 June 1906.

78 PAR, 1/MPO Add. 1/1/1 Natal Mounted Rifles Intelligence Book, Report, Tom Khuzwayo, 26 June 1906.

79 PAR, SNA 1/1/343 Statement, Mabeza, 23 June 1906.

80 PAR, SNA 1/1/352 3440/1906 RM Lower Tugela to USNA, 16 October 1906 to 16 April 1907; 1/MPO 5/4 Report, Somveli, 23 July 1906.

81 PAR, SNA 1/1/352 3440/1906 Depositions, Sambana ka Gunjini, Zwelabo ka Fingwana, et al., 16 October 1906.

82 PAR, SNA 1/1/399 1476/1908 Statement, Meseni, 20 March 1907.

83 Marks, *Reluctant Rebellion*, 321–26.

84 PAR, SNA 1/1/352 3440/1906 RM Lower Tugela to USNA, 16 October 1906 to 16 April 1907.

85 PAR, SNA 1/1/352 3440/1906 Depositions, Sambana ka Gunjini, Zwelabo ka Fingwana, et al., 16 October 1906.

86 Marks, *Reluctant Rebellion*, 325n3.

87 Ibid., 324.

88 Marks, "Class, Ideology, and the Rebellion," 358. See also Marks, *Reluctant Rebellion*, 313–14.

89 PAR, 1/MPO Add. 1/1/1, Natal Mounted Rifles Intelligence Book, Statement, Levu, 19 June 1906; Statement, John Hlonono, 25 June 1906; Statement, Tom Khuzwayo, 26 June 1906; Statement, Gaba ka Gebula, 29 June 1906.

90 Marks, *Reluctant Rebellion*, 245, 313.

91 Ibid., 78, 80–81, 330–31; Switzer, "The Problems of an American Mission in a White-Dominated, Multi-Racial Society," chaps. 3–4, 8.

92 PAR, SNA 1/1/352 3322/1906 Statements, Mahlubi et al., 11 October 1906.

93 PAR, SNA 1/4/17 C60/1907 Statement, Meseni, 20 March 1907.

94 PAR, AZM A/5/65 Transcript of notes taken at an interview between the MNA and Revs. Goodenough and Taylor, 26 February 1907.

95 PAR, SNA 1/1/352 3322/1906 Statement, Billy Mkwanazi, 11 October 1906.

96 PAR, AZM A/5/65 Statement of Billy Mkwanazi, n.d.; Annotated statement of Elijah, n.d.; Native men of Esidumbini said to have joined rebels, n.d. See also PAR, 1/MPO, Add. 1/1/1, Natal Mounted Rifles Intelligence Book, Statement, Mvakwendlu Sivetshe, 16 May 1906.

97 Marks, "Class, Ideology, and the Bambatha Rebellion," 357, 367.

98 Ibid., 358. Marks made the same point sixteen years earlier in her exhaustively researched masterpiece on the rebellion, *Reluctant Rebellion*, 313–14.

99 Carton, *Blood from Your Children*, 3.

100 Scott, *Weapons of the Weak* and *Domination and the Arts of Resistance*.

101 The best estimates for the size of the various rebel forces are to be found in Marks, *Reluctant Rebellion*, 174–76, 206, 209, 230, and 232.

102 This interplay of geography, economics, and culture is discussed more thoroughly in chapters 4 and 5.

EPILOGUE

1 La Hausse, *Restless Identities*, 207.

2 Renan, "What Is a Nation?"

3 Marks, *The Ambiguities of Dependence*; Cope, *To Bind the Nation*.

4 La Hausse, *Restless Identities*.

5 La Hausse, "The Message of the Warriors," esp. 30, 37.

6 McClendon, *Genders and Generations Apart*.

7 La Hausse, "The Message of the Warriors," 44–47.

8 Bradford, *A Taste of Freedom*.

9 Hunter, "The Materiality of Everyday Sex" and "Cultural Politics and Masculinities."

10 La Hausse, "The Message of the Warriors," 39.

11 Marks, "Patriotism, Patriarchy, and Purity."

12 For the Inkatha Women's Brigade, see Waetjen, *Workers and Warriors*; Bonnin, "Claiming Spaces, Changing Places"; Shireen Hassim, "Family, Motherhood, and Zulu Nationalism." For virginity testing and its political and social context, see Scorgie, "Virginity Testing and the Politics of Sexual Responsibility."

13 Jung, *Then I Was Black*.

14 Sitas, *Black Mamba Rising* and "Traditions of Poetry in Natal."

15 Oomen, *Chiefs in South Africa*; Williams, "Leading from Behind."

16 Nhlapo Commission on Traditional Leadership Disputes and Claims, "Deter-

mination on AmaZulu Paramountcy," Media statement by the Minister for Provincial and Local Government, Sydney Mufamadi, on the Findings of the Commission on Traditional Leadership Disputes and Claims, 30 April 2008, at the website for South Africa's Department of Cooperative Governance and Traditional Affairs, http://www.thedplg.gov.za/. See also Canaan Mdletshe, "AmaHlubi Reject Zulu Links," *The Sowetan*, 3 August 2007; Bheko Madlala, "Court to Decide on AmaHlubi Monarchy," 11 August 2005, Independent Online, http://www.iol.co.za; Agiza Hlongwane, "Twelve Kings Saga Sparks KZN War Talk," *Tribune*, 8 July 2007; Jan Hennop, "Nhlapo Quits Commission," *Dispatch Online*, 28 November 2007, http://blogs.dispatchnow/.

BIBLIOGRAPHY

ARCHIVAL PRIMARY SOURCES

Pietermaritzburg Archives Repository (PAR), Pietermaritzburg, South Africa

American Zulu Mission Collection (AZM)
  A/5/65: Papers relating to the rebellion, 1906–7
Attorney General's Office (AGO)
  1/7/52: Proceedings of the Special Court, Zulu Rebellion, 1908–9

Colonial Secretary's Office (CSO)
  1806–1814: Miscellaneous Records, 1906
  2580–2599: Minute papers, 1899–1906
Government House (GH)
  1041: Minutes from the Prime Minister, Natal, 1894–1910
  1465–1472: Memoranda Military Affairs Bambata Rebellion, 1906–7
  1549–1550: Memoranda Native Affairs, 1906–7
Mapumulo Magistracy (1/MPO)
  1/4/1/1: Martial Law Note Book, 1906
  5/4: Martial Law Miscellaneous Reports, 1906
  Add. 1/1/1: Natal Mounted Police Intelligence Book, 1906
Native High Court (NHC)
  II/7–II/8: Riot and homicide case records (High Treason), 1880
  II/9–II/11: Civil case records, 1894
Prime Minister (PM)
  61: Minute papers, 1906
  102: Confidential minute papers, 1906
Secretary for Native Affairs (SNA)
  1/1/1–1/1/414: Minute papers, 1846–1908
  1/3/30: Letters from magistrates, 1878
  1/4/1–1/4/20: Confidential papers, 1898–1910
  1/6/11–1/6/16: Papers on Native levies in the Zulu War, 1878–1879

Theophilus Shepstone Papers
Zululand Archive (ZA)
  34: Confidential correspondence, 1904–5

Killie Campbell Africana Library, Durban, South Africa

Marwick Papers
Nembula File
Stuart Papers
Zulu Tribal History Essay Competition

Durban Archives Repository, Durban, South Africa

Durban Corporation Letterbook (DCL)
Durban Magistracy (3/DBN)
Durban Magistrates Correspondence (DMC)
Durban Superintendent of Police Report Book (PRB)

Transvaal Archives Repository, Pretoria, South Africa

Colony of Transvaal, *Mining Industry Commission: Minutes of Evidence with Appendices and Index* (Parts 1–4, TKP 266–7, Pretoria, 1908)
Colony of Transvaal, Native Affairs Department, *Treatment of Complaints of Natives Employed on Mines and Improvements Effected in their General Living Conditions since the Assumption of Control by the Native Affairs Department* (Johannesburg, 1904) (TKP 241)
Colony of Transvaal, Report of the Transvaal Labour Commission (Johannesburg: Argus, 1903)
Department of Justice, Union of South Africa (JUS)
Industrial Commission of Enquiry, Transvaal, 1897
Johannesburg Census, 1896–1904
Johannesburg Public Library, Johannesburg City Archive
Law Department, Transvaal Colony (LD)
Mining Industry Commission Evidence, 1908 (TKP 266) and Report
Native Grievances Commission, 1913–4 (K 358, vols. 1–2)
Native Grievances Enquiry Report
Secretary for Native Affairs, Transvaal Colony (SNA)
Secretary of Mines, Transvaal Colony (MM)
Sekretaris voor Naturellen, Zuid-Afrikaansche Republiek (SN)
Staatsekretaries Afdeling Buitelandse Sake, Zuid-Afrikaansche Republiek (SSA)
Staatsprokureur, Zuid-Afrikaansche Republiek (SP)
Union of South Africa, Department of Justice, *Annual Report for the Calendar Year 1912* (Cape Town, 1913)
Union of South Africa, *Report of the Native Grievances Inquiry, 1913–14*
Witwatersrand Chamber of Mines, Annual Reports

Houghton Library, Cambridge, Massachusetts

American Board Mission (ABM) records

GOVERNMENT PUBLICATIONS

Colony of Natal (Natal Colonial Publications, NCP)

Blue Book on Native Affairs (1879–1886, 1894–1898, 1901–1905)
Blue Book for Native Affairs: Departmental Reports
Census of the Colony of Natal, 1904
Correspondence Relating to Granting to Natives in Natal of Documentary Tribal Titles to Land (1890)
Correspondence Relative to the Eviction of Native Occupants from Crown Lands (1883)
Department of Native Affairs Annual Report (1905–1909)
Evidence before the Natal Native Affairs Commission, 1881–2
Evidence Given Before the Lands Commission, 1901
Evidence Taken before the Natal Native Commission, 1881
Natal Government Gazette Supplement, 1852
Natal Legislative Assembly Debates (1900), v. 29
Natal Legislative Council Debates (1900), vol. 9
Natal Legislative Council Sessional Papers. (1890), no. 22–3
Natal Parliamentary Papers. vol. 156, no. 18, 1891
Native Affairs Commission 1906–7: Evidence (Pietermaritzburg, 1907)
Report of the Natal Native Commission, 1881–2
Report of the Secretary for Native Affairs for the Years 1899–1900
Statistical Year Book for the Year 1906
Supplement to the Blue Book for the Colony of Natal: Departmental Reports (1884, 1889)

Cape Colony

Report and Proceedings, with Appendices, of the Government Commission on Native Law and Customs, 1883

Colony of the Transvaal (Transvaalse Koloniale Publikasies, TKP)

Reports of the Transvaal Labour Commission: Minutes and Proceedings of Evidence (1904)

PUBLISHED SECONDARY SOURCES

Abadan-Unat, Nermin. "East-West vs. South-North Migration: Effects upon the Recruitment Areas of the 1960s." International Migration Review 26.2 (1992): 401–12.
Adas, Michael. Prophets of Rebellion: Millenarian Protest Movements against the European Colonial Order. Chapel Hill: University of North Carolina Press, 1979.

Akyeampong, Emmanuel. *Drink, Power, and Cultural Change: A Social History of Alcohol in Ghana, c. 1800 to Recent Times.* Portsmouth, N.H.: Heinemann; Oxford: James Currey, 1996.

Alford, C. Fred. "What Would It Matter If Everything Foucault Said about Prison Were Wrong?: *Discipline and Punish* after Twenty Years." *Theory and Society* 29.1 (February 2000): 125–46.

Anderson, Benedict. *Imagined Communities: Reflections on the Origin and Spread of Nationalism.* London: Verso, 1983.

Atkins, Keletso. *The Moon Is Dead! Give Us Our Money! The Cultural Origins of an African Work Ethic, Natal, South Africa, 1843–1900.* Portsmouth, N.H.: Heinemann, 1993.

Ballard, Charles. "Traders, Trekkers, and Colonists." *Natal and Zululand from Earliest Times to 1910*, ed. Andrew Duminy and Bill Guest, 116–19. Pietermaritzburg: University of Natal Press / Shuter and Shooter, 1989.

Beinart, William. "The Origins of the Indlavini: Male Associations and Migrant Labour in the Transkei." *African Studies* 50 (1991): 103–28.

———. "Political and Collective Violence in Southern African Historiography." *Journal of Southern African Studies* 18.3 (1992): 455–86.

Berglund, Axel-Ivar. *Zulu Thought-Patterns and Symbolism.* Cape Town: David Philip, 1976.

Berry, Sara. "Hegemony on a Shoestring: Indirect Rule and Farmers' Access to Resources." *No Condition Is Permanent: The Social Dynamics of Agrarian Change in Sub-Saharan Africa*, 22–42. Madison: University of Wisconsin Press, 1993.

Bhana, Surendra, ed. *Essays on Indentured Indians in Natal.* Leeds: Peepal Tree Press, 1990.

Bhana, Surendra, and Joy Brain. *Setting Down Roots: Indian Migrants in South Africa, 1860–1911.* Johannesburg: Witwatersrand University Press, 1990.

Bhana, Surendra, and Goolam Vahed. *The Making of a Political Reformer: Gandhi in South Africa, 1893–1914.* New Delhi: Manohar, 2005.

Bird, John, ed. *The Annals of Natal.* Pietermaritzburg: P. Davis and Sons, 1888.

———. *Is the Kafir Population in Natal Alien or Aboriginal? A Brief Inquiry.* Pietermaritzburg: City Printing Office, 1890.

Bonner, Philip. "African Urbanisation on the Rand between the 1930s and the 1960s: Its Social Character and Political Consequences." *Journal of Southern African Studies* 21.1 (March 1995): 115–29.

Bonnin, Debby. "Claiming Spaces, Changing Places: Political Violence and Women's Protests in KwaZulu-Natal." *Journal of Southern African Studies* 26.2 (2000): 301–16.

Bradford, Helen. "Peasants, Historians, and Gender: A South African Case Study Revisited, 1850–1886." *History and Theory* 39.4 (2000): 86–110.

———. *A Taste of Freedom: The ICU in Rural South Africa, 1924–1930.* Johannesburg: Ravan Press, 1987.

Breckenridge, Keith. "Migrancy, Crime, and Faction Fighting: The Role of the Isitshozi in the Development of Ethnic Organizations in the Compounds." *Journal of Southern African Studies* 16.1 (March 1990): 55–78.

Brookes, Edgar, and Colin Webb. *A History of Natal*. Pietermaritzburg: University of Natal Press, 1965.

Bryant, Alfred T. *Olden Times in Zululand and Natal*. London and New York: Longmans, Green and Co., 1929.

——. *A Zulu-English Dictionary*. Pietermaritzburg: P. Davis and Sons, 1905.

Bundy, Colin. *The Rise and Fall of the South African Peasantry*. Berkeley: University of California Press, 1979.

Burke, Timothy. *Lifebuoy Men, Lux Women: Commodification, Consumption, and Cleanliness in Modern Zimbabwe*. Durham: Duke University Press, 1996.

Campbell, James T. *Middle Passages: African-American Journeys to Africa, 1787–2005*. New York: Penguin, 2006.

Carton, Benedict. *Blood from Your Children: The Colonial Origins of Generational Conflict in South Africa*. Pietermaritzburg: University of Natal Press, 2000.

Carton, Benedict, John Laband, and Jabulani Sithole, eds. *Zulu Identities: Being Zulu, Past and Present*. Scottsville: University of KwaZulu-Natal Press, 2008.

Chanock, Martin. *Law, Custom, and Social Order: The Colonial Experience in Malawi and Zambia*. Cambridge: Cambridge University Press, 1985.

Clegg, Jonathan. "*Ukubuyisa isidumbu*—'Bringing Back the Body': An Examination into the Ideology of Vengeance in the Msinga and Mpofana Rural Locations, 1882–1944." *Working Papers in Southern African Studies*, ed. Philip Bonner, 2:164–98. Johannesburg: Ravan Press, 1981.

Cobbing, Julian, "A Tainted Well: The Objectives, Historical Fantasies, and Working Methods of James Stuart, with Counter-Argument." *Journal of Natal and Zulu History* 11 (1988): 115–54.

Cohen, Abner. *Custom and Politics in Urban Africa: A Study of Hausa Migrants in Yoruba Towns*. Berkeley: University of California Press, 1969.

Colenbrander, Peter. "The Zulu Kingdom, 1828–79." *Natal and Zululand from Earliest Times to 1910*, ed. Andrew Duminy and Bill Guest, 83–115. Pietermaritzburg: University of Natal Press / Shuter and Shooter, 1989.

Colenso, Frances E. *My Chief and I*. 1879. Reprint, Pietermaritzburg: University of Natal Press, 1994.

Colenso, John. *Langalibalele and the Hlubi Tribe*. London: Spottiswoode, 1874.

Comaroff, John L., and Jean Comaroff, *Of Revelation and Revolution*. 2 vols. Chicago: University of Chicago Press, 1991–1997.

Conklin, Alice. *A Mission to Civilize: The Republican Idea of Empire in France and West Africa*. Stanford: Stanford University Press, 1997.

Cooper, Frederick. "Conflict and Connection: Rethinking Colonial African History." *African Historical Review* 99.5 (December 1994): 1516–45.

Cooper, Frederick, and Rogers Brubaker. "Beyond Identity." *Theory and Society* 29.1 (2000): 1–47.

Cope, Nicholas. *To Bind the Nation: Solomon ka Dinuzulu and Zulu Nationalism, 1913–1933*. Pietermaritzburg: University of Natal Press, 1993.

Crehan, Kate. *Gramsci, Culture, and Anthropology*. Berkeley: University of California Press, 2002.

Crush, John, and Charles Ambler, eds. *Liquor and Labour in Southern Africa*. Athens: Ohio University Press; Pietermaritzburg: University of Natal Press, 1992.

Delius, Peter. "Sebatakgomo: Migrant Organisation, the ANC, and the Sekhukhuneland Revolt." *Journal of Southern African Studies* 15.4 (1989): 581–615.

Dirks, Nicholas, ed. *Colonialism and Culture*. Ann Arbor: University of Michigan Press, 1992.

Doke, C., D. M. Malcolm, J. M. A. Sikakana, and B. W. Vilakazi. *English-Zulu Zulu-English Dictionary*. Johannesburg: Witwatersrand University Press, 1990.

Elder, Glen. "Malevolent Traditions: Hostel Violence and the Procreational Geography of Apartheid." *Journal of Southern African Studies* 29.4 (2003): 921–35.

Eldredge, Elizabeth. "Delagoa Bay and the Hinterland in the Early Nineteenth Century: Politics, Trade, Slaves, and Slave Raiding." *Slavery in South Africa: Captive Labor on the Dutch Frontier*, ed. Elizabeth Eldredge and Fred Morton, 127–65. Boulder: Westview, 1994.

Epstein, A. L. *Politics in an Urban African Community*. Manchester: Manchester University Press, 1958.

Etherington, Norman. *Great Treks: The Transformation of Southern Africa, 1815–1854*. London: Longman, 2001.

——. "Natal's Black Rape Scare of the 1870s." *Journal of Southern African Studies* 15.1 (1988): 36–53.

——. *Preachers, Peasants, and Politics in Southeast Africa, 1835–1880: African Christian Communities in Natal, Pondoland, and Zululand*. London: Royal Historical Society, 1978.

——. "The 'Shepstone System' in the Colony of Natal and beyond Its Borders." *Natal and Zululand from Earliest Times to 1910*, ed. Andrew Duminy and Bill Guest, 170–92. Pietermaritzburg: University of Natal Press / Shuter and Shooter, 1989.

——. "Why Langalibalele Ran Away." *Journal of Natal and Zulu History* 1 (1978): 1–24.

Fanon, Frantz. *Black Skins, White Masks*. 1967. Reprint, New York: Grove Press, 1982.

Feierman, Steven. *Peasant Intellectuals: Anthropology and History in Tanzania*. Madison: University of Wisconsin Press, 1990.

Ferguson, James. "The Bovine Mystique: Power, Property, and Livestock in Rural Lesotho." *Man* 20.4 (1985): 647–74.

Fields, Karen. *Revival and Rebellion in Colonial Central Africa*. Princeton: Princeton University Press, 1985.

Foucault, Michel. *The History of Sexuality*. Vol. 1. New York: Pantheon, 1978.

Freund, Bill. *Insiders and Outsiders: The Indian Working Class of Durban, 1910–1990*. London: J. Currey; Portsmouth, N.H.: Heinemann, 1995.

Fuze, Magema M. *The Black People and Whence They Came: A Zulu View*. 1905. Translated by H. C. Lugg. Edited by A. T. Cope. Reprint, Pietermaritzburg: University of Natal Press; Durban: Killie Campbell Africana Library, 1979.

Gilligan, James. *Violence: Reflections on Our Deadliest Epidemic*. London: Jessica Kingsley, 1992.

Ginzburg, Carlo. *The Cheese and the Worms: The Cosmos of a Sixteenth-Century Miller*. Translated by John Tedeschi and Ann Tedeschi. New York: Penguin, 1982.

Glassman, Jonathon. *Feasts and Riot: Revelry, Rebellion, and Popular Consciousness on the Swahili Coast, 1856–1888*. Portsmouth, N.H.: Heinemann, 1995.

Gluckman, Max. *Analysis of a Social System in Modern Zululand*. Manchester, U.K.: Manchester University Press, 1940.

——. *Custom and Conflict in Africa*. Oxford: Basil Blackwell, 1963.

——. "The Kingdom of the Zulu in South Africa." *African Political Systems*, ed. Meyer Fortes and E. Evans-Pritchard, 25–55. London: Oxford University Press, 1940.

——. *Order and Rebellion in Tribal Africa*. London: Cohen and West, 1963.

——. *Politics, Law, and Ritual in Tribal Society*. Oxford: Basil Blackwell, 1965.

Golan, Daphna. *Inventing Shaka: Using History in the Construction of Zulu Nationalism*. Boulder: Lynne Rienner, 1994.

Gramsci, Antonio. *The Antonio Gramsci Reader*. Edited by David Forgacs. New York: New York University Press, 2000.

Guest, Bill. *Langalibalele: The Crisis in Natal, 1873–1875*. Durban: University of Natal Press, 1976.

——. "The New Economy." *Natal and Zululand from Earliest Times to 1910*, ed. Andrew Duminy and Bill Guest, 302–23. Pietermaritzburg: University of Natal Press / Shuter and Shooter, 1989.

Guha, Ranajit. *Dominance without Hegemony: History and Power in Colonial India*. Cambridge: Harvard University Press, 1997.

——. *Elementary Aspects of Peasant Insurgency in Colonial India*. Delhi: Oxford University Press, 1983.

Gump, James. "Ecological Change and Pre-Shakan State Formation." *African Economic History* 18 (1989): 57–71.

Guy, Jeff. "Analysing the Pre-Capitalist Societies in Southern Africa." *Journal of Southern African Studies* 14.1 (1987): 18–37.

——. *The Destruction of the Zulu Kingdom*. London: Longman, 1979.

——. "Gender Oppression in Southern Africa's Precapitalist Societies." *Women and Gender in Southern Africa to 1945*, ed. Cherryl Walker, 33–47. Cape Town: David Philip; London: James Currey, 1990.

——. *The Heretic: A Study of the Life of John William Colenso*. Johannesburg: Ravan Press; Pietermaritzburg: University of Natal Press, 1983.

——. *The Maphumulo Uprising: War, Law, and Ritual in the Zulu Rebellion*. Pietermaritzburg: University of KwaZulu-Natal Press, 2005.

——. *The View across the River: Harriette Colenso and the Zulu Struggle against Imperialism*. Cape Town: David Philip, 2001.

Hamilton, Carolyn. *Terrific Majesty: The Powers of Shaka Zulu and the Limits of Historical Invention*. Cape Town: David Philip, 1998.

Hamilton, Carolyn, and John Wright. "The Making of the *AmaLala*: Ethnicity, Ideology and Relations of Subordination in a Pre-colonial Context." *South African Historical Journal* 22 (1990): 3–23.

Hammond-Tooke, W. D. "Descent Groups, Chiefdoms and South African Historiography." *Journal of Southern African Studies* 11.2 (April 1985): 305–19.

——. "In Search of the Lineage: The Cape Nguni Case." *Man* 19 (1984): 77–93.

——. "Kinship Authority and Political Authority in Pre-colonial South Africa." *Tradition and Transition in Southern Africa*, ed. Andrew Spiegel and Patrick McAllister, 185–99. New Brunswick: Rutgers University Press, 1991.

——. "Who Worships Whom: Agnates and Ancestors among Nguni." *African Studies* 44.1 (1985): 47–64.

Hanretta, Sean. "Women, Marginality, and the Zulu State: Women's Institutions and Power in the Early Nineteenth Century." *Journal of African History* 39 (1998): 389–415.

Harries, Patrick. "Imagery, Symbolism, and Tradition in a South African Bantustan: Mangosuthu Buthelezi, Inkatha, and Zulu History." *History and Theory* 32 (1993): 105–25.

——. *Work, Culture, and Identity: Migrant Laborers in Mozambique and South Africa, c. 1860–1910*. Portsmouth, N.H.: Heinemann, 1994.

Hassim, Shireen. "Family, Motherhood, and Zulu Nationalism: The Politics of the Inkatha Women's Brigade." *Feminist Review*, no. 43 (spring 1993): 1–25.

Herd, Norman. *The Bent Pine: The Trial of Chief Langalibalele*. Johannesburg: Ravan Press, 1976.

Herskovits, Melville J. "The Cattle Complex in East Africa." *American Anthropologist* 28 (1926): 230–72, 361–80, 494–528, 630–34.

Holm, John. *Pidgin and Creole Languages*. 2 vols. New York: Cambridge University Press, 1988.

Huffman, T. N. "Archaeological Evidence and Conventional Explanations of Southern Bantu Settlement Patterns." *Africa* 56.3 (1986): 280–98.

——. "Archaeology and Ethnohistory in the African Iron Age." *Annual Review of Anthropology* 11 (1982): 133–50.

Hughes, Heather. "'The Coolies Will Elbow Us Out of the Country': African Reactions to Indian Immigration in the Colony of Natal, South Africa." *Labour History Review* 72.2 (August 2007): 155–68.

Hunt, Nancy Rose. *A Colonial Lexicon of Birth Ritual, Medicalization, and Mobility in the Congo*. Durham: Duke University Press, 1999.

Hunter, Mark. "Cultural Politics and Masculinities." *Culture, Health, and Sexuality* 7.4 (2005): 389–403.

——. "The Materiality of Everyday Sex: Thinking beyond 'Prostitution.'" *African Studies* 61.1 (2002): 99–120.

Isaacman, Allen. "Peasants and Rural Social Protest in Africa." *Confronting Historical Paradigms*, ed. Frederick Cooper, 205–317. Madison: University of Wisconsin Press, 1993.

Jacobson, Matthew Frye. *Special Sorrows: The Diasporic Imagination of Irish, Polish, and Jewish Immigrants in the United States*. Cambridge: Harvard University Press, 1995.

Jeffrey, Anthea. *The Natal Story: Sixteen Years of Conflict*. Johannesburg: South African Institute of Race Relations, 1997.

Jung, Courtney. *Then I Was Black: South African Political Identities in Transition*. New Haven: Yale University Press, 2000.

Kaplan, Robert. "The Coming Anarchy." *Atlantic Monthly* 273.2 (February 1994): 44–76.

Kennedy, Phillip. "Mpande and the Zulu Kingship." *Journal of Natal and Zulu History* 4 (1981): 21–38.

Kertzer, David. *Ritual, Politics, and Power*. New Haven: Yale University Press, 1988.

Krige, E. J., and D. J. Krige. *In the Realm of the Rain Queen*. London: Oxford University Press, 1943.

Krikler, Jeremy. *Revolution from Above, Rebellion from Below: The Agrarian Transvaal at the Turn of the Century*. Oxford: Clarendon, 1993.

Kunene, Mazisi. *Emperor Shaka the Great: A Zulu Epic*. London: Heinemann, 1979.

Kuper, Adam. "The 'House' and Zulu Political Structure." *Journal of African History* 34.3 (1993): 469–87.

——. "Lineage Theory: A Critical Retrospect." *Annual Review of Anthropology* 11 (1982): 71–95.

——. "Symbolic Dimensions of the Southern Bantu Homestead." *Africa* 50.1 (1980): 8–23.

——. *Wives for Cattle: Bridewealth and Marriage in Southern Africa*. London: Routledge and Kegan Paul, 1982.

La Hausse, Paul. *Brewers, Beerhalls, and Boycotts: A History of Liquor in South Africa*. Johannesburg: Ravan Press, 1988.

——. "'The Cows of Nongoloza': Youth, Crime and Amalaita Gangs in Durban, 1900–1936." *Journal of Southern African Studies* 16.1 (March 1990): 79–111.

——. "Drink and Cultural Innovation in Durban: The Origins of the Beerhall in South Africa, 1902–1916." *Liquor and Labor in Southern Africa*, ed. John Crush and Charles Ambler, 86–88. Athens: Ohio University Press; Pietermaritzburg: University of Natal Press, 1992.

——. "The Message of the Warriors: The ICU, the Labouring Poor, and the Making of Popular Political Culture in Durban, 1925–1930." *Holding Their Ground: Class, Locality, and Culture in Nineteenth and Twentieth Century South Africa*, ed. Philip Bonner, 19–57. Johannesburg: Witwatersrand University Press; Braamfontein: Ravan Press, 1989.

——. *Restless Identities: Signatures of Nationalism, Zulu Ethnicity, and History in the Lives of Petros Lamula (c. 1881–1948) and Lymon Maling (1889–c. 1936)*. Pietermaritzburg: University of Natal Press, 2000.

Laband, John. "The Cohesion of the Zulu Polity under the Impact of the Anglo-Zulu War." *Kingdom and Colony at War*, ed. John Laband and Paul Thompson, 1–33. Pietermaritzburg: University of Natal Press, 1990.

——. "The Cohesion of the Zulu Polity under the Impact of the Anglo-Zulu War: A Reassessment." *Journal of Natal and Zulu History* 8 (1985): 33–62.

——. *The Rise and Fall of the Zulu Nation.* London: Arms and Armour, 1997.

——. *Rope of Sand: The Rise and Fall of the Zulu Kingdom in the Nineteenth Century.* Johannesburg: Jonathan Ball, 1995.

Lambert, John. *Betrayed Trust: Africans and the State in Colonial Natal.* Pietermaritzburg: University of Natal Press, 1995.

Larson, Pier. "'Capacities and Modes of Thinking': Intellectual Engagements and Subaltern Hegemony in the Early History of Malagasy Christianity." *American Historical Review* 102.4 (October 1997): 969–1002.

Liebenberg, B. J. *Andries Pretorius in Natal.* Pretoria: Academica, 1977.

Lockman, Zachary. "The Social Roots of Nationalism: Workers and the National Movement in Egypt, 1908–1919." *Middle East Studies* 24.4 (1988): 444–59.

Lonsdale, John. "The Moral Economy of Mau Mau: The Problem." *Unhappy Valley*, ed. Bruce Berman and John Lonsdale, 2:265–314. London: Cambridge University Press, 1992.

——. "The Moral Economy of Mau Mau: Wealth, Poverty, and Civic Virtue in Kikuyu Political Thought." *Unhappy Valley*, ed. Bruce Berman and John Lonsdale, 2:315–504. London: Cambridge University Press, 1992.

Mahoney, Michael R. "The Millennium Comes to Mapumulo: Popular Christianity in Rural Natal, 1866–1906." *Journal of Southern African Studies* 25.3 (September 1999): 375–91.

——. "Racial Formation and Ethnogenesis from Below: The Zulu Case, 1879–1906." *International Journal of African Historical Studies* 36.3 (2003): 559–84.

——. *The Zulu Past in the Present: What Zulu History Means for Zulus Today.* Forthcoming.

Mamdani, Mahmood. *Citizen and Subject: Contemporary Africa and the Legacy of Late Colonialism.* Princeton: Princeton University Press, 1996.

Maré, Gerhard. *Ethnicity and Politics in South Africa.* London: Zed, 1993.

Maré, Gerhard, and Georgina Hamilton. *An Appetite for Power: Buthelezi's Inkatha and the Politics of Loyal Resistance.* Bloomington: Indiana University Press, 1987.

Marks, Shula. *The Ambiguities of Dependence in South Africa: Class, Nationalism, and the State in Twentieth-Century Natal.* Baltimore: Johns Hopkins University Press, 1986.

——. "Class, Ideology, and the Bambatha Rebellion." *Banditry, Rebellion, and Social Protest in Africa*, ed. Donald Crummey, 351–72. London: James Currey, 1986.

——. "Natal, the Zulu Royal Family, and the Ideology of Segregation." *Journal of Southern African Studies* 4 (1978): 172–94.

——. "Patriotism, Patriarchy, and Purity." *The Creation of Tribalism in Southern Africa*, ed. Leroy Vail, 225–34. Berkeley: University of California Press, 1989.

——. *Reluctant Rebellion: The 1906–8 Disturbances in Natal.* Oxford: Clarendon, 1970.

Marks, Shula, and Dagmar Engels, eds. *Contesting Colonial Hegemony: State and Society in Africa and India.* London: I. B. Tauris, 1994.

Martens, Jeremy. "Settler Homes, Manhood, and 'Houseboys': An Analysis of Natal's Rape Scare of 1886." *Journal of Southern African Studies* 28.2 (2002): 379–400.

Martin, Phyllis. "The Violence of Empire." *History of Central Africa*, ed. David Birmingham and Phyllis Martin, 2:1–27. London: Longman, 1983–1998.

McAllister, Patrick. *Building the Homestead: Agriculture, Labour, and Beer in South Africa's Transkei*. Aldershot, U.K.: Ashgate, 2001.

McClendon, Thomas V. *Genders and Generations Apart: Labor Tenants and Customary Law in Segregation-Era South Africa, 1920s–1940s*. Portsmouth, N.H.: Heinemann; London: James Currey; Cape Town: David Philip, 2002.

McCord, Margaret. *The Calling of Katie Makanya*. Cape Town: David Philip, 1995.

Mesthrie, Rajend. "The Origins of Fanakalo." *Journal of Pidgin and Creole Languages* 4.2 (1989): 211–40.

Mitchell, J. Clyde. *The Kalela Dance: Aspects of Social Relationships among Urban Africans in Northern Rhodesia*. Manchester: Manchester University Press, 1956.

Mitchell, Timothy. *Colonising Egypt*. Cambridge: Cambridge University Press, 1988.

Mofolo, Thomas. *Chaka*. 1925. Reprint, London: Oxford University Press, 1931.

Moroney, Sean. "Industrial Conflict in a Labour Repressive Economy: Black Labour on the Transvaal Gold Mines, 1901–12." Undergraduate honors thesis, University of the Witwatersrand, 1976.

Msimang, C. T. "Impact of Zulu on Tsotsitaal." *South African Journal of African Linguistics* 7.3 (July 1987): 82–86.

Mzala. *Gatsha Buthelezi: Chief with a Double Agenda*. London: Zed, 1988.

Odendaal, André. *Vukani Bantu! The Beginnings of Black Protest Politics in South Africa to 1912*. Cape Town: David Philip, 1984.

Okoye, Felix. "Dingane: A Reappraisal." *Journal of African History* 10.2 (1969): 221–35.

Omer-Cooper, J. D. *The Zulu Aftermath: A Nineteenth-Century Revolution in Bantu Africa*. Evanston, Ill.: Northwestern University Press, 1966.

Oomen, Barbara. *Chiefs in South Africa: Law, Power, and Culture in Post-Apartheid South Africa*. Oxford: James Currey; Pietermaritzburg: University of KwaZulu-Natal Press; New York: Palgrave, 2005.

Parle, Julie, and Michael Mahoney. "An Ambiguous Sexual Revolution: Intra-generational Conflict in Late Colonial Natal, 1879–1906." *South African Historical Journal* 50 (2004): 134–51.

Pearse, R. O., et al. *Langalibalele and the Natal Carbineers: The Story of the Natal Rebellion, 1873*. Ladysmith, South Africa: Ladysmith Historical Society, 1976.

Rabinow, Paul. *French Modern: Norms and Forms of the Social Environment*. Cambridge: Massachusetts Institute of Technology Press, 1989.

Ranger, Terence. "African Reactions to the Imposition of Colonial Rule in East and Central Africa." *The History and Politics of Colonialism in Africa*, ed. L. H. Gann and Peter Duignan, 1:293–324. Cambridge: Cambridge University Press, 1969.

——. "The Invention of Tradition in Colonial Africa." *The Invention of Tradition*, ed. Eric Hobsbawm and Terence Ranger, 211–62. Cambridge: Cambridge University Press, 1983.

———. "The Invention of Tradition Revisited: The Case of Colonial Africa." *Legitimacy and the State in Twentieth-Century Africa*, ed. Terence Ranger and Olufemi Vaughan, 62–111. London: Macmillan, 1993.

Redding, Sean. "A Blood-Stained Tax: Poll Tax and the Bhambatha Rebellion in South Africa." *African Studies Review* 43.2 (September 2000): 29–54.

Rees, W., ed. *F. S. Colenso: Letters from Natal*. Pietermaritzburg: Shuter and Shooter, 1958.

Renan, Ernest. "What Is a Nation?" *Becoming National: A Reader*, ed. Geoff Eley and Ronald Grigor Suny, 41–55. New York: Oxford University Press, 1996.

Rodney, Walter. *How Europe Underdeveloped Africa*. Washington: Howard University Press, 1972.

Scorgie, Fiona. "Virginity Testing and the Politics of Sexual Responsibility: Implications for AIDS Intervention." *African Studies* 61.1 (2002): 55–75.

Scott, James C. *Domination and the Arts of Resistance: Hidden Transcripts*. New Haven: Yale University Press, 1990.

———. *Weapons of the Weak: Everyday Forms of Peasant Resistance*. New Haven: Yale University Press, 1985.

Shepperson, George. "The Comparative Study of Millenarian Movements." *Millennial Dreams in Action*, ed. Sylvia Thrupp, 44–52. The Hague: Mouton, 1962.

———. "Nyasaland and the Millennium." *Millennial Dreams in Action*, ed. Sylvia Thrupp, 144–59. The Hague: Mouton, 1962.

Shepperson, George, and Thomas Price. *Independent African: John Chilembwe and the Origins, Setting, and Significance of the Nyasaland Native Rising of 1915*. Edinburgh: Edinburgh University Press, 1958.

Simon, Roger. *Gramsci's Political Thought: An Introduction*. London: Electric Book Company, 2001.

Simons, H. J. *African Women: Their Legal Status in South Africa*. London: C. Hurst, 1968.

Sitas, Ari, ed. *Black Mamba Rising: South African Worker Poets in Struggle*. Durban: Culture and Working Life Publications, 1986, 1990.

———. "Class, Nation, and Ethnicity in Natal's Black Working Class." *The Societies of Southern Africa in the Nineteenth and Twentieth Centuries*, 267–68. London: Institute for Commonwealth Studies, 1990.

———. "Traditions of Poetry in Natal." *Journal of Southern African Studies* 16.2 (June 1990): 307–27.

Slater, Henry. "Land, Labour, and Capital in Natal: The Natal Land and Colonisation Company, 1860–1948." *Journal of African History* 16.2 (1975): 257–83.

Stoler, Ann Laura. *Race and the Education of Desire: Foucault's History of Sexuality and the Colonial Order of Things*. Durham: Duke University Press, 1995.

Stuart, James. *A History of the Zulu Rebellion, 1906*. London: Macmillan, 1913.

Stuart, James, and D. McK. Malcolm, eds. *The Diary of Henry Francis Fynn*. Pietermaritzburg: Shuter and Shooter, 1950.

Takaki, Ronald. *Pau Hana: Plantation Life and Labor in Hawaii, 1835–1920*. Honolulu: University of Hawaii Press, 1983.

Thompson, Paul. *The Natal Native Contingent in the Anglo-Zulu War, 1879*. Pieter-maritzburg: University of Natal Press, 1997.

Tönnies, Ferdinand. *Community and Society*. 1887. English edn. edited and trans-lated by Charles P. Loomis. East Lansing: Michigan State University Press, 1957.

Turner, Victor. *The Ritual Process: Structure and Anti-Structure*. Ithaca: Cornell, 1969.

Vail, Leroy, ed. *The Creation of Tribalism in Southern Africa*. Berkeley: University of California Press, 1989.

Van Onselen, Charles. "Crime and Total Institutions in the Making of Modern South Africa: The Life of 'Nongoloza' Mathebula, 1867–1948." *History Workshop Journal* 19 (1985): 62–81.

———. *New Babylon, New Nineveh: Everyday Life on the Witwatersrand, 1886–1914*. 1982. Reprint, Johannesburg: Jonathan Ball, 2001.

———. "The Regiment of the Hills—*Umkosi Wezintaba*: The Witwatersrand's Lump-enproletarian Army, 1890–1920." *Past and Present* 80 (August 1978): 91–121.

———. *The Small Matter of a Horse: The Life of "Nongoloza" Mathebula, 1867–1948*. Johannesburg: Ravan Press, 1984.

Vaughan, Megan. *Curing Their Ills: Colonial Power and African Illness*. Stanford: Stanford University Press, 1991.

Waetjen, Thembisa. *Workers and Warriors: Masculinity and the Struggle for Nation in South Africa*. Urbana: University of Illinois Press, 2004.

Walker, Cherryl. "Gender and the Development of the Migrant Labour System, c. 1850–1930." *Women and Gender in Southern Africa to 1945*, ed. Cherryl Walker, 168–96. Cape Town: D. Philip; London: J. Currey, 1990.

Wallerstein, Immanuel. "Ethnicity and National Integration in West Africa." *Cahiers d'Études africaines* 3 (1960): 129–39.

Walter, E. V. *Terror and Resistance: A Study of Political Violence with Case Studies of Some Primitive African Communities*. New York: Oxford University Press, 1969.

Warwick, Peter. "Black Industrial Protest on the Witwatersrand." *Essays in Southern African Labour History*, ed. Eddie Webster, 20–31. Johannesburg: Ravan Press, 1978.

———. *Black People and the South African War, 1899–1902*. Cambridge: Cambridge University Press, 1983.

Webb, C. De B., and J. B. Wright. *The James Stuart Archive*. 5 vols. Pieter-maritzburg: University of KwaZulu-Natal Press, 1976–2001.

Weber, Eugene. *Peasants into Frenchmen: The Modernization of Rural France, 1870–1914*. Stanford: Stanford University Press, 1976.

Weir, Jennifer. "'I Shall Need to Use Her to Rule': The Power of 'Royal' Zulu Women in Pre-Colonial Zululand." *South African Historical Journal* 43 (2000): 3–23.

Welsh, David. *The Roots of Segregation: Native Policy in Colonial Natal, 1845–1910*. Cape Town: Oxford University Press, 1971.

White, Luise. *Speaking with Vampires: Rumor and History in Colonial Africa*. Berkeley: University of California Press, 2000.

Williams, J. Michael. "Leading from Behind: Democratic Consolidation and Chieftaincy in South Africa." *Journal of Modern African Studies* 42.1 (2004): 113–36.

Willis, Justin. *Potent Brews: A Social History of Alcohol in East Africa, 1850–1899*. London: James Currey; Athens: Ohio University Press, 2002.

Wilson, Bryan R. *Magic and the Millennium: A Sociological Study of Religious Movements of Protest among Tribal and Third-World Peoples*. London: Heinemann, 1973.

Wright, Gwendolyn. *The Politics of Design in French Colonial Urbanism*. Chicago: University of Chicago Press, 1991.

Wright, John. "Control of Women's Labour in the Zulu Kingdom." *Before and After Shaka: Papers in Nguni History*, ed. J. B. Peires, 82–99. Grahamstown: Rhodes University Institute of Social and Economic Research, 1981.

——. "Political Transformations in the Thukela-Mzimkhulu Region in the Late Eighteenth and Early Nineteenth Centuries." *The Mfecane Aftermath*, ed. Carolyn Hamilton, 163–81. Johannesburg, South Africa: Wits University Press, 1995.

——. "Politics, Ideology, and the Invention of the Nguni." *Resistance and Ideology in Settler Societies*, ed. Tom Lodge, 96–118. Johannesburg: Ravan Press, 1986.

Wright, John, and Carolyn Hamilton. "Traditions and Transformations: The Phongolo-Mzimkhulu Region in the Late Eighteenth and Early Nineteenth Centuries." *Natal and Zululand from Earliest Times to 1910*, ed. Andrew Duminy and Bill Guest, 59–67. Pietermaritzburg: University of Natal Press / Shuter and Shooter, 1989.

Wright, John, and Andrew Manson. *The Hlubi Chiefdom in Zululand-Natal: A History*. Ladysmith: Ladysmith Historical Society, 1983.

Wrong, Dennis H. *Power: Its Forms, Bases, and Uses*. New York: Transaction, 1996.

Wylie, Dan. *Myth of Iron: Shaka in History*. Pietermaritzburg: University of KwaZulu-Natal Press, 2006.

——. *Savage Delight: White Myths of Shaka*. Pietermaritzburg: University of Natal Press, 2000.

UNPUBLISHED SECONDARY SOURCES

Carton, Benedict. " 'Blood from Your Sons': African Generational Conflict in Natal and Zululand, South Africa, 1880–1910." PhD diss., Yale University, 1996.

Cohen, Brett. "Something Like a Blowing Wind: African Conspiracy and the Coordination of Resistance to Colonial Rule in South Africa, 1876–1882." PhD diss., Michigan State University, 2000.

Cubbin, Anthony. "Origins of the British Settlement at Port Natal, May 1824–July 1842." PhD diss., University of the Orange Free State, 1983.

Devermont, Judd. "Refining Racial Identities on the South African Sugar Belt, 1851–1913." Master's thesis, Yale University, 2004.

Fourie, J. J. "Die koms van die Bantoe na die Rand en hulle posisie aldaar, 1886–1899." Master's thesis, Rand Afrikaans University, 1976.

Guy, Jeff. "An Accommodation of Patriarchs: Theophilus Shepstone and the Foundations of the System of Native Administration in Natal." Paper presented at the University of Natal-Durban African Studies Seminar, 20 August 1997.

Hamilton, Carolyn. "Ideology, Oral Traditions, and the Struggle for Power in the Early Zulu Kingdom." Master's thesis, University of the Witwatersrand, 1985.

Hedges, David. "Trade and Politics in Southern Mozambique and Zululand in the Eighteenth and Early Nineteenth Centuries." PhD diss., University of London, 1978.

Hemson, David. "Class Consciousness and Migrant Workers: Dock Workers of Durban." PhD diss., University of Warwick, 1979.

Hlongwane, Herbert Themba. "An Insight into the Causes and Events of the Zulu Rebellion of 1906 from the Black Point of View." Undergraduate honors thesis, University of Zululand, 1987.

Hughes, Heather. "Politics and Society in Inanda, Natal: The Qadi under Chief Mqhawe, c. 1840–1910." PhD diss., University of London, 1995.

Kennedy, Phillip. "The Fatal Diplomacy: Sir Theophilus Shepstone and the Zulu Kings, 1839–1879." PhD diss., University of California, Los Angeles, 1976.

Kubeka, Isaac Sibusiso. "A Preliminary Survey of Zulu Dialects in Natal and Zululand." Master's thesis, University of Natal, Durban, 1979.

——. "The Struggle for the City: Alcohol, the Ematsheni, and Popular Culture in Durban, 1902–1936." Master's thesis, University of Cape Town, 1984.

Mael, Rosalind. "The Problem of Political Integration in the Zulu Empire." PhD diss., University of California, Los Angeles, 1974.

Mahoney, Michael R. "Between the Zulu King and the Great White Chief: Political Culture in a Natal Chiefdom, 1879–1906." PhD diss., University of California, Los Angeles, 1998.

Moroney, Sean. "Industrial Conflict in a Labour Repressive Economy: Black Labour on the Transvaal Gold Mines, 1901–12." Undergraduate honors thesis, University of the Witwatersrand, 1976.

O'Laughlin, M. Bridget. "Mbum Beer-Parties: Structures of Production and Exchange in an African Social Formation." PhD diss., Yale University, 1973.

Ownby, Carolan. "Early Nguni History: The Linguistic Evidence and Its Correlation with Archaeology and Oral Tradition." PhD diss., University of California, Los Angeles, 1985.

Parle, Julie. "States of Mind: Mental Illness and the Quest for Mental Health in Natal and Zululand, 1868–1918." PhD diss., University of KwaZulu-Natal, 2004.

Parle, Julie, and Fiona Scorgie. "Bewitching Zulu Women: *Umhayizo*, Gender, and Witchcraft in Natal." Paper presented at the History and African Studies Seminar, University of KwaZulu-Natal at Howard College, 2001.

Slater, Henry. "Transitions in the Political Economy of Southeast Africa before 1840." D.Phil. diss., University of Sussex, 1976.

Switzer, Les. "The Problems of an African Mission in a White-Dominated, Multi-Racial Society: The American Zulu Mission in South Africa, 1885–1910." PhD diss., University of Natal, 1971.

Wright, John. "The Dynamics of Power and Conflict in the Thukela-Mzimkhulu Region in the Late Eighteenth and Early Nineteenth Centuries: A Critical Reconstruction." PhD diss., University of the Witwatersrand, 1989.

——. "Notes on the Politics of Being 'Zulu,' 1820–1920." Paper presented at the Conference on Ethnicity, Society, and Conflict in Natal, University of Natal, Pietermaritzburg, 14–16 September 1992.

INDEX

MICHAEL R. MAHONEY is an adjunct professor at Ripon College, and a visiting assistant professor at Lawrence University.

Library of Congress Cataloging-in-Publication Data

Mahoney, Michael R.
The other Zulus : the spread of Zulu ethnicity in colonial South Africa /
Michael R. Mahoney.
p. cm.—(Politics, history, and culture)
Includes bibliographical references and index.
ISBN 978-0-8223-5295-2 (cloth : alk. paper)
ISBN 978-0-8223-5309-6 (pbk. : alk. paper)
1. Zulu (African people)—Ethnic identity.
2. KwaZulu-Natal (South Africa)—Ethnic relations—History.
3. Great Britain—Colonies—Africa—Administration.
I. Title. II. Series: Politics, history, and culture.
DT1768.Z95M36 2012
968.'004963986—dc23
2012011588